ROMANTIC
WEEKENDS

# SAN FRANCISCO
# *&* the Bay Area

PHYLLIS & ROBERT WHITE

**HUNTER**
PUBLISHING

Hunter Publishing, Inc.
130 Campus Drive, Edison NJ 08818
(908) 225 1900, (800) 255 0343, Fax (908) 417 1744

*In Canada*
1220 Nicholson Rd., Newmarket, Ontario
Canada L3Y 7V1, (800) 399 6858

ISBN 1-55650-772-0
© 1997 Hunter Publishing, Inc.
Maps by Kim André and Lissa Dailey

For complete information about the hundreds of other travel
guides and language courses offered by Hunter Publishing,
visit our Web site at:
**www.hunterpublishing.com**

To Helen Chang and
Anne and Steve White
whose knowledge of San Francisco
and help we appreciate.

Every effort has been made to ensure that the information in this
book is correct, but the publisher and authors do not assume, and
hereby disclaim, liability to any party for any loss or damage
caused by errors, omissions, misleading information or potential
problems caused by information in this guide, even if such errors
or omissions are a result of negligence, accident or any other cause.

Grateful acknowledgment is made to the Regents of the University
of California for permission to reprint poems 123 and 152 from
*Songs of Gold Mountain: Cantonese Rhymes From San Francisco
Chinatown*, translated by Marlon K. Hom. © 1987 by The Regents
of the University of California.

1 2 3 4 5

# Contents

# Maps

# The Bay Area

California's first love story, one that's been sighed over for almost two hundred years, can still evoke a tear. It's actually a true story.

In 1806, Count Nikolai Petrovich Rezanov, an emissary of the Czar in charge of the Russian fur trading post in Sitka, sailed down the coast to try to negotiate trade with the Spanish. The King of Spain had a long-standing law that these far-flung, remote colonies were forbidden to deal with foreigners.

The Commandant of the Presidio was away when Rezanov sailed through the Golden Gate, but the Russian was welcomed by the Commandant's family and the officers of the garrison. The middle-aged Count attended a welcoming reception at the Presidio that first night and danced with Concepcion Arguello. Concepcion was the Commandant's dark-eyed daughter, only 15 years old, but already reputed to be the most beautiful girl in the province.

Rezanov was overwhelmed! During his stay, he wooed and won her. Despite the difference in ages and religions, he gained the consent of her father. The Count sailed away, after promising Concepcion that he would return for her as soon as he received the permission of the Russian Orthodox and Catholic churches for their mixed-faith marriage. Concepcion swore she would wait for him.

Due to the long and tedious nature of travel at that time, Concepcion knew that her wait would be at least several years. But a decade passed, and more, and still she waited. It was 1842 when Sir George Simpson of the Hudson's Bay Company arrived in San Francisco with the news that Rezanov had fallen ill and died. The tragedy had occured at the border of Siberia on his return trip home, 36 years before.

As one writer told the story, a shocked listener said, "But, his *enamorada* is here... in this room."

After a deathly silence, the faded Concepcion spoke. "No, she died, too."

## San Francisco Bay Area

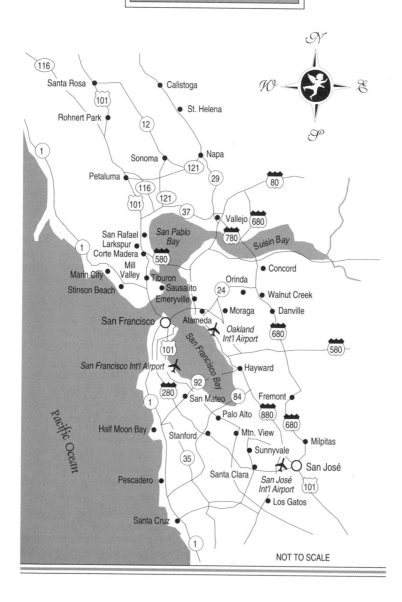

NOT TO SCALE

San Francisco Bay was discovered late in history, considering how long explorers sailed up and down this coast, and how often they missed finding it. Juan Rodriguez Cabrillo was the first, in 1542. He almost reached the great bay when severe storms drove him south. A half-dozen others, including Sir Francis Drake, who actually went ashore just a few dozen miles north in Marin in 1579, had no idea they had sailed past the greatest protected anchorage on the Pacific Coast. Not until 1769 was its existence known. During Gaspar de Portola's overland expedition a scout saw the big bay from a hill down the peninsula.

A Presidio and the Mission Dolores were established in what was called Yerba Buena, later renamed San Francisco. The peninsula was mostly sandy so the Mission Fathers pastured cattle on the rolling hills across the bay in what is now called Oakland. When wood was needed for building, or new spars and water for visiting ships, they sailed up the bay to Marin, or Napa Valley.

After Spanish rule ended in 1820 and independent Mexico relaxed trading restrictions, more American ships from New England arrived to trade hides and tallow. The Spanish and Mexicans did little farming and mostly ran cattle, which is about all they had to trade for manufactured goods. This was the time of Dana's *Two Years Before the Mast*, a good look at the life of the early *Californianos*.

Another romance we know of had a much happier ending. It took place in the 1820s when Maria Antonia Martinez, whose father was the new Commandante, met William Richardson, the first foreigner to settle here. (Apparently, all commandantes had beautiful, nubile daughters.) Richardson deserted from the whaler *Orion*. Within a year he was acting as "Captain of the Bay," teaching the populace carpentry, caulking, navigation and making time with Maria.

Two years later, William and Maria were married. William, now baptized "Antonio," became a naturalized citizen, which put him in line to receive a big land grant. Don Antonio was a busy lad indeed. If you take the Marin ferry, look around before you arrive in Sausalito; you are in Richardson Bay.

Gold was discovered in 1848, about a hundred miles east of Sacramento. Tens of thousands of men flocked here from all over the world, each determined to dig the yellow metal from the earth. For some, there was another reason for taking off for the distant "Cal-if-or-ny-ay": it seemed to be a good chance to start over after a few mistakes had been made. A popular gold rush ballad went:

*Oh, what was your name in the States?*
*Was it Thompson or Johnson or Bates?*
*Did you murder your wife and flee for your life?*
*Oh, what was your name in the States?*

The few women who came also planned to find gold, although they had no intention of digging in the dirt for it. Instead, most made their fortunes by establishing "Houses of Horizontal Pleasure."

In the century and a half that followed, San Francisco became a big city. The other areas around the bay, like Marin, Sonoma Valley, Napa Valley, Berkeley, Oakland and Half Moon Bay down the peninsula, developed into unique places, each with its own charm.

This book offers a number of different ways to achieve a romantic weekend in any one of these locales. The choice is yours.

# B & Bs, Inns, Hotels

❦ *I have seen purer liquors, better segars, finer tobacco, truer guns and pistols, larger Dirk and Bowie knives, and prettier courtesans here in San Francisco than in any other place I have ever visited, and it is my unbiased opinion that California can and does furnish the best bad things that are obtainable in America.*

Hinton R. Helper, 1855, *Land of Gold: Reality vs. Fiction*

Some places call themselves bed and breakfasts, some inns, and others hotels. "Inn" seems to be the preferred title, since both hotels and B&Bs sometimes call themselves that. "What's the difference anyway?," you may ask. Strictly speaking, a bed and breakfast is someone's home; a place where the owner actually lives and rents out a spare bedroom or two to make extra money. This arrangement stems from a concept started long ago in Europe. In this home-like setting, prices are often much lower than commercial alternatives. In the US, the last 20 years have seen the number of bed and breakfasts explode. People have purchased large, older homes, specifically to establish a bed and breakfast. The result has often been that rates are as high or even higher than those found at nearby hotels.

According to the dictionary definition, an inn is "a commercial establishment that provides lodging and food for the public, especially travelers." The majority of inns listed here fit that description well. Most actually provide a complimentary breakfast and a few serve three meals a day. The three-meal plan is a convenient option when you don't feel like going out for lunch or dinner. Many inns are set in beautifully refurbished classic homes; often old Victorian mansions. There is a decidedly different feeling that goes along with staying at a well-appointed inn, rather than at an ordinary hotel.

San Francisco is blessed with more pleasant, small hotels than any other city in the US. The other areas around the bay do not have as much to offer as of yet. The so-called "boutique hotels" of San Francisco will frequently serve wine and cheese in the afternoon in addition to a bountiful breakfast. High levels of service can be expected and rooms are furnished with antiques or good reproductions.

You will find many examples of all three types of accommodations here. We have tried to describe each facility in detail, ranging from practicality to atmospheric characteristics. Whatever type of lodging you select, you'll have a pretty good idea which one will be best for *your* romantic weekend.

## Booking Inns & Hotels

Most inns and hotels are full in the summer months. It is always best to reserve ahead, especially for weekends when vacationers flood the area. A one-night minimum deposit via a credit card is almost always requested. Once upon a time, September and October were the best months to visit San Francisco. Summer vacations were completed, rooms were easily found, and the weather was beautiful. The weather is still delightful, but the rooms are scarce and business conventions have increased in popularity at this time of the year. During the winter months, availability is usually no problem. Beware of large conventions descending upon the city. Again, reservations are a must.

## Restaurants

> ❦ *It is impossible to reminisce about San Francisco without thinking of food. As an international overeater, I would not hesitate to take any European gourmet and invite him to lean his paunch against the tables set by the restaurants there.*
>
> Paul Gallico

One of the great reasons for coming to the Bay Area is for the opportunity to eat in its restaurants. Ever since the Gold Rush, the quality and variety of the food has become legendary. A huge amount of wealth poured into the area; first by the gold strikes, then by the immense silver strike at Comstock, and subsequently as the region became the shipping and financial center of the West Coast. There have always been enough monied people to demand the best.

The variety of cuisines was assured when over 55,000 men and a few thousand women arrived here in the 1850s from France, Germany, Great Britain and China. Still more immigrants came from all over South America. The diversity of palates was guaranteed in later years when thousands of Italians arrived, first from northern Italy and later from the southern climes. Ever since that time, the area has celebrated a wide assortment of ethnic restaurants.

Also lending a hand is the unusually broad range of local resources. No town in the area is more than a half-hour's drive from the bay or the ocean, and most are within minutes. San Francisco Bay originally teemed with seafood. Before Jack London became a writer, he made his living as an oyster pirate, sailing out into the bay from Oakland. As recently as 50 years ago, the saloons along San Francisco's Embarcadero had heaping bowls of fresh bay shrimp on the bar instead of free pretzels.

Though their stocks are declining, there are still masses of fish in the Delta, and oysters, mussels and abalone are grown in western Marin County. In addition to Napa and Sonoma's famed vineyards, many varieties of lettuce and vegetables are grown in Sonoma and Half Moon Bay, reaching the Bay Area's restaurants within a few hours of being picked. After all, this is where the term, "California cuisine" originated and gave new meaning to cooking lightly with fresh, local ingredients. Add to that the culinary traditions of Europe, the Orient, the Near East and even Africa, and you have a cornucopia of places to dine.

You may notice, as you read through this book, that we praise most of the restaurants we review. If you begin to wonder whether there are any lousy restaurants in the Bay Area, we assure you there are. We just did not put them in this book.

A final note about food indicates the results of a recent survey by Club Med. It found that couples who dieted on vacation argued three times more often than those who did not, and those who did not diet had three times as many romantic moments.

Now it's up to you.

## Best Time to Come

🐞 *I prefer a wet San Francisco to a dry Manhattan.*

    Larry Geraldi

September and October are still the best months weatherwise. June, July and August are the foggiest months. March, April and May sometimes start with the tail end of winter storms and always end with the onset of summer. In between foggy periods, the weather can be perfectly balmy. The period from November through February sees most of the year's rainfall.

## What to Pack

Many times over the years, San Francisco and the Bay Area have wound up with a negative reputation. Yes, there is fog, but only during part of the year. Yes, there is rain, but generally during a different part of the year. Most travel destinations, with the exception of Death Valley, present the traveler with similar conditions. The climate is, to say the least, unpredictable. You can bring a bathing suit and expect to be able to use it, especially during September and October. But, also pack a sweater. An umbrella might well be needed from November through February. However, you may also be fortunate enough to encounter brilliantly clear, warm weather on your entire weekend. Ignore packing for the extremes. It won't be bitterly cold – this isn't Chicago! It won't be scorchingly hot or humid – this isn't Chicago!

## Other Useful Information

**Credit Cards:** There is a great range of who will take what. We list them specifically.

**Prices:** To save you the bother of trying to remember what $$ means, or if two-rosettes-and-a-half is better than two forks, we lay out the actual prices or price range.

**Phone Numbers:** San Francisco and Marin have a 415 area code. In Sonoma and Napa, the area code is 707; Oakland, Berkeley and the East Bay are 510. Starting August 2, 1997, the area code in San Mateo County, which includes Half Moon Bay, will be changed from 415 to 650. In this case, either area code may be used until January 2, 1998.

**Directions:** Generally, the owner will send you a map, or give directions on the phone when you make reservations.

A heart ♥ next to an inn or restaurant indicates one we think is especially romantic.

## Getting Anywhere from San Francisco International Airport

**Airporter:** ☎ 415-673-2432. $9 to downtown San Francisco and Fisherman's Wharf hotels; request rates for other cities.

**Super Shuttle:** ☎ 415-558-8500. Price depends on destination.

**Taxi:** $25 is the flat rate to downtown San Francisco. Higher rates to other cities.

## Ferries

You'll probably want to take at least one ferryboat ride. You can travel to San Francisco, Oakland and Sausalito, Larkspur, Tiburon and Angel Island by water. In addition, there are a number of Bay excursions available. There are several different companies and a maze of schedules.

**Blue & Gold Fleet:** ☎ 415-705-5444. Oakland, Alameda service, Bay excursions.

**Red & White Fleet:** ☎ 415-425-2131. Angel Island, Tiburon.

**Golden Gate Ferry:** ☎ 415-332-6600. Sausalito, Larkspur.

## For More Information

San Francisco's Visitor Information Center maintains 24-hour telephone hot lines. For a three-minute tape of "What's On," ☎ 415-391-2001.

## About This Book

We include a list of all the inns featured in San Francisco and the page numbers where you will find their descriptions at the beginning of the San Francisco chapter. Lists of all city restaurants and night spots are there too. The same format is followed for the other regions.

We hope you experience the ultimate romantic weekend in the Bay Area and enjoy this whole region as much as we do.

*Phyllis and Robert White*

# San Francisco

## An Introduction

❦ *Fair city of my love and my desire.*

Ina Coolbrith, California Poet Laureate, 1915-1928

San Francisco is a huge tourist attraction. It is the city that travelers from all over the world most want to visit in America. Because there is such a need for tourist activities, supply has naturally followed demand. Pier 39 did not spring to life without reason. Those tacky stores on and off Market Street that sell San Francisco-emblazoned T-shirts and ashtrays painted with the Golden Gate Bridge, exist because San Francisco is a magnet for tourists.

There are lots of reasons it worked out this way. The city is downright beautiful, for one thing. Only Vancouver and Hong Kong come close to matching its setting on an interesting bay dotted with islands, complete with hills and a skyline. It has a fascinating history, with peaceful Indians, not-nearly-so-peaceful Spanish, and even more warlike Americans. The Gold Rush definitely molded this region and the people living here today. The crucial postwar decision that shaped the city as we know it today was made in the 1960's. Ever since the Gold Rush, San Francisco was the West Coast's largest port. Banks and financial companies flourished on or near Montgomery Street. But post-World War II, a clever person came up with the concept of containerized shipping. This idea would eventually revolutionize ocean traffic. The drawback was that a lot of space was required to stack the containers waiting to be loaded. The city's government decided that the financial busi-

*Market Street sweeps down to the Ferry Building on the bay. The San Francisco-Oakland Bay Bridge is visible at right.*

ness was enough and that the city did not need to cater to grubby freighters anymore. Therefore, all container shipping (and all other shipping) is done across the Bay in Oakland, which jumped at the windfall and built enough container space to take all the business. Ironically (don't tell us the gods don't have a sense of humor), most of the banking and financial business moved to Los Angeles and elsewhere, never to return. So, San Francisco is very much in the tourist trade by necessity.

It is still the most beautiful city in the US. If Seattle wants to argue about this they'll have to write their own book! It does not have as many gargantuan hotels as Las Vegas (no city does), but there are many more romantic inns and comfortable boutique hotels here than in any other city in the country. And, incredibly, one can find the best food at affordable prices. New York thinks it has the best food, but its famous restaurants all cost an arm and a leg and a few other body parts!

Among the more interesting features of the area are the city's hills and its neighborhoods, which appear to be all mixed up with one another. The people who live on Telegraph Hill are very conscious of that fact. If asked, they would never say, "Oh, I live over that way" or "Just past downtown." They live on Telegraph Hill and know it well. It's a definite community. Most would never live in any other part of town. The same sense of community exists in Pacific Heights. North Beach, after more than a century, is still a small, cohesive, mostly Italian district. Chinatown is a real community full of Chinese grocery stores, theaters and temples. More people of Chinese ancestry live in this community than anywhere else outside of China.

Neighorhoods can be big and sprawling, like The Richmond, north of Golden Gate Park, or small and tightly knit like Cow Hollow. But they all have romantic bed & breakfasts, inns or small hotels. They also have good local places to eat, and wonderful Victorian homes, which only San Francisco has preserved. Views of the Bay, romantic strolls, pubs where one-of-a-kind beer is brewed by the batch right on the premises, and... the list goes on.

# Getting Around

**MUNI:** The bus system is extensive, reaching into all neighborhoods. It is perfectly possible to get around without a car in San Francisco, particularly the downtown area. A single fare is $1. For a few days of concentrated sightseeing, you are better off with a One Day Passport for $6. A Three Day Passport is $10 and a Seven Day Passport is $15. You can request a transfer to any other line or cable car. You may purchase the Passports at the Visitors Information Center, Hallidie Square (Powell and Market, below street level).

**Cable Cars:** Cable cars are tied in with the MUNI system. A single ride costs $2 and transfers may be made to the bus line. Passports are also valid.

**Taxis:** Since a parking spot is difficult to find, the taxi is a reasonable alternative. The flag drop rate is $1.90, with each mile charged at a rate of $1.50.

**BART:** Trains cover Oakland and the East Bay, tunnel under the Bay and run under Market Street. The basic fare is $1, with rates increasing dependent on the length of trip.

**Bay Bridge:** Highway 80 crosses the Bay Bridge to Oakland and to the East. A toll of $1 per car is collected on the in-bound lanes (towards San Francisco).

**Golden Gate Bridge:** This bridge has Highway 101 running across it to Marin and the North. Take Lombard Street from downtown or Highway One (Park Presidio Blvd.) from western San Francisco and follow the signs. A toll of $2 is collected in-bound.

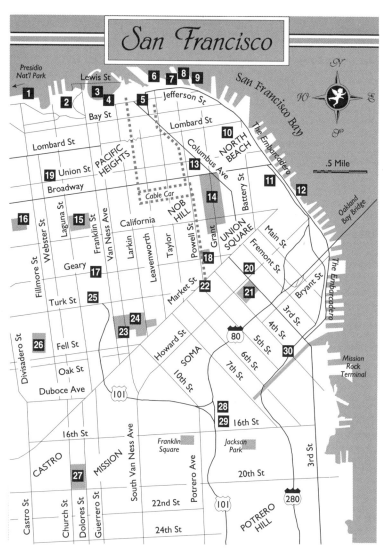

1. Marina Green
2. Ft Mason Military Reserve
3. Aquatic Park
4. Ghirardelli Square
5. The Cannery
6. Fisherman's Wharf
7. Ferry to Sausalito,Tiburon & Alcatraz
8. Pier 41
9. Pier 39
10. Coit Tower

11. Embarcadero Center
12. Ferry to Sausalito, Tiburon & Larkspur
13. Washington Square
14. Chinatown
15. Lafayette Park
16. Alta Plaza
17. Japantown
18. Union Square
19. Union Street Shops
20. Museum of Modern Art

21. Moscone Convention Ctr
22. Visitors Center
23. War Memorial Auditorium
24. Civic Center, Brooks Hall, Davies Hall, Opera House
25. Jefferson Square
26. Alamo Square
27. Mission Park
28. The Concourse
29. Galleria
30. CalTrain

# Inns & Small Hotels

❦ *The cool, grey city of love.*

George Sterling

San Francisco is a city full of places to stay. Not all, of course, would be your first choice to spend a romantic weekend. Some cater to business travelers and have a different atmosphere. Others are booked most of the time with minimal effort and thereby feel they do not have to go through the trouble of pampering guests. We look for an atmosphere that is genuinely friendly, not just efficient.

If we find ourselves saying, "Let's go home" when it's time to return to our hotel after a day of sightseeing or an evening out we know it's a good place. These are the inns and hotels we recommend. We have stayed in most, or thoroughly checked them out on the recommendation of someone we know who has stayed there. All were chosen for their appeal to couples.

There are two collateral reasons for a place to be included here. Geography is one reason. We made sure to find special places in each of San Francisco's neighborhoods. If you choose to stay in a hotel right next to Union Square, in the middle of downtown, or would prefer a meticulously preserved Victorian "painted lady" up in Pacific Heights, you will find it here.

The hotels we include are, for the most part, small and centrally located. These boutique hotels range from 40-50 rooms to 200 rooms, like Hotel Monaco. We know from personal experience that these hotels treat guests like individuals. They do not cater to conventions. Every one of the staff will try very hard to get you whatever you desire. There are usually staff members who speak several languages, particularly in the hotels. You may find assistance in French, German, Italian or Japanese. Each tries to create a friendly ambiance, usually with a continental or better breakfast in the morning and wine available by the fireplace in the afternoon.

## Details of Listings

All local phone and fax numbers have a 415 area code.

Where only the number of rooms is given, it means that each has its own private bath. If it says "eight rooms, seven baths," that indicates two rooms share a bath. This arrangement is usually less expensive.

We note if children are accepted as guests. Some inns, particularly those with only a few rooms, do not want noisy children disturbing other guests, who tend to be mostly romantic couples. If the whole idea of a romantic weekend is to get away from children, note that some of the places welcome children and others don't.

# Alamo Square

One of the postcard pictures of San Francisco is known all over the world. It displays a row of beautifully restored, brightly colored Victorian houses against a backdrop of the city and the Bay beyond. That photo of "Post Card Row" is shot from Alamo Square Park, within a half-hour walking distance of the Civic Center and downtown. It is a quiet, remote area and truly another world.

The area was well known in the city's early days. From the time San Francisco was founded in 1776 to about 1835, the Mission Dolores and the Presidio were the only settlements. The old Divisidero Trail ran between the two, passing through brush-covered sand dunes where deer were plentiful. Halfway down the Trail was a prominent landmark called Alamo Hill. At what is now Di-

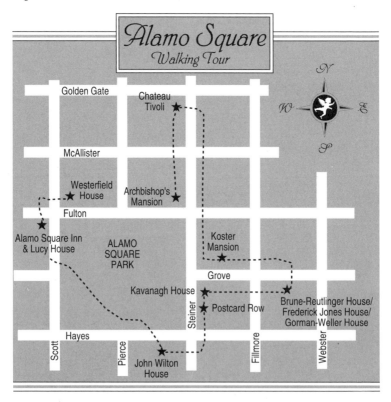

Alamo Square
Walking Tour

visidero and Fulton Street, just a block from the hill, was San Souci, a roadhouse established as a rest stop. This was the first permanent building in San Francisco, other than the Mission and Presidio.

After the Gold Rush and the city's expansion, the Comstock silver boom pushed San Francisco west, past Van Ness to what still is known as the Western Addition. The early way out from the city was on a horse-drawn trolley down McAllister Street. The 12-acre park here was created in 1856. In 1906, it became a tent city, sheltering hundreds made homeless by the earthquake and fire.

At the start of World War II, the Japanese, many of whom were living in this neighborhood, were taken away and put in concentration camps in the desert. These were euphemistically called "Relocation Camps." The area, and all of the Western Addition, went downhill. But it is in a good location, close to downtown, and has a good climate. It is now under redevelopment. We do not want to oversell the renaissance of the Western Addition. Most of the area is safe, but there are pockets that have bad reputations. If you are staying here, check with the inn's owners before you go strolling too far in the wrong direction at night.

## Inns

### Alamo Square Inn

The beautifully restored, three-story Queen Anne Victorian house is on an extra-wide lot with a driveway and parking. Next door, on the corner, is the Tudor Revival house that is also part of this fine Inn. It is across the street from Alamo Square Park and only 10 blocks from the Civic Center. You enter up the usual Victorian front steps, with a massive locked door at the top. As a guest, you will get a front door key as well as a room key. Inside is a generous entry room with a 15-foot ceiling. The Victorians, who had to heat with fireplaces, had a perverse generosity with room heights, thus allowing the heat to rise above where it would do humans any good. You can feel the opulence that went along with beautifully built houses in the late 19th century. Details like oak flooring, oriental carpeting and the curved grand staircase add to the age-old charm. To the left is the parlor, with its fireplace and sofas. The chandelier in here is not an original piece, but it is a dead ringer for the gas/electric combination chandelier that would have hung here a century ago. Through the wide sliding door is a large dining room, now used as a sitting room, with comfortale sofas in front of the fireplace. This is where guests sip wine and chat in the late afternoon and evenings. Wine sipping time seems to be rather open-ended and always enjoyable!

The Tudor house next door has its own sitting room and parlor, so there is no shortage of places for a couple seeking a quiet, private place to browse through a library or perhaps just be by themselves.

The Victorian, originally known as the Baum House, cost all of $6,400 when it was built in 1895. Charles Baum, a prominent businessman, had come to San Francisco from St. Petersburg, Russia, where his father was in the employ of Catherine the Great's court. He arrived in 1849 and later married the daughter of the first Mexican Consul to San Francisco. The house stayed in the family for quite a few years. After World War II, it gradually went downhill and was in sad shape when Wayne Corn and Klaus May bought it and the house next door. They restored them to their present fine condition.

The Tudor house was built in 1896 for the even smaller sum of $4,950, by George D. Lucy, a local soap manufacturer. The design is clean and simple, unlike the excessively florid Victorian styles. The present owners have not fussed with the interior, choosing to leave it in the pristine condition in which they found it. There are five bedrooms in the Tudor house. All the original bedrooms in the Victorian were on the second floor; two more have been added in what was the attic under the peaked roof. Some of the bedrooms are small and cozy. The largest, Mr. and Mrs. Baum's original bedroom and sitting room across the front of the Victorian, is large indeed. It boasts a massive bed, equally grand armoires, a fireplace and a circular bay, wrapped in a 180-degree window on the corner of the house and overlooking the park. Other rooms are smaller, but all are furnished with antiques, chandeliers, and lace curtains. Every bit of decor makes the guests feel as though they are staying in a welcoming, well-to-do home in the last half of the 19th century.

The houses are joined by the solarium and breakfast is served in what was once the carriage house. Quite a few weddings have been held here. The owners will make all the arrangements, including the food, which will be prepared by Klaus May. Chef May was formerly a chef at the Kahala Hilton, which accounts for the fine breakfasts.

- ❏ *719 Scott St., San Francisco, CA 94117;*
     ☎ *415-922-2055, fax 415-931-1304.*
- ❏ *Rooms: 14 rooms in two connected 1890s houses.*
- ❏ *Prices: $85-$275.*
- ❏ *Credit cards: All, except Diners.*
- ❏ *Reservations: Highly recommended; weekends require longer advance notice than weekdays; holidays are booked far in advance.*
- ❏ *Minimum stay: Two nights on weekends and holidays*
- ❏ *Deposit: First and last night.*
- ❏ *Check-in time: After 2 pm.*
- ❏ *Check-out time: Noon.*

❑ *Breakfast: Full American breakfast in the old carriage house, 8 am-10 am.*
❑ *Wine: Starting at 5 pm.*
❑ *Handicapped accessible: No access, due to stairways.*
❑ *Smoking: In solarium only.*
❑ *Children: Yes.*
❑ *Pets: No.*
❑ *Parking: Off street and without charge.*

## ♥ *The Archbishop's Mansion*

How about sleeping beautifully, or even sinfully, in a room that was a former chapel, with a king-size bed where the pews once were? Would it help to hear that the chandelier in the parlor is from the set of *Gone With The Wind,* the mirror in the Great Hall is from Mary Lincoln's home and the piano, occasionally played by a guest in the evening, is a 1904 Bechstein baby grand, once owned by Noel Coward and, it is rumored, played by George Gershwin? If you look closely, there is a picture of Cardinal Pacelli, who stayed here when he came to bless the newly opened Golden Gate Bridge in 1937. He later became Pope Pius the XIIth.

Then there is the Carmen Suite. You will discover a fireplace in the bathroom, close to the extra-large, claw-footed tub. This is the most asked-for suite, no doubt by those who like warm baths. The former library is now an eight-sided panelled bedroom.

The Archbishop's Mansion was indeed made for an archbishop and it is definitely a mansion, in the style of a French chateau from the Belle Epoque. It was built in 1904 as a residence and guest house for the Archbishop of San Francisco, Patrick Riordan, when Alamo Square was one of the most fashionable and expensive neighborhoods in town.

In 1944, the Archdiocese moved its headquarters to Pacific Heights, which had become the new most fashionable and expensive neighborhood. Later, the old mansion was sold to Jonathon Shannon and Jeffrey Ross, the present owners, who spent 2½ years renovating it. Their work has included furnishing the interior with European antiques which fit the spirit of the property perfectly.

We were shown into the Don Giovanni Suite (the 10 rooms and five suites are each named after an opera), former personal quarters of the archbishop. We had to hide our gasps; actually, we didn't hide them, we just gasped! The bedroom is huge. The living room had hosted a birthday party here the night before for over 50 and it wasn't crowded. The bedroom is dominated by the bed. It is a four-poster from France, fully canopied, intricately carved, and so high that a small stepstool is provided on each side to help you get into it. There are cupids cavorting all over it and angels carved into

*The Archbishop's Mansion.*

the headposts. The headboard sports a family crest and the date of 1630 is carved into the footboard. Two oversized bedside tables are done in the same fashion and tall enough so that everything is within easy reach, even from your elevated altitude. There is a cozy fireplace and fresh flowers on the table where breakfast is served by the corner windows.

The bathroom is commensurate in size with the claw-footed tub and extra-large cabinets built into the wall with their own large mirrors. A separate shower room has a seven-headed shower – one overhead, three in front and three behind. Sheer luxury. The parlor is furnished with twin eight-foot leather couches, a 10-foot-long walnut table, five-foot-high Chinese vases and other equally imposing antiques. It is overwhelming.

If you are looking around for other guests, your best chance of finding them is at the "wine hour," which actually lasts an hour and a half before everyone scatters for dinner. Most often, the place looks empty because people tend to stay in their rooms. Robes are provided so you can kick back and put your feet up. Breakfast is served in the dining room, but manager Rick Janvier is surprised when anyone comes down. "People seem to like our rooms," he says. Small wonder!

- ❏ *1000 Fulton St., San Francisco, CA 94117;*
  ☎ *415-563-7872 or 800-543-5820.*
- ❏ *Rooms: 15, including five suites.*
- ❏ *Prices: Rooms $129-$189; suites $215-$385.*
- ❏ *Credit cards: AE, Discover, MC, V.*
- ❏ *Reservations: Definitely.*
- ❏ *Minimum stay: Two nights on weekends.*
- ❏ *Breakfast: Continental.*
- ❏ *Wine: 5:30 pm-7 pm.*
- ❏ *Amenities: Robes, in-room breakfast.*
- ❏ *Handicapped accessible: No.*
- ❏ *Smoking: In dining room.*
- ❏ *Children: Yes.*
- ❏ *Pets: No.*
- ❏ *Parking: Private lot.*

# *Things to Do*

## *Strolling Around the Square*

Even if you are not staying on Alamo Square, you should stroll around it to see some of the marvelously restored Victorian homes there. After all, this is San Francisco's most famous Victorian neighborhood.

**The Archbishop's Mansion,** 1000 Fulton, the corner of Steiner and Fulton, was built in 1904 for San Francisco's second Catholic Archbishop, Patrick Riordan. It is now a bed and breakfast, with each of its spacious rooms named after a famous opera. See page 17. Walk two blocks north on Steiner to Chateau Tivoli.

**Chateau Tivoli,** 1057 Steiner, is probably the most elaborate Victorian of them all, with cupolas, witch's towers, balconies and gabled roofs. The equally busy color scheme has assorted shades of brown, green and turquoise. Return on Steiner one block past Fulton to Grove Street for the Koster Mansion.

**Koster Mansion,** 926 Grove, is one of the most dramatic structures in San Francisco, occupying five city lots with an impressive view of the city. Continue east on Grove a half-block past Fillmore to the Brune-Reutlinger House.

**The Brune-Reutlinger House,** 824 Grove, the **Frederick Jones House** at 817 Grove and the **Gorman-Weller House** at 823 Grove are a magnificent collection of homes. These Italianate Victorians are smaller than many of the houses lining the square, but show their authenticity inside and out. Back on Steiner, just off Grove, is The Kavanagh House.

**The Kavanagh House,** 722 Steiner, built before the neighboring "Painted Ladies," is free of the heavy applied woodwork that was typical of that period. It is a simpler house with an octagonal Victorian bay and subtle ornamentation. Now, you may move on to the infamous Postcard Row.

**Postcard Row,** the "Painted Ladies," has adorned San Francisco's promotional material for many years. The five Queen Anne Victorians are the best known for their dramatic position in front of the city's skyline. Built by various architects in the mid- to late 19th century, they reflect the different aspects of Queen Anne design. Walk on and turn right at the corner to see the John Wilton House.

**The John Wilton House,** 1017 Hayes, flanks the square on the south side. Built in 1891, it is a prime example of opulent Victorian architecture. Now take a stroll across the park to the corner of Scott and Fulton.

**The Alamo Square Inn** and **The Lucy House**, which are connected through the conservatory, have two addresses, 719 Scott and 1201 Fulton, respectively. They are very obviously two entirely different styles of architecture, a traditional Queen Anne and a classic Tudor Revival. They blend nicely into a comfortable bed and breakfast. See page 15. Located catty-corner across Fulton is the Westerfield House.

**The Westerfield House,** 1198 Fulton, is a spectacular home with a square lookout tower. It was built in 1875 and sold in the 1920s to the White Russian consular corps, which opened a restaurant called "Dark Eyes" in the basement. Later, it was occupied by a magician who kept 500 candles burning continually in the tower room. The notorious murderer, Charles Manson, lived here for awhile in the 1960s.

On that cheery note, we leave Alamo Square with all of its history and all of its beautiful Victorian houses.

# The Barbary Coast

❦ *(San Francisco) is a moral penal colony. It is the worst of all the Sodom and Gomorrahs in our modern world.... It is the paradise of ignorance, anarchy and general yellowness.... It needs more than all else a steady trade wind of grape-shot.*

Ambrose Bierce

For 75 years, the name of San Francisco evoked three words: The Barbary Coast. To the law abiding citizens, it was a prime dwelling place of crime and corruption. To the devout, it was a pit of evil and abode of the devil. But to many it conjured up a thrilling image of an area that thumbed its nose at conventional morality and got away with sinning. It was "the wickedest city on earth" or "the most dangerous city in the world," or both.

In the 19th century, New York's Hell's Kitchen was renowned for its violence and New Orleans' Storyville was known for wide-open prostitution. But the infamous Barbary Coast came to have, from the early 1850s on, more of each of those vices. Adding to the Sodom and Gomorrah reputation was the presence of gambling casinos, honky-tonks, melodeons, cribs, low saloons with obscene entertainment and gangs eager to shanghai unwary victims.

Before 1849, there was no Barbary Coast. This was not because the inhabitants of old San Francisco were without sin, but there simply were not enough of them to support a district devoted solely to it.

Once the Gold Rush was well under way, the lack of feminine companionship was soon remedied. The first women were from Mexico, Peru and Chile. They all came to be called "Chilenos," regardless of their ethnic background. These pioneer women set themselves up in tents and board shanties on the slopes of Telegraph Hill and went into business. Between this center of prostitution and the saloons and gambling halls of Portsmouth Square, the Barbary Coast was created. That was roughly its area for the next 75 years.

The greatest economic mainstay of the area was prostitution. Following the Chilenos, 2,000 women arrived from New Orleans, the East Coast and France. Of these, the most eagerly patronized were the French, *femmes de joie*, who had a long-standing reputation for being uncommonly ardent and sexually adept. For their presence, the impatient argonauts could thank the French government, which raised a fund to ship poor but virtuous girls to this city of opportunity. They would, theoretically, make a fresh start in life. Actually, it was a scheme to rid Paris of its oversupply of prostitutes. *La Belle France* disposed of 900 of its harlots by shipping them to The City by the Bay.

Another economic prop for the Barbary Coast during the rest of the century was supplying seamen for sailing ships. Many men jumped ship when it arrived in San Francisco. Working conditions on vessels in those days were so brutal that it was almost impossible for captains to find enough hands to man their vessels. A number of thugs based in the Barbary Coast went into business to remedy that deficiency.

In the early years, it was a lengthy, roundabout voyage to get to Shanghai. When a ship started on any long and hazardous cruise, she was said to be making a "Shanghai Voyage." Eventually, the men forcibly impressed were said to be "shanghaied." A citizen named Kelly, who was very successful in that trade, kept a saloon and boarding house at 33 Pacific St. by the Bay. Once, in the 1870s, there were three ships anchored off the Heads, outside the Golden Gate Bridge, all needing full crews. Kelly could not lay his hands on a single man, but he was nothing if not resourceful. He chartered the *Goliah*, an old paddle-wheel steamer and let it be known he was going to celebrate his birthday with a picnic aboard her, complete with free liquor and women. Everyone was invited. The riff-raff of the Barbary Coast greedily lined up to board. Kelly counted them as they walked up the gangplank and when 90 men were on deck, he cast off. The *Goliah* puffed away from the dock, sailed down the Bay, under the Golden Gate Bridge and out into the Pacific. The picnickers drank to Kelly's health with free beer and whiskey, all of which was heavily drugged. Within a short time every man on board, except for Kelly and his hoodlums, was unconscious.

Whereupon the *Goliah* turned and made for the three crewless ships, where the new crews were hoisted aboard. Kelly, paid handsomely, steamed back into San Francisco and was forevermore regarded with awe for his astuteness. From that time on he was known as Shanghai Kelly.

🐝 *The Barbary Coast is the haunt of the low and the vile of every kind. The petty thief, the house burglar, the tramp, the whoremonger, lewd women, cutthroats, murderers, all are found there.... Licentiousness, debauchery, pollution, loathsome disease, blasphemy, and death, are there. And Hell, yawning to receive the putrid, is there also.*

B.E. Lloyd, *Lights and Shades in San Francisco*, 1876

It is not known who named the area or when, but it was undoubtedly a seaman comparing the perils of the district with the dangerous, pirate-infested waters of the Mediterranean off the Barbary Coast. There were some odd saloons to be found in this second Barbary Coast. One owner had plates of sheet metal installed in front of the bar and in the wall between his saloon and the even more violent one next door. The goal was to save bartenders by stopping stray bullets.

The there was The Cobweb Palace, opened by Abe Warner in 1856 and managed by him until 1897. Warner bought monkeys, parrots and birds from sailors and kept them in rows of cages. One parrot, not confined in a cage and with the run of the saloon, had a taste for liquor and could curse in four languages. A feature that attracted many patrons was the thousand garish paintings of nude women crowded onto the walls. But the reason for the name was that Warner had an unusual fondness for spiders and refused to interfere with one when it started to spin a web. As a result, the interior was a mass of cobwebs that hung from the ceiling, covered the lighting fixtures and obscured the paintings so their charms could hardly be appreciated.

Generation after generation of San Francisco's respectable real estate tycoons made money from the buildings they secretly owned in the Barbary Coast. Many generations of politicians raked in so much graft that the district was exempt from the usual political pressure to clean it up.

The Barbary Coast seemed like a force of nature, with its heart found on Pacific Avenue. On one block alone, you might have found 10 saloons, many of them side by side. One chained a grizzly bear beside its entrance. Some had musicians blaring away. Others, according to *Scribner's Monthly* in 1875, "keep a female staff capable of waking thirst in a stone." Nature itself was finally the force that accomplished what all the efforts of morality could not. The 1906 earthquake and subsequent fire wiped out most of the area. The few buildings left standing were in and around Pacific Avenue. The Hippodrome bar and dance hall, with plaster bas-reliefs of dancing girls on doorway pillars (see North Beach, page 107) is one of the best remaining examples.

The Barbary Coast tried to come back, but it was vanquished in 1913 when a wave of morality engendered by some of the city's clergymen dovetailed with the efforts of a reformist politician. This was, finally, the end of one of the longest-running sin cities in American history.

# At the Beach

It is called Ocean Beach, which sounds redundant, but probably was not when there was also a North Beach. It is a wide beach with dark, golden sand and runs for five miles from the Cliff House, a few blocks north of Golden Gate Park, to Fort Funston, where hang gliders soar. It is not ideal for swimming, since it is very cold even in the summer months. There are also dangerous riptides. But it is a great location for walking, jogging, or letting a dog run.

## The Cliff House

The present Cliff House is the latest in a succession of buildings of that name which have stood on the same spot by Seal Rocks. It has been a leisure-time destination for generations of San Franciscans. The first Cliff House was built by Adolph Sutro, a mining engineer, who made millions in Nevada's Comstock silver mines. At first, only well-to-do people with a horse and buggy and the time to take a long, long drive out of town could enjoy the beach. Sutro built a train, with the fare only a nickel, so even the masses could reach his resort. He built extensive gardens, where visitors could stroll amid flowers and statuary. He had the world's largest indoor swimming complex constructed. Six saltwater swimming pools and a huge, spring-fed fresh water plunge, all maintained at different temperatures under a glass-domed roof, could accomodate 25,000 people at one time. After the first place was destroyed by fire in 1894, Sutro built the second in 1896, modeled on a French château, though it out-châteaued any of the châteaux in France. It was eight stories high with spires and an observation tower 200 feet above the sea – a favorite destination for elegant dining, dancing and entertainment. After surviving the earthquake, it too was destroyed in a fire the following year.

Today's Cliff House was built by Sutro's daughter, Emma, in 1909. This version was neoclassic in design. It had several owners and ups and downs during wars and the Great Depression. The National Park Service bought it in 1977 and made it a part of the Golden Gate National Recreation Area. This is the place to see the ocean and the beach from a high vantage point. It is a good place for lunch or dinner (see below). Outside, you can walk down to the terrace, built out over the waves below the restaurants. There is a Visitors Center here where you can see a map and get directions for a walk. There is a camera obscura in the basement and a Mechanical Museum that features arcade games from the past.

❑ *1090 Point Lobos (at Ocean Beach), San Francisco, CA 94121;* ☎ *415-386-3330.*
❑ *Parking: Roadside and parking lot.*

## Restaurants

The Cliff House sits on the rocks at the edge of the Pacific Ocean, around the corner of the Bay from the Golden Gate Bridge and north of Golden Gate Park. Inside, you will find four places to eat. The phone number to reach each of the dining rooms is ☎ 415-386-3330.

### Seafood & Beverage Company Restaurant in the Cliff House

(Seafood)

This is a romantic place to sit and toast the sunset. Seal Rocks are at your feet, perhaps a ship is headed for the Bay, and foam curls over the coastline. Leon Gregory always plays, "Sunrise, Sunset" from "Fiddler on the Roof" and times it so that the last note sounds as the sun goes over the edge.

The Seafood and Beverage Company (an apt but curious name) is handsome. It is a long, rather narrow room, to take advantage of the full windows on three sides. These tower 20 feet in height, joined by a lovely painted ceiling and accented with squarish art-deco chandeliers. There is a long, raised portion of the room that gives those seated away from the windows a good view too. Plenty of couples come here. Alan Goldstein, the sociable British manager, says that at least once a month there is a proposal of marriage either here or in the more intimate restaurant, Upstairs at the Cliff House. To help the atmosphere of romance along, Leon Gregory plays familiar show tunes during the dinner hours.

Since seafood is in the name, you know pretty much what to expect on the menu. We always start with a few Preston oysters from Bodega Bay, which is just up the coast. Try them with lemon juice and a bit of garlic or request the house tomato and horseradish sauce (take care, it is potent horseradish).

There is a tasty Greek-style appetizer of prawns with Kalamata olives, garlic and feta cheese. Crab cakes are different here, combined with salmon for a salmon-crab cake with Cajun aioli, which lends a spicy flavor. We enjoyed this dish so much, that when we mentioned it to Alan Goldstein, he gave us the recipe so we could make them at home. You might want to do that too.

## Salmon & Crab Cakes

1 lb salmon (poached or grilled)

½ lb crab meat

1 small red onion, finely diced

2 green onions, finely diced

1 tbsp Worcestershire Sauce

1 tsp Tabasco Sauce

1 tsp dry mustard

½ tsp dillweed

salt and pepper to taste

¼ stick whole butter, room temperature

½ cup mayonnaise

1 cup seasoned breadcrumbs

1 tsp Thai chili paste (or your own hot sauce)

¼ cup olive oil

Make sure cooked salmon is picked clean of bones. Flake crab meat and salmon into medium size mixing bowl and set aside. In a small mixing bowl, mix remaining ingredients (reserve ¼ cup of breadcrumbs). Blend well and add to salmon and crab mixture. Mix together lightly, without overworking. Shape salmon mixture into 4 oz. balls and press into patty shapes. Coat with remaining breadcrumbs. Heat ¼ cup olive oil in medium sauté pan and brown cakes on both sides. Serve with your choice of sauce. Sauce suggestion: Mix ½ cup of mayonnaise with 2 tbsp Cajun spice.

The scallops sautéed in butter with white wine, garlic and parsley are good. Herbed snapper, which sounds delicious, was a disappointment when we ordered it. The usual delicate taste of the fish was gone. It was bland and the herbs did not make up for it. But this was just one dish among a number of winners.

There is a Sunday brunch which presents a good time to see Seal Rocks. Not a buffet (see The Terrace Room for a buffet), the offerings include the typical eggs Benedict, French toast and salads.

The Cliff House has been around so long that some old line San Franciscans tend to forget about it, but the food is as good as almost any in San Francisco, which is to say in the country.

□ *Open: Weekdays 11 am-10:30 pm, Saturday 10-11, Sunday 9-11.*
□ *Lunch menu until 4 pm, dinner from 4. Sunday brunch 9-2.*
□ *Prices: Appetizers, soups and small salads $3.45-$9.95; entrées, pastas, house specialties $10.50-$19.95.*
□ *Reservations: Recommended.*

## *Upstairs at the Cliff House*

(California cuisine)

The ceiling is lower here, with small tables and a more intimate setting. It is great for viewing the sea and a wonderful choice for a later supper. The menu features pastas, seafood and chicken. Breakfast and lunch are also served.

□ *Open: Weekdays 8 am-3:30 pm, 5 pm-10:30 pm, Saturday and Sunday 8 am-4 pm and 5 pm-11 pm.*
□ *Prices: Lunch $6-$9. Dinner averages $15.*
□ *Reservations: Not usually necesssary.*

## *Benjamin J. Butler Room*

This room is named after a seal who somehow got a toilet seat stuck over its head and hung around this end of the Cliff House thereafter. An unlikely story, but we were told that it's true.

A nice, comfortable, circular room offers seating with good views of the sea. It is dedicated to drinking while grazing, or gazing into each other's eyes – both satisfying experiences. Appetizers and snacks are available all day and a pianist appears on weeknight evenings.

□ *Open: Weekdays 11 am-1:30 am, Saturday 10 am-1:30 am, Sunday 9 am-1:30 pm.*

## The Phineas T. Barnacle Bar & Deli

(Light fare)

This bar and deli is a more casual setting than the other rooms, but still has its own sea-gazing windows. There is an oyster bar and a television that is almost always turned to sports channels. The idea is to drink beer, munch pretzels and cheer or boo a team. There is also a fireplace, which invites sitting and sipping as you whisper to one another. If the sports crowd gets rowdy, you will have to whisper more loudly. After all, this is a neighborhood hangout.

Snacks like seafood, chicken wings, nachos, sandwiches and clam chowder are readily available. Espresso, Irish coffee and cocktails are served.

❑ *Open: Daily 10 am-1:30 am.*

## The Terrace Room

(Sunday Champagne Buffet)

This is where you will find the big Sunday buffet. The Terrace Room is a level lower than the Seafood and Beverage Company Restaurant, but it still has good views of Seal Rocks and the ocean. You will be serenaded by a delightful harpist while you take in the view. The menu includes breakfast fare, pastries, salads, prawns, salmon, pasta, London broil and more. Of course, there is an ample supply of champagne.

❑ *Open: Sunday 10 am-3 pm.*
❑ *Price: $24.50.*

# Things to Do

Just offshore are the Seal Rocks. For as many years as anyone can remember, sea lions have been here. Sea lions are not to be confused with seals – the name of the rocks may be misleading. People have been coming out to the Cliff House to see the sea lions for years. Then, in 1994, the sea lions suddenly disappeared. It was at that same time that hundreds of sea lions began spending their days at Pier 39. While no one has directly accused the Pier of bribing the animals with a daily bucket of fish, the timing is decidedly suspicious.

Farther out to sea (27 miles to be exact) are the Farallon Islands. They are desolate, uninhabited chunks of jagged rocks. In the first half of the 19th century, Russian fur traders based up the coast at Fort Ross, wiped out the seals and sea otters who lived on the rocks.

After 1850, when San Francisco was booming, commercial egg companies did the same to the millions of birds who made their home here. The birds that most commonly nested on the Farallons were the murres. Their eggs were taken to feed the city population. The seals and murres have fortunately returned, but not the otters.

On most clear days you can see the islands from the Cliff House and Point Lobos, but do not count on it. Even when it is clear here on the coast, it is often fog-shrouded around the Farallons.

## Farallon Islands National Wildlife Refuge

The Oceanic Society provides cruises for bird, whale and marine-mammal watching on a 63-foot boat. The Farallons are the largest seabird rookery in the eastern Pacific, with tufted puffins, pigeon guillemots, rhinoceros auklets, murres, oystercatchers and cormorants. Also seen are sea lions, elephant seals, humpback or blue whales and porpoises. Leave from Fort Mason Center at 8:30 am for a fascinating eight-hour trip. Cruises depart on Saturdays, Sundays, occasional Mondays and Fridays from June through November. Bring lunch, beverages, binoculars and warm clothes. Rates for Friday and Monday cruises are $58, with Saturday and Sunday rates at $62. ☎ 415-868-1221 for information, ☎ 415-474-3385 for reservations.

## Sutro Heights Gardens

These gardens are inland and above the Cliff House, where Adolph Sutro's elaborate mansion stood. Not as lavish as they once were, but they are well worth seeing.

## Walking Tour, Cliff House to Lands End

Walk up from the Cliff House to the ruins of the Sutro Baths. Then take the stairs up to Merrie Way parking lot, pick up the trail at the north end of the lot and follow it to Lands End. Part of it uses the abandoned roadbed of Sutro's old Cliff House and Ferries Railroad. Many of the dirt sidepaths leading down toward the water are unstable and dangerous. The walk is generally easy with wonderful views overlooking the ocean. Giant freighters and tankers come in toward the Golden Gate Bridge and continue down the cliffs to where many ships piled up on the rocks at Lands End.

# *The Castro*

❦ *What fetched me instantly (and thousands of other newcomers with me) was the subtle but unmistakable sense of escape from the United States.*

H.L. Mencken, writing of San Francisco

A very pretty young woman came out of a boutique in front of us as we strolled down Castro Street after seeing "Hello, Gorgeous!" – the Barbra Streisand Museum. She was very blonde, wore black leather pants and a white blouse cut full in the sleeves with long collar points. A casual dusting of colors sparkled across her cheeks, silver, gold and pink. At that moment another young woman came toward us. She was tall with a regal bearing, fine features and lovely lavender hair. Talking over a glass of wine in The Sausage Factory later, we realized why we came over here every once in awhile. It just feels good to be walking along and enjoying life in The Castro.

The Castro District was not always a gay neighborhood. The street names laid out to sell lots give a clue as to the origin of the area: Castro, Noe, Sanchez, Dolores, Guerrero, and Valencia, all families from the Spanish and Mexican eras.

The neighborhood was really a village way outside of the City. That was when the folks who lived down by the Bay used to make the long trek on horseback or by buggy on a Sunday. They would come to see the Mission, or take in a bull and bear fight in the 1850s-60s, then in the 1870s-80s to stroll the gardens. There was always plenty of entertainment around the Mission. The Castro was even farther away, over the hill in the next valley.

The boom came after the cable car line constructed in 1887 made quick transportation down Market to the Ferry Building possible.

The Castro, like Noe Valley and Haight-Ashbury, was spared from fires and earthquakes. It survived a post-World War II slump and then was revitalized in the 1960s and 1970s. Gay couples were particularly strong forces in the rebirth of all these neighborhoods, but nowhere as much as in The Castro.

In 1972, San Francisco was the first American city to ban discrimination against homosexuals in housing or employment. For the first time, after a history of discrimination and often brutal oppression, gays found a city where couples could openly avow their love and achieve economic and political power.

## *Parking & Getting Around*

There are a few small, metered lots on Castro in the first block off Market between 17th and 18th and on 18th between Castro and Collingwood. Be warned that they are most often full. We have never known anyone who found a space in either one and suspect the cars you see there are permanently occupying the parking spots. Perhaps both lots are in reality outdoor galleries and the cars are *objets d'art*. If you are going to drive here, it is always possible to find a parking space on one of the side streets, eventually. What is needed, above all else, is patience.

❦  *... patience, patience everywhere like a fog.*

Graham Greene, *The Potting Shed*

The K, L and M MUNI cars run under Market Street to Castro. San Franciscans, quoting Herb Caen, a former *Chronicle* columnist, call it the route for Dutch tourists – the KLM line.

## *Restaurants*

### *The Sausage Factory*

(Southern Italian)

When we walked into The Sausage Factory the first time, guess what music was playing? Tony Bennett singing "I Left My Heart in San Francisco." An omen.

The Factory is one block from the famed Castro Theater and just a couple of doors from "Hello, Gorgeous," the Barbra Streisand Museum. It is old-fashioned in appearance with high ceilings, mirrors in elaborately carved frames and 1890s chandeliers. Lighting is kept low in the booths and on the tables. Singles come here, especially at lunch, and there are lots of dating couples at night.

The prices are so reasonable! At lunch, $4.50 will get you a nice plate of spaghetti, and ravioli is only $5.50. There are dinner specials every day. Monday night features saltimbocca at just $12.95, Tuesday has chicken cacciatore for $11.95, and Wednesday's special is veal scallopini for $12.50. It continues throughout the week and your wallet and palate will both be pleased.

The wine list consists of house red, white or rosé – a glass is $2, a half-liter is $4 and a liter is $8. It is a modest wine with, excuse the old wine joke, much to be modest about. There are big liter bottles of red on the table with small glasses, just as you would find in bistros or ristoranti in France and Italy.

A basket of sourdough bread arrives at the table first. Last time we were here, half the loaf was gone by the time the meal arrived and we weren't hungry any more. This time we ordered the very basic spaghetti and ravioli dishes without any accompaniments. Both came on platters mounded high with a ground beef and red sauce.

Are you seeking sheer nirvana? It's not that the food is so exceptional; the nostalgia is what counts here. This was a childhood treat for both of us. We shared memories of going out to an Italian restaurant with red-checked tablecloths, spaghetti piled high and tasting exactly like this. These memories precede the nefarious 1980s when basket-woven chianti bottles hanging from the ceiling were replaced by the spare, unadorned, clean Northern Italian restaurants with their imaginative dishes.

The Sausage Factory actually was a sausage factory in the 1960s. The sausage-making machinery is still back in the kitchen. Originally, there was a barber shop in the front of the factory. While you are sipping and waiting for your order to arrive, talk to Ray Laird who's been here, first as a customer then as a waiter, for 20 years. We learned from him that during the 1970s, when The Castro was really jumping, there was a candle on every table. As it dripped down, another was just stuck on top, and on and on. The dripping wax spread farther over each table and the candles got larger and larger until finally the fire department decided they were a hazard and ordered the candles taken out, forever. Too bad, it must have been quite a sight.

□ *517 Castro St.;* ☎ *415-626-1250.*
□ *Open: 11:30 am-1 am, seven days a week.*
□ *Prices: Lunch entrées from $4.50. Dinner, anti-pasto, Baby $8.95; Mama $9.95, pasta from $7.95-$9.95; other dishes $10.95-$11.95.*
□ *Credit cards: None.*

# *Things to Do*

## *A Different Light Bookstore*

489 Castro St., ☎ 415-431-0891. Gay and lesbian couples will find this an especially good place to spend a little time browsing, as this bookshop specializes in books written by, or about, homosexuals. All couples will find the free newspapers, fliers and posters handy to see what is happening in San Francisco's theater, dance and music scenes.

## *Castro Theater*

429 Castro St., ☎ 415-624-6120. Built in 1924, the grand era of theater building, this is done in a Spanish-Renaissance style with a unique interior resembling a Bedouin tent. Instead of a dozen tiny screens, there is one huge screen that shows old films, foreign films, art films, American classics and plays host to part of the San Francisco Film Festival (phone for dates). It attracts an appreciative and lively audience who are likely to talk back to the films. An organist plays a giant Wurlitzer during intermissions on weekends.

## *Hello, Gorgeous!*

549 Castro St., ☎ 415-864-2678, open Monday-Thursday 11 am-7 pm, Friday-Saturday 11 am-8 pm, Sunday 11 am-6 pm. No admission charge. Ken Joachim was a Barbra Streisand fan at age 16. He grew into a Barbra Streisand nut 23 years later when he hocked his Sonoma wine country home to finance his dream of building a tribute to her. Now, we have the only museum dedicated to Barbra Streisand in the world.

Proceed up the stairs and find the rooms filled with photos and posters of Barbra. In addition to the pictures, you will find amazingly similar looking mannequins in gowns that you will recognize. There is a TV set running continuously, showing a 1965 CBS special featuring guess who?

Downstairs is a store that sells nothing but memorabilia like audio tapes, videos, framed photos, and posters, some of which are rare. Shirts and blouses like the ones she has worn are also available for purchase. They look good, by the way. The costumes displayed on the wall are for real, but not for sale. And there's another TV set showing *Funny Girl*, most likely for the 1,000th time. We love Barbra, too, but think of that long-suffering clerk. If you're in The Castro, be sure to drop in. It's a lot of fun.

## In-Jean-ious

432 Castro St., ☎ 415-864-1863. In-Jean-ious has been here quite awhile, but it first hit public attention just before Christmas of 1996. It sold Barbie dolls that had slightly different lifestyles than the usual ones. There was, for instance, Trailer Trash Barbie, Hooker Barbie, Big Dyke Barbie and Drag Queen Ken, all in appropriate costumes and make-up. Bill Tull, In-Jean-ious' owner, quickly learned that his shop was being publicized in newspapers all over the world. That publicity also meant that he caught the attention of Mattel, Square Barbie's maker. Bill heard from their legal deparment in nothing flat.

Meanwhile, the shop is still a great place to browse for men's clothes. Most of the clothes are unisex, so lots of women shop here too. It is mostly active wear, casual and trendy. If a night dancing is on your agenda, this is the place to look for the perfect clubwear outfit.

Plenty of novelty items are to be found here as well. You will probably find something to take home to that person who is hard to shop for. How about a T-shirt with "I can go from zero to bitch in .5 seconds" printed on the front? You must know someone who fits that description. They can ship anywhere.

## Liberty Street Walk

Walk uphill one block south of Castro on Liberty Street to Noe. Fine Victorian houses and late 19th-century "cottages" line the street. Go up the flight of steps to the top for a wonderful view of downtown San Francisco.

## Names Project: Memorial Quilt

2362 Market St., ☎ 415-863-1966. This is where new panels are created for the moving, nationwide response to AIDS. Panels are made by family and friends to commemorate a person who has died of AIDS, then added to the enormous and, unfortunately, still growing quilt. Visits and donations are welcome.

# Annual Events

## June

You will see the Gay and Lesbian Freedom Day Parade in June. It is San Francisco's largest annual celebration (the second largest in California after the Rose Parade in Pasadena). Dates vary, but it is always held in late June. The parade route is usually up Market Street from the Ferry Building to the Civic Center. ☎ 415-864-3FREE (3733).

## First Sunday in October

See the Castro Street Fair, featuring crafts, food booths, outrageous costumes and lots of fun.

## October 31st

Halloween is celebrated in a big way in San Francisco, like no other city in the country. Last Halloween, we were in North Beach at night and the number of elaborately-costumed adults on the street was amazing. You will see celebrations everywhere in the city, but nothing can hold a pumpkin to The Castro. The crowd was getting so large that in 1996 the city threw an officially sponsored Halloween street party in the Civic Center, just to spread things out. The Castro celebration is still bigger.

## November 27th

The Harvey Milk-George Moscone Memorial March takes place with everyone holding lighted candles. The marchers go down Market Street to City Hall. Harvey Milk was San Francisco's first openly gay member of the Board of Supervisors. He and Mayor George Moscone were assassinated in 1978. There is a plaque honoring Milk above the subway entrance at Castro and Market streets.

# *Chinatown*

❦ *A beautiful woman, sheltered in a gilded mansion.*
*A nuptial union, celebrated under the bright lights*
*of wedding candles.*
*Together we'd sleep, sharing pillow and bed.*
*To my heart's content, I'd caress her tender breasts.*
*O, moments such as this –*
*I just don't know this joy that I can get.*
*Instead I came to live alone in the West.*
*And betrayed sixteen years of my youthful best.*

*Songs of Gold Mountain, Cantonese Rhymes from San Francisco China-town*

In coming to Chinatown, you will find **Grant Street** lined with shops selling clothes, antiques, tea and herbal medicine. What can you take home as a souvenir? Here's an idea that's colorful, educational and inexpensive all in one. Buy a Chinese calendar. This special calendar started 5,000 years ago when Buddha called all the animals together, but only 12 came. To reward their loyalty he named a year after each of the 12, in the order of their arrival. Ever since that time, the years have run in sequence of those 12, over and over. First, the year of the Rat, then the Ox, Tiger, Rabbit, Dragon, Snake, Horse, Goat, Monkey, Rooster, Dog and Pig. From the

*Chinatown.*

calendar, you can learn which you are, and which you partner is, depending on the year you were born.

With that serious matter out of the way, how to see Chinatown? It is best to leave your car at the hotel, get here by taxi or public transit and then walk. One side of Chinatown rubs up against the Union Square area and on the other side you will run into North Beach. You can make a day of it, with plenty to see.

Walking offers choices. You can go around the area on your own and linger as long as you like in a shop. Or you may hook up with a walking tour, where you will hear a lot about the beginnings of this area, and how the Chinese got here. Over 300,000 Chinese arrived between 1850 and 1900. Most were young men hoping to make their fortune and return to China.

The area that came to be called Chinatown expanded from a few blocks to take in the 16 blocks from Kearny to Stockton and Bush to Broadway, as it does today. You should know that this part of town is really the site of the beginnings of San Francisco. It all started around **Portsmouth Square**, at Kearny between Clay and Washington. It was not anything as grand as a square at first. It started as a cow pen. But Yerba Buena Cove was close by, and when building began around here the space became the town's plaza. It's where Captain John Montgomery, commander of the *USS Portsmouth*, raised the American flag on July 9, 1846 and declared California a possession of the United States. As the town's center, it was also the scene of mass meetings, public whippings and, with the Vigilantes a bit later, public hangings.

It is a bit less exciting here these days. Like Union Square, this too was dug up, a big public garage stuck underneath and the Square put back on top. There are two levels to the Square on this sloping street. Off Kearny Street, where the entrance to the garage is, you will find a play area for kids. There is also a plaque commemorating the first cable car line. Another plaque marks the site of first Public School in California erected 1847. There is no plaque for the bordello that once stood here.

On the larger and livelier upper part of the square you'll find groups of Chinese men playing Chinese checkers and mah jong or talking. Plenty of conversation is exchanged in these parts. A bridge over Kearny leads to the third floor of the Holiday Inn, where the **Chinese Cultural Center** is found. The Center organizes walking tours of Chinatown from this location. In the northwest corner of the Square, a bronze galleon with golden sails set, represents the *Hispaniola*, from Robert Louis Stevenson's book, *Treasure Island*. The inscription is from *"A Christmas Sermon."* Stevenson lived nearby on Bush Street between 1879 and 1880 and became a good friend of many Chinese people in an era when that was unusual.

Walk uphill on Washington almost to Grand. The **Bank of Canton** is located at 737 Washington and was built after the earthquake in an effort to make Chinatown look more "Chinese." They certainly succeeded! This was the Chinese Telephone Exchange. Operators had to be proficient in English, five Chinese dialects *and* know every subscriber's name. The exchange was closed in 1949 when it was converted to rotary dialing.

Cross Grant Street and the next lane is **Waverly Place**, a famous place indeed. By the end of 1850, when there were 781 Chinese, only two were women. This created an obvious problem. At first, it seemed fortunate for the frustrated men that one of the two was a stunning young woman named Ah Toy. She had been bought in China and sent as a slave to serve as the city's first Chinese prostitute. But rich and prominent white men, who could pay much more for her affections, completely monopolized her time from the beginning. As a result of their favors, Ah Toy was able to buy her freedom and become the owner of her own brothel on Waverly Place, stocked with girls she bought and imported. Madame Ah Toy eventually sold out and returned to China a wealthy woman.

After Ah Toy's success, this narrow two-block street was lined with brothels in the later years of the century. All were destroyed in 1906. After that time, several temples were built along here; two can be visited. **Tin How Temple** is on the top floor at 123-29 Waverly Place. You will have to ring the bell. The red and gold altar is dedicated to Tien Hon, goddess of sailors, fishermen, travelers, wandering minstrels and prostitutes. It was built by those who arrived safely after crossing the Pacific in 1852. **Morras Temple** is at 109-11 Waverly Place.

Back on Grant Avenue, this is the oldest street in San Francisco, originally called *Calle de la Fundacion*. On the corner of Grant and California is **St. Mary's Church**. It was the first Catholic cathedral on the West Coast, built by Chinese construction workers from 1852-54. The granite foundation and the trim came from China and the bricks came around the Horn. It has been home of the Paulist Fathers since 1894. Up high under the clock, you will see the inscription, "Son Observe the Time and Fly from Evil," facing the brothels which stood across the street where St. Mary's Square is now located.

The Paulist Fathers petitioned the city in 1895 to raze the brothels and replace them with a badly needed park. Their prayers were not answered until the earthquake and fire took care of the matter and St. Mary's Square became possible. There are no tables for mah jong to be found here. Instead, there stands a statue of Dr. Sun Yat-sen, China's early revolutionary, who lived in San Francisco and started a newspaper here to support his cause in 1910. He then returned to

China and succeeded in overthrowing the Qing dynasty in 1911. The handsome statue is made of stainless steel and pink granite. The WPA accomplished this good deed by commissioning Beniamino Bufano to sculpt it in 1938. The plaque and bronze screen on the opposite side of the park honors Americans of Chinese descent who died serving the US armed forces in World Wars I and II.

Walk on down Grant to Bush and see the **Chinatown Gate**, built in 1970. This Gate is at a strategic spot at the Union Square entrance to Chinatown, serving as a device to promote the community and tourism. The foo dogs flanking the flaming red gate are mythical creatures to ward off evil spirits. The fish symbolize abundance and prosperity. The dragons on the green tile-capped top represent power and fertility, with the ball symbolizing the earth.

You might notice an anomaly here. When you step through the gate expecting everything from here on to be Chinese, the first thing you see is the Sabra Café to your left. "Glatt Kosher-Falafel-Shish Kebab" are the specialties there. Who said this was not a cosmopolitan city?

## Restaurants

Dining in Chinatown is a problem, brought about by the success of Chinatown itself. Everyone who visits San Francisco wants to see the neighborhood, and most want to eat here. For the most part, you can forget romance. The best Chinese restaurant, Tommy Toy's, is just outside Chinatown in the financial district. The menu is French-Asian and it's very romantic. Brandy Ho's fine Hunan fare is half a block outside in North Beach on the opposite side of Chinatown.

## Brandy Ho's

(Hunan Chinese)

There are two Brandy Ho's locations. The "other" Brandy Ho's has been around for 16 years. It is crowded, noisy and successful. *Our* Brandy Ho's (run by the same family) has been here for only seven years. It is smaller, quieter and has a dramatic red, black and white decor. It is peaceful, just the slightest bit formal, and is well-nigh perfect for eating and romance.

Three brothers in the Ho family started the first restaurant. The eldest brother, Brandy, was the chef, with family members working other jobs in the restaurant. Jack, the second brother, now runs both restaurants. Sedgwick, the third brother, is the chef at the new restaurant.

Here's a recipe Sedgwick Ho suggested for those who those who enjoy the smoked ham with fresh cloves of garlic. You can buy the Hunan smoked ham as a take-out item, or substitute Virginia ham.

## *Brandy Ho's Smoked Ham with Fresh Garlic*

2 cups smoked ham, sliced
1 medium onion
¾ cup of bamboo shoots (you can get canned)
6-8 garlic cloves
¾ cup scallions
2 tbsp cottonseed oil
¼ cup white wine
⅓ cup chicken broth
3 tbsp soy sauce
1 tsp tapioca or corn starch

Heat oil in a very hot wok. If you don't have a wok, use a frying pan. Add whole crushed garlic. Stir quickly, only allowing the cloves to brown lightly. Add julienne strips of onion and stir. Add cut bamboo shoots and stir for 30 seconds. Then add strips of sliced ham stirring constantly. When everything is well coated, add the wine, stirring continuously. Add the soy sauce and then the broth. When liquid is reduced to ½ cup, add the scallions and stir vigorously for one minute. Add tapioca or corn starch.

This is authentic Hunan food. The western boundary of Hunan, in southeast China, has an abundance of wild game. The family's smoking process comes from there, as much of the game is traditionally smoked to preserve it. The Hos never used MSG in China and see no reason to use it here.

It is difficult to suggest just a few items from the long menu, because practically everything we have had could be recommended. But to start out simply, the cucumber and bean sprout salad (which is enough for two) is wonderfully fresh tasting. The wok-cooked shrimp has a medley of flavors. The smoked ham is a surprise when you are used to the American-smoked product. The Hos smoke this the Hunan way, over hardwood until it has a much stronger smokey flavor. Then they wok-cook it with cloves of garlic, spring onions and bamboo shoots. Chicken and duck are also available smoked Hunan-style.

We have found the dish listed as "Brandy's Dinner" a good choice because of its variety – a fusion of beef, scallops and shrimp stir-fried in wine sauce with bamboo shoots, onion, ginger, garlic and bell pepper. Despite the fact that they are all cooked together, the taste of each remains distinctive.

Hunan, on China's south-central coast, has one China's great cuisines. The emphasis is on seafood and fresh vegetables with very hot spices. If you are not used to that much chili, just tell your waiter/waitress how hot you want it. They will adjust accordingly.

On our last visit we sat at a table by the back window looking up at the cliff face. The big windows look out on the sheer rock of Telegraph Hill. We chopsticked our way through dish after dish. When we were on our first or second (or third?) appetizer, the young couple seated at the next table rose to leave. The man spotted Jack, the second Ho brother. Deliberately eavesdropping, we heard the man tell Jack that this was the best Chinese meal he had ever had in his life. After we had finally stopped eating, we agreed completely.

- ❏  *450-452 Broadway;* ☎ *415-362-6268.*
- ❏  *Open: 11:30 am-11 pm, daily.*
- ❏  *Prices: Appetizers from $1.75, soups from $2, salads from $4.75, half-order $2.75, entrées $7.50-$11.50.*
- ❏  *Credit cards: All major.*
- ❏  *Reservations: Suggested.*
- ❏  *Parking: Street.*
- ❏  *Directions: A half-block east of Broadway and Columbus.*

## Pearl City Seafood Restaurant

(Dim sum)

We consulted with knowledgeable friends, including Chinese friends, who eat often in Chinatown and know their restaurants. They agreed that, although this restaurant lacks the outward trappings of romance, it is the best at what it does.

The specialty of the house at breakfast and lunch is dim sum – a style of cooking that allows you to taste a broad variety of succulent dishes. Dim sum, in case you are not acquainted with it, started as small samples of dumplings stuffed with different ingredients. Although dumplings are served all over China, the Cantonese make the most. The Cantonese also claim that they offer the finest varieties of dumplings. Dim sum now includes lots of other dishes besides dumplings.

Pearl City is a long, narrow place with three rows of tables. The food is on carts, wheeled between the rows, each in its own small dish. You make your selections and the check is figured by counting the empty dishes when you are finished.

The room is reasonably attractive, the food very good and the price, at $2 per dish and up, is right. Incidentally, no tourists come here. In fact, you will probably find that everyone in the restaurant is Asian, which is a sign that you are in the right place. Dim sum is served from 8 am to 3 pm and there is a full Cantonese menu for dinner. If you really want to emulate the Chinese while you are in Chinatown, show up for breakfast.

- ❏ *641 Jackson St. (between Grant and Kearny);* ☎ *415-398-8383.*
- ❏ *Open: 8 am to 10 pm. Dim sum at breakfast and lunch; full menu at dinner.*
- ❏ *Prices: $2 per dish (you'll need six or so).*
- ❏ *Reservations: No.*

♥ *Tommy Toy's*

(Chinese-French)

This is the restaurant Chinatown should have, but does not. Tommy Toy says there are two great cuisines in the world: French and Chinese. So, he combined them.

It is a place where business people bring customers to impress them. But it is also a great place to take a significant other. Tommy Toy's *is* special. There is no doubt about it. The decor is fashioned after the 19th-century Empress Dowager's reading room. Along with 300-year-old tapestries on the wall inlaid with hand-silvered mirrors, "powder paintings" framed in sandalwood, carved wooden archways and silk draperies, there is Tommy's collection of Chinese fans.

Use the street level entrance of the tall commercial office building at Montgomery and Washington in the Financial District. Once inside, any hint of commercialism vanishes. A small bar, just off the entry, is a quiet place to sip 30-year-old malt Scotch while waiting for your table.

The restaurant holds 160, but you would not know it. With several rooms and small, separated areas, it seems intimate and cozy. The lighting is dim, with perhaps a tall candle behind you and another on the table. Read the menu by the flickering light and enjoy it all.

The *prix fixe* dinner gives you a sampling of many things. It starts with lobster pot stickers and chili sauce for appetizers, followed by seafood bisque served in a coconut shell with puff pastry sealing in all the subtle flavors.

Wok-cooked tiger prawns show up on a bed of spinach, a delicious contrast in tastes and textures. Peking duck is not something you eat all the time, unless you happen to live a wealthy life in Beijing. On the rare occasion when it comes along, you want it to be perfect. This is not a whole duck. You will be served slices that taste like heavenly morsels.

The pork medallions with a glazed cassia sauce on a bed of sliced oranges are excellent. Cassia is a variety of cinnamon, sometimes called Chinese cinnamon. The sauce is made, not from ground powder, but from the pulp found inside large pods. The flavor is similar, but unlike any you have tasted before.

Then it's on to dessert! One night for us, it was a peach mousse on a strawberry compote. We will not go on. Let it be said that the endings are as good as the beginnings.

The restaurant attracts a late dinner crowd, with 9 pm being the busiest time. At 6 pm, you would probably be dining alone. At any rate, if this weekend is to be the big seduction, the honeymoon or the 20th anniversary celebration, this may very well be *the* restaurant of choice.

Order the *prix fixe* dinner and be dazzled by the seven courses accompanied by seven complete sets of silver. Expect your water or wine glass to be refilled a dozen or so times. You will be presented with a fresh, hot, moist towel a good five or six times throughout the meal. It is awesome.

- *655 Montgomery St., (Corner Montgomery and Washington);* ☎ *415-397-4888.*
- *Open: Lunch served Monday-Friday, 11:30 am-3 pm. Dinner served Monday-Saturday, 6 pm-10 pm, Sunday 6 pm-9:30 pm.*
- *Prices: Dinners, appetizers and soups $4.95-$7.95; entrées $11.95-$14.95; prix fixe $38 and $48.*
- *Credit cards: AE, Diners Club, MC, V.*
- *Reservations: Definitely.*
- *Parking: Valet.*

# Things to Do

## The Chinatown Kite Shop

717 Grant Ave., near Sacramento Street, ☎ 415-989-5182. This kite shop is a great place to find a gift for a child (prices start at $1.89) or an adult (prices go up to $300). There are kites made of paper and others made of silk in China. There are kites in the shape of butterflies, airplanes, diamond kites and box kites. Good kite flying areas in San Francisco are Marina Park, north of North Beach,

Golden Gate Park and the beach. But, if you get a stunt kite, which has two lines and can dive and loop, you only need the space of a yard for it to fly.

The Double-Nine Festival, which falls on the ninth day of the ninth month in the lunar calendar, is the day to drink chrysanthemum wine and fly kites. Ask Albert Chang for the exact date when you visit the shop.

## The Wok Shop

718 Grant Ave., ☎ 415-989-3797. Toll-free information from out-of-town ☎ (888) 780-7171. The Wok Shop is a fascinating place for anyone who loves to cook. Here is where you will find those hard-to-find kitchen tools and, despite the name, implements from every country are in stock here. If you have questions about any aspects of cooking, Tane Chan, the owner, is very knowledgeable and helpful. Actually, it is fun to browse, pick something up and say to your partner, "What the hell could *that* be for?"

## Chinese Cultural Center Walking Tour

750 Kearny St., ☎ 415-986-1822. The Cultural Center, with its gallery of Chinese and Chinese-American art, is on the third floor of the Holiday Inn and directly connected to Portsmouth Square by a bridge. The walks, which take 1½ to two hours, meet here Saturdays at 2 pm and cost $15. You will visit temples, tea shops, investigate the street life and learn Chinatown's history. Call for reservations.

## City Guides Walking Tour

☎ 415-557-4266 for recorded update; Internet address http://www.hooked.net/users/jhum. City Guides do a good job of exploring the essence of Chinatown, its alleys, side streets, sewing shops, medicinal herb shops and produce stores. Sweat shops are omitted, though they are an unfortunate part of Chinatown. The tour participants meet at Kearny and Clay, edge of Portsmouth Square, Saturday mornings at 10 am. The tours are led by docents from the Public Library.

## GGO Tour Chinatown

☎ 888-446-8687. Chinatown definitely has a plethora of tours. This one is a combination – on your own, with the benefit of some guidance. You rent a tape recorder with a headset and, as you walk, you hear about what you are seeing. Rental is $12, or $19 for two headsets.

## Chinese New Year Celebration

This colorful celebration goes on for two weeks sometime between late January and February. The exact date of New Year depends upon the lunar calendar. There is a carnival in Portsmouth Square with street vendors selling candy, flowers and red envelopes on the already-packed Stockton Street and Grant Avenue. The color red is thought to bring good luck. You are supposed to give little red envelopes (known as *lai see*) with a dollar bill inside to children and unmarried friends for good fortune.

The culmination of this event is the parade featuring a 60-foot-long sinuous, dancing dragon (known as *gum lung*). This is the largest celebration in San Francisco all year. The parade usually starts at Market and Second, weaves along the streets of Chinatown and ends at Kearny and Stockton at a reviewing stand. The incessant popping and crackling of thousands of little firecrakers is definitely part of the fun.

## Parking

Parking is available at Portsmouth Square Garage with an entrance off Kearny between Clay and Washington. It is the most convenient garage, but usually crowded. Midday is the best time or on weekends. Chang's parking is a commercial lot across Washington from the Square. The public Sutter-Stockton Garage, between Sutter and Bush, Stockton and Grant, is only a block from the Chinatown Gate at Grant and Bush. The entrance is on Bush Street going north. You can always find parking here.

# Civic Center

❦ *There is almost nothing to see in San Francisco that is worth seeing. I think I may say that strangers will generally desire to get out of San Francisco as quickly as they can.*

Anthony Trollope

You probably will not be spending much time here unless you are going to a concert. The United Nations Charter was signed in the Opera House in 1945. The Civic Center Plaza, in front of City Hall, is the ending point of parades that come up Market Street. It is also the site of protests and demonstrations.

We have an oblique insight into some of the problems because Anne, our daughter-in-law, works here. This area sits on the edge of The Tenderloin, resulting in an abundance of homeless people and a fear of crime. As a result, we hesitate to make a date with her for lunch in the Union Square area, where most of the good restaurants are. She is uneasy about walking even a few blocks because of problems she might encounter en route.

There are, however, several buildings that may interest you. The Opera House is home to one of the great opera companies. The San Francisco Ballet has its own theater and Davies Symphony Hall is also here. Check the newspaper to see what's playing.

The old Public Library, a venerable and much-loved building, was closed when a new library was built next door. The new building, which has much more space for equipment, allowing for internet surfing, does not have enough space for all the books from the old library. As a result, thousands were quietly disposed of, many into landfills. Every once in awhile San Francisco, in its march forward, falls on its face. Amid all this negative talk there are, however, a few bright spots in the Civic Center that you will discover as you read on.

## Inns

### Abigail Hotel

The Abigail and the Inn at the Opera are both in the Civic Center. Other than their location, they have nothing in common. We are listing the Abigail primarily because the Millenium restaurant is in the hotel and has a once-a-month aphrodesiac dinner, which includes staying overnight at the hotel. This incredible dining experience occurs only on the night of the full moon. (See Millenium, page 49.)

If you're interested in spending a few days in San Francisco at bargain prices, it is hard to beat this place and its $79 rooms. It's even possible to get a better price and a better room, as long as you don't mind sharing the bath. (See Inn 1890, page 78.)

What you will find here are small rooms, half with queen beds, half with double beds. Each has a dresser and a small television set, without cable. The shared bathroom has a tile bathroom/shower. The deluxe rooms, $10 more, have queen beds and most rooms front onto McAllister Street. They have a round marble-top table and two chairs in a bay window overlooking the street. This is an old, narrow, tall brick building, put up after the 1906 fire. You remember the old black and white films, where the private eye hero goes into a cheap hotel that has a small lobby with linoleum on the floor (in this case it is marble). The guy behind the cramped desk wears an eyeshade and expects to be beaten to a pulp before he'll tell the hero what room the bad guy's in? Remember the narrow, creaking elevator the hero, like Edmond O'Brien, takes upstairs? The Abigail has this kind of character. Beware of another character lurking around here, known as the "The Christmas Ghost." You will have to ask that guy at the desk with the eyeshade to tell you about it.

- *246 McAllister;* ☎ *800-243-6510.*
- *Rooms: 64.*
- *Rates: Rooms $79-$89, suites $139. Aphrodesiac Package $95, including dinner, deluxe room, parking.*
- *Credit cards: All.*
- *Reservations: For a room, absolutely required. For Aphrodesiac Package, at least one week in advance, four weeks in advance during the summer.*
- *Breakfast: Continental breakfast included.*
- *Handicapped accessible: Inquire for specifics.*
- *Smoking: Both smoking and non-smoking rooms.*
- *Children: One per room.*
- *Pets: No.*
- *Parking: $8 for 24 hours, in and out. Street parking difficult in daytime, easy at night.*
- *Walking: Two blocks from Market St.*

## ♥ Inn at the Opera

Walking into the Inn at the Opera is like entering a really good European hotel. It is small with an attentive staff ready to pamper and care for your every need. In the attractively decorated lobby, we heard Mozart chamber music in the background. Continuing through the lobby, you will find the small but luxuriously appointed bar and dining room.

The individual attention is exemplary. An employee will drive you anywhere in downtown San Francisco. There are fresh flowers in every room and 24-hour room service. Our suite was attractively furnished in pastels of pink, blue and green. There were oversized pillows on the queen bed and a half-canopy draped it. There was a phone in the bedroom as well as the sitting room. Two white terry cloth robes waited and the bedside tables were equipped with good reading lamps. There's an honor bar with the usual goodies plus little delicacies like duck pâté ($5) and brie ($4.50). A microwave oven and a sink made it a useful nook.

Rooms are categorized as standard, moderate or superior. None are really large, but the standard-size rooms have little space left after the queen bed, chair and armoire have filled the floor. But the price, at $115, is so good it may make up for that drawback.

People come here for a gracious and elegant atmosphere with a very professional staff that gives wonderful service as a matter of course. Another attraction is the location, just two minute's walk from the opera or ballet.

The Inn was built in 1926 as the New Alden Hotel. From the earliest years, it has always been known as the home of jazz musicians, performing artists playing at the San Francisco Opera and pop singers playing at the Civic Center. Music critics and writers all show up at this hotel. Artists check in and ask, "Who's in town?"

"It's great to see Michael Tilson Thomas (conductor of the San Francisco Symphony) on stage at night and then see him here in the small dining room at breakfast," said a guest who has been coming here for years.

You might see Jerry Hadley (tenor), Samuel Ramey (basso), Frederica Van Stade (mezzo soprano) all in the bar together and feeling right at home. Since the hotel is right behind City Hall, it is not surprising to find the Mayor, the Lieutenant Governor and assorted councilpersons and legislators in here for breakfast or lunch.

The complimentary breakfast, in the Act IV restaurant downstairs, is far more than simple continental fare. We were delighted to find a big buffet with fresh-squeezed orange juice, berries, papaya, freshly baked scones and muffins, sliced ham, cereal, cheese and yogurt.

The bar and restaurant are always full during opera, ballet and symphony seasons, but empty out by 7:30 pm, leaving plenty of seats for the non-theater-going guests. It is customary to have a pre-theater meal, go to the opera and return for dessert.

A "Romantic Interlude" package includes a chilled bottle of Domaine Chandon Champagne with berries and cream waiting in your room.

Be warned that the Inn is booked heavily in September and February for the opera and ballet seasons. December is also very popular for the Nutcracker Suite performances.

It is said that Tony Bennett, who sings about leaving his heart in San Francisco, actually left it here.

- *333 Fulton St.;* ☎ *415-863-8400; California outside San Francisco, dial 800-423-9610; rest of country, dial 800-325-2708.*
- *Rates: $125-$220. Romance package $190 and $240, depending on room selection. Stay two nights on the package and receive 10% off both nights. Stay a third night and get 20% off all three nights.*
- *Reservations: Recommend two weeks in advance, easier on weekdays.*
- *Breakfast: Large continental buffet.*
- *Amenities: Robes, honor bar, microwave, shoe shine, driver to downtown, bar, lunch and dinner in restaurant.*
- *Handicapped accessible: Two rooms; entire hotel is accessible.*
- *Smoking: Rooms on two floors. Bar allows smoking.*
- *Children: Yes.*
- *Pets: No.*
- *Parking: Valet $19 for 24 hours in and out.*
- *Directions: Go to City Hall and look behind it.*

# *Restaurants*

## ♥ *Act IV at Inn at the Opera*

(An American grill)

The room is clubby, intimate and very comfortable. A short bar on one side has a few bar stools. The richly hued walls are hung with oil paintings, and the dozen tables are flanked with comfortable chairs and leather settees. It is a place made for lingering.

Right off the top, you will dawdle over the menu. Do not be surprised if you change your mind several times before settling on something.

You may wish to start with a mixed green salad with a mustardy caper vinaigrette that lends a tart sharpness. One night, we discovered fried green tomatoes with a smokey bacon that set them off beautifully.

The Caesar salad, with its crisp green romaine, has croutons that actually taste deeply of fresh garlic. Top it off with some freshly grated parmesan cheese and you have achieved a delicious, full flavor. You might like the baked goat cheese in a biscuit crust with olives served on fresh, crunchy watercress.

Then we get down to serious business. A wild king salmon is grilled to a crusty tenderness and served with a roasted corn salad accompanied by a basil and garlic mayonnaise that manages not to overwhelm the corn flavor. Perhaps two crisp crêpes will tweak your appetite. One is filled with roasted yams and corn and the other with red lentils and herbs, served with a roast garlic sauce, which lends its own rich taste.

For the meat and potatoes person, horseradish mashed potatoes is just the right accompaniment to a fork-tender loin of beef. Another choice is a roasted chicken breast stuffed with crayfish and served with ancho chili dumplings, light and plump in pan gravy.

You can see the pattern here: tomatoes, bacon, corn, yams and lentil beans – all straightforward American fare with a gourmet touch.

- *333 Fulton St.;* ☎ *415-553-8100.*
- *Open: Breakfast, 7 am-10 am daily. Lunch, 11:30 am-2:30 pm, Monday-Friday and Sunday. Dinner served Sunday-Thursday, 5:30 pm-10 pm, Friday-Saturday, 5:30 pm-10:30 pm.*
- *Prices: Appetizers $5-$9.50; entrées $16-$26.*
- *Credit cards: AE, MC, V.*
- *Reservations: Recommended.*
- *Parking: Complimentary valet.*

## Millenium in the Abigail Hotel

(Gourmet vegetarian)

This is the place that features an Aphrodesiac Menu one night a month, with a stay at the hotel as part of the package. Dinner for two is reminiscent of the *Tom Jones* movie, with Albert Finney and Joyce Redman staring into each other's eyes as they erotically tore food apart and stuffed it into their mouths. We'll get to that later.

Like most people, we do not ordinarily rush to vegetarian restaurants. The first time we got to Millenium was strictly because it was recommended by someone knowledgeable about vegetarian food. After that, it was voluntarily, because what we had was light, different and tasty.

Dinner here might start with a grilled and smoked portobello mushroom, served with a sweet Moroccan sauce (not too sweet), which enhances the earthy tones of the mushroom. It comes with toast which tastes of fresh garlic. There is a warm spinach salad with red onions and smoked tofu. The spinach is crisp and fresh tasting, nothing like that terrible soggy spinach served in so many restaurants.

The next course could be a filo purse filled with wild mushrooms, leeks and butternut squash; a veritable stew of flavors, each coming through without blanketing the others. There is a tofu ricotta and barley pilaf, both served on French lentils with a fine Dijon mustard sauce. The polenta torte is another winner. But, even though it is called a torte, it is really rosemary polenta served with a basil tofu ricotta, mushroom duxelles and a tomato putanesca sauce. What they do with vegetables here is astounding!

The Aphrodesiac Dinner is a special menu served on the Sunday nearest to the full moon. We confess that we haven't tried it, so we can't guarantee that passions will flame higher between you with every bite. But if you are in San Francisco at the right time, the deal is hard to resist. How about an Aphrodesiac Dinner for two, beverage and room for the night at the Abigail for $95?

The Aphrodesiac Package includes parking and amenities like razors, toothbrushes and toothpaste. Small items like these are in case the dinner has the desired aphrodesiac effect and you decide on the spur of the moment to stay overnight. Technically, of course, you are supposed to have reserved the whole package in advance.

The Abigail is conveniently located at the same address as the Millenium, but with a different phone number. It is on McAllister, just off Market Street, in the middle of the Civic Center, an area awash with busy people and endless cars from Monday through Friday. At night or on a weekend, you can shoot a cannon and won't even wing a Democrat. You can even find a parking place on the street.

❑ *246 McAllister St. (between Larkin and Hyde);*
 ☎ *415-487-9800, fax 415-487-9921. Abigail Hotel,* ☎ *800-243-6510.*
❑ *Open: Lunch 11:30 am-2 pm, Tuesday-Friday. Dinner 5 pm-9:30 pm, Tuesday-Sunday.*
❑ *Prices: Lunch, salads $5.95, entrées $6.95-$7.95. Dinner, salads $6.25-$7.25, entrées $11.75-$15.25. Menu is constantly changing, so prices vary, but this is the usual range. Aphrodesiac Dinner for two includes beverage, room and parking for $95.*
❑ *Credit cards: All major.*
❑ *Reservations: Recommended. Required for Aphrodesiac Dinner package.*
❑ *Parking: Street or in one of the closed lots.*

## *The Emperor of San Francisco*

*San Francisco is a mad city, inhabited for the most part by perfectly insane people.*

Rudyard Kipling

His real name was Joshua Abraham Norton, but for the last 25 years of his life he was addressed as "Emperor" or "Your Highness." This was Emperor Norton, self-proclaimed Emperor of the United States and Protector of Mexico. Most cities would have tossed him into a loony bin. The citizens of San Francisco took him into their hearts.

The future Emperor came to California from his native England in 1849 and set himself up as a real estate entrepreneur with $40,000 in capital. He made a fortune. Then, he lost it in an unlucky investment. They say his mind was unbalanced by this turn of bad luck and that he went mad. Or did he? What is known is that after disappearing for a few months he resurfaced on September 17, 1858. He sent an announcement that he had been appointed Emperor of the United States to the newspapers of the city. His announcement included an admonition that he must hereafter be addressed by the proper title; and so he was. The miracle is that everyone in San Francisco went along with it. He could eat and drink wherever he chose, free of charge. When his "uniform" of red-striped trousers and gold-plated epaulets wore out, the Board of Supervisors bought him a newly tailored uniform. With impeccable royal manners, he sent a gracious note of thanks and a patent of nobility for each Supervisor.

Whenever Emperor Norton needed money, he issued bonds of 10, 25, and 50 cents which were accepted everywhere in the city. Now and then, he drew a check for a small amount and it would be honored by the banks. He promenaded the streets downtown, always carrying a cane, with a long, red-hilted sword in his belt. He nodded in a kingly manner to his subjects, who bowed gravely in return.

When he died, the city's flags were lowered to half-mast and the whole town turned out for his funeral. He left an estate of one $2½ gold piece, three dollars in silver, an 1828 franc and 98,000 shares in a worthless gold mine.

Was Joseph Abraham Norton insane or a great actor? Did he "take" the city of San Francisco for all those years by putting on a fine show? Madman or con man? We'll never know. But is there another city in the world that would have gone along with the joke for decades? It could only happen in lovely, eccentric San Francisco.

# Cole Valley

❦ *Marriage among us seems to be regarded as a pleasant farce – a sort of laughable afterpiece to courtship.*

*San Francisco Chronicle*, 1854

The neighborhood folks call this place Cole Valley. It is a one-block business district with cross streets going uphill away from it. There is one saloon, **Finnegan's Wake**, 937 Cole St., ☎ 415-731-6119; **EOS Restaurant and Wine Bar**, dinner only, 901 Cole St., ☎ 415-566-3063; **Bambino's Pizza Restaurant**, an Italian place, 945 Cole St. ☎ 415-731-1345; **Grandehos Kamekyo**, a Japanese restaurant, 943 Cole St., ☎ 415-759-8428; and **Zazie**, very French (941 Cole St., ☎ 415-564-5332). This is one lucky neighborhood!

Actually, it is only a few blocks from Haight-Ashbury, but the people who live in Cole Valley definitely do not want to be identified with that neighborhood. Their houses are up on the hill above The Haight with higher rents and higher property values. There are no T-shirt shops and no tourist buses. They have a really nice little spot, with just enough friendly restaurants and busineses. Of course, it's a problem parking your car. This is San Francisco. What else is new?

## Restaurant

### Zazie

(French)

Catherine Opoix owned and ran Zazie many moons ago in this very same location. Then she got tired of the restaurant business and sold. It became a Tex-Mex café for a few years. Then, about the time they were ready to say adios, Catherine got bored with doing nothing and was ready to go back into the business. Thus the rebirth of Zazie.

The room is long and thin, about 15 feet wide. The ceiling is high, maybe two stories, and there is a garden in the back with a few tables – a most pleasant spot for lunch on warm days. It is little more than a storefront, but the food is as sumptuous as if you were on the continent. There is sometimes flamenco dancing on Sundays, and French-speaking dinner nights (when enough French-speakers sign up). The clientele consists mostly of students and locals who take advantage of their proximity, along with knowledgeable San Franciscans from other neighborhoods.

The soft, taped vocal music in the background is French. We tried the soup du jour which was leek-yam, a new combination for us. It turned out to be good, with a smooth texture and a delicate taste.

Salads are fresh greens of a half-dozen varieties accented with a light, non-destructive vinaigrette. The last time we had lunch here, the pasta was farfalle, or bow ties, that were cooked briefly with a sparse handful of spinach and a sauce of tomato, garlic and basil. There was a Provençal fish soup with mussels and fresh fish, and a roasted free-range chicken marinated in orange balsamic vinegar. The latter was a fine example of the chef's imagination. The chef is Eleanor Triboletti and she is to be complimented.

A few good beers are offered: local Anchor Steam, Sierra Nevada and Red Hook from Seattle, all in bottles. There is an uncomplicated wine list and wine by the glass.

They have live music every Sunday evening, always something different. Selections include harp and guitar, music of Broadway, flamenco, jazz, blues, tango and opera. At some point, you will hear each type of music. There are special days too, such as Valentine's Day, Beaujolais Night (third Thursday of November), New Year's Eve or French-speaking night. Call to see what's happening.

- ❑ *941 Cole St., between Carl and Parnassus, Cole Valley;* ☎ *415-564-5332.*
- ❑ *Open: Monday-Thursday 8 am-2 pm, 6 pm-9:30 pm; Friday 8 am-2:30 pm, 6 pm-10 pm; Saturday 9 am-3 pm, 6 pm-10 pm; Sunday 9 am-3 pm, 6 pm-9:30 pm.*
- ❑ *Prices: Lunch, tapas $3.95, vegetarian petit pain $4.95, trout $9.95. Dinner entrées $9.95-$12.95.*
- ❑ *Credit cards: MC, V.*
- ❑ *Reservations: No.*
- ❑ *Entertainment: Live music Sundays.*
- ❑ *Parking: Street.*

# Cow Hollow

Cow Hollow is old-time vernacular for the valley lying west of Van Ness Avenue between Russian Hill and the Presidio. The name today is applied mainly to the strip of Union Street's 1600 to 2200 blocks and a few blocks on either side of that. In post-Gold Rush days, this district was a green dale watered by small creeks seeking the bay. The first dairy was established here in 1861, and others followed. Soon hundreds of cows shared the grasslands with wild ducks, quail and rabbits. Besides supplying San Francisco with its milk, the Hollow was the communal wash basin. Fresh water was scarce along the Barbary Coast so Laguna Pequena, the little lake beyond the city limits, was used by the washerwomen. These working women took in laundry from the Presidio officers, the city's miners and businessmen (a disproportionate number of whom were saloonkeepers in those days).

By the 1890s, the cows were gone and the Hollow became a so-so residential neighborhood until the late 1950s. At that point, the affairs of god and man and Cow Hollow took a Cinderella turn. Imaginative merchants, mostly decorators, began to see possibilities in Union Street's old clapboard Victorian buildings, its converted carriage houses and surviving stables and barns. A few stylish antique shops and home furnishings showrooms moved in. By 1964, it had evolved into a neighborhood with flair, including a flourishing shopping center with a turn-of-the-century flavor.

Cow Hollow is best done on foot because its charms are pretty much tucked-away. Passages lead between buildings to flower-

*Cow Hollow, along Union Street.*

filled courtyards bordered by boutiques. Tiny brick-paved patios host tables for lunch guests. The real shopping stretches from the 1800 block at Octavia for five blocks to the 2200 block. This is where you will find art objects, handicraft galleries, antiques, custom clothes, feminine fripperies, books, gifts, linen, specialty foods and candies.

Restaurants abound – mostly Italian (so many that it is like an extension of North Beach), Japanese and Chinese. Many have garden or veranda service. You will find pubs and café-delicatessens tucked away in crannies and cul-de-sacs, so walk slowly and look sharp!

All this is possible because of the abundance of old Victorian buildings, artfully transformed into smart shopping compounds. Fine old facades are painted in subtle shades with contrasting gingerbread trim. Wrought iron fences have been retained, and in some places gas lights reintroduced.

## Inn

### Four Charlton Court Inn

Charlton Court is a cul-de-sac off the south side of Union Street's 1900 block. It was a milk wagon loading yard back when Cow Hollow was so aptly named. Two- and three-story Victorian houses

*Four Charlton Court Inn.*

on both sides of the court have been recycled to become an inn. They blend well and are painted a bluish gray with white trim.

The Garden Suite has two bedrooms. The master is in front with a queen bed and the other is in a loft above the world's largest luxury bathroom. You will especially like the double jacuzzi with its own windows looking out over the rear garden. There is a small library, warm and inviting, a full kitchen, small sitting room and a solarium partly in the garden so one can take the sun.

Another suite is very modern with a large L-shaped living room, several soft sofas, a full kitchen and a deck with plants. An incredibly narrow spiral staircase leads up to a loft, a big, wide area under sloping eaves fitted with a bed of many pillows which looks perfect for wrestling and romping. Another huge bathroom under the eaves has a tub big enough for two, soft, furry rugs and a long, low couch with its own big pillows by the tub. These are highly recommended for romance, although we still have not figured out how to get the luggage up that staircase. Oh well, just leave it downstairs.

There are other, smaller rooms with a shower, no tub, and equipped with phone and TV. Four less expensive rooms have sinks and vanities in the rooms and share three bathrooms with toilets and showers. Breakfast is an "extended" continental, with lots of sliced fruit. If you prefer something like hot oatmeal, simply tell Frankie Stone, the friendly woman who runs this nice place. Breakfast, by the way, is served in the dining room or in your own room. Take your choice.

□ *4 Charlton Court, San Francisco, CA 94123;* ☎ *415-921-9784.*
□ *Rooms: 11.*
□ *Rates: Five rooms with private bath, phone, TV $115-$140; Mayfair Suite and The Garden Suite $215-$275; four "Pension" rooms with shared bathrooms $70-$90.*
□ *Credit cards: None.*
□ *Reservations: Call "way ahead" for weekends.*
□ *Breakfast: Complimentary extended continental.*
□ *Handicapped accessible: No.*
□ *Smoking: No.*
□ *Children: Rarely.*
□ *Pets: No.*
□ *Parking: Public garage, $10 for 24 hours.*

# Restaurants

## Antipasti Ristorante

(Italian)

There are so many restaurants in Cow Hollow that it is fun just to stroll around and pick one out. You cannot go wrong. We particularly like this place. We limped in after a long morning's walk and were greeted so warmly we felt right at home immediately. It is a modern, yet old Italian style restaurant showcasing a long mahogany bar with a mirrored back and glasses hanging upside down overhead. There are blond wood tables and an area out front where you can eat.

Both of us had vegetable soup and shared a big antipasti misto, with calimari, caponata, grilled eggplant, potato salad, carrots marinated in herbs and roasted red pepper. You will have to ask for this dish, as it is not on the menu. *Zuppa de vegetables* is a specialty and if it is on the bill of fare we urge you to try it. It is both creamy and a bit spicy, but good.

Pasta is another specialty here and is homemade every day. The least expensive pasta is penne arrabbiata, which is a typical Roman dish. It is made with tomato sauce, seasoned with basil and red peppers (chilis). *Arrabbiata* means angry, so if you do not want the top of your head taken off, tell the waiter you would like it a little less *furioso*.

*Coniglio* is rabbit, which a lot of people do not care much for. As a result, you will not always find it on the menu. Here, it is braised in a white wine sauce and served with polenta.

There are eight pizza selections, but the Margherita is definitely at the top of the list. In the last century, Queen Margherita of Italy was known for her frequent travels around the country. Chefs everywhere vied in honoring her with special dishes. In 1889, when she arrived in Naples, Senor Brandy, the owner of a lowly pizzeria, created a pizza made with tomatoes, mozzarella, basil and garlic. The Queen liked it so much it became known as the "Margherita Pizza" from then on.

There is a modest wine list, with a dozen bianchi, half from California and half from Italy, priced from $19 to the low $20s. The two dozen rossi are mostly Italian, with chianti priced a bit higher. There is a selection by the glass at $4.50, and a full bar.

- ❑ *1838 Union St. (between Octavia and Laguna);* ☎ *415-921-3097.*
- ❑ *Open: 11:30 am-10 pm.*
- ❑ *Prices: Antipasti are $5-$7.50, pastas $9.25-$12.95, secondi piatti $11.25-$14.95, pizza and calzone $9.25-$11.95.*
- ❑ *Credit cards: AE, MC, V.*
- ❑ *Reservations: Not necessary.*
- ❑ *Parking: Street.*

## Strolling, Looking, Perhaps Shopping

At the corner of Gough and Union, starting the 1700 block, is the **Octagon House**. It is a perfectly preserved 1861 heirloom restored inside and out. It is open to the public on the second and fourth Thursdays of the month from 12 noon until 3 pm. The National Society of Colonial Dames of America do not insist upon a donation, but would be pleased if you would contribute.

1887 Union Street is where you will find **Noah's New York Bagels**. Eighteen different kinds are available along with a half-dozen types of knishes and coffee.

1954 Union Street is home to **Prelude Boutique**, geared towards women who dress for success.

1974 Union Street is where **Kinder Toys** offers an assortment of delightful children's toys. This is where you will find just the right thing to take home to the kid you left behind.

1980 Union Street is a striking Victorian compound fashioned from three circa 1870 residences. The ensemble includes a pair of "wedding houses" which are identical bungalows, joined by a common center wall. They are now home to several shops and restaurants.

1981 Union Street is the old **Laurel Vale Dairy** building, virtually all that remains of Cow Hollow's dairy industry. Now Earthly Goods sells women's apparel here.

Ar 2040 Union Street is a three-story mansion, originally built in 1870 by James Cudworth, one of Cow Hollow's first dairymen. It now shelters numerous boutiques.

2044 Union Street was originally the barn belonging to the big house at 2040 Union Street. It served as a first aid station during the 1906 earthquake and fire, and for awhile, was a hideout for a pair of notorious looters, the "Gas Pipe Thieves."

At 2068 Union Street you will find **Solar Light Books**, downstairs, off the street, in a basement. It is good place for browsing through an eclectic collection. There are always plenty of sale items, starting with what may be found on the tables in front.

2164-66 Union Street was originally a carriage yard and barn. It is now shared by two stores, **Ted Singer Flowers & Urban Nursery** and **Valentino and Rei**.

2184 Union Street is where you will discover **La Nouvelle Patisserie**. Small, round, marble-top tables are reminiscent of a soda shop of days gone by. They don't serve lime rickies, but dozens of different pastries. Buy something fattening, a cup of coffee and sit and enjoy.

2250 Union Street is the place to stop for chocolate lovers. **The Chocolate Bear** is a small place, but, "oh my!" The candy sold here is so good that tour buses have this little shop as a regular stop on their route. While the salesperson, Pat O'Brien, was pointing out different kinds and shapes of chocolates, we felt ourselves putting on weight just by breathing in the aroma. The shop makes its own hand-dipped chocolates in a variety of styles. We gave in to temptation and tried a couple shaped like a cable car and the Golden Gate Bridge. There are cute and tasty gifts – if you can resist eating them yourself. ☎ 415-922-5711, fax 415-922-6930.

2191 Union Street, on the corner of Fillmore, is a local hangout known as **Union Street Coffee Roastery**. You will find dozens of fresh roasted coffees, pastries and quiches.

2095 Union Street, on the corner of Webster, is home to a boutique called **Bebe**. They sell slinky evening gowns, in case you want to knock 'em dead at the country club back home.

While you are at the corner of Webster, walk north to the next corner, which is Filbert. There is a magnificent Queen Anne Victorian house with a red onion-shaped roof and balconies all around the third floor. Just stare and admire it.

# The Embarcadero

❦ *It has been said that all great cities of history have been built on bodies of water – Rome on the Tiber, Paris on the Seine, London on the Thames, New York on the Hudson. If this is a criterion of a city's greatness, surely San Francisco ranks in the first magnitude among cities of the world. For never was a metropol more dominated by any natural feature than San Francisco by its bay.*

Harold Gilliam, San Francisco Bay

When the first settlers arrived, the shoreline was seven blocks farther into the city. Of course, there were no city blocks at that time. Instead, there were dunes, a few small streams and a lot of mudflats when the tide was out. There was a cove, just past where Montgomery Street is now, with the shore in the middle of the block between Washington and Pacific. That is where tents were pitched, and later adobe and wooden shacks built because it was easiest to land rowboats and small launches there.

Filling in Yerba Buena Cove and building wharves out into deeper water started even before the Gold Rush. Development increased greatly as soon as thousands of men and shiploads of supplies began arriving from all over the world. The mountainous sand dunes that covered much of downtown San Francisco were leveled to provide fill. In fact, a large part of the east side of Telegraph Hill was dynamited for it. As ships arrived, their gold-hungry crews deserted en masse for the mining camps. The abandoned vessels eventually sank into the mud and became part of the fill.

The stone seawall was started in 1877 and was not finished until 1914. Long before that, the Embarcadero was established as a street to run along the entire 12½-mile length of the waterfront. It was wide enough for the drays and later for the big trucks and railroads to handle freight from the ships.

It is a broad, wonderfully scenic place for a long stroll.

## Inn

♥ Dockside Boat & Bed

This is a different kind of "B&B" because it all takes place on a boat. The boat is docked at Pier 39. You can spend part or all of a day looking over the Pier itself, where there are restaurants, shops and sea lions to watch.

*Sea Ghost*, a 42-foot Beneteau sailboat, has a spacious aft cockpit and is in a slip with good views of the central bay. Below, there are two staterooms, fore and aft, and two heads, each with a shower. The salon features a dining table with settee seating, color TV, VCR and a stereo tapedeck. On the port side is a galley with a refrigerator, microwave and coffeemaker.

*Athena* is a 51-foot Bluewater motor yacht with three staterooms, two with queen beds and one with a full bed. There are two heads with showers and the salon features an entertainment center with color TV, VCR and CD/cassette player. It has a complete galley and a dining alcove. An upper sundeck with chaise longues has great bay views.

You could choose the *C Love R*, a 36-foot Carver motor yacht with a queen bed in the master stateroom. *Integrity*, a 50-foot motorsailer ketch, is another option. Its master stateroom is aft, while forward and below is a full galley. The *Attitude* is a smaller 33-foot sailboat. It has a small head with a shower and a cozy double VB berth.

Don't forget breakfast, which is delivered on deck or in the salon whenever you choose. Freshly squeezed orange juice, just-baked sweet breads and rolls, and freshly made coffee slip on board in the morning hours. If it is great to sleep on a boat, think how grand it is to wake up to this.

You may choose to take advantage of the package deals. A candlelit dinner catered on board or a special "snooze and cruise" combination are available.

□ *Pier 39, C Dock office;* ☎ *415-392-5526.*
□ *Boats: Six.*
□ *Rates: Weekdays $95-$225, weekends $125-$275.*
□ *Credit cards: All major.*
□ *Reservations: Usually necesssary.*
□ *Minimum stay: Two nights over holidays.*
□ *Smoking: On deck only.*
□ *Children: No small children.*
□ *Pets: No.*
□ *Parking: Public garage.*
□ *Walking distance: Next to Pier 39, a 10-minute walk to Fisherman's Wharf and Ghirardelli Square.*

# ℛestaurants

## ℬoulevard

(American-Continental)

This waterfront "boite" is not romantic in the sense of a candle on the table with an atmosphere so quiet that you can hear a soufflé drop. To the contrary, Boulevard is noisy and crowded. After high recommendations from several sources, we went on a Monday night, with reservations in place. Every table was filled and we had to wait 10 minutes at the long bar, sipping a perfect martini.

At the foot of Mission Street, where it intersects with Stewart and catty-corner from the Ferry Plaza, there is a three-story building. It was erected in 1899, in the style of Parisian commer-

*Boulevard.*

cial buildings of that era, with a mansard roof and brick exterior. It was the Bulkhead Coffee Parlor, actually a saloon, when the earth shook in 1906. There is a much-told tale, perhaps even true, that when firemen came to dynamite the French-style Audiffred Building, as it has always been known, the saloon keeper promised them two quarts of whiskey apiece to spare it. As a result, it's the only building around here that pre-dates the fire, proving the restorative powers of spirits, we suppose.

Boulevard occupies a long, narrow space on the ground floor at the end of the building. There's lots of glass and diners look out on the Ferry Plaza and Ferry Building, outlined with lights, from most tables. You can also see the Bay Bridge, all lit up at night, from the front (Embarcadero) end of the room.

The chef's repertoire is wide ranging. There are a dozen appetizers to choose from. The menu includes oysters, caviar, sweetbreads, hot smoked sturgeon, foie gras and more. Fresh chanterelle mushrooms on a mashed potato ravioli taste much better than they sound. Maine lobster macaroni and cheese is also served as an appetizer, but it can be doubled to make a delicious entrée. We can testify that the red and yellow tomato pistou is a deeply satisfying way of rendering tomatoes into soup. This contains vermicelli and has pounded garlic and grilled tomatoes mixed with oil, all contributing to the deep flavor.

In the entrée department, duck is served three ways in one dish. 1) a boneless breast adorned with truffles which Phyllis enjoyed the most; 2) crispy confit leg with shallots, which Bob claimed for his own; 3) sautéed livers on caramelized onion and apple crostini that we both relished.

You can see that we ordered two entrées and then split them, which we have found is a good way for each to get a variety of tastes. If you order fish, the Alsation Pinot Blanc wine the waiter recommended is a perfect match. It is a fine wine list, by the way, one of the best you will see anywhere, with scores of reds, whites, California wines, French and Italian available by the bottle, half-bottle or glass. A half-dozen draft beers and dozens of bottled beers from boutique breweries also await consumption.

- ❏ *One Mission St.;* ☎ *415-543-6084.*
- ❏ *Open: Lunch, Monday-Friday, 11:30-2 pm; bistro, Monday-Friday, 2 pm-5:15 pm; dinner, Monday-Sunday, 5:30 pm-10:30 pm. Dessert menu, Monday-Sunday, 5:30 pm-11:30 pm.*
- ❏ *Prices: For dinner, soups $5.95, salads $8.25-$9.25, appetizers $8.95-$14.75, entrées $16.25-$23.25. Lunch quite a bit less.*
- ❏ *Credit cards: All.*
- ❏ *Reservations: Best to call four to six weeks ahead.*
- ❏ *Parking: Valet or street.*

## Buena Vista Café

(Breakfast)

Irish coffee is available all day and most of the night. This has been a favorite spot of San Franciscans for breakfast since 1941. The fine old Edwardian building, with charming bay windows, dates back to 1911. We will return to the subject of breakfast, but first we must deal with their famous Irish Coffee. It is what they are really known for. Visitors from the Far East and Germany alike land in San Francisco and head straight for this place because they've heard about the Irish Coffee. The brew started in the early 1950s when a *Chronicle* columnist told the owner about the yummy hot drink he had tasted in Ireland. The owner fooled around with it and finally duplicated the taste. Here's the recipe:

## *Irish Coffee*

coffee
3 cocktail sugar cubes
1 oz Irish whiskey
whipping cream

Fill glass with very hot water to pre-heat, then empty. Pour hot coffee into hot glass until it is about ¾ full. Drop in sugar cubes. Stir until sugar is thoroughly dissolved. Add jigger Irish whiskey. Top with collar of lightly whipped whipping cream by pouring gently over a spoon. Enjoy while piping hot. (Note: Cream should be 48 hours old and lightly frothed to float on top.)

You will find Irish coffee served in quite a few other places these days. But, if you hear the "fizz-fizz" of an aerosol spray can instead of the "whip-whip" of real whipping cream being frothed, you know it will not be as good as the Buena Vista version.

Buena Vista is not known for any unusual dishes at breakfast, just good solid food at good prices. It has been enough to keep people coming back for 56 years. Their menu offers all the different eggs, the bennies (short order lingo for eggs benedict) and anything you would expect at a full breakfast place, except for pancakes and waffles.

- *2765 Hyde St.;* ☎ *415-474-5044.*
- *Open: Monday-Friday 9 am-2 am, Saturday-Sunday 8 am-2 am.*
- *Prices: Irish coffee $3.75. Omelets with ham, peppers, sausage, hash brown potatoes, toast and coffee is $6.29.*
- *Reservations: Not necessary.*
- *Parking: Street.*

## *Equinox Restaurant in the Hyatt Regency Embarcadero*

(California cuisine)

The Hyatt Regency Embarcadero is the hotel with the spectacular atrium. Eighteen floors of balconies rise straight up with plants dripping down from each one. You will get a crick in your neck trying to see it all at once, but it is worth a try. When you are finished staring, take the elevator up 19 floors to the Equinox Room, Northern California's only revolving restaurant. It too, is memorable. You discover the Bay Bridge is right in front of you, outlined in lights. This view gives way to Market Street and then you are looking into windows of buildings that tower over you. In an occasional office, we saw a lone person sitting at a desk, working late. Less often, we spotted a cleaning person, but for the most part, the offices are empty. Surely all those lights are not on just to give diners at the Equinox something to look at?

The crab cakes appetizer is a real bargain at only $9.50, considering that the entrées are in the $20s and $30s. It turns out to be two crab cakes, remoulade, corn relish and a fresh Sonoma green salad. This can make for full meal when accompanied by their thick clam chowder. The shrimp cocktail is another biggy, with a good, old-fashioned cocktail sauce. The linguine sauce has fresh cherrystone clams. Oven-roasted rack of pork is tender and crusty, but it has a curious potato pumpkin purée with it. All in all, revolving and eating here is a pleasure. One revolution of the room takes 45 minutes. The meal, with martinis to start and coffee to end, took us a little more than two rotations.

After they stop serving dinner at 10 pm this place really comes into its own. Most couples have quiet, intimate conversations at tables for two and there is an occasional boisterous party of six celebrating a birthday or promotion. Sunday brunch is popular; not buffet-style, but ordered from the menu. This is definitely a place for couples to come for dates, anniversaries and special nights on the town. We would not want to mislead you. The food is OK, nothing special. It is the revolving restaurant, with its ever-changing views, that is the real attraction.

- ❑ *5 Embarcadero Center; ☎ 415-788-1234.*
- ❑ *Prices: Appetizers $5.50-$9.50, entrées $23-$38.*
- ❑ *Open: Dinner 6 pm-10 pm, cocktails to 11:30 pm on Sunday to Thursday, 1:15 am Friday and Saturday.*
- ❑ *Reservations: Recommended.*
- ❑ *Parking: Valet at Hyatt Regency Embarcadero.*
- ❑ *Directions: Located at the bottom end of Market St.*

## Neptune's Palace

(Seafood)

Neptune's Palace is on the second floor of Pier 39 and everyone who eats here has a great view of the bay. Our corner table also had a close view of sea lions basking in the sun. There are several rafts just 100 feet from the end of the pier where the sea lions congregate. The rafts are so crowded that when one animal heaves himself up from the water and jostles his way on, another is pushed off. Phone ahead and make a reservation for a window table at the left (north) end of the restaurant so you can enjoy watching them while you are eating.

The restaurant is fairly quiet after the joyous clamor of Pier 39. The service is good and the food, mostly seafood, is excellent. There is a seafood stew (not a ciopino), which is about as close to bouillabaisse as a cook can get without stepping over any country's borders. This stew has mussels, crab, shrimp, scallops and clams, all cooked for seemingly scant seconds, just to the point of tenderness, in a deliciously fishy broth. If you are in the salad mood, you will find a sort of seafood Caesar with shrimp and Dungeness crab nestled in the romaine among the garlic croutons. It is more like a marine salad, but the end result is so good it does not really matter what they call it.

The menu is long, both at lunch and dinner, with a variety of seafoods and various fish prepared any of several ways: steamed, baked, pan-fried or grilled. There is a full bar that prides itself on the large number of mostly California wines that may be served by the glass. This is a good opportunity to try, at a small price, some vineyard or vintage you might have wondered about, without investing in an entire bottle.

- ❏ *Pier 39, second level, all the way back;* ☎ *415-434-4424.*
- ❏ *Open: 11:30 am-10 pm.*
- ❏ *Prices: Dinner entrées $16.75-$25.*
- ❏ *Credit cards: All major.*
- ❏ *Reservations: Recommended.*
- ❏ *Parking: Public garage across street from Pier 39.*

## *Waterfront Restaurant*

(Seafood)

"Hide this ring in the dessert!" is a request this restaurant hears often. Proposals are common here because it is a seriously romantic place. After all, no matter where you sit, you are looking through windows at San Francisco Bay. Ferries and sailboats dot its white-capped surface. We are even tempted to say that the view from this Embarcadero restaurant can't be beat, but we could say the same about many restaurants in San Francisco. The difference is that here the view is from close to water level, rather than from high up.

There is a second floor, really more of a mezzanine level, with a few tables and a slightly higher view. Most couples ask for a window table, either upstairs or down, but some want a booth at the back, on the lower level, because it is more private.

The menu is heavy on fresh fish, seafood and shell fish. A bowl of New England clam chowder is thick with clams and the shrimp sandwich on focaccia at lunchtime is lovely and sweet. Salad greens are from a kitchen garden. There are a dozen varieties of fresh Pacific oysters and abalone. Daily specials feature fish in season. It might be broiled sea bass with a sun-dried tomato basil vinaigrette, or sautéed red snapper with crab meat and scallions in a spicy meunière sauce.

The Waterfront Restaurant is very popular on Sundays for brunch. There is no buffet, but there is a champagne and seafood brunch menu in addition to the regular selection. You might try Eggs Waterfront, which is a filet mignonette on an English muffin with mushroom sauce, topped with poached egg and Béarnaise sauce. Or try the Hangtown Fries made with sautéed fresh oysters and bacon with scrambled eggs (see page 258). There is a small bar facing out over the water and a good beer list with British draughts and boutique local beers.

◻ *Pier 7, on the Embarcadero at the foot of Broadway;* ☎ *415-391-2696.*
◻ *Open: Monday-Saturday 11:30 am-10:30 pm, Sunday 10 am-10:30 pm.*
◻ *Prices: Clam chowder $3.50, entrées $11-$20. Sunday brunch menu $7.95-$12.95, champagne extra.*
◻ *Credit cards: All major.*
◻ *Reservations: Suggested.*
◻ *Smoking: At bar.*
◻ *Parking: A small lot to the right side, free of charge.*

# Things to Do

## Embarcadero Center

This is a self-contained area, with more than 120 shops and restaurants and a five-screen cinema immediately next to Ferry Plaza (in front of the Ferry Building). There are also several special things to take note of here.

The **Skydeck**, an indoor/outdoor observation deck on the 41st floor of One Embarcadero Center, has the only 360° view of the Bay Area. It is open Wednesday-Friday, 5 pm-10 pm, and Saturday, Sunday and holidays from 10 am-10 pm. The cost is $4, with seniors 62 and older admitted for $3.50.

There are **Sculpture Walk Guided Docent Tours** of the Center's extensive sculpture collection, featuring works of Louise Nevelson, Jean Dubuffet and others. On the last Saturday of summer months, meet at 2 pm in the lobby of the Park Hyatt Hotel. The tour takes about one hour.

The **Outdoor Ice Rink** opens in November for the holidays and is located in Justin Herman Plaza, next to Ferry Plaza.

☎ 800-733-6318 for information about any of the above.

*The view from the Embarcadero Center Sky Deck.*

## Farmers' Market

It is a crisp Saturday morning and color is everywhere, thrown with an extravagant hand over dozens of stalls. Flower vendors arrange vases of delicate blossoms, gold and creamy, blue and purple. Tiers of deep red tomatoes, careless piles of orange carrots, pyramids of yellow, green and almost lavender peppers complete the rainbow. There is a line for double lattes and sticky buns. We find we have followed a tempting scent to a tent where buttered corn revolves as it roasts. Teamed with a grilled salmon sandwich from another tent, we have the perfect combination. We wander among the stalls, pausing to watch a man grilling eggplants, the long, rounded bodies revolving while the purple skin chars to crinkly black. We listen to a strolling accordion player on one side and a pair of violinists on the other. We glance at the clock on the Ferry Building tower and decide to walk along the Embarcadero. We stroll out to the end of Pier 7 to sit on a bench for awhile and watch the whitecaps appear and disappear on the gray water. We see a line of racing sailboats leaning over on their sides. The view includes the immense Bay Bridge arches, Yerba Buena Island's green woods, and on it goes. What a nice way to spend a Saturday morning!

❑ *At Ferry Plaza*
❑ *Open: Every Saturday, 8:30 am-1:30 pm, Tuesdays 11 am-3 pm, early April to late November.*

## *Ferry Building*

The first Ferry Building was built at the foot of Market Street in 1875. The present one, dating from 1898, was home to dozens of ferry boats that made 50,000,000 passenger-trips a year across the Bay, before the Bay Bridge was completed in 1936 and the Golden Gate Bridge in 1937. It is still home dock for a few ferries that once again ply the Bay. After the bridges were built, all the ferries were stopped and it was thought to be the end of them. But it turned out that traffic can gridlock on bridges. Thousands of people find a cruise across the Bay a lot more pleasant than breathing smelly gasoline fumes. We find the return of the ferries one small step for mankind.

Dozens of buses coming from all parts of the city end their routes here and a BART station for underground trains from the East Bay is just up Market Street. Just to the right (south) of the Ferry Building is a multilevel promenade, an excellent place to gawk at the immense arches of the Bay Bridge that seems so close. Also within viewing distance are the boats coming and going, the towering skyline of the city behind you and plenty of funny people passing. (Funny = everyone else except me and thee.)

## *Fisherman's Wharf*

 *...a fog-misted dream world.*

Herb Caen, *San Francisco Chronicle*

How would you like to go to the tackiest tourist attraction in San Francisco? Or, would you rather visit the number one tourist attraction in San Francisco? You can do both at the same time. Just take yourself to Fisherman's Wharf.

Little did Harry Meiggs know, when he built an 1,800-foot wharf at the end of present-day Powell Street in 1853, what he was starting. Ship builders were busy along sandy North Beach, but when the Great Seawall was constructed, North Point Cove was quickly filled in. All the flat blocks from Bay Street north became landfills and businesses started moving in around the wharf. After Meiggs Wharf disappeared under the fill, the fishing fleet moved here in 1900 and it became known as Fisherman's Wharf.

Flash forward to the 1960s when the Bay was nearly fished out and the fleet had to go outside the Golden Gate to find a catch. This was still a place where you could "go to eat and see." There are still plenty of places to eat. The grandsons and granddaughters of those original Genoese fishermen, and the Sicilians who came along behind them, decided that what San Francisco needed was one or two or 16 more Italian cafés. The names of the present-day restaurants reflect their origins. Alioto's, Tarantino's, Castagnola's and more, all have their specialties and serve their versions of seafood and sometimes friendliness. Lou's Pier 47 simply says "cool music and hot food."

What happened to the fishermen? In 1970, there were about 300 boats left of the hundreds that used to dot the bay. This year, there are about 140, only a third of which fish year round. They are mostly Korean and Vietnamese fishermen now. We look forward to the next logical step, which would be a rash of Korean and Vietnamese restaurants appearing on Fisherman's Wharf.

## Ghirardelli Square

It is not exactly a full city block devoted to chocolate, although the word "Ghirardelli" does conjure up thoughts of rich, dark, delectable bars of the stuff. This is a block of buildings that were once a chocolate factory, now filled with shops and places to eat, built around plazas and open spaces. Sometimes, there are clowns blowing up balloons for children, street vendors selling delicious soft pretzels, splashing fountains and always something more to see. There are always plenty of people, mostly tourists, for the shops. Locals come here too, for restaurants like Ghirardelli Chocolate Manufactory (first floor, Clock Tower Building) with its gobs of hot fudge on banana splits. Another restaurant is called Ghirardelli's Too! (West Plaza), known for espresso, chocolate and yogurt. An unusual eatery is Timo's Norte (second floor, Mustard Building), with an international fare. Have a tuna ceviche with avocado, Quintana Roo-style, or maybe monkfish curry with a Canadian accent. They try to have a dish from every country. If you are ready for a serious meal, try the Mandarin Restaurant (fourth floor, Woolen Mill Building) for Chinese food, or McCormick & Kuleto's Seafood Restaurant (Beach Street, Wurster Building).

It's not all food here. There are many more shops and galleries than cafés, among them The Clever Shepherd (third floor, Woolen Mill Building) for British sweaters, China Jade & Art Center (third floor, Woolen Mill Building), Xanadu Gallery (second floor, Cocoa Building), African and Oceanic art, and The Glass Sculptors (Fountain Plaza), a glass art gallery.

Stop at the Information Booth (Fountain Plaza) for a map.

Why is all of this in a defunct chocolate factory? It seems Domenico Ghirardelli was an apprentice confectioner in Genoa in the 1820s. He took a detour to South America, where he Spanishized his name to Domingo. He eventually ended up owning a general store in Stockton, California during the Gold Rush, but still made chocolate.

His sons came into the business, bought land on North Point Street in San Francisco and built the first of these buildings. The 15-foot illuminated letters spelling out "Ghirardelli" welcome ships passing through the Golden Gate and date back to 1923. In the 1960s, after the chocolate manufacturing moved, this "festival marketplace" was created. The Ghirardelli sign flashed into life again in 1966 after being dark during World War II.

It is a nice place to shop, eat and enjoy life.

❑ *900 North Point St.; ☎ 415-775-5500.*
❑ *Open: Shops are generally open 10 am-9 pm. Some close at 6 pm weekdays. All shops are open Sunday, 10 am-6 pm year round.*
❑ *Parking: Underground garage, entrances Larkin and Beach streets; validated in many shops and restaurants.*

## The Last of the Liberty Ships: SS Jeremiah O'Brien

You walk around the corner of the San Francisco warehouse and there she is, high in the water and still painted war-time gray. The *SS Jeremiah O'Brien* is the last unaltered Liberty ship in existence. She was built in South Portland, Maine, in 1943. Her construction took only 44 days. She was just one among 2,741 identical cargo ships slapped together during the war with riveted plates and a short, stubby bow. Stories still circulate around the waterfront of how they could pitch and roll in a blow! All the other Liberties are gone now. Some went to the bottom during the war and others have been cut up for scrap. The *SS Jeremiah O'Brien* was saved and declared a National Monument in 1978. Now she can be found and thoroughly explored at Pier 32, just a small tugboat's toot down the Embarcadero from Ghirardelli Square and Fisherman's Wharf. You can wander the deck from bow to fantail, plunge two decks down into the engine room or climb all the way up to the top deck to check out the wheel house, the chart room, radio room or captain's quarters. Nooks and crannies are everywhere.

The ship is open to visitors almost every day (359 days a year). On the third weekend of each month, she comes alive. Down in the engine room, you will find the huge triple expansion steam engine running. In the galley, the original coal stove will be in operation and the "slop chest," the seaman's store, will be open for business. On these weekends, there are usually special events like live band music with sea chanties being sung or perhaps exhibits illustrating shipboard life in the war years. You might meet Captain George Jahn, who was Master of the Liberty ship *William Matson* during the war, and retired from the sea after long service as a San Francisco Bay pilot. He took command again in 1994 to take this ship back to Normandy for the re-creation of the D-Day landing.

This old ship got banged up some during the war. She made 11 round trips from England to the Normandy beachheads during the D-Day invasion. She took part of General Patton's Fifth Division to Normandy and later she sailed from the West Coast to Australia. After the war, the SS *Jeremiah O'Brien* spent the next 33 years rocking gently in the calm waters of Suisun Bay, an arm of San Francisco Bay. She was all closed up, waiting and waiting. Finally, volunteer workers climbed aboard and started the hard task of putting her back into shape. In October 1979, she sailed out of Suisun Bay under her own steam.

Four days each year, all the hard work is made worthwhile. On a Saturday and Sunday in May and again in October, the Chief Engineer gives orders to "get up steam" from down in the engine room. On the bridge, Captain Jahn makes a long, triumphant blast on the ship's whistle and the First Mate gives the orders to cast off. Deckhands haul in the lines that have held her immobile at the dock and the SS *Jeremiah O'Brien* moves out into San Francisco Bay.

Almost 1,000 passengers are aboard each cruise when she steams out under the Golden Gate Bridge toward the Farallon Islands. In May, she will pause between Point Diablo and Point Bonita where a memorial service is held to honor the men and women who built, sailed and repaired Liberty ships during World War II. This is in conjunction with Maritime Day, declared by Congress to honor the 5,662 merchant seamen lost during that war. A higher percentage of merchant seaman were killed than any other branch of the services, except the Marines. Then, she will turn back and cruise the Bay, going under the Bay Bridge, up the Oakland Estuary to Jack London Square, north to Angel Island, through Racoon Strait and back across the Bay past Alcatraz to her pier on the Embarcadero.

You may be wondering who the ship was named after, and why. She was named for a Maine hero. Jeremiah O'Brien led some of his fellow villagers from the settlement of Machias, Maine, to capture the British armed vessel *Margaretta* in 1775 in the first American naval victory of the Revolution. When the armed cruiser *Diligent* and her tender *Tapnaquish* were sent from Halifax "to bring the obstreperous Irish Yankee (meaning O'Brien) in for trial," O'Brien turned the tables by capturing both of those ships instead. Jeremiah O'Brien's ship was named *Machias Liberty*, and she was America's first armed cruiser.

❑ *Ship at Pier 32. Mailing address: Purser, SS Jeremiah O'Brien, Landmark Building A, Fort Mason Center, San Francisco, CA 94123;* ☎ *415-441-3101.*
❑ *Open at dock: Monday-Friday 9 am-3 pm, Saturday-Sunday, 9 am-4 pm.*
❑ *Cruises: Third Saturday and Sunday in May and October. Can board at 7:30 am (coffee and doughnuts available), shove off at 9 am and return at 3:30 pm.*

❑ *Cost: At dock $5, seniors $3. Cruise, $100 tax deductible donation.*
❑ *Reservations: Needed for cruise.*
❑ *Parking: On the pier, free.*
❑ *Directions: Pier 32 is the fourth pier south of the Bay Bridge.*

## *Pier 39*

This is not a place where couples go to be alone, since it is the world's third most popular attraction (Disney World in Florida and Disneyland in Southern California are first and second). It is San Francisco's top attraction. (Fisherman's Wharf disputes this.) In fact, four out of every 10 visitors are locals. Just to increase the noise and confusion level, Pier 39 is the favorite place of the Bay Area's kids. You will understand better when you see them here in feral packs and ravening hordes.

After World War II, shipping slacked off at San Francisco's once-bustling docks so badly that the piers of the several-mile-long Embarcadero were deserted to the point of falling apart. A group of entrepreneurs rescued this pier and opened it in 1978 as a sort of open-air mall on pilings out over the bay. It had two levels, over 100 shops and a dozen or so restaurants. That is how Pier 39 came into being. Business got a big boost seven years ago when sea lions started showing up and hanging out here. First, just a few came and now there are at least 100. Pier 39 cooperates with the Marine Mammal center, which trains docents to give information about sea lions on weekends from 11 am-5 pm. (See the section on Sea Lions, page 76.) There is a Marine Mammal Center Store and Interpretive Center on the second level.

Pier 39 keeps adding attractions every year. Now, there is a wide-screen theater showing a movie about San Francisco. The most recent addition is an underwater aquarium. Actually, you are on a moving walkway traveling through a glass tube and the fish are all around in the water peering in at you. It is called **Underwater World**. Admission is $12.95, seniors $9.95. ☎ 888-732-3483.

As a romantic couple, you might very well want to look in the **Midsummer Night's Lingerie** shop on the second level, left side. As you would expect, couples usually come in together and he buys something seductive for her to wear. In addition to silk and satin lingerie, you will also find bath salts, scented candles and scents to put into panty drawers. Edible oils are popular and so are board games like "Getting To Know You Better," and "Bedroom Adventures." There is a Weekender Kamasutra Kit, fore-playing cards and books like *101 Nights of Grrreat Sex.* ☎ 415-788-0992.

Down on the first level, we could not resist **Chocolate Heaven**. Chunks, bars, boxes and individual chocolates were all enticing.

Mmmmm. Or, try the **Left Hand World**, which sells everything for a left-handed person. There are things you would never imagine are made separately for right- and left-handed people. How about playing cards, cork screws, spatulas and toothbrushes?

There are restaurants and lots of fast-food joints where you can saturate yourself with sugar, fat, cholesterol and all that good stuff. Scores of shops sell souvenirs of Pier 39 and San Francisco. There is a two-tiered Venetian carousel in case you want to go around together a few times.

❑ *Pier 39;* ☎ *415-705-5500, 800-325-7437.*
❑ *Open: Shops 10:30 am-8:30 pm, restaurants 11:30 am-11:30 pm.*
❑ *Parking: Garage with a pedestrian bridge connection. $5 an hour, but full restaurants validate your ticket.*

## Embarcadero Walks

### Ferry Building to SS Jeremiah O'Brien Walk
*(Length: about ¾ of a mile, another half-mile to Mission Creek. Flat.)*

Instead of the more usual, better-known and longer walk up toward Fisherman's Wharf, try going the other way for a short and easy stroll. It is only three blocks to the San Francisco-Oakland Bay Bridge (to use the full name no one ever utters). The small pier underneath, Pier 24 (piers have odd numbers north of the Ferry Building, even numbers south), is the Fireboat Dock. The *SS Jeremiah O'Brien* Liberty ship is at Pier 32. If you walk past a few more piers, you will come to the South Beach Marina, where the Embarcadero officially ends, though the waterfront goes on. That is the Mission Creek Inlet where the narrow strip of water pushes inland. There once was a real Mission Creek, but it is long gone. On the other side is China Basin.

### Ferry Building to Fisherman's Wharf Walk or Bicycle
*(Length: 1½ miles. Flat.)*

Start at Ferry Plaza, turn to the north (left, if you are facing the Ferry Building) and start walking. The big vessel that looks like a ferry boat docked at Pier 3 was once just that. The *Santa Rosa* transported commuters and their cars to and from Sausalito from 1927 until 1937, when the Golden Gate Bridge was built. Visitors can board from 8 am-5 pm to look her over. These days, she does not ever leave the dock.

Detour for a walk out onto the next pier. **Pier 7** is strictly for leisure-seeking people, like us. Its planks are wooden, railings are ornate bronze and seagulls compete with the local fishermen for

*Biking along San Francisco's northern waterfront.*

what is swimming out there. Romantic couples share benches under the bronze lampposts and dreamily watch the boats go by. You might join them, or even bring a sandwich along and have lunch out here. You will be joined by office workers who walk down from the Financial District to get a little peace and quiet along with pastrami on rye.

There is a longish parade of derelict piers after that, most being used for parking space and offices; only an occasional cruise ship ties up on nautical business. If you get tired of walking, the number 32 bus comes by about every 10 minutes. But you will soon be at Pier 39, with all of its attractions; visual and gustatory in nature.

From here on, the next chunk is all considered part of **Fisherman's Wharf**. At Pier 45, is the *USS Pampanito*, a World War II fleet submarine that sank six Japanese ships. You can board to see how compact and cramped the innards of a sub really are. Past that, at the Hyde St. Pier, are several historic sailing ships, the 301-foot, square-rigged *Balclutha*, which sailed around Cape Horn and was the fastest windjammer in the Alaska Packer fishing fleet. The *Eureka*, one of the largest ferryboats in the world in her day (1890-1940), is also on view along with a century-old lumber schooner. Next to the pier, on the shore of Aquatic Park, is the **National Maritime Museum**, built by the WPA in 1939. You cannot miss its Streamline Moderne design that looks like a cruise ship. It has rounded ends, stepped decks and round porthole windows. As a maritime museum, it is filled with anchors, winches and prows of clipper ships. You will want to spend time here if you are at all interested in boats.

The *USS Pampanito* is open 10 am-5 pm, admission $3, seniors $1. Hyde Street Pier is open 10 am-5:30 pm, admission $2, seniors free. The National Maritime Museum is open 10 am-5 pm and is free of charge. For all three, ☎ 415-929-0202.

Also on the Hyde Street Pier is **The Maritime Store**, a non-profit bookstore with an extensive selection that promises hours of browsing time to anyone interested in the sea. If you want to order nautical books by mail, request their catalogue by writing to 2905 Hyde Street Pier, San Francisco, CA 94109; ☎ 415-775-2665. A good place to end your walk is at the Buena Vista Café, right here at Hyde and Beach streets (see page 62).

## Golden Gate Promenade Walk

*(Length: 2½ miles from Fort Mason, another mile from Fisherman's Wharf. Mostly flat.)*

If you are a walker, not a hiker, and looking for something easy but scenic, either this or walking across the Golden Gate Bridge (see page 138), are your best choices. This path leads along the shoreline of the bay. You can pick it up at four different places and parking is available.

Start either at Fisherman's Wharf, where you walk west to Aquatic Park or next door, along the rim and to Fort Mason. The latter is probably your best choice because the parking is easier. The piers extending into the bay here were the main embarkation centers for the military from 1910 to 1963, when the Fort was turned over to the city. The warehouses have been converted into museums, theaters, class-rooms and restaurants. It is a really active community place.

Follow the signs with the blue and white sailboat logo which lead to Marina Green. This is a big, grassy field where there are usually kite-flyers taking advantage of the ever-present winds. Go along the pathway on the bayfront and past St. Francis Yacht Club. Do not miss the wave organ at the end of the Yacht Club's outer sea wall. If the tide is right, the water surging through submerged pipes makes a weird tune. To the left is where the 1915 Panama Pacific International Exposition was held. The Palace of Fine Arts is still standing. Stay with the signs, "San Francisco Bay Trail." Crissy Field was the first of the military airfields here, built in 1920. Now, the big action is out in the water, seeing the windsurfers defy the strong winds that usually blow off this point. There is a par course with exercise stations along this stretch, for those feeling particularly frisky. The path dodges a parking lot and fishing pier, then leads to the Fort Point National Historic Site, under the Golden Gate Bridge.

It was here, in 1794, that the Spanish built Castillo de San Joaquin to defend the Presidio. There was never a gun fired in anger. That first adobe fort was replaced by this brick and granite structure constructed by the US Army Engineers in 1853 and named Fort Point. When the•Civil War started, its 120 cannons were manned by 150 Union soldiers to protect the entrance to San Francisco Bay from a Southern attack, which never came. The museum holds a lot of history, with Civil War relics and a gift shop.

Return the same way.

❑ *Parking: At Fort Mason or at a parking lot at this end of the Golden Gate Bridge. Take final exit off 101 before the bridge.*
❑ *Getting here: The Powell Street cable cars (start at Powell and Market). Powell/Mason cars end at Aquatic Park.*

## *Sea Lions*

Among the biggest attractions at Pier 39 these days are the sea lions. A merchant's dream come true, they first started showing up in 1990. Before they appeared, the area next to the pier was a marina. People liked to eat on the pier and look at the boats, while other people liked to eat on the boats and look at the pier. This was an arrangement that made everyone happy. Then the pinnipeds showed up.

Most boat owners tend to think wet, slobbery, noisy sea lions smelling of spoiled fish make terrible neighbors. But the boaters could not get rid of them, because the beasts are protected by law. Management lost some rents at first, but after awhile realized that more people were coming to see the sea lions than the boats.

They started publicizing the animals and adopted one of them, nicknamed Salty, as the pier's mascot. They even published a book, *Salty, the Sea Lion,* which they give to kids.

Since then, millions of visitors have flocked here to see those "cute little fellas," each leaving a few bucks behind. Of course, Salty is an imaginary sea lion, but the noisy, messy mammals are fun to watch. There are several rafts where they congregate, just 100 feet from the end of the pier. All you get here are males from the Channel Islands off Santa Barbara in Southern California. Females stay at home and tend to the nest. Fewer are seen in May, June and July, although there are always some. There is a cooperative program with the Marine Mammal Center, which trains docents who are on the dock to talk about sea lions on weekends from 11 am-5 pm.

# Haight-Ashbury

Its most famous era was three short years from 1964-67. The corner of Haight and Ashbury was the center of the Hippie movement. The Haight was important to San Francisco for a century before that. After Golden Gate Park was built in the 1870s, people rode their buggies out from the city to spend the day and picnic. Stables and bars, cafés and bicycle rentals sprang up along Stanyan, at the end of the park. Then, a cable car came down Haight Street. An amusement park was built, as well as a baseball stadium at Stanyan and Waller. The great rivals, Stanford and Berkeley, played a famous "delayed" game in 1902. That Sunday afternoon, the Stanford team arrived at the field drunk. Their coach saw they could hardly play, let alone win. That was when the ball was conveniently "lost." There was a fan in the stands who owned a sports equipment shop. He volunteered to go downtown, open his shop and get a new ball. By the time he returned with it, the Stanford team had sobered up, and they won the game. It was even an upset.

The **Stanyan Park Hotel** was built on that corner of Stanyan and Waller in 1904. At 1749 Waller, now Park Cyclery, was a Chinese laundry in the 1890s. Laundry was one of the few business options for the Chinese.

An alternative hippie lifestyle was established here in the 1960s. It was grounded in a philosophy that rejected an overly commercialized way of life and was meant to change society by persuading each individual to become a tolerant and loving person. Some people, who later became pretty well known, lived here during that time. Young people were flocking from all over the country to this suddenly famous spot, or infamous, depending on your point of view.

Two blocks east of Stanyan and a half-block south of Haight, at 636 Waller St., is where Charles Manson lived in the early 1960s. It is here where he gathered his "tribe," before gracing Southern California with his presence.

A block further east, the yellow building on the corner of Waller and Belvedere is where, in July of 1967, Rudolph Nureyev and Margot Fontaine were busted for possession of "12 joints, marijuana, two tablets of an unknown substance and two rolls of pornographic film." They were released from jail a few hours later and danced that night at the Opera House in top form. Nureyev was even said to have floated a little higher than usual in his leaps.

Keep walking two blocks further to Ashbury, just north of Haight Street. On the west side, at #555, is where Timothy Leary lived for a time, practicing his creed, "Tune in, turn on, drop out."

Still on Ashbury, cross Haight and you will see the Edwardian building at #635 where Janice Joplin lived in the mid-1960s. She also stayed in a Victorian at 112 Lyon St. for awhile. That is three more blocks east and on the other side of the panhandle.

Stay on Ashbury and walk another block. Look at that row of similar Queen Anne Victorian houses built about 1890 on the east side of the street. The one painted grayish-greenish-blue at 710 is where the Grateful Dead group was formed and where they lived for several years. They were busted here in 1967.

Before you get that far, on Masonic south of Haight Street, mid-block on the west side of the street, the mauve house with window boxes is where Patty Hearst holed up after robbing the bank with the Simbionese Revolutionary Army.

The neighborhood is far different now than it was 30 years ago, but some of the old spirit is still here. The people who live in The Haight fought fiercely in the old days to keep chain stores out. Ben & Jerry's ice cream shop finally broke the barrier and put in a big place right on the corner of Haight and Ashbury. At first furious locals vowed never to patronize it; now it's a popular hangout.

# *Inns*

## ♥ *Inn 1890*

As we drove up Page Street we saw the house. A stunning Victorian stood on a corner lot. Corner lots were more expensive in those days and that usually meant a more expensive house. Inside, it has been much refurbished, but the high ceilings and good architectural breeding are still here. While one room has a private bath, there are two toilets and two showers for the other four bedrooms. That is the reason that the rates are so low (starting at $59). This is a real bargain, even if the rates have gone up a bit by the time you phone for a reservation.

The house was built as a private residence by Dr. Carl Salfield, who identified himself on the original deed as a "Physician and capitalist." He did not live here, but rented it out. He renovated the house in 1922. The suspicion is that he used it as an abortion clinic for unmarried women. That went on for years, kept secret, of course. Clinics of that kind, run by private doctors, were common in those days.

In the past 40 years, the house had deteriorated badly. Win Schachter wondered about its past as he peeled and scraped different layers of paint and wallpaper. He became so curious he hired a search organization which turned up much of this history. Win is the former Executive Director of the California Psychological Association. Because he has narcolepsy, a sleep disorder, he decided that owning and running an inn would be the perfect vocation in his retirement years. He lives in the inn now and is happy to help visitors with advice for restaurants, entertainment and directions.

There is a small library with a fireplace and so a large jar of chocolate kisses in the entry hall. What a temptation every time you pass by! Each room has a kitchenette built into a former closet with a sink, microwave oven, toaster, refrigerator and dishes. There are two robes in each room with "Inn 1890" embroidered on the breast pocket. Every room has its own private phone. As of now, most of the furniture throughout is of a solid, standard type and not antique. Win is slowly replacing some of the pieces.

Breakfast consists of muffins, three or four kinds of breads, Danish, bagels, cream cheese, cold cereals, juice, fresh fruit and yogurt. Trays to take breakfast back to your room are a thoughtful touch.

All the rooms have queen-sized beds, down comforters, and brass or iron bedsteads. Rooms Two and Three on the Shrader Street side have lots of windows and are very bright. Room Eight (ours) has an original 1890 wood floor. The hardwood floors in the other rooms were put in during the 1920s. We were on the second floor in the corner room, made bright with three windows. The bed angles into the room with its head to the windows, the fireplace a few feet to one side. We lit the fire and got into bed – flames danced in the darkness as we went to sleep. Very nice!

There is an unusual carved mantel over the tile hearth with a big horizontal mirror above and two tall, slender mirrors on each side, set into intricate carvings. A low red-cushioned rocking chair matches the low dresser. There are plants on the dresser and on either side of the hearth and a small TV beside the bed. Antique lamps are on bedside tables, and there is a desk with the private-line phone and an answering machine to record your own message.

The inn has a good location with shopping and restaurants on Haight, just a block away. Golden Gate Park is also just one block. You can bicycle, walk, see the museums, Japanese garden, or stroll hand in hand on secluded paths through the trees. Inn 1890 is like some of the small hotels we go to in Europe for their quaintness and to save money. Many have one room with tub and one with toilet for an entire floor, sometimes two floors. Inn 1890 has two showers (no tubs) and two toilets for only four rooms. A vast improvement!

❑ *1890 Page Street, San Francisco, CA 94117;*
   *Local* ☎ *415-386-0486, reservations 888-INN-1890, fax 415-386-3626.*
❑ *Rooms: Five.*

❑ *Rates: $59 without fireplace, $69 with fireplace. These were rates in October, 1996 when the inn first opened. We expect rates will be raised by perhaps $5.*
❑ *Reservations: Advised.*
❑ *Credit cards: MC, V.*
❑ *Minimum stay: Two nights on weekends.*
❑ *Breakfast: 8 am-10 am, large continental.*
❑ *Amenities: Robes, kitchenettes, washer/dryer in basement.*
❑ *Handicapped accessible: No.*
❑ *Smoking: On back deck only.*
❑ *Children: Older than eight years of age.*
❑ *Pets: If well-behaved.*
❑ *Parking: Some private parking, plus street parking.*
❑ *Directions: Four bus lines within a block or two.*

♥ *The Spencer House*

There is no sign outside this Victorian mansion to hint that it is an Inn. It is not listed in the phone book and Barbara Chambers does not advertise. We cannot think of any other bed and breakfast which discourages guests this way, but Barbara regards the Spencer House as her home, not a business.

The house was built in 1887 by the Spencer family. It was always a private residence, but deteriorated badly during the last few decades. When Barbara and Jack bought it in 1984, the lights, plumbing and gas did not work. There had been what looked like roller skating parties on the hardwood floors. Barbara and Jack moved into the basement while they fixed the place up. Later, they decided to open it as a bed & breakfast. Now the housekeeper and his family live in the basement and the Chambers are living luxuriously in what was the attic. The six rooms in between, all on the second floor, are for guests.

As you enter, the portraits that face you are of the Spencers. The staircase, hand-carved of honeywood oak, is original, as is the quarter-sawn parquet floor. In the living room, off the entry, are green velvet sofas and a tall Eastlake bookcase against the front wall. In the bay window looking out on Haight Street is a handy oval "partners" writing desk with a Tiffany lamp. Stained glass windows crown regular panes. There are Oriental carpets and a big fireplace. True to the Queen Anne style, Corinthian columns separate the living room from the back parlor, where there is a Stroud player piano with lots of rolls to play. This room also holds the oak dining table, always set for 12, with silver, fine china and a lace tablecloth. "I like it to look as though people are coming for dinner, whether they are or not," Barbara told us. This is also where breakfast is served. The 12-foot-high cabinet is from the 1700s and is French in origin. The honeywood hutch is built-in, another original that matches the entry staircase. The chandeliers are original to the house, with "Edison filaments."

There are two robes in every room with the "coat of arms" of the Spencer family embroidered on their pockets. Each of the rooms is different. The French Room, where we stayed, has a large four-window bay overlooking Baker Street and is frilly enough to fit its name. The gold chandelier, with its 1906 light bulbs, came from Sally Stanford's house, downtown on Pine Street. Gold cupids support the candle-shaped bulbs, while matching cupids are carved into the head- and foot-boards of the king-size bed. We really were taken aback by the sight of the bed. It is big to begin with, and then swells to a dome in the center. It looks as though a couple getting in on opposite sides will roll downhill away from one another. Actually, the mattress is, in the Victorian tradition, overstuffed with feathers that flatten out softly when one lies on them. It turned out to be very good for snuggling. The triple armoire is massive, at least eight feet tall with two large closets. A pattern of vases, bouquets, garlands and bows done in several colors cavort around the ceiling and chandelier. One painter who specializes in this kind of style took six weeks to do this ceiling by hand. This is one of the reasons why refurbishing old Victorians is a bottomless money pit. The smallish bathroom is very modern, with a shower, but no tub.

The Queen Anne Room is in front with big corner bay windows, roomy enough to hold a table and two chairs. A carved maple bed matches the triple armoire. This is very much a Victorian room.

In the Garden Room, a large closet has been cleverly converted into a wet bar. The bathroom has a tub and shower while a second former closet now holds the sink. There is a carved wood queen-size bed, an armoire from Scotland and rose-patterned wallpaper.

The Victorian Room has a corona over the bed, a triple armoire and closet. You will need to bring a few extra suitcases of clothes to make use of them all. The king-size bed makes this room look smaller than it is. Call it cozy, because it is very nice.

During November and December, the house is decorated in an incredibly beautiful holiday fashion. Magazines ask to photograph it. There are few guests from late November to Christmas, so that would be a wonderful time to come.

Several buses pass by here and restaurants and shopping are within three blocks.

- *1080 Haight St., San Francisco, CA 94117;*
  ☎ *415-626-9205, fax 415-626-9230.*
- *Rooms: Six.*
- *Rates: $115, $145, $165.*

□ *Credit cards: AE, MC, V.*
□ *Reservations: Four weeks in advance, August to October. Much easier from November to February. Weekends need more time than weekdays.*
□ *Minimum stay: Two nights on weekends.*
□ *Cancellations: $10 fee if you cancel less than five days before; if room is re-rented there is no fee.*
□ *Breakfast: A fine, imaginative breakfast is included.*
□ *Wine: Barbara does not have a wine license and the decanter of port is for her and Jack's personal use, but if you happen to have a glass in the afternoon or when you return from dinner, well that's OK.*
□ *Handicapped accessible: No.*
□ *Smoking: No.*
□ *Children: Yes, but only two people in one room; no rollaways or cribs.*
□ *Pets: No.*
□ *Parking: Three spaces and street.*

## Victorian Inn on the Park

*Victorian Inn on the Park.*

Although the front of this Italianate Victorian is on Fell Street, facing the panhandle of Golden Gate Park, the entrance is on Lyon Street. Go up a half-dozen steps to the door, which is locked at night (each guest gets a key). After the entry, there is a curious arrangement with an office to the right and the dining room for breakfast past that. The parlor, with fireplace, is to the left, furnished with comfortable chairs, books and music playing softly. There is also a library with more chairs, reading lamps and bookshelves. But past all these is a hallway with yet another fireplace blazing merrily.

The original staircase marches up, with royal red carpeting, to the second and third floors. There are portraits of ancestors on the walls, all bought at auction.

It was built in 1897 as the Clunie House. A base of concrete was troweled to look like rusticated stone, then brick, then it's topped off by the typical Victorian embellished wood. In this case, the crowning achievement is the open belvedere at the very top; one of only two in San Francisco. A belvedere is an octagonal tower with a curved roof. Guests occupying the Belvedere Suite on the third floor can sit out and enjoy the view of the city and park. The house is on a corner, and is therefore larger than most Victorians. It was fully restored and declared an Historic Landmark in 1981, when Shirley and Paul Weber opened it as an elegant inn. It had been several things over the years, including a commune for hippies in the 1960s. Haight-Ashbury was full of communes then.

There are 12 rooms, each different. But the following are representative examples. We stayed in Room 102, the only non-smoking room. Larger than most, it is in the front corner of the building with wide bay windows overlooking the park. The windows are double-glazed to reduce the noise from cars on Fell Street. There is another tall window on the Lyon Street side and more windows in the large bathroom. A queen bed, very comfortable, has large bedside tables with tall, fringed lamps, throwing off plenty of light for nighttime reading. A soft peach wallpaper (or pinkish beige, we disagreed) complements the red velvet chairs by the fireplace. The bathroom looks very 19th century. It is probably not the original sink, but it is from that era, with a narrow, deep bowl. The tub is an old-style claw foot, with a shower added over it.

Another room that also looks out on Fell and the park from tall windows is small, but with enough space for several chairs and a table. There is a sextet of Great Musicians portraits on the wall, only one of whom is smiling. Several rooms are larger than that and have bay windows, with a wicker sofa in the bay, a four-poster bed and very different bathrooms.

Room 111 is the smallest. A queen bed is set at an angle under small windows looking out on the park. It has a surprisingly large bathroom with a modern glass-doored shower.

We went downstairs to the living room for a while after 5 pm to enjoy a glass of wine. It was an inexpensive California Burgundy, but mellow enough that we took a second glass back upstairs to sip next to our own fireplace. The fireplace is one reason this room is priced higher. It's worth it.

We had a reservation at Tommy Toy's restaurant downtown on Montgomery Street at 8 pm. The staff arranged for a cab to pick us up at 7:30 pm and it was only a 15-20-minute ride downtown from here. In many of the inns, you will notice college students getting room and board and a stipend to be on call all night for little duties such as these. Next morning, there was a prompt wake-up call. We hustled out early to get to Powell Street. The bus is at Hayes, the next corner, and goes right down Market to Powell. This is a good location, with buses and nearby shopping.

❑ *301 Lyon St., San Francisco, CA 94117;*
☎ *415-931-1830; for reservations,* ☎ *800-435-1967.*

- Rooms: 12.
- Rates: $99-$320. 10% discount for seniors, Sunday-Thursday, November to March.
- Reservations: One month for weekends; "weekdays better."
- Minimum stay: Two nights on weekends.
- Cancellation: There is a charge if cancelled one week before date, two weeks for holidays.
- Breakfast: Complimentary continental breakfast.
- Packages: Will arrange roses, candy, champagne, caviar – whatever you wish – for an extra charge.
- Wine: After 5 pm; sherry always available.
- Handicapped accessible: No.
- Smoking: OK, except for Room 102.
- Children: "Allowed, but rarely."
- Pets: No.
- Parking: $10 a night on lot, free on street.

# Restaurants

## Cha Cha Cha

(Caribbean)

Colorful, loud and garish. Everyone in San Francisco (at least, all the younger people) knows about Cha Cha Cha as a place to go with a date for a noisy time. The food is Caribbean and decorations are as loud as the conversations shouted over the music. Fake palm trees, fake hibiscus and plenty of purple-yellow-red things make up the incredible display. Highly recommended as lots of fun, but depends on what you're looking for. At lunchtime it's just a place to eat.

- 1801 Haight St.; ☎ 415-386-7670.
- Prices: $7-$10.
- Open: 11:30 am-11:30 pm.
- Parking: Street.

## Zare Garden Grill

(Contemporary American)

You might wonder what "Zare" means. Abbassali Zare, the owner, is from Iran, where his grandfather was a farmer. Zare means "farmer" in Farsi.

The dining room is two stories high with a balcony. The room is painted white and it is bright and airy. There are paintings on the walls by local talent, all for sale. When we were there last, the paintings were by San Francisco Impressionist Ben Dominguez.

The salads are good. A Greek version is available with mixed greens, kalamata olives, dressed with feta cheese and the house dressing of oil and vinegar with touches of tarragon, mustard and basil adding some subtle flavors. There is also a wonderful spinach salad with a balsamic vinaigrette. The onion soup is thick with sweet onions. The spoon does not quite stand up in it, but it almost does.

If you are in the mood for a burger, how about a salmon burger, buffalo burger or venison burger? Venison burger? Are you sure you want to eat Bambi? The best Italian food is generally found in a restaurant where a godfather eats, or at least a cappo. We make it a rule not even to order pasta in a place where the chef doesn't at least have an Italian accent. But here we make an exception. Though without accents (at least, not Italian), they actually make several good pasta dishes here. Cheese-filled spinach tortellini with gorgonzola cream sauce or smoked chicken linguine with garlic, onion, shittake mushrooms, sun-dried tomatoes and a white wine cream sauce are delicious choices. When you are tired of all that cream sauce, a simple spaghetti with basil, pine nuts, tomato, roasted garlic, olive oil and parmigiana makes an excellent selection.

- *1640 Haight St.;* ☎ *415-861-8868.*
- *Open: Lunch 11:30 am-6 pm, dinner 6 pm-10:30 pm.*
- *Prices: Soups $3.25-$4.50, salads $6-$6.50, burgers $5.75-$7, pastas $7.50-$9.50.*
- *Credit cards: All major.*
- *Reservations: Not necessary.*
- *Parking: Street.*

# Things to Do

## Haight-Ashbury Flower Power Walking Tour

Bruce Brennan, artist and sculptor, first saw the Haight in 1967; Pam Brennan got here in 1973. Both have been deeply involved in this village within a city ever since. Once you have taken this tour, you will have learned a lot about the neighborhood and will have had fun in the process. You will learn from Bruce and Pam, who are brother and sister, how all this went from sand dunes and scrubby hills to fine Victorian homes after Golden Gate Park was created in the 19th century. The most fascinating part and the era they focus on, is the Flower Power period of the 1960s. This few-block area was the epicenter of it all. You'll see where the Grateful

Dead, Janis Joplin and Timothy Leary lived. You will walk down Haight Street, still the mecca for thousands who make their pilgrimages looking for what is now only a ghost of that era. You'll explore the new Psychedelic History Museum, not yet open to the public but open to this tour. Primarily, Bruce and Pam want you to go away knowing why it all happened here and what the participants really wanted to accomplish.

Haight-Ashbury is included on several bus tours, but seeing all this from inside a bus with a large group of people is no substitute for the up-close and hands-on walking tour they offer. Whether you lived through those times or only heard about them, you will find this tour delightful.

❑ *PO Box 170106, San Francisco, CA 94117.*
❑ ☎ *415-221-8442; fax 415-553-8541.*
❑ *Price: $15 per person.*
❑ *When: Tuesdays and Saturdays, 9:30 am, for approximately 2½ hours. Meet at Stanyan and Waller streets (across from Golden Gate Park). Tours operate more often during the summer and by appointment.*

## Haight Street Fair

The Haight Street Fair is held on the second Sunday in June. It was started 20 years ago as a way to "save" The Haight. After the heady days of the 1960s had crashed with drugs and crime, the neighborhood was at its nadir with boarded-up store windows and homes owned mostly by elderly people whose children had moved to the suburbs, while real estate bottomed out. People from other parts of the city were afraid to come here. There was even talk in the government offices in Sacramento of bulldozing a strip through it for a new freeway. Pablo Heising, unofficial "Mayor of The Haight," and some friends, knew something had to be done to save the neighborhood and show others that Haight-Ashbury was safe to visit. So the Street Fair was born. Haight is closed off for five blocks from Masonic to Stanyan, with two stages providing live entertainment, a few hundred booths for arts and crafts, food, etc. Thousands attend. It is colorful and fun. If you happen to be in San Francisco at that time, you will enjoy it.

# Golden Gate Park

❦ *A cool breeze, a warm day,*
*A leisurely walk around the New Garden*
*Willows green, peaches red, all are marvelous sights;*
*I don't mind the fragrant paths leading a distance away.*
*All the more delighted,*
*I wander along, to the east, to the west.*
*Each blade of grass and every blooming flower can cheer a troubled*
*mind.*
*O, why not take it easy and enjoy everything all over again?*

("New Garden" was the term used for Golden Gate Park by the Chinese in
the early 1900s.)

*Songs of Gold Mountain, Cantonese, Rhymes from San Francisco Chinatown*

It is a half-mile wide and three miles long, with an extension one
block wide and eight blocks long. This is called Golden Gate Park
because San Franciscans, early and late, have always been fascinated by the term and stick it on anything big. That includes a
bridge, a street and one of the largest urban parks in the world. The
extension is called the Panhandle, an apt name because it sticks out
to the east through the Haight-Ashbury like a handle on a frying
pan. The park came first and the neighborhood grew up around it,
At first this area was way outside the city. It was originally called
the Outside Lands, with mostly sand dunes to the west.

Then, the people of San Francisco wanted a park. In all the hysteria
of the Gold Rush, no one had thought of keeping land for something like that, and the city owned the Outside Lands anyway. The
smart money men blocked anything from happening until the city
gave them 90% of the city's own land and the taxpayers got to keep
10%. That is how Golden Gate Park was born.

Some people's early idea was to grade everything flat and put in
the usual formal gardens. Fortunately, a surveyor named William
Hammon Hall got the contract with his plan to leave the land as
nature had created it. He followed the contours that were already
there and put in a "natural" park. The first task was to hold down
the sand, which had the habit of moving with every wind. That was
accomplished by planting barley and lupine. Barley sprouted
quickly and held things in place while the slower-growing lupine
rooted and then spread. Then bushes and trees could be planted. It
took decades.

In the meantime, Hall was replaced by John McLaren, who spent
the rest of his life building and defending the park. It takes constant
defending. As soon as the park became successful, which was

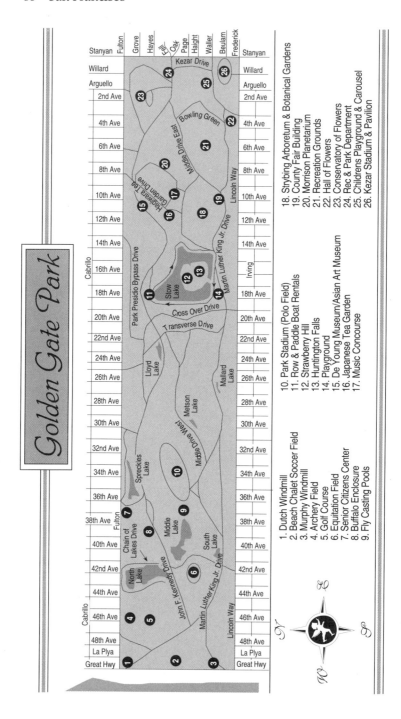

Golden Gate Park

18. Strybing Arboretum & Botanical Gardens
19. County Fair Building
20. Morrison Planetarium
21. Recreation Grounds
22. Hall of Flowers
23. Conservatory of Flowers
24. Rec & Park Department
25. Childrens Playground & Carousel
26. Kezar Stadium & Pavilion

10. Park Stadium (Polo Field)
11. Row & Paddle Boat Rentals
12. Strawberry Hill
13. Huntington Falls
14. Playground
15. De Young Museum/Asian Art Museum
16. Japanese Tea Garden
17. Music Concourse

1. Dutch Windmill
2. Beach Chalet Soccer Field
3. Murphy Windmill
4. Archery Field
5. Golf Course
6. Equitation Field
7. Senior Citizens Center
8. Buffalo Enclosure
9. Fly Casting Pools

defending. As soon as the park became successful, which was almost immediately, San Franciscans loved it. They still love *their* park. Everyone, it seemed, wanted to stick something there. Politicians and ethnic groups were always campaigning to put up a statue or a monument to someone. When they succeeded, over McLaren's strenuous objections, he would promptly plant bushes and trees around the thing so it could hardly be seen. Unfortunately, since his death 50 years ago, that commendable practice has not been followed.

The **Midwinter Fair,** built in the park in 1894, was copied after the famous 1893 Universal Exhibition in Chicago. The theme of the Fair was a high-minded one. Since electricity was the new phenomenon of the age, the centerpiece was the Electric Tower, which McLaren blew up after the Fair. The Japanese Tea Garden and Fine Arts Museum (now the M.H. de Young Memorial Museum) are almost the only parts that remain. In fact, the hit of San Francisco's Fair had been the same act that had drawn nationwide attention to Chicago's – a belly dancer called "Little Egypt" (a.k.a. Catherine Devine), with a lissome troupe, allegedly from Cairo. More than a few observers speculated that her undulating dance in a semi-transparent skirt had much more to do with the Fair's success than the Asian artwork on display.

When John McLaren was 70 years old, the compulsory retirement age for city employees, the Board of Supervisors asked him to step down. The people of San Francisco, who called him "Uncle John" and loved him for always standing up to any who would exploit the park for their own purposes, protested loudly. The Supervisors backed down. McLaren died at the age of 97, still in charge.

A final story started in December of 1943 as McLaren lay dying in McLaren Lodge. It had been built at the edge of the park for him and his family. He asked if the stately Monterey cypress that grows in front of the lodge could be hung with colored lights. Even though San Francisco was blacked out for the duration of the war, it was done. Ever since, every December "Uncle John McLaren's Christmas Tree" is covered with lights.

Get information and a map ($2.25) from the Recreation and Park Commission, McLaren Lodge, 501 Stanyan St. (across from end of Fell Street at the Haight-Ashbury end of the park), ☎ 415-666-7200. Open 8 am-5 pm, Monday-Friday. Information is also available at Beach Chalet Visitors Center, 1000 Great Highway, 8 am-6 pm, seven days a week. Parking may be found along the sides of the roads in the park. Paid parking in the Music Concourse area, weekends and holidays. Please note that on Sundays and holidays, Kennedy Drive between Kezar Drive and Transverse Drive within the park is closed to auto traffic. As a result all the bicyclists and roller bladers in the world have a grand time. Handicapped accessible parking is available in the Music Concourse.

## *Things to See*

The **Arboretum** and **Botanical Gardens** together hold over 6,000 species of plants. Special gardens within the 70-acre display include a Biblical Garden, an Asian Garden and the Garden of Fragrance. The latter is designed for the blind, with scented and fragrant flowers and medicinal plants identified with braille labels. These attractions are located near South Drive off the Ninth Avenue entrance to the park.

The **Beach Chalet** faces the Great Highway and the sea, across J.F. Kennedy Drive from the Dutch Windmill. It had been closed for years and was just reopened in January, 1997. Downstairs there is a Visitors Center where you can buy a map of Golden Gate Park and get directions. Upstairs is a brew pub with windows facing the beach and on the ground floor are the Lucien Labaudt murals. They were executed in 1936-37 as a Federal Art Project. The theme of the murals is San Francisco itself and there are scenes showing many areas of the city, including Golden Gate Park. In the short time this building has been reopened, it has become very popular. Often, especially on weekends, it can get crowded. Open 10 am-5 pm.

The **Garden of Shakespeare's Flowers** contains nothing but the 150-odd plants named in The Bard's plays and sonnets. Near the California Academy of Science.

The **Music Concourse** was the site of the Midwinter Fair of 1894. There is a Pavilion where concerts are held at 2 pm on Sundays in the summer, with the "Opera Concert in the Park" in August and September.

**California Academy of Science** borders the Music Concourse and contains an aquarium, planetarium, and the Museum of Natural Science. The Hall of Man traces man's and woman's evolution. The African Hall displays dioramas of fauna and the Earth and Space Halls are true to their names. They are open daily from 10 am-5 pm, with later hours in the summer. Admission is $7. An "Explorer Pass," good for admission to the Academy of Science, de Young Museum, Asian Art Museum and Japanese Tea Garden, is $12.50; available at the McLaren Lodge and Beach Chalet Visitors Center. ☎ 415-750-7145.

The **M.H. de Young Memorial Museum** is across from the Academy of Science. Michael Harry de Young, along with his brother, Charles, started the *San Francisco Chronicle* in 1865 and donated this fine art collection to the city. It is open Wednesday-Sunday from

10 am-5 pm, with a $6 admission charge (or the $12.50 Explorer Pass). ☎ 415-863-3330.

The **Asian Art Museum** is housed in a wing of the de Young Museum and built around the original collection by Avery Brundage. Forty countries, 6,000 years of history and a spectacular Jade Room are sure to intrigue you. The Museum is open Wednesday-Sunday from 10 am-5 pm. A $6 admission includes entry to the de Young Museum, or use the $12.50 Explorer Pass (available at McLaren Lodge or Beach Visitors Center). ☎ 415-668-8921.

The **Japanese Tea Garden** was originally the Japanese Village, a part of the 1894 Midwinter Fair. It was so popular that it was retained and has been one of Golden Gate Park's most popular attractions since. A Japanese gardener, Makato Hagiwara, created it. Along with his family, he kept it beautiful for 47 years until 1942, when the Japanese on the Pacific Coast were interned in "relocation camps." When the war was over, the Hagiwara family was refused permission to move back to the park. Not until 29 years later, in 1974, was their devotion to the city recognized when a plaque was installed in the Garden. "To honor Makato Hagiwara and his family, who nurtured and shared his garden from 1895 to 1942."

Miniature trees, wooden bridges arching over still pools, make it a beautiful place, especially in March and April when the cherry trees blossom. The nine-foot-tall "Buddha who sits unsheltered from the wind and rain" was cast in Japan in 1790. An open air Tea Shop sells tea and cokes, $2.50 with cookies and crackers, served by waitresses in kimonos. People seem to find eating the cookies and crackers more fascinating than anything else in the Garden. The Garden is pretty well surrounded by roads and parking lots that undermine the tranquil setting. If possible, come early on a non-weekend, non-summer day for best results. Yet, even if you cannot make that, in spite of the museums, band concerts, crowds and autos around it, this small space provides paths to stroll to pagodas, waterfalls, a zen garden, dwarf tree forest and beauty in general.

In addition to his other accomplishments, Mikato Higawa is the man who invented the fortune cookie, to be served at the Midwinter Fair. Chinese restaurants in San Francisco began to serve them as well and they became known all over the world as Chinese fortune cookies.

The Garden is open 9 am-6:30 pm daily, admission $2.50, or $12.50 Explorer Pass.

The **Buffalo Paddock** is on the west side of Kennedy Drive, near Spreckles Lake. It is rather startling to suddenly come upon a small herd of bison in the middle of the city. These were donated by Richard Blum, husband of California Senator Dianne Feinstein, to replace the original herd that had been here since 1892. It is rather sad to see normally active, big animals who naturally migrate long distances for food, standing inert and abject in this small enclosure.

The **Conservatory of Flowers**, a duplicate of the original in London's Kew Gardens, was badly damaged in the storms of 1996. There are no plans at present to reopen.

## Sports & Recreation

**Archery.** 47th Avenue near Fulton Street. Bales are provided but bring your own targets, bows and arrows. No reservations required. Free.

**Bicycling.** 7½ miles of paved trails. (See Rentals, below.)

**Boating.** Pedal, electric and row boats are for rent at Stow Lake. Snack bar. (See Rentals.)

**Fly Casting.** Opposite Buffalo Paddock. Bring your own equipment. Free. ☎ 415-386-2630 on Saturdays.

**Golf.** Opposite 47th Avenue. A short but tricky nine-hole course with par three holes. No reservations required. Green fees. ☎ 415-751-8987 daily.

**Horseback Riding.** 12 miles of bridle paths, guided rides daily. (See Rentals.)

**Horseshoe Pitching.** Off Conservatory Drive. Bring your own horseshoes. No reservations required. Free.

**Jogging.** Many miles of jogging trails at Polo Field Parcourse.

**Exercising.** Senior citizen exercise course behind Senior Center, 36th Avenue and Fulton Street.

**Picknicking.** May be done throughout the park; hundreds of beautiful spots to choose from.

**Tennis.** 21 courts off Kennedy Drive opposite the Conservatory. Reservations required. For rates and weekday reservations, ☎ 415-753-7100, Tuesday-Sunday, 9 am-5 pm. For weekend reservations, ☎ 415-753-7101, starting previous Wednesday 7 pm-9 pm.

## Rentals

**Golden Gate Skate & Bike**, 3038 Fulton St. Mountain bikes $5 per hour, $25 per 24-hour day; tandem bikes $10-$50, helmets included (no locks). Regular skates, the old-fashioned kind, $4-$12; in-line skates $6-$24, pads included. Open 9 am-5 pm daily, 9 am-6 pm during daylight saving time. ☎ 415-668-1117.

**Lincoln Cyclery**, 772 Stanyan St. Mountain bikes or hybrid $5 per hour, $25 per day, helmets included (no locks; you have to stay with bikes). Open Wednesday-Saturday, Monday 9 am-5 pm, Sunday 11:30 am-5 pm, closed Tuesday. ☎ 415-221-1415.

**Park Cyclery**, 1749 Waller St. Scott 21-speed mountain bikes $5 per hour, $25 per day; tandem bikes $10-$50 (includes helmets, locks, map). In-line skates $6-$30, including pads. Open 10 am-6 pm, seven days a week. ☎ 415-221-3777 or 751-7368.

**Stanyon Street Cyclery**, 672 Stanyan St. Mountain bikes $14 for two hours, $18 for four hours, $25 for 24 hours, $250 credit card deposit, helmets and racks included, no locks. Open April through October, Monday-Friday, 9 am-7 pm; November through March, Monday-Friday, 11 am-7 pm; all year Saturday 10 am-6 pm, Sunday 10 am-5 pm. ☎ 415-221-7211.

**Stowe Lake Boat House**. Electric motorboats $13 per hour; rowboats $9.50; pedal boats $10.50. No credit cards. Open 9 am-5 pm, mid-June to Labor Day, 9 am-4 pm during the winter. ☎ 415-752-0347.

**Golden Gate Park Stables**. Guided one-hour horseback rides every day, 9 am-3 pm, $25. ☎ 415-668-7360.

# *Mission District*

In the beginning, of course, was the Mission Dolores. The Spanish arrived in 1776. They established the Presidio at the edge of the Bay by the Golden Gate to protect the harbor and they built a mission a few miles inland where there was a spring.

When the Americans arrived in the 1840s, and in a torrent after gold was discovered, this area, far outside the city that still hugged the Bay, became a favorite place for outings, especially on Sundays. The terrain in between was still hilly, windswept and sandy, but the land around the Mission became the Coney Island of early San Francisco, with roadhouses, racetracks and two bull rings. Later, elaborate gardens and "palaces" were built, a kind of early Disneyland.

Now, the Mission District is once again a neighborhood in transition, but that is nothing new. In the late 1800s and up to the 1940s, it was home to successive waves of working-class Irish, German and Italian families. For the last few decades, it has been San Francisco's Hispanic neighborhood. Some of the best burritos in town are found at Taquerias La Cumbre on 515 Valencia Street. Lately, especially since Willie Brown has been Mayor, there has been a push to open up the district to the rest of the population, with city-wide events and cultural activities. A few hot new restaurants are attracting people from other neighborhoods.

A continuing problem is that the Mission District is not a "good" neighborhood. There are still boarded-up storefronts and some run-down houses. The crime rate is perceived to be high. The worst part is around 16th and Mission Streets. Farther on, by 24th Street, it is much better, and some good restaurants are starting to locate around there. Do not be dissuaded from coming here. Remember, there is also the Mission, the murals and other sights well worth seeing. If you are going to the Mission District by underground, there's a BART station at 16th and Mission and another at 24th. Get off at 24th.

# *Inn*

## *Inn San Francisco*

Within the Mission District, Inn San Francisco is well removed from the problem area – several blocks south of Mission Street on a wide boulevard in a neighborhood of fine Victorian homes. Walk up the two short flights of stairs between Corinthian columns and enter the narrow, tall front door with its lace curtains. To your right is the formal front parlor, with a piano, fireplace and four bay windows. Beyond is the sitting room, with another fireplace. A fruit bowl and refrigerator with sodas are for guests to help themselves. Both rooms are replete with grand coffee table books about San Francisco, many of which we had never seen before. This is where, while sipping sherry from a delicate glass, we found the oversized *Landmarks of San Francisco* by Patrick McGrew. The book contains a large photo of the Havens Mansion taken just a few blocks from here. It is almost identical to this house, also built by Charles Havens in the 1870s. Havens was the City Architect for 12 years and everything he designed reflected the upper-middle class lifestyle of that era.

The house has certainly been imaginatively rebuilt. Room 10 was the dining room originally. It now has a shower and hot tub. Room 11, the original kitchen, also has a hot tub. Room 12 is tiny; it was the pantry, now made cozy and with a deep tub/shower. We think it's very romantic. After all, who needs room to swing a cat on a romantic weekend? Leave the cat at home.

The Oriental Room is the wedding night suite. There is a fireplace, four-poster bed, jacuzzi and shower, with oriental touches like vases and paintings. Upstairs, is a small, "cute" room with a plumped up feather bed, fireplace, jacuzzi and private deck over the garden. Watch for the raccoons on the deck. They walk along the railing to get to the fig tree.

There is a hot tub in the quiet garden for all to use, which is surrounded by camellias, the big fig tree and a walnut tree. Most rooms have queen beds, although a few smaller rooms have double beds.

Breakfast is really the star of the show here. Served in the sitting room, it is sumptuous, with soft, classical music playing somewhere in the background. The local papers and *The New York Times* are on hand. On the sideboard are three or four kinds of homemade breads, a pitcher of freshly squeezed orange juice and a pot of jam. On the marble mantel over the fireplace is a basket of fresh fruit, several plates of sliced fruit, and a just-made quiche. You will not go hungry. There are another half-dozen dishes of sliced fresh fruit like green kiwis, oranges, melons, red grapefruit and yellow pineapple. An indication of the number of European guests who stay here, are the platters of sliced meats, cold cuts, and cheeses, plus a bowl of hard boiled eggs.

The Mission District is generally considered a less favorable area than the more chic neighborhoods north of Market. This is one reason that this very nice inn is a bargain.

❑ *943 South Van Ness Ave., San Francisco, CA 94110;*
   ☎ *415-641-0188, 800-359-0913 for reservations, fax 415-641-1701.*
❑ *Rooms: 21 (15 in main building, six in adjoining building).*
❑ *Bathrooms: 20.*
❑ *Rates: $85-$225.*
❑ *Credit cards: All.*
❑ *Packages: Request romance package for champagne, flowers.*
❑ *Reservations: Weekdays, two to three days; weekends, two weeks.*
❑ *Minimum stay: On weekends and holidays, two days.*
❑ *Breakfast: Large, extended continental.*
❑ *Wines: Sherry.*
❑ *Handicapped accessible: No.*
❑ *Smoking: OK in rooms, gardens and balconies; not in parlor or hall.*
❑ *Children: Yes.*
❑ *Pets: Occasionally.*
❑ *Parking: Garage $10 per day.*

# Things to Do

## Mission Dolores

Welcome to La Mision de Nuestro Serafico Padre San Francisco de Asis a la Laguna de Nuestra Senora de los Dolores. If you can say

*Mission Dolores.*

that without breathing heavily, you are a better person than the two of us, Gunga Din. Take the easy way and call it simply the Mission.

It is the oldest building in San Francisco. That is not saying a lot considering the 1906 earthquake and fire. But, the Mission rode that one out without major damage. The first mass was celebrated here by Father Francisco Patou in 1776, before there was a United States. The building itself was completed in 1791 and has stood here ever since, with its four-foot-thick walls resisting decay and earthquakes.

The present Basilica dates from 1918. Pope Pius XII designated it a Basilica, an honorary Church of the Pope, in 1952. Beautiful stained glass windows commemorate Father Patou, the missions, and founder Father Junipero Serra.

Through 220 years the Mission has remained the parish church and is still the baptistry. A fine Venetian glass bowl serves as the baptismal font. There is a cemetery next to the Mission, a small part of the huge one which was streeted over. The first mayor of San Francisco lies here, as does the first Governor of Alta California. There is a larger-than-life-size monument to Father Serra in the cemetery's garden and the grounds are kept up admirably.

This is the best preserved of all California missions. Although it has gone through a lot, many of the adobe walls, redwood beams and original roof tiles are still in place.

❑ *320 Dolores St.;* ☎ *415-621-8203.*
❑ *Open: May through October, 9 am-4 pm; November through April, 10 am-4 pm; New Years and Easter, 10 am-1 pm.*
❑ *Admission Fee: $2 to garden and cemetery.*
❑ *Parking: On street.*

## Mural Tours

These tours are famous in Europe and their fame is spreading to Asia. As a result, many Japanese tourists come to see them. Yet for some reason, you would not have found the fabulous murals that are everywhere in the Mission District in any guidebook until now. Every Saturday at 1:30 pm the Mural Walk takes place. Though only eight blocks long, you will see over 75 outdoor artworks. Walks are led by experienced muralists. You may even witness a mural being created before your eyes. The subject matter ranges from world politics to neighborhood issues. The cost is $4, seniors $3. Meet at Precita Eyes Mural Arts Center, 348 Precita Ave. (at Folsom Street, one block south of Cesar Chavez Street). If you prefer to be picked up downtown, meet the bus on the last Saturday of each month at 9:30 am in front of SF MOMA (Museum of Modern Art), 151 Third St., for transportation and the Mural Walk. Cost is $15 and includes refreshments. It takes 2½ hours to complete the tour.

To make it a mural cycle tour, bring your bike to 348 Precita Ave. on the second Saturday of the month at 11 am. Cost is $10 and a helmet is required. No reservations are necessary for either tour.

An extended bus tour of murals throughout the city is held on the third Saturday of the month. Start the tour at 12:30 pm by meeting in front of the SF MOMA, 151 Third Street. Or meet the tour at 1 pm at the Precita Eyes Mural Arts Center, 348 Precita Avenue. Cost is $30 and includes refreshments. You will see over 100 murals in three hours. ☎ 415-285-2287 for more information.

## Good Vibrations

You would be surprised at the number of couples with romance on their minds who drop into this big, well-lit store on Valencia Street near the Mission. It is an emporium of sex toys, books, videos and all romantic things. The patrons we found browsing were typically heterosexual women under 40; most looked like students and businesswomen, with a fair sprinkling of men and couples. There is a big section of educational books, like *Celebrating Orgasm*, by Betty Dodson, PhD., and fun reading like *Best American Erotic Literature of 1996*. You will find book signings taking place here. There are CDs and audio tapes to listen to in the car while driving back home. There is a big selection of games – board games like *An Enchanted Evening* and card games like *Romantic Sensations* that many couples are now taking along in their luggage to while away those vacation nights.

Good Vibrations has been here for 20 years and is well-known in San Francisco for its Vibrator Museum. It is the only one in the world, for all we know, with antique hand-cranked models from the 19th century and a large, hands-on display of new types for sale.

Another unusual offering is the Bridal Registry. We know couples who are each on their second or third marriage and have all the toasters, blenders and china patterns they will ever need. Come to think of it, if either of them had used this registry sooner they might still be on their first marriage.

❑ *1210 Valencia St.;* ☎ *415-974-8980.*
❑ *For a catalog: 938 Howard St., Suite 101, San Francisco, CA 94103, 800-289-8423, fax 415-974-8989, e-mail goodvibe@well.com, Web site http: //www.goodvibes.com.*
❑ *Open: 11 am-7 pm, daily.*

## Dog Eared Books

Dog Eared Books is not a very large or distinguished new and used book store on Valencia Street. But, if you are in the neighborhood and are feeling romantic, they have a section labeled, "Desire," and another named, "Lust." Actually, those are "fun signs," it was explained, as we were pointed to the "Gender Relations" shelves, where there are lots of volumes on sexual relations. Topics cover men and women, men and men, women and women and probably a few other combinations. You can also buy a tome or two on how to become functional if dysfunctional.

❑ *1173 Valencia St.,* ☎ *415-282-1901.*
❑ *Open Monday to Saturday, 10 am-9 pm, Sunday 11 am-6 pm.*

# Nob Hill

❦ *The hill of palaces.*

Robert Louis Stevenson

First known as "the California Street hill," it was simply a very large sand dune, too steep to build on. Then, in 1873, the cable car was invented. Immediately, the rich built their own system called the California Street Cable Railroad, primarily so their "palaces" could rise on Nob Hill. The name may have come from British India's nabobs (a slang name for millionaires), or perhaps it was a takeoff on British nobility, or it could have come simply from nob, meaning hill or mountain. In any case, the original derivation is lost now.

The Big Four, the railroad barons Mark Hopkins, Leland Stanford, Charles Crocker and Collis Huntington, built their homes on acres of land at the very top of the hill, as befitted their exalted positions. The poor came to stare at their outrageous architecture. The Big Four were soon joined by silver barons, James Flood and James G. Fair, former bartenders who suddenly became Kings of the Comstock Lode. Their new homes rose on the hill and were no less ostentatious than the others. Flood constructed a mansion on a square block of land, put a brass railing around it and hired a servant to keep it shiny. That was his only duty, 10 hours a day. The big quake and fire took care of all the wooden structures in

1906, but Flood's brownstone mansion survives to this day. Now home to the Pacific Union Club, it is a refuge for latter day magnates and is often dubbed the "PU" by the disrespectful.

The Mark Hopkins hotel stands where Hopkins' mansion once held sway. The manicured greenery of Huntington Park is where the Huntington palace stood. The Fountain of the Turtles, a copy of an original in Rome, was a gift of the Crocker family to the park. Fairmont Hotel and Tower occupies the block James Fair left to his children.

# *Restaurant*

## *Venticello*

(Italian)

We first stopped here because we had the San Francisco curse, i.e., we were in a car at dinner time and, of course, couldn't find a parking place within marathon runner distance of a restaurant. It was on narrow, hilly Taylor Street that we passed what looked like our salvation – valet parkers in front of what looked like it might be... a restaurant of some kind! It was. It was also $6 to the green-jacketed youths who would take the car away and put it God knows where.

We soon realized it was not only the car parkers who contributed to the restaurant's jammed condition, but the fact that it is on the Powell/Hyde Street cable car line – built for smart people who don't try to drive cars in San Francisco.

It is a tall, narrow room on the corner of Taylor and Washington streets. Washington is on a hill, so the top part is 10 feet higher than the bottom section. There are a few tables in the upper room and more down below. The lower part seems preferable, but do not quibble. Take whatever you can get. A blue-tiled *forno* (oven) is constantly in use and extends halfway along one wall in the lower room.

Without a reservation, we had a long wait but finally ascended to the status of table-occupants. It was then that we discovered the other, and probably more basic reason, for the restaurant's popularity. The food is good. It starts with a basket of focaccia bread, a plate of good extra virgin olive oil (is there any other kind?) and black Kalamata olives. Tear off a chunk of bread, dip it in the green oil and taste. It is hard to stop, once you start.

To start with, there were salad selections. Fresh tomatoes, cucumbers and red onions were set off by aged ricotta cheese and a light extra virgin olive oil dressing. The couple at the next table kept raving about the house salad – the Venticello, with its gorgonzola and honey-mustard dressing, to say nothing of the roasted walnuts. They kept offering us tastes, which we could not resist. We also tried the spinach with caramelized onions and garlic, which was fresh as it could be, and found it to be irresistible.

The pastas were next. Pasta entrée portions are huge. You might consider ordering one for the two of you. Their *bucatini alla carbonara* comes with a cream sauce. We hesitated at that and the waiter agreed, "OK, we'll make it without the cream." We were right. The cream would have gotten in the way of the pancetta and fresh (never frozen!) peas. Both are tastes that should not be interfered with. But that is our personal preference. To each his own. If you prefer penne, it is tossed with wild mushrooms in a marinara sauce.

After all that pasta, a little meat seemed in order. Phyllis had veal scaloppine. The veal was sautéed with prawns in a basil sauce with Sambuca. It is amazing how much flavor the liqueur brings out of that tender veal. The ahi tuna Bob had was crusty with rosemary and pepper, seared and served with a lemon-butter sauce and capers.

- ❑ *1257 Taylor St., (corner Washington);* ☎ *415-922-2545.*
- ❑ *Open: 5:30 pm-10 pm.*
- ❑ *Prices: Antipasti $6-$7; insalate $5.50-$6.50; pasta $11.50-$13; secondi piati $15.50-$16.50.*
- ❑ *Reservations: Yes.*
- ❑ *Parking: Valet, $6.*
- ❑ *Directions: It's on the Powell Street cable car line.*

# ᴼᶰ𝒩ightlife

## ♥ 𝒯op of the 𝒩ark

The address is Number One Nob Hill, or you can just say "The Mark" to a cab driver. Thousands of former servicemen will never forget the Mark Hopkins Hotel and its top floor cocktail lounge. This was *the* place to come with your wife or girlfriend, if you were here in World War II. San Francisco was a staging area then and men in uniform practically had to fight to get in here. If you were out of uniform, forget it.

One of our favorite old movies, *One Way Passage*, gave the Top of the Mark some of its fame. It starred William Powell and Kay Francis. They met on a luxurious cruise ship coming back from Hong Kong. He was an escaped criminal who had been caught and was going back to prison and she, although gorgeous, was terminally ill. Neither of them knew the other's plight. They fell in love and promised to meet on "New Year's Eve at the Top of the Mark." The last scene of the picture showed New Year's Eve at the Top of the Mark. On an empty table with a white table cloth, two empty martini glasses fall and break with their stems crossing, as the clock strikes midnight. The End. It is guaranteed to produce some misty eyes.

After over 50 years of daily and especially nightly service, the Top of the Mark endured its share of wear and tear. It closed for a complete renovation and opened again in August of 1996. For those who knew it, the old central circular bar is gone. The new bar, called the Herb Caen Bar, is very small and is set in a corner. Caen, the long beloved *San Francisco Chronicle* columnist, spent much time here and wrote about the place many times. There is a pianist where the old bar was. Orchestras appear on weekends – Latin, Big Band, and various others. Any day or any night, there are small tables by the windows where a couple can order a drink, look out at that fabulous bay and think nice thoughts about each other. It's even better to say nice things *to* each other.

The Mark Hopkins was built in 1925. The original Mr. Mark Hopkins made his millions from the Southern Pacific Railroad, which had a stranglehold on California's economy and was dubbed "The Octopus" by Frank Norris, the muckraking author. Hopkins, despite his wealth, lived in a $30-a-month cottage and saved string. When he died, his widow made up for lost time by building a hell of a French chateau on top of Nob Hill and marrying her interior decorator. They lived happily every after. The Mark Hopkins Hotel was built on the site of the château. It would seem more appropriate to us that it should have been called the Mrs. Mark Hopkins. Some years after the hotel was built, the top floor, which had been a penthouse, was turned into the most popular and best known cocktail lounge west of New York's Rainbow Room.

The Mark Hopkins sits on top of the tallest of San Francisco's hills and rises another 20 stories higher. The view of San Francisco Bay and the two bridges was entirely unimpeded back during World War II. It became a tradition to have a farewell drink at the Top of the Mark on a serviceman's last night in town. Then the next day, the wife or girlfriend would come back up here and watch his ship sail out of the bay and off to war. If the one left behind received the dreaded telegram saying he was missing or dead, it became a tradition for her to come back here where they had spent so many happy hours. In the corner of the room closest to the Bay, called the Weeping Widows Corner, a final, private toast would be made to him. Now, that is romantic. Sad, but romantic. The corner is still here.

- *One Nob Hill;* ☎ *415-392-2424 before 2 pm, 415-616-6916 thereafter.*
- *Open: Cocktails, Sunday-Thursday, 5 pm-midnight; Friday and Satur-day, 5 pm-1 am; Monday-Friday Tea, 3 pm-5 pm; Sunday Brunch, 10 am-2:30 pm.*
- *Prices: Cocktails after 8:30 pm, $6 cover charge; Tea, $20, Sunday Brunch $39 or $45 with sparkling Piper Sonoma wine.*
- *Reservations: Necessary for Tea and Sunday Brunch.*
- *Parking: Valet or self-parking in hotel at $5 an hour; no validation.*

## *The Cable Cars*

*They take no count of rise or fall, they turn corners almost at right angles, cross other lines, and, for aught I know, may run up the sides of houses.*

Rudyard Kipling, after riding a cable car

Some years ago, a woman named Gloria Sykes went to court following an accident and claimed she had been turned into a nymphomaniac after being struck by a cable car. The jury awarded her $500,000. We were amazed at the verdict. We would not have been surprised if instead, they had exiled her from San Francisco for her crime of possibly damaging the cable car. For if there is anything San Franciscans love more than cable cars, we can't imagine what it is.

Back in 1947, the city budget was tight and Mayor Roger Lapham decided it would help to get rid of the damn things. "They are old, outmoded, expensive and inefficient," he declared. He proposed to replace them with cheaper modern buses. The people of San Francisco, who had not thought one way or another about the subject for years, rose up in their wrath to demand that not a single car be thrown on the scrap heap. Millions of dollars were raised to refurbish the system and Mayor Lapham was lucky not to be impeached. A transportation system that uses cable cars only makes sense in a city built on hills. Since Rome has only seven and San Francisco has 42 hills, it is not surprising that this is the only place in the world to have them.

It all started back in 1869, when public transportation consisted entirely of horse-drawn streetcars. An engineer, named Andrew Hallidie, was out one rainy day and watched a streetcar being pulled by four horses. The horses were struggling over the wet cobblestones as they labored to pull the car up a steep hill on Jackson Street. Suddenly, one of the horses slipped and fell. As Hallidie watched in horror, the heavy car slid back down the hill all the way to the bottom, dragging the poor horses after it. At that moment, the idea for a system of streetcars that could surmount San Francisco's hills was born. The concept was to lay narrow gauge rails and dig a narrow trench up the center. An endless, immensely strong cable would run through the trench at just over nine miles an hour. When the "gripman" on the cable car pulled a lever, a device like a pair of pliers would grip the cable and the car would be pulled along with it. To stop, the gripman would release the cable and use a brake.

It all seems so obvious now, and easy. It did not seem so at the time. First, Hallidie could not get investors. It was an expensive proposition to dig up the streets and construct the machinery, with no guarantee, only a hope, that the public would want to risk their lives on steep hills. Some were calling the idea "Hallidie's Folly." When the skeptical Board of Supervisors finally gave him a franchise, it had a clause that said an actual car had to be tested to prove its safety by August 1, 1873 or his rights would expire.

At 4 am on August 2nd (he actually missed the deadline by a few hours), the only cable car to be built so far stood at the brow of the steepest hill on Clay Street. It was ready to plunge down the slope for the first time. Hallidie rode as a passenger, along with the group of investors. He told the young man, who had been hired to be the world's first gripman, that they could not wait any longer. They had to go now! The young man looked down to where the tracks disappeared into an impenetrable fog that concealed the lower half of the hill and jumped off the car. Seeing this, the passengers were understandably ready to get off too. Then Hallidie himself released the brake, used the lever to grab the cable, and the car moved forward. It tipped over the edge of the hill and rode smoothly to the bottom. Within days of its official opening, the cable cars were crowded on every trip. New lines were soon built. At one time, there were 22 lines, making it possible to live on the steepest hills.

The Powell/Mason and Powell/Hyde lines both start at Powell and Market streets. They are "single-enders." The gripman's controls are only at one end of the car, so a turntable is needed at each end of the line. The gripman or conductor gets out and pushes the car around in a circle to point back up the opposite way. This is a sight that never fails to delight the hundreds of tourists who are usually waiting there with cameras poised. The Powell/Mason line runs up Powell, past Union Square, over part of Nob Hill. It then switches over to Mason as far as Columbus and ends at Victoria Park at Taylor and Francisco streets, a few blocks from Fisherman's Wharf. The Powell/Hyde line's route is up Powell the same way, then over to Hyde Street and to the end, closer to Fisherman's Wharf, across from the Buena Vista Café, at Beach and Hyde.

The California line starts at California and Market, near the Ferry Building, and runs straight out over Nob Hill, to Van Ness Avenue. Its cars are larger and "double-enders," so there is no need for turntables. This makes it less alluring to camera-toting visitors.

The two Powell Street lines are by far the most crowded, especially in the summer and on the weekends. The line of people waiting their turn to board, especially at Powell and Market, is sometimes several hundred people long. It is a much shorter wait to board in the middle of the run, and the California line is usually less crowded.

The powerhouse, where the cables are wrapped around big verticle wheels that provide power to all three lines, is at Mason and Washington streets and can be visited. The cable car museum is also here and can be toured.

Because the gripmen use their bells quite a bit, the way car drivers use their horns to warn other traffic, most of them have become very adept, almost playing tunes with the clanging. So, every year in July, there is a cable car bell ringing contest. It pits the gripmen against one another to see who is the most accomplished.

Fares are $2, and you can transfer to another cable car or bus. A better deal is a one-day pass for $6, or a three-day pass for $10. These may be purchased at the Visitor's Center, downstairs in Hallidie Square, at Powell and Market.

There is a plaque in Portsmouth Square that reads: "Andrew Smith Hallidie – Site of Eastern Terminus First Street Cars in world propelled by cable – Commenced August 1, 1873, ceased February 15, 1942."

We do not want to forget Gloria. This is not Gloria the nympho, but Gloria the heroine. She was a college student and one fine day in the 1960s she jumped onto the step of a California Street cable car. The conductor told her to move inside. She refused. He told her it was the law. Ever since cable cars first started running, females had to ride inside. Gloria not only refused this time, but she went on to deliver a speech about her rights as a woman to stand on the step if a man could. Meanwhile, the cable car stood there, not moving, and a crowd gathered. The exasperated conductor called the cops. Gloria, just getting wound up, told the police about the constitution and the rights of womankind. The police, wanting very much by now to charge her with something, looked up the ordinance about women not being allowed to stand outside on the step of a moving cable car. They discovered it did not exist. For 90 years, they had been enforcing a tradition, not an actual law. Ever since that day, women ride on the outside step just like men. Gloria's last name has been lost (at least, we cannot find it), but there should definitely be a plaque somewhere for San Francisco's own Rosa Parks.

# ℅Ⅴoe Valley

🐾  *San Francisco has only one drawback – 'tis hard to leave.*

Rudyard Kipling

Some areas of San Francisco have an exciting, spectacular, often lurid, history. Fires and earthquakes, vigilantes hanging miscreants on street corners, prostitutes and venal politicians holding sway all play into the general fun and games that have occurred down through the years. All that time, little Noe Valley has gone about its own quiet affairs, not attracting any notice and liking it just that way. To give you an idea where it is, turn west on 24th if you are in The Mission (on Valencia or Mission streets) and go up a steep hill. At the top, you will see a peaceful, sheltered valley below, known as Noe (pronouned No-ee). Back when California was part of Mexico, San Francisco's last *alcalde* (colonial mayor) was Jose de Jesus Noe. He was granted the 4,000-acre Rancho San Miguel in 1845. Don Noe built his adobe ranch house near what is now 24th and Noe streets.

There was little development until 1887, when the Market Street Cable Railway was extended all the way to 26th Street. It is hard to believe, but in those days, over 100 years ago, there was at least five times as much cable car trackage as there is now. In the next 20 years, all of the Victorian houses you see blanketing the hills and going down into the narrow bottom land were built. Over the years, young professionals moved here, beautifully restoring the old Victorians and bringing new life in the still peaceful valley.

Parking is metered on 24th, the commercial street. A few metered off-street spaces are available and no meters are to be found on the other streets.

Directions: Take the J line down Church from Market Street. then bus #48 up 24th.

## Inn

### ℅Ⅴoe's ℅Ⅴest

The inn is on 23rd Street. It is the house with the green garage and steps beside it. This is not one of the old refurbished Victorian houses. Instead, it is more or less modern, an ordinary two-story house on a hill. The owners live in it and rent out five rooms to guests.

The Garden Room on the first floor is $125 and is spacious and bright. It has a big deck overlooking the garden (thus the name), which is great for having breakfast in the sun. The bathroom has a shower with a full-length window that also looks out on the garden.

The Oriental Room is in the front with not as much light and no view, but it does have good looking Oriental furniture and extends onto its own very private front deck. It is also inexpensively priced at $85.

The Castaway Room on the second floor in the front has a big skylight, which makes it bright. It is a terrific bargain at $95.

We stayed in the one called the Penthouse. Actually, it is a lovely suite. You walk into a room with low ceilings and a thick green carpet. A white and gold desk is in the room along with a queen bed under a sloping ceiling over at one side. There is a very handy bathroom with lots of counter space and double sinks. You step down to a sunken shower/steam bath, which holds two easily. We discovered how great that steam bath was the last thing before going to bed – very relaxing! Past the room divider, which incorporates a 35-gallon tank of exotic fish, step down into a sunken bedroom with a wall of glass, a king-size bed and a TV. You will also discover a VCR with tapes of classic movies, a full-length mirror and a wide dresser with many drawers, white and gold to match the desk. It is all air-conditioned. That glass wall is made up of sliding doors that lead out onto a big deck overlooking the city and the garden. The deck is furnished with a table, umbrella, chairs and chaises. It is a beautiful spot for lounging and looking out to the hills on the other side of the valley. This is the $150 room and worth every penny.

All the rooms have padded wall paper. It is a quiet hilltop neighborhood and an even quieter house. The hot tub in the back yard is for the use of all guests.

Sheila Ash, the host, puts out a complimentary breakfast on the counter in the kitchen early in the morning. It is a matter of helping yourself, whenever you are up. You will find several kinds of breads (some homemade, some from local bakeries), a pitcher of juice, fresh fruit, coffee, and something she has made the night before. We were greeted with a quiche on the morning we had our breakfast there. You can also help yourself to the morning paper.

It is very hard to get a taxi to come up here at rush hour without a long wait. If you are going downtown to dinner, give yourself a half-hour. Drive to where you are going if they have valet parking or park in a public garage and take a taxi from there.

❏ *3973 23rd St., San Francisco, CA 94114;* ☎ *415-821-0751.*
❏ *Rooms: Five.*

- *Rates:* $85-$150.
- *Credit cards: All.*
- *Reservations: Yes.*
- *Minimum Stay: Two nights on weekends.*
- *Breakfast: Complimentary, extended continental.*
- *Wine: No.*
- *Amenities: Hot tub.*
- *Handicapped accessible: No. Many steps.*
- *Smoking: No.*
- *Children: Yes.*
- *Pets: No.*
- *Parking: A few spaces in garage, otherwise on street.*
- *Walking distance: Noe Valley shopping is two blocks downhill.*

## Things to Do

A half-dozen blocks along 24th Street contain all the commercial life, as well as enough shops, several nondescript cafés, and some good bars. If you are in the mood to mingle with the local citizens, take a stroll down this street and enjoy yourself.

**Noe Valley Cyclery** is strictly for sales and repairs. Rentals are not available, which is not surprising in a tiny valley surrounded by steep hills.

The **San Francisco Mystery Bookstore**, 4175 24th St., ☎ 415-282-7444; storybooks@aol.com; http://www.MysteryNet.com/sfmb. If you are a mystery fan, this is a place you will love. Thousands of new and used mystery books will intrigue you. Open 11:30 am-5:30 pm, Wednesday-Sunday.

**Irish Bars**. Noe Valley was largely settled by working-class Irish in the last part of the 19th century. This led to quite a few saloons along 24th Street. Many Irish descendents still live here, which is why there are still several Irish bars on 24th Street. For a usually friendly atmosphere and sometimes good conversation, try **Dubliner** at 3838 24th Street. ☎ 415-826-2279.

# North Beach

When you get to the triple corner of Columbus, where it crosses Pacific and Kearny, you will see a street sign, "Corso Cristoforo Columbo." That is when you will definitely know you are in North Beach. If you have any ideas about bringing a bikini along and tanning your bod on the sand, be aware that, while there once was a North Beach here, that was a long time ago. Tons of fill were dumped into the water, one wagonload at a time. By the 1880s, the beach and a little cove had disappeared and another four blocks had been added to San Francisco. This is why the city ends where the Embarcadero is now.

Back during the Gold Rush, the neighborhood was a red light district – the home mostly of prostitutes from Chili. Since they were the first group of women to arrive, they might be called San Francisco's Founding Mothers. When the area was cleaned up during one of the city's short-lived morality campaigns, Irish and Mexican workers moved into the cheap housing, along with Peruvians, French, Basque and Portuguese. Then after 1860, the influx of Italians who arrived with entire families, changed the neighborhood for good.

North Beach was leveled in the earthquake and fire. Most of the buildings you see now are three and four stories and were built soon after 1906. The quarter next gained national attention in the 1950s as one of the three enclaves of the Beat Generation. The other two enclaves were New York and Venice in Southern California. Lawrence Ferlinghetti founded City Lights and published Allen Ginsberg's "Howl." The beat poets sat with berets and goatees in Tosca and Vesuvio Café, eating spaghetti and drinking red wine. Why here in North Beach? Mainly because pads, spaghetti and red wine were all cheap.

The beatniks are mostly long gone, though their spirit lives on, along with City Lights, Tosca and Vesuvio Café. The word "beatnik" was coined by *Chronicle* columnist, Herb Caen. The Soviet Union had put up "sputnik" and "nik" was tagged onto anything new. The explosion of entertainment that also infused that time in San Francisco has not fared as well. The Purple Onion nightclub is located downstairs at 140 Columbus and is famous as the place where Lenny Bruce and Woody Allen got their starts. The Hungry I, where Mort Sahl began, is still here as well. The Purple Onion is a rock venue now, and the once-venerated Hungry I features "live exotic strippers." A few places remain, notably Finocchio's, a long-time institution with its transvestite shows.

It is still a vibrant, lively neighborhood, with old, old restaurants continuing alongside as fresh ones open to become San Francisco's hot, new places – for awhile at least. The coffee houses are many, and undoubtedly the best in the city. There are still funky places to shop and music to hear in funny little dives at night. Don't miss North Beach.

For more information, request a free *North Beach Guide*. For specific questions, contact the North Beach Chamber of Commerce at ☎ 415-403-0666/0660. Contents of the guide and much more may be found on the Internet at http://www.sfnorthbeach.com.

There is a large public garage at Powell and Vallejo (766 Vallejo), plus a number of commercial garages and lots. There is also street parking, if you are lucky.

Public transportation is available through four bus lines and a cable car from almost anywhere in the city. ☎ 415-673-MUNI (6864) for details.

# *Inn*

## *Hotel Boheme*

It is a three-story building on Columbus and had several incarnations before being completely remodeled in 1995. The halls are lined with photos of North Beach in the 1950s when the beatniks were here. It could be considered a shrine to the beatnik generation. Alan Ginsberg stayed here. Francis Ford Coppola, whose production offices are just down the street, sends people here. A lot of honeymoons and anniversaries are celebrated here. Those couples find complimentary champagne waiting in their rooms. There is a high nostalgia quotient, with guests returning and wanting the same rooms they had before, even when they were here during the hotel's previous life.

All rooms have queen beds. The furniture is not expensive. There are few authentic antiques. It is much more prosaic than that, but they are all nice rooms. A typical room is smallish, with tomato walls and a green ceiling. It sounds garish but, surprisingly, it works. There is an armoire with mirrors and a tile bathroom with a shower, no tub.

You are sure to receive a lot of attention from the staff, if you want it. But, if you would rather have complete privacy with no attention at all, hey, that is part of the service too. If you want to be in the middle of everything – restaurants, late night clubs, floor shows, and coffee houses – anytime you step out the front door, this is the place.

- ❑ *444 Columbus Ave., San Francisco, CA 94133;* ☎ *415-433-9111.*
- ❑ *Rooms: 15.*
- ❑ *Rate: All $115.*
- ❑ *Credit cards: All.*
- ❑ *Reservations: At least one week ahead for weekends, weekdays are easier to get.*
- ❑ *Breakfast: No, but 10% off breakfast at Café Malvina, 1600 Stockton St. at Washington Square.*
- ❑ *Wine: Sherry 6 pm-10 pm.*
- ❑ *Handicapped accessible: No.*

❑ *Smoking: No.*
❑ *Children: Yes.*
❑ *Pets: No.*
❑ *Parking: North Beach Garage is 1½ blocks away; $20, 24 hours.*
❑ *Directions: Public transportation access is excellent, three buses ply this stretch of Columbus.*

# Restaurants

## Rose Pistola

(Northern Italian-Ligurian and Californian cuisine)

It's hard to equate a bright, noisy restaurant with romance. But, in the case of Rose Pistola, we will make an exception. We think you will too once you have eaten here. It is a long place, going from Columbus Avenue to Stockton Street, with the tables arranged in several sections. There are big windows at each end. The furniture is in light, blond wood with white walls. When Rose Pistola had only been open for a month, reservations were already necessary for dinner. Lunch is easier, but you may have to wait.

Why Ligurian-style cooking? Well, Italians who first settled North Beach were from the Ligurian region around Genoa. They were mostly farmers and fishermen and their cooking was not really refined, more down-home. For example, a thick soup called ciuppin was made of whatever fish was left over from the catch and available vegetables. This name became corrupted in San Francisco to cioppino.

They do have cioppino! With Dungeness crab, monkfish, mussels and calimari each contributing its own flavor to the broth, the cioppino is subtle and engaging.

The simplest appetizer is focaccia, made with the rind of parmigiana cheese, which gives the bread an extra sharp flavor. The first words spoken at our table when we took a bite were, "Gee, that's good!" Zuccini chips are very thinly sliced, dredged lightly in flour and briefly deep-fried. Watch out. You simply cannot stop eating them! Pickled crab salad? Maybe the idea is a bit off-putting to some, but we like crab and we like pickles, so why not? It's an old Italian dish. They serve it cold, and we found many more flavors than simple crab. The pickle taste does not dominate at all. Bean soup is often on the menu. It contains pasta shells, a melange of several kinds of beans, diced root vegetables and a great flavor brought out by chicken stock and court bouillon.

As in Genoa, with the exception of a few meat dishes, fish dominates the menu. The fish of the day is roasted three different ways with three different sauces. Or it is grilled with garlic, potatoes and lemon oil. Our method of choice was fish braised with garlic, anchovy and lemon.

Peter Birmingham, the maitre d', gave us this recipe.

## Ligurian Seafood Salad

¼ cup cooked octopus
¼ cup rock shrimp
¼ cup cleaned calamari, cut into rings
4 mussels
4 clams
octopus court bouillon (see recipe following)
pinch of chopped Italian parsley
pinch of spring garlic or white garlic
¼ cup extra virgin olive oil
½ lemon
salt and pepper

Separately poach calamari, shrimp, clams and mussels individually in the octopus court bouillon. Do not overcook the shellfish. Drain, cool and place in a bowl. Discard any mussels that do not open.

## Octopus Court Bouillon

1 onion
1 sprig of rosemary, thyme & marjoram
1 celery rib
1 carrot
1 cup chopped tomato
1 clove garlic
½ cup dry white wine

Chop the vegetables coarsely and sweat* the onion, carrot, celery and garlic together. After sweating the ingredients and they have become aromatic, add the tomato, herbs and wine. Cook the wine to concentrate the flavors of the vegetables. Add the octopus and cover with cold water. Raise the temperature until just below the simmering point. Do not boil! Octopus becomes tough if boiled. Simmer for one hour or until tender. Cool, strain and reserve for recipe.

* Sauté until translucent, when they release liquid.

The wine list has a good selection by the glass and a very good range of both California and Italian wines. Some, however, are overpriced

As for the name, Rose Pistola is a crusty, tough woman who ran a bar and grill from 1950 to 1974 on the site of what is now the Washington Square Bar and Grille. Her name is Rose, but she got the moniker Pistola from her husband, who got that nickname after chasing a cook with a pistol. Rose was bartender, bouncer and sometimes cook herself, although she never had a menu. She would simply cook up a batch of something when she had the time. She was a fixture in North Beach for many years and still is. Still alive at 89, she embodies the spirit of North Beach. The owners of this place thought she should be celebrated, so they used her name. She drops in every once in awhile.

- ❑ *532 Columbus Ave.;* ☎ *415-399-0499.*
- ❑ *Open: Weekdays, 11 am-midnight, weekends, 11:30 am-1 am.*
- ❑ *Prices: Appetizers run from assorted marinated olives, $2.75, to prosciutto with persimmons, $4.35, and pickled crab with fennel, $9.75. Entrées include roast quail with chanterelles, $14.75, and cippino, $16.50.*
- ❑ *Credit cards: AE, MC, V.*
- ❑ *Reservations: Needed for dinner, especially Thursday through Sunday about two weeks ahead. Okay to drop in for lunch.*
- ❑ *Parking: Valet, $4 lunch, $7 dinner.*

## The San Francisco Brewing Company

(Pub grub)

At first glance, it seems like an ordinary corner pub, except for that big window in the corner room that looks out on Columbus Street. Behind it they make the beer, in those giant, hand-made copper brew kettles. The bar in the big room, when you enter, strikes you right away. It is a long, mahogany single plank of a bar with columns and mirrors that have been here since the beginning in 1907. That was just after the Big Quake, when this odd corner was the last gasp of San Francisco's fabled Barbary Coast.

It opened as the Andromeda Saloon and gained wide respect when Jack Dempsey was employed as a bouncer, before he became World Champion. Prohibition closed down most of the city's old saloons, but the Andromeda kept going by serving clams and oysters and calling itself a "café." They still served alcohol, but for purely "medicinal" purposes. During this period, the bar received its first coat of paint. It survived many owners and many slapdash changes until, in 1977, new owners decided to restore it to its former glory. The original ceiling was discovered under many coats of paint. There was even a skylight up there. The bar itself was brought back to life, and the mahogany columns polished to reveal the grain of wood surging upward as fiery flames. Once more, the beautiful stained glass windows welcomed all who came through its big oak doors.

Allen Paul started in the brewery trade as a home brewer. On his third batch, he won an award. That was when he got fanatical and he has been doing it ever since. In 1985, he acquired the property and opened The San Francisco Brewing Co.; the first brew pub in San Francisco. It was a struggle against the Big Guys and the bureaucrats who hand out licenses, as none of them saw much use for a micro-brewery "on the premises." But Paul persisted.

Smoked ribs became a speciality. They may be the best in town. Chicken salad is tasty with honey poppyseed dressing. There is also grilled fish, breaded and Italian-seasoned calamari, gumbo and various sandwiches and salads. He makes his own pork sausage for those who delight in home-made sausage.

Couples seem to gravitate to this place. Quite a few spend a sizeable portion of their courtship here. They often come back after the ceremony for their reception. A few have even been married beside the brewtank.

Which beer to try? You can always suggest a taste of everything being brewed. It is a big production and lots of fun. A batch of smaller glasses, (you don't want to stumble out of here), is lined up in front of you. All the beers, ales, stouts and porters brewed currently are poured. Taste them in order, from the mildest to the strongest and compare your preferences. We found that choosing a favorite was more difficult than we had expected.

Following are the beers made right here on location:

*Albatross*, a golden lager.

*Emperor Norton*, another lager, the most popular.

*Pony Express Amber*, the lightest, named because the real Pony Express ended its cross-country dash just two blocks away.

*Winter Wheat*, amber, seasonal.

*Gripman's Porter*, very dark.

*King of the Hill Stout*, dark, seasonal. Brewed in the Russian Imperial Stout style, 9% alcohol, aged in the keg three months and very strong. It is a sipping beer, served in small portions.

Each February, in honor of Chinese New Year, Paul makes a special brew named after the year. 1997 is the Year of the Ox.

These are unfiltered brews. The liquid is alive and not preserved with chemicals. It has a shorter shelf life, but much more flavor. When you get stout, it's in the keg and tapped by the glass when ordered. All the others are in stainless steel, 200-gallon tanks in the

cellar (which used to be a pool hall and prior to that, an opium den).
Things change! Pipes lead up to the taps behind the bar and nothing
is bottled.

- *155 Columbus Ave.; ☎ 415-434-3344, fax 415-434-2433,
  http://www.sfbrewing.com.*
- *Open: Weekdays, 11:30 am-past midnight, weekend, 12 pm-past midnight.*
- *Parking: Street.*
- *Directions: On the triangular corner of Columbus, Pacific and Kearny.*

## Coffee Houses

San Francisco is *the* city for coffee houses in the United States. Two
out of the three big coffee makers started in San Francisco: Folgers
and Maxwell House. When the Italians arrived in the 1870s and
1880s, they started up coffee houses. They sprang up right here in
North Beach, fashioned after the ones back in the old country.
Today, there are over 100 in the city. A minority belong to chains.
The homegrown chain of choice in other parts of the city is Peet's.
But at the moment there are only eight Peet's coffee houses in all of
the city. There are no chains in North Beach. The city will not allow
them, in order to protect the traditional, individual coffee houses.
Isn't this a lovely city?

While you are visiting coffee houses and choosing among that
huge, confusing range of blends, remember that the darker beans
have less caffeine. Most people think it's just the opposite.

### Café Trieste

Café Trieste has only been here at 601 Vallejo St. (corner of Grant)
for 41 years, but it's already a San Francisco institution. It could be
the excellent espresso or Café Vienna negro or bianco that they
serve. It may be the pastries, antipasto or sandwiches that can
accompany the coffee. But we have a hunch that what is most
important is the atmosphere of this warm, inviting place. One wall
of the not-very-large corner shop is covered with old photos,
mostly of Italian families who have gathered here over the years.
Giannni Giotta is up on the wall singing with Pavarotti. He was a
tenor in the Trieste Opera Company before he emigrated to San
Francisco and started Café Trieste in 1956. The fellow with the
typewriter is Francis Ford Coppola, who has lived in North Beach
a long time. Xolanda Giotta, Gianni's sister, who still works here
five days a week, told us Coppola used to come into Trieste a lot.
Finally, he brought his portable typewriter and left it. He then came
in every day to write *The Godfather*. That other photo is of Gianni
leaning over Coppola's shoulder while he types.

The jukebox is filled with mostly operatic tunes. Sometimes, a family member or a friend like Matteo, who has been coming in since the place opened, will play a mandolin, as he did while we were having coffee and schmoozing. Saturdays from two to five is regular opera day. Musicians and semi-pro singers come in. Coffee, wine and pastry are consumed. The atmosphere is delightful. Get here early for Saturday afternoon. It is a small place and always packed. ☎ 415-392-6739.

## Caffe Greco

Caffe Greco is possibly the most popular in North Beach. It is a small, oddly shaped place at 423 Columbus Avenue with a dozen tables close together inside and another half-dozen out on the sidewalk. It is named after the oldest café in Rome. Customers from the neighborhood sit here and read the newspaper by the hour. Students study with cups of coffee perched precariously on top of their books.

Homemade tiramisu and cannolis, Italian cakes and focaccia sandwiches are available along with the coffee, of which there are a multitude of different blends. Sandy Suleiman, who was an engineer in Milano until he and Hanna moved here nine years ago and started Caffe Grecco "out of love for coffee," told us he uses mainly Illy coffee. He imports it from Trieste, "because it's the best in the world." Our favorite here is affogato espresso with gelato. "Affogato" means, "to choke." The richness of the espresso and ice cream taken all at once are wonderful. ☎ 415-397-6261.

## Caffe Roma

"Black as Night, Strong as Sin, Sweet as Love, Hot as Hell" is a pretty good motto for this coffee house. Located at 526 Columbus Avenue, they offer a wide range of coffees roasted and ground every day in the front window. The store goes through the block to Stockton. ☎ 415-296-ROMA.

# Nightlife

## Beach Blanket Babylon

(Theater)
The first shock comes when you notice that the street where you turned off Columbus Avenue is named Beach Blanket Babylon Boulevard. When Steve Silver, creator of Beach Blanket Babylon,

died in 1995, the San Francisco Board of Supervisors simply wanted to do something to honor the man who had brought laughs to so many people. We suppose it is only right. This is, after all, the longest running musical revue in the history of American theater. There are other shocks still to come during the evening, but they are all wonderfully entertaining.

Club Fugazi is like an old odeon or vaudeville theater, with small tables in front of the seats, so you can order drinks during the performance. The show itself is a series of wildly colorful musical numbers, spoofing political and social topics. It features outrageous costumes. One of the hats (all are large, a signature of the show) is billed as the biggest hat ever on a stage. Ever! Would they lie?

Jokes are fast and furious. The packed house was laughing so hard from the very beginning to the standing ovation at the end that we wondered how anyone heard the punch lines. After 24 years, everyone who lives in San Francisco has seen this show. Because it keeps changing, some have seen it many times. We recommend it highly as it makes a great night out. Have dinner at the place of your choice and then see Beach Blanket Babylon. Afterward, walk a block or two down Columbus and have coffee or a glass of something while listening to some good jazz. Oh, by the way, there is a story line, something about Snow White, but it doesn't really matter.

- ❑ *Club Fugazi, 678 Green St.;* ☎ *415-421-4111, fax 415-421-4817.*
- ❑ *Prices: Weeknights, from rear balcony, $23, to front cabaret, $31. Weekends, $26 to $35.*
- ❑ *Reservations: Recommended.*
- ❑ *Credit cards: MC, V.*

## La Bodega

With nightly flamenco, guitar and dancers, it is also a restaurant.

- ❑ *1337 Grant Ave.;* ☎ *415-433-0439.*
- ❑ *Open: 5 pm to 1:30 am weekends, 5-12 weekdays.*

## O'Reilly's Pub

Contemporary Celtic and traditional Irish music along with Guinness and Irish coffee can be a pleasant combination. It is also a restaurant, with Irish food prepared by an Irish chef. You may have gathered this is an Irish sort of place.

- ❑ *622 Green St.;* ☎ *415-989-6222.*
- ❑ *Open: Daily, lunch and dinner; Sunday brunch 10 am-1:30 am.*

## Purple Onion

This was the famous launching pad for numerous stars back in the 1960s. Now it favors whatever the latest trend is in the evolving rock scene, plus lots of 60s rock and early Beatles. Must be 21 or older. Beer only.

- ❑ *140 Columbus Ave.;* ☎ *415-398-8415.*
- ❑ *Open: Friday-Saturday, 9 pm-2 am.*

## The Saloon

Besides being the oldest saloon in San Francisco, this is deliberately the raunchiest joint in town. Vesuvio runs a close second. Built in 1861, it was one of the few things around here to escape the earthquake and obviously has not been improved since. You could probably still find some soot from the fire in the corners. But, the place is absolutely jammed every night – a stop on everyone's night-time prowl through North Beach. There is live music, mostly rock, sometimes rhythm and blues, and down home blues. The live music is on Sundays, 4-8 pm.

- ❑ *1232 Grant St. (at Fresno Alley, just off Columbus near Vallejo);* ☎ *415-989-7666.*
- ❑ *Open: 12 pm-2 am, daily, music every night.*

## Tosca

This is where, for a lot of years, people have been ending up every night after everything else. It is a long, narrow room with a long, narrow bar along one wall. The opposite wall is covered with faded photos of opera stars. In the back, behind all this, is a cavernous room with high ceilings. The house drink is known as White Nun.

### White Nun

1 oz Kahlua
1 oz brandy
steamed milk

Pour Kahlua and brandy into coffee glass. Add steamed milk to fill. Stir and serve. It is a great way to finish the night off.

The tables are usually full with couples, whether he-she, he-he or she-she. Looming over everyone on the big back wall is a 20-foot-long, eight-foot-high, underwhelming painting of Venice's lagoons. The juke box, though, is world-class. Maria Callas sings from La Boheme. The next record is Bunny Berrigan's, "I Can't Get Started." Franco Corelli does Cavalleria Rusticana and then Patti Page warbles "Tennessee Waltz." Rather eclectic.

❑ *242 Columbus Ave.;* ☎ *415-986-9651.*
❑ *Open: 5 pm-2 am.*

# *Things to Do*

## *Blazing Saddles Bike Rentals*

This shop is located at 1095 Columbus Ave. (at Francisco Street), ☎ 415-202-8888. A map, helmets and bike locks are included in the rate. You are almost at the end of Columbus Avenue here, edging Fisherman's Wharf. It is a good place to start off by following the Bay Trail which leads to the Golden Gate Bridge. You are off to Sausalito and can return by ferry. Shop hours: daily, March-October 9 am-7 pm, November-February 9 am-5 pm. Mountain bikes are $5 per hour, $25 per day; road bikes and tandem bikes, $10 and $45.

## *City Lights*

Located at 261 Columbus Ave., ☎ 415-421-4219, City Lights is open from 10 am-midnight daily. Lawrence Ferlinghetti opened his doors in 1953 as the first bookstore in the country to sell nothing but paperbacks. He made enough to support a literary magazine that he was publishing. It was also the world-wide headquarters of the beat generation. You will find a good general bookstore on the ground floor filled with literature, history and current affairs categories. Downstairs in the basement is a great selection of books about film, plays, jazz, women's studies, and myteries for a fun weekend read.

## *Columbus Day Festivities*

These are big events in North Beach. If your visit happens to coincide, you can join in on the fun. It begins a week before, with a blessing of the fishing fleet at Fisherman's Wharf. Festa Italiana is several days of ethnic food, street dances and bocce ball tournaments. There are various banquets and balls leading up to a high mass on the Sunday closest to Columbus Day, October 12th, at 10 am. The high mass is held in Saints Peter and Paul Church, 666 Filbert Street. Then, the Italian Heritage Parade starts, usually around 1:30 pm. It begins at the Embarcadero at Fisherman's Wharf and ends at Washington Square at Columbus and Filbert streets in front of the church.

For information about all the events, call the Columbus Day Celebration Committee, ☎ 415-434-1492. (Notice that clever phone number?)

## Columbus Tower

The Columbus Tower is at 906 Kearny St. (where Kearny crosses Columbus and Pacific). Be sure to take a look at it since it is one of San Francisco's favorite buildings. It is a seven-story edifice with a dome on top, clad in white tile and copper that has acquired a fine green patina. The building was under construction, with scaffolding around it, when the earthquake struck in 1906. One of the few buildings downtown left standing, it was finished in 1907.

Around the turn of the century this was the headquarters of a political boss, Abe Ruef, who finally went to prison for bribing various officials. Francis Ford Coppola bought the building in 1970 and it is the headquarters for his production company.

## Godwana Gallery

Find 241 Columbus Ave., ☎ 800-831-1952, if you are interested in African tribal art.

## Javawalk

This is a coffee house walking tour of North Beach. Elaine Sosa says she started this walk "to legitimize my coffee house addiction." We are happy she did. Though only indifferent coffee drinkers ourselves, by the end of two hours, we feared we were in danger of becoming addicts. In Elaine's own hyper-enthusiastic way, she filled us up with coffee lore, coffee history and coffee house culture. Elaine will happily do the walk with just one couple (which is much more likely to happen off-season), though usually there are four to six people.

The walk ambles through Chinatown and wide swathes of North Beach. Some days, she stops at an inn for a tour, other times at some local landmark. The heart of the walk, though, are the sessions in four or five coffee houses (cost of coffee extra). You can meet the owners and learn the stories behind the coffee or the places themselves, while you sip their best brew. Usually included in the tour is the block of Kearny Street that is so steep the city had to put in steps. (Tip: count the number of steps on the way up. There will be a quiz at the top and the winner gets free coffee at the next stop. We won't tell you the correct answer. You have to do some things for yourself!)

☎ 415-673-WALK, $20. Tuesday and Saturday, 10 am. Fewer walks take place in the winter. Meet at Mark Reuben Gallery, 334 Grant Ave., near the Chinatown entrance arch.

## Matteucci's Clock

The clock is at 450 Columbus Ave., across the street from Caffe Greco, on the sidewalk in front of R. Matteucci & Co. Jewelers. The very traditional jewelry store has been here since 1887. The clock is a late-comer as it was only installed in 1908. Look closely at this beautiful work of art. It is a Seth Thomas spring-wound clock that is wound by hand once a week. It is a duplicate of a clock in Times Square and is the only working four-faced clock in San Francisco. There are two on Market Street but they are owned by the city and have not worked for years. Has anyone told Mayor Willie Brown about this?

If you have coffee at one of the sidewalk tables at Caffe Grecco, you can spend your time observing this lovely clock right across the street.

## Molinari's Delicatessen

Molinari's opened 101 years ago and has been fulfilling culinary dreams ever since. Once you step inside the door, you are doomed. We were. What food-lover can resist that aroma? It is a wonderful mixture of garlic, a dozen kinds of sausages, and many dozen types of cheeses. They make their own ravioli and handmade prosciutto-filled tortellini every day, along with their own Italian dry salami.

There is a good selection of Italian wine, especially strong in the reds. A bottle of your favorite wine, a couple of sandwiches ($3.75 to $6.50) made to order, a pint of salad and a half-pint of one of the half-dozen varieties of olives would be great to take along for an *al fresco* lunch in the park.

If you left a gourmet behind when you came to San Francisco, perhaps instead of taking home a T-shirt saying, "I Survived Alcatraz," a two-pound ball of provolone cheese ($11.98) would make a good gift. Or, you may choose a three-pound, whole Molinari salami ($11.50). Be sure to wrap them tightly before you get on the plane. It is better to keep that aroma to yourself, if you don't want dirty looks from the flight attendants.

❑ *373 Columbus Ave. (at Vallejo);* ☎ *415-421-2337.*
❑ *Open: Monday-Saturday, 8 am-5:30 pm.*

## North Beach Festival

How about the oldest urban street fair in the country? If you have plans to be here in June, have we got a festa for you! It starts at noon on Saturday with the blessing of the animals in honor of St. Francis of Assissi, whose parish this is. Then, throughout two days, there will be chalk art, with contests for the best art executed on the pavement with colored chalks. Chalk art is called "arte di gesso" in North Beach. A new event will be olive oil tasting. There will be food vendors by the score, *al fresco* dining in the streets, and arts and crafts booths. Other attractions include a poetry stage, ethnic dancing of the tarantella and flamenco, plus three music stages with blues, jazz and a dance floor for the swing stage. Remember, this is the fair that put "street" into street fair!

For information, contact North Beach Chamber of Commerce, 253 Columbus Ave., San Francisco, CA 94133. ☎ 415-403-0666. Internet address: http://www.sfnorthbeach.com.

## Thomas E. Cara, Ltd.

This item is strictly a quirk of ours because we are fascinated by any culinary gadget. If you have ever thought of buying an espresso maker, or simply would like to see the most beautiful coffee machines in the world, this is the place for you.

During World War II, Thomas Cara was with US Army Intelligence in Italy. In Milan, he met the Pavoni family who, for 100 years, had been making espresso machines. They were not being exported to the US, and though they are expensive, now ranging from $450 to $2,000, Cara thought they were so wonderful that he surely could sell them here. And so he has for 51 years, since 1946. Now his son Christopher carries on. For people who are going to use them every day, be assured that they will last 25-30 years. Others buy them as art. Christopher told us, "When people buy and don't ask how to steam, I know they're not going to use it."

Without waxing too lyrical, when you walk into this small shop and see what is on display, perhaps you will agree with us that it is an experience more fulfilling than many an art gallery can offer. While you are at Thomas Cara's, you might take note of the building next door at 555 Pacific. It is the Hippodrome, which is now being rebuilt. During the latter part of the 1800s, it was the largest bordello on the Barbary Coast. After the earthquake, it was rebuilt as the Bella Union, a lavish saloon-gambling house. That was when the nude nymphs and female torsos you see outlining the front door were sculpted. Inside were more sculptures and the ceiling was ablaze with rows of light bulbs. Much of it is being carefully preserved by the new tenants.

❏ *517 Pacific Ave. (between Columbus and Montgomery);* ☎ *415-781-0383, fax 415-781-7224.*
❏ *Open: Monday-Friday, 9:30 am-5 pm, Saturday 12 pm-3 pm.*

# *Pacific Heights*

❦ *San Francisco is a mad city, a city inhabited for the most part by perfectly insane people whose women are of remarkable beauty.*

Rudyard Kipling

This area historically has ranged from Van Ness Avenue on the east to Presidio on the west, and from Green on the north to California on the south. It is hilly with relatively sunny uplands and two delightful parks known as Alta Plaza and Lafayette, situated on hilltops. The 1906 fire was stopped at Van Ness by dynamiting all the Victorian mansions that stood on the east side of that broad avenue, which saved the mansions to the west of it.

Lower Pacific Heights is a fairly recent enclave. Actually, San Francisco's sharply defined neighborhoods are multiplying as the people who live in a portion of a community form their own neighborhood. For example, the southern boundary of Pacific Heights was always California Street. Now, the area from there down to Sutter is known as Lower Pacific Heights. The Queen Anne Hotel is here (page 125), while The Mansions Inn (see below) is in the middle of the older district, near Lafayette Park.

There are bus tours of Pacific Heights, though walking it is better. Walking with a knowledgeable guide is best of all. (See Jay's Victorian Tour, page 127.) If you are near Lafayette Park, you might want to go to the east side and look across Washington Street, on the corner of Octavia. The big white building with ionic columns at number 2080 is not, as you would expect, a public museum or library. It is the Spreckles Mansion, built by an older mega-million-aire for his young bride. Adolph Spreckles went into the sugar business and did very well. In 1908, at age 50, he married 24-year-old Alma de Bretteville, who's sylph-like figure was the model for the statue of Victory atop the Dewey Monument in Union Square. In 1913, they built this reinforced-concrete building faced with white Utah limestone as their house in town. It has 26 bathrooms and a swimming pool. Today, it is the home of novelist Danielle Steel, who lives here with her 13 children, each of whom has two bathrooms.

# Inns

## The Mansions

Do you want to stay in a haunted Victorian house with a documented ghost, Claudia, who has been seen or felt by accredited demonologists? She was the niece of mining baron, State Senator Charles Chambers, who built the twin-turreted Queen Anne mansion in 1887. Poor Claudia lived here with him, kept a pet pig in the house and collected all sorts of

*The Mansions.*

pigobelia, including statues of pigs, paintings of pigs and lots of kitschy, piggy things.

There is a magic show every night in the front parlor at which Claudia makes an invisible appearance and performs on the Swine-way, her grand piano. She participates in mind reading along with the resident magician, and ends it all by creating a snow storm. It is all very impressive! You do not have to believe in Claudia, but it helps.

The owner, Bob Pritikin, joined the Chambers mansion with the equally opulent 1880s Judge Black Victorian next to it and turned them into the present 30-room inn. In the tiny front garden you will see a towering figure of St. Francis of Assisi, patron saint of San Francisco, by Geniamono Bufano, a well-known 20th-century sculptor. The really huge doll house in the billiard room/porcine museum is from the Broadway production of Edward Albee's play, *Tiny Alice*.

The impressively large blue and gold live macaw you are sure to run into is named Senator Chambers. Close by his perch is the Celebrity Wall, signed by guests Barbra Streisand, Robin Williams, Andre Sakharov and John F. Kennedy, Jr., among others. In the East Wing is the parlor containing collections of historic documents, tables for chess, and the dining room looking out on the garden. The Magic Museum is in the library, with memorabilia of magicians Houdini, Blackstone, Thurston and Herman the Great. Every room in the inn has a 1920s Thomas radio with the gothic arched cabinet. All ceilings and carpets are red. All toilets are old-style and almost all beds are double.

The Crocker Room in front on the second floor is fairly typical, with a brass bed, sofa, comfy chairs, an ottoman and a coffee table. There is a mural of "Mrs. Charles Crocker, grand dame of San Francisco society at the golden turn of the century." Mrs. Crocker wears a long, formal gown, a few drops of fabulous jewelry and a benign expression.

The Muir Room has three windows with window seats overlooking the garden. It has a big, colorful print of the old Sutro Baths. The sunny Jim Rolph Room is a bit smaller, but the walls are alive with a mural of tycoon S.J. Rolph near a photo of W.C. Fields. It is obvious they were not soul mates.

Some of the rooms, like the Emperor Norton Room, have fireplaces. That one also has a beautiful floor-to-ceiling, gold-framed mirror and a mural of Emperor Norton (see page 50 for more about his slightly eccentric personality). There are some small rooms on the third floor, formerly servants' quarters. They are now fixed up nicely and are actually romantic in their coziness.

- 2220 Sacramento St., San Francisco, CA 94115; ☎ 415-929-9444.
- Rooms: 30.
- Rates: $129-$350.
- Credit cards: All major.
- Reservations: Two weeks ahead for weekends; weekdays are easy.
- Minimum stay: None.
- Breakfast: Full, meaning juice and toast, ham and eggs, potatoes, fruit, danish – the works.
- Wine: Yes.
- Amenities: Dining room is open for dinner; complimentary admission to the magic show.
- Handicapped accessible: No.
- Smoking: Yes.
- Children: Yes.
- Pets: Yes.
- Parking: Garage (reserve when you call) and street.
- Walking distance: Two blocks to Fillmore's restaurants and shops.

## Queen Anne Hotel

This exceptionally large Victorian was built on the corner of the tony, expensive Pacific Heights neighborhood, not as a private residence, but rather as a tony, expensive private girls' shool. The public rooms on the ground floor, unusually large for a Victorian building, were originally designed as play areas and ballrooms. The present owners gave it a new identity as the Queen Anne Hotel and removed everything, stripping coats of enamel paint away and opening flues that had been closed for decades. The Queen Anne opened in 1981 as a luxury guest house.

Now there is a front hall with a desk, concierge and elevator with wide doors capable of taking a wheelchair. Behind this is a large parlor with a fireplace. The library has another fireplace. These rooms are very popular, especially from 4 pm-6 pm when the guests take sherry here. Both rooms are furnished with beautiful antiques that fit the period exactly. An original staircase of Spanish cedar rises to the upper hall, which is spacious enough for an unusual, carved triple-chair and other lovely period pieces. The dining room off the parlor, where guests have breakfast, is not a standard Victorian dining room by any means. It is more like a restaurant, and not nearly up to the standards of the rest of the house. All rooms have TV, phone, second phone in the bathroom, a minibar and a hair dryer.

Room 404, a one bedroom suite, is typical. The sitting room, with four windows that make it bright and cheerful, looks out on the street. There is a table and chairs in the bay window niche. A big ivy-like plant looks as if it is trying to escape from the room. A very green carpet goes well with the striped couch, sideboard and minibar and continues into the bedroom with its green floral comforter, armoire and tall dresser.

Room 414 has the same green carpet and a king bed with a very bright, big bedroom. Not a suite, it costs less but it is a spacious corner room.

Perhaps atypical is room 201, the so-called Garden Suite. It actually looks out on Octavia Street, not on a garden, from four tall windows. The name comes from the plants on the armoire top and those growing in a marble section of colonnaded railing. A tree (artificial) "grows" beside the fireplace with colorful leaves and a few silent (also artificial) birds. Another tree lounges by the door to an impressive bathroom. There is another fireplace in the bedroom and antique furniture in window bays. The queen bed has a draped canopy. It is a beautiful room, pick of the litter in our opinion.

This is a very nice hotel, with comfortable, good-looking rooms. But try not to make any phone calls while you are here, especially long distance. A 30% surcharge is applied.

- *1590 Sutter St., San Francisco, CA 94109;*
  *☎ 415-441-2828, reservations 800-227-3970, fax 415-775-5212.*
- *Rooms: 49 on four floors; 55 bathrooms (extras in halls and on first floor).*
- *Rates: $110-$275.*
- *Reservations: One week ahead for weekdays, one month for weekends.*
- *Breakfast: Continental, 7 am-9 am; afternoon coffee, tea, cookies, 4 pm-6 pm.*
- *Wine: Carafe of sherry is always on the sideboard.*
- *Handicapped accessible: Two rooms.*
- *Smoking: In library and fourth-floor rooms.*
- *Children: Yes.*
- *Pets: No.*
- *Parking: In hotel's own lot, $12 for 24 hours.*

## Restaurant

### The Mansions

(Turn of the century upper class dining)

First, you gather with the other guests in the 1880s parlor of a gorgeous Victorian home and sip wine poured from a cut-glass decanter, while leafing through tintypes of San Francisco's early days. Then you go down the hall to another room where you see a magic show and perhaps a ghost. You proceed to a lovely garden room for a leisurely dinner. We had heard, of course, about the magic show and the ghost and were looking forward to it, but we did not anticipate how good the dinner would be!

The sourdough fresh-baked bread with extra-virgin olive oil, flavored with Italian olives and fresh herbs, starts things off. We knew we would have to control ourselves or we would go through loaves of it and not eat any dinner. So, we restrained ourselves; sort of. We still had healthy appetites for the Mansions' own Victorian salad, a simple bed of greens with a light lemon garlic vinaigrette.

The pasta course that evening was angel hair with tomatoes and shrimp in a light garlic sauce. There was a salmon that was beautifully done. A filet was roasted and served in a parchment "waistcoat," which holds in all the flavors of the shallots, dill, white wine and bay laurel until you open it up and the aroma bursts forth in all its glory.

There was also Frisco Chicken with herbal stuffing, Steak Wellington and fresh water prawns in garlic sauce. Gold Rush Desserts this night were chocolate mousse and San Francisco cheesecake. We each chose a different one. The mousse was creamy and rich and the San Francisco cheesecake lighter than the New York version. The "Gold Rush" came in because both were sprinkled with gold dust.

We don't care whether the mansion is really haunted. We'll go back for dinner any time.

- ❑ *2220 Sacramento St.;* ☎ *415-929-9444.*
- ❑ *Open: Arrive 7 pm for wine, followed by magic show. Dinner at 8:15 pm.*
- ❑ *Prices: Friday and Saturday $47 prix fixe menu includes show; other days, à la carte, entrées $23-$32.*
- ❑ *Credit cards: All major.*
- ❑ *Reservations: Required.*
- ❑ *Parking: Street.*

# Things to Do

## Jay's Victorian Walking Tour

We met Jay Gifford in the lobby at the St. Francis Hotel on Union Square "under the clock." This is where San Franciscans have been meeting since 1907. It was August and our walk was set to take place from 11 am-2 pm. As Jay explained, "If there's fog on summer days, it's most likely in early morning and late afternoon. 11 am-2 pm is our window of sunshine, if we're lucky." We were lucky. There were some clouds, some sun and a bit of breeze. But, just in case, bring a sweater or jacket.

Jay is in his early 30s. He has lived in San Francisco for 15 years and obviously fell in love with the city. This is a common reaction, but not everyone figures out a way to make a living out of that devotion. There are companies that make these tours by bus, but Jay goes to special neighborhoods, where tour buses are not allowed. He takes only small groups (never more than six or eight people). There were three people this day: the two of us and a single young woman from St. Louis.

When the time came, we walked with Jay out of the St. Francis Hotel, turned left and went up a block to Sutter. There, we got on a bus (Jay paid the fare, which was included in our tour) and rode west about 10 minutes to Lower Pacific Heights. We started our education with the magnificent Queen Anne Inn at Sutter and Octavia streets as he explained its century-old features. He took us inside, where we could marvel at some of the highlights of its public rooms. In the meantime, he entertained us with history of all that we were seeing. (See page 125 for much more about the Queen Anne Inn as a place to stay.)

Still in Lower Pacific Heights, Jay's tour takes in Laguna Street, especially the block between Bush and Pine, one of the best blocks in the city to see restored Victorians. Gradually we learned to pick out the Italianate, Stick or Queen Anne styles ourselves, and could even identify the decade of the 19th century when they were built. He showed us one of the few remaining Folk Cottages, predating the Victorian era.

We saw the house, on the corner of Steiner and Broadway, where a part of *Mrs. Doubtfire*, the 1995 movie with Robin Williams and Sally Field, was filmed. The exterior of the house was used in the film.

We ended up at the top of Pacific Heights, looking out over the Bay amid the grander, eclectic houses of that section. We then returned to Union Square where we had started about 2½ hours earlier.

Walking along streets lined with gorgeous 19th-century Victorian houses was infinitely more satisfying than a bus tour would have been. The homes all had bay windows with gingerbread, painted white, blue or yellow and immaculately kept up. We strolled hand-in-hand behind Jay, as he pointed out the features we would never have noticed on our own. He did a fantastic job of explaining the history of Victorians in San Francisco. Although we did get a crash course in 19th-century architecture, that is not really the purpose of the tour.

For more information about San Francisco's architecture, and especially its Victorians, see "Painted Ladies," below.

- ❑ *2226 15th St.; ☎ 415-252-9488.*
- ❑ *Cost: $20.*
- ❑ *When: Daily.*
- ❑ *Reservations: Required.*
- ❑ *Length of tour: 2½ to 3 hours.*

## *Painted Ladies*

*A Little Old Lady had been watching two painters at work on a Victorian house on Page Street. On the fourth day, as they were applying a fourth color, she yelled up: 'Now you boys stop dropping acid – you've got enough colors up there already!'*
Herb Caen, *San Francisco Chronicle*

One of the three things that make San Francisco the most popular city in America to visit are the Painted Ladies. This is the city's name for its wonderfully colorful Victorian houses. There are more here than anywhere else in the world. They have been called one of the world's architectural treasures.

A definition of a Victorian is a building of a certain style built during the 64 years that Queen Victoria reigned over the British Empire. Queen Victoria influenced, or downright dictated, much of the Western world's tastes in dress, manners, morality and architecture. That period coincided with San Francisco's incredible boom in population and the consequent, necessary building frenzy. At first, newly wealthy San Franciscans copied New England gothic houses, and even had them shipped ready-made around The Horn. But the city's regulations called for 25-foot lots, which meant no side yards and few side windows. Victorian houses with bay windows in front fit the narrow lots better. A whopping 48,000 were built between the Gold Rush in 1850 and the Panama Pacific International Exposition in 1915. When you travel around the city and start to notice them, at first they are all just "Victorians." Tall, wooden, lots of windows, a plenitude of carvings, columns and decorations, and painted a range of colors. It is usually only after you go on a walking tour (like "Jay's Victorian Walking Tour," see above, or "Haight-Ashbury Walking Tour" in that section) that you begin to see the differences.

The Italianate style was used in the 1860s and 1870s. It is characterized by a straight, vertical look with tall narrow doors and windows, flat roof lines and always Corinthian columns on the porches. The tops of Corinthian columns are elaborately carved into curling leaves and petals. Early ones had flat windows, built flush with the front of the house. Later, bay windows were slanted out.

Stick style was used in the 1880s and developed by local craftsmen. These homes were still tall and narrow, but with square bay windows. Windows, doors and the framework of the house were outlined with narrow strips or sticks.

The Queen Anne style came in the 1890s, when angles got rounded out. You will see a round tower above the roof and a steep, pointed gable. By this time, technology made curved glass possible, so there are round bays on the corner with curved windows. Walls were usually shingled along with the roof.

The large number of original Victorians has been drastically depleted. Thousands were lost in 1906 when everything south of Van Ness was destroyed by the earthquake or deliberately dynamited to stop the subsequent fire. In the 1930s and 1940s, more were lost to misguided modernization. Stucco, asbestos and aluminum siding salesmen convinced thousands of home owners that those "old-fashioned" houses would look better with all their details covered up! Worst of all, perhaps, because it was a deliberate local government policy, was the Urban Renewal of the '50s and '60s, when 28 blocks in the Western Addition were bulldozed. To drive through that area now and see the results is enough to make you weep. But the 1960s also saw the birth of the "colorist" movement, when all the details of a meticulously refurbished Victorian were highlighted with paint. Sometimes, you will see as many as a dozen different colors and shades on one house. The results, strange as it seems, can be wonderful. But, you will have to see for yourself!

# SOMA

☙ *If every man was as true to his country as he is to his wife – God help the USA.*

Sampler on the wall of a San Francisco cat house parlor

It means, "South of Market" and it is literally south of the tracks, the streetcar tracks that run along Market Street. SOMA is a new, yuppie term. Actually, this area has been called South of the Slot ever since cable cars were invented, referring to the slot in the middle of Market Street where the cable runs.

Originally, when the early Gold Rush fortunes were made, this neighborhood was where the lucky ones built mansions. Those who struck it rich were especially attracted to Rincon Hill. But the area, because it was handy to the harbor, also attracted warehouses and riffraff. After the invention of the cable car made living on Nob Hill practical, the swells abandoned everything south of Market to move north and higher. Today, even Rincon Hill is gone, leveled to make room for more industry.

For the next 100 years, South of Market was San Francisco's prime slum area. Factories, flop houses, greasy spoon cafés and "sawdust joints" (cheap saloons with sawdust on the floor) prevailed. Nothing changed until the 1970s when the city cleared the area from Market to Harrison and from west of Fourth to east of Third in one of the rare redevelopment projects that was a success.

# Nightlife

## The Mexican Bus

☙ El Volado: "One who lives a wildly romantic life, who revels in romantic illusions."

Salsa music blares from the loudspeaker over the driver's head. Couples dance in the aisles to the pounding beat as the bus drives to another of San Francisco's hottest clubs. For those couples who like to dance, who love to be in the thick of where the action is, it is time to get on El Volado, The Mexican Bus.

You meet at Chevy's Café, Fourth and Howard, (that's south of Market) at 9 pm. Too early for anything to be happening? It will start as soon as you get there. If the outside of the bus looks garish, the inside is more so. Despite the kitschy interior, it is well, sort of nice through it all. Because it's a different world, a world of music, the driver's tape provides all the latest latin dances. Toni Hafter goes down the aisle pouring Cuervo Gold into proffered shot glasses. You are on your way to three clubs. It may be Bahia Tropical or Bahia Cabana to dance to a Brazilian beat, Sol y Luna for rhumba, Café du Nord for mambo, or Tu Pueblo for merenque.

It is not all Latin. On Blues Night, you will probably be at The Saloon in North Beach to crowd onto their tiny dance floor. On East Bay Nights, the tour may take in Larry Blake's in Berkeley.

The tours are run by Toni Hafter and her husband, Lalo Obregon, who modeled the bus after the buses that used to ply Mexico City's streets during the 1930s, 1940s and 1950s. A muralist painted the inside and posters of Latin films and knicknacks kitsch up the interior the way the drivers of those buses did.

The night will end around 1:30 am. You will visit three clubs and spend about an hour in each. But right now, everyone wants to dance the salsa. So, the first stop is for those who are not so sure of their technique and want a salsa class. Wherever the bus goes, the emphasis is all on having fun and doing what the passengers want. If the music is good in one club and no one wants to leave, that's OK.

It happens Saturday nights and some Fridays for a cost of $30. This charge takes care of admission and cover charge at the clubs. ☎ 415-546-3747.

# Things to Do

## The Cake Gallery

There are some great bakeries in San Francisco whipping up haute cuisine pastries. We must admit that this is the boulangerie that is closest to our hearts. Here are cupcakes with imagination and tarts that really know what the name means. It is probably better known than any other bakery in town because, for 20 years, the crew here has been whipping up X-rated cakes to order. Actually, you can order a cake, or buy chocolates, made to any degree of sexuality you are comfortable with (G, PG, R or X rating). Practically all their business is for birthdays, anniversaries and special events. They are ethnically correct, with breast-shaped cakes coming in chocolate, tan or pink. Chocolate (candy) penises are a popular item. John, the guy behind the counter, used to tell people he modeled for it until a woman customer mentioned she was disappointed. She had expected it to be bigger. You will find a good line of greeting cards ranging from tame to "Oh, my God!"

They take orders over the phone from out of town and then deliver to the hotel where you are staying. They will also ship. Jerry Carson, the owner, told us of a cake he sent recently in the shape of a rear end with the outline of lipsticked lips on it. It was sent by an attorney to a judge, with the card signed "anonymous."

- *290 Ninth St. (three doors from Folsom Street);* ☎ *415-861-2253.*
- *Prices: 50¢ to $7.50 for chocolate confections, $12.95 and up for cakes. Free delivery anywhere in San Francisco.*
- *Open: 9 am-6 pm, Monday-Saturday.*
- *Parking: If you are coming off the 101 freeway stop and park as soon as you see the Ninth St. sign. You can almost always park on the street within a block. Have a quarter for the meter.*

## Cartoon Art Museum

If one or both of you reads the funnies, here is an intriguing place to spend an hour. POW! If either of you absolutely cannot start the day until you have devoured your favorite strip along with your morning coffee, this is a must destination. ZOWIE!! After all, it is the only West Coast museum "dedicated to the collection, preservation, study and exhibition of original Cartoon Art." ZAP!!! It was founded in 1984 by a small group of cartoon afficionados and started out with traveling exhibitions. In 1987, with donated funds, including some from Charles Schulz, creator of Peanuts, this downtown space was found in the historic Print Center Building.

In the last few years, the museum has had numerous displays on its walls. Among them were: "Pogo's Golden Anniversary Exhibition from the Walt Kelly Family Archives," "With a Smile and a Song: The Animation Art of Snow White," "Good Grief, You're 45 Charlie Brown," and dozens of retrospectives of comic books, animation studios (a Hanna-Barbera Retrospective will be staged this year) and individual artists. BOING-G-G-G!!!!

- *814 Mission St. (one block south of Market between Fourth and Fifth);* ☎ *415-CAR-TOON.*
- *Open: Wednesday-Friday, 11 am-5 pm, Saturday 10 am-5 pm, Sunday 1 pm-5 pm.*
- *Admission: $4, seniors $3.*

## San Francisco Museum of Modern Art (MOMA)

MOMA just opened in 1996. The building itself is already acclaimed as San Francisco's best piece of modern architecture. Inside are six floors of eclectic art.

- ❏ *Street Address: 151 Third St.; ☎ 415-357-4000.*
- ❏ *Open: Friday-Tuesday 11 am-6 pm, Thursday 11-9. Closed Wednesday.*
- ❏ *Admission: $8; Seniors $5.*
- ❏ *Parking: You can actually find street parking south of Market, and there is a large public garage between Fourth and Fifth on the south side of Mission St.*
- ❏ *Directions: Take any bus that goes down Market, get off at Fourth or Fifth and walk one block over.*

# Telegraph Hill

🐝 *A bachelor is one who has lost the opportunity of making a woman miserable.*

Lillie Coit

It is the tallest of San Francisco's 42 hills. At first, it was called Alta Loma, and in Gold Rush days a part of it on the slope facing the Bay, was called Little Chile. It was so named for the women who reached San Francisco first in response to the need for ladies to staff the "houses of horizontal pleasure." Later, when the Italians arrived from Liguria, it became known as Goat Hill for the herds of goats grazing on the slopes. The morning milk was delivered on the hill by Italian women who milked their goats on the buyer's doorstep. During the Gold Rush, a wooden semaphore was built on top of the hill. When a ship was approaching the Golden Gate, the semaphore arms would signal the news to the city below. In 1853, a telegraph was installed up there and the hill acquired its permanent name. You can see a bronze plaque in a granite monument to Guglielmo Marconi, near where Telegraph Hill Boulevard meets Lombard Street.

About the time writers Mark Twain, Joaquin Miller and Bret Harte lived up here, an eight-year-old girl named Eliza Wychie Hitchcock became involved in a chain of events that led to the erection of perhaps San Francisco's most famous landmark. Lillie, the name she was called all her life, was playing in the under-construction Firzmaurice Hotel when it caught fire. Two girls who were with her were killed. Lillie was saved by a volunteer fireman from Knickerbocker Engine Company Number Five (all the members were from New York). He cut through the roof and hauled her to safety on his shoulders. After that, whenever Lillie saw Number

Five racing to a fire, she ran along with them to help, and she became the mascot of the volunteer company. Her parents were horrified. Girls did not do things like that, but they could never stop her. Lillie would have been much more at home in our times than in those. She made herself a fireman's uniform with a helmet, a red shirt and a black skirt that was way too short for that time. As she grew older, she sneaked into back rooms to play poker, smoke cigars and drink bourbon with the men. She even had "5" embroidered on her underwear in honor of Engine Company Number Five. At the same time, Lillie definitely had her feminine side. She went to all the balls in her Paris gowns (fortunately, her parents were wealthy), had many beaus, and in her 20s married Howard Coit, a businessman who was older than she was. But Howard had a roving eye and after a few years of marriage began straying. Lillie tried, heaven knows, she tried! But, after several separations and reconciliations, she finally divorced the cad. Howard never married again. When he died 20 years later, he left his entire fortune to Lillie. Lillie never remarried either. She never forgot the firemen she had idolized most of her life. Nor did they forget her. When she died, years later, her funeral procession was led by a contingent from the San Francisco Fire Department, including three white-haired men who had known her from the beginning. She left a hefty bequest in her will for the bronze statue of three firemen that stands in Washington Square in North Beach. The most important bequest was the money to build Coit Tower, the 210-foot-tall fluted cement column that stands on top of Telegraph Hill. The observation room at the top has the best view of the Bay in the city. You can see Marin County, the East Bay and far down to South Bay. The striking murals as you enter were done by local artists in 1933, paid for by the WPA.

It has been generally believed in San Francisco all these years that the tower is built in the shape of a firehose nozzle. The designer denied it. In this case, we would prefer to believe the myth.

Parking here is difficult during the daytime, but possible at night. It's easiest to avoid the crowds on winter weekdays or at night. Traffic can be bumper to bumper, both for cars and buses, during the summer; summer weekends are murder.

## Restaurant

### ♥ Julius' Castle

(Italian)

Yes, there was a man named Julius and yes, this was his castle. He was Julius Rozk, a former counterman and Italian immigrant who had a dream of building a castle on Telegraph Hill and did. In 1920, the finest craftsmen using the finest materials, rich redwoods and elegant maples rescued from the demolition of the Pan Pacific Exposition, built a landmark that was to become known around the world as Julius' Castle. It became the carriage trade's favorite speakeasy during Prohibition and remained an "in" place ever since. This is where Sam Spade and his secretary, Effie Perrine, ate lunch in Dashiell Hammett's short story, *A Man Called Spade*. Diners at the window table here have watched everything from the building of the Bay Bridge in 1936 and the Golden Gate Bridge a year later to the ferries plying their way across the Bay today.

It is said that you can fall in love all over again here. Now that we have seen it, we believe it. We were lucky. We had an early dinner reservation because we were going to the theater after, so we got the daytime view, followed by the night time lights – the best of both worlds.

And then there was the food, the reason for Julius' Castle's fame. Soups are excellent, with combinations like leek and red lentil balanced perfectly. Garden lettuce salad with pear, walnuts and gorgonzola cheese with a light dressing is typical. Entrées include a simple roasted salmon and a "crispy" caponata streudel with grilled portobello mushroom and tomato coulis. We have tried both and they are excellent. There is also a roasted breast of pheasant or Maine lobster poached in a buttery herb broth.

The streets are steep, narrow, winding and tend to dead-end around here. The restaurant is at the end of a narrow cul-de-sac lane on a cliff. In the 1920s, a turntable in the street was the only way to turn cars around. For a romantic setting, this simply can't be beat.

- *1541 Montgomery St.; ☎ 415-362-3042.*
- *Open: 5 pm-10 pm.*
- *Prices: Appetizers mostly around $9.50, soups and salads $7, entrées $23-$29, with lobster $39. (Minimum charge for dinner $12.)*
- *Credit cards: AE, Carte Blanche, Diners Club, Discover, MC, V.*
- *Reservations: Essential.*
- *Parking: Valet only $6; no street parking.*

# Things to Do

## Coit Tower

Summit of Telegraph Hill. Open 10 am-6 pm daily. Fee to ride elevator to top $3, seniors $2.

## Lombard Street

This part of Lombard, down the slope of Telegraph Hill, is very steep, so the street is a series of switchbacks. There is often a line of cars driving down it. People like to say that they have driven "the crookedest street in the world."

## Greenwich Steps

This walk starts at the Coit Tower parking lot. You will see lots of landscaping with beautiful trees and flowers, as you go all the way down the hill. Steps go off in all directions, so you will probably take detours. You end up in the Embarcadero near Levi's Plaza. There are about 500 steps in all.

## Filbert Steps

Walk down Telegraph Hill Boulevard from the Coit Tower parking lot until you see the Filbert Street sign at the top of the steps. Follow them down until Filbert turns into a real street again. That also takes you to Levi's Plaza.

# The Bridges

❧ *I don't know who decided to paint it orange, but God bless them. When you drive up over Nineteenth Avenue and see the bridge rising before you, it's like seeing the towers of Chartres when you're driving out of Paris.*

Susan Cheever

Each of the towns in the Bay Area is unique in its own way. There is one quality common to all that has done more to shape what attracts visitors than anything else: San Francisco Bay. What would San Francisco and Oakland and Sausalito and the rest be without the Bay and its bridges?

## The San Francisco-Oakland Bay Bridge

As long ago as 1856, there was talk about building a bridge to connect San Francisco with Oakland, Alameda and Berkeley. Nothing happened until 1933. Then, it took four years to build and cost $70 million. When it was finally done, the San Francisco-Oakland Bay Bridge was magnificent in its simplicity. Suspension spans (all

2,300 feet of them) are joined in the middle of the channel at Yerba Buena Island, which is pierced by a tunnel. The four great piers of the spans have huge braces which create an overlapping grid pattern as you drive underneath. No pedestrians or bicycles are allowed.

The ferries that had handled all the traffic across the Bay for 100 years were cancelled once the bridge was completed. But such an outcry resulted from outraged citizens who loved their ferries that some schedules were reinstated. It has since turned out to be a good thing. Ferries do not get tied up in gridlock.

## The Golden Gate Bridge

It reaches from San Francisco to Marin over one of the best known stretches of water in the world. The bridge is the symbol of San Francisco. Easily identified by its art deco design and its international orange color, the Golden Gate Bridge almost didn't get built. The powers that be had lots of doubts. But Joseph Strauss, the engineer brought in to survey the situation, was a visionary. It was his tenacity and persistence that persuaded the citizens of San Francisco and the surrounding counties (Marin, Napa, Sonoma) that it could be done. In the end it took only 52 months to design and build, opening in 1937. The total cost was $33 million, about what it would cost today to repair one pylon!

*The Golden Gate Bridge.*

*Walking, Jogging or Bicycling the Golden Gate Bridge*

This is something many people want to do just to be able to say that they have done it. Why not?

There is a viewpoint parking lot just south of the toll plaza. It is as good a place as any to leave your car. Or, you may walk to the beginning of the bridge from Fisherman's Wharf or Fort Mason along the bayside trail. From Fort Point, a road leads up to a statue of Joseph Strauss, the bridge's creator, where you start your real walk or bike trip. Pedestrians can walk on either side, but bicycles are restricted to one side on weekdays and the other side on weekends.

From the east side of the bridge, you will get a fine view of Fort Point, Alcatraz, San Francisco's skyline and, on a clear day, Oakland and the Berkeley Hills. You will see the ships passing underneath. If you are lucky, you'll see lots of ships. Many things necessary to life in California sail in under the Golden Gate Bridge.

The second high tower (65 stories high, with the top often lost in a fog) marks the beginning of Marin County and the end of your walk or ride. Either turn around and do it again in reverse, or continue on to Sausalito and take the ferry back.

A word of caution. The bridge is 260 feet above the water. If you are afraid of heights, you will probably be queasy out there. The way the wind blows in through the Golden Gate, we advise you to bring a sweater and windbreaker.

# *Union Square*

🌿 *San Francisco is a money-rattling city of nouveaux riches, a panorama of swells who dress to show themselves, feeding their vulgar desire to be seen. These are the mediocre people who will sink into oblivion within a few years.*

Martha Hitchcock, mother of Lillie Coit (who donated Coit Tower to San Francisco)

When Jasper O'Farrell laid out, in 1847, the plan that would shape San Francisco for good or for ill and for all time, he provided only two open spaces for parks. Union Square was one. At that time, it did not look like a park. It was a sandy hillock with a deep gully on the west side, with a stream running along the bottom. That is what is now Powell Street, where the cable cars clang. It was not even called that at first. The name was hung on it because of all of the violent pro-Union rallies staged here on the eve of the Civil War.

In the early years, it was bordered on all sides by the city's principle churches, synagogues and posh private clubs. A few remain, but most moved west after the St. Francis Hotel was built in 1908 and commercial stores started crowding in.

❦ *I'd rather be a lamppost on Powell St. than own all of San Mateo County.*

Tessie Wall

If you stand across the street and look at the handsome building at 535 Powell St., a bit up from the square itself, you will see the only surviving downtown structure that was built as a single-family home. Even greater fame comes from the fact it was bought by Frank Daroux, a local politician, for his bride, Tessie Wall, who owned a lodging house on O'Farrell Street. Of course, Frank was not only a politician. He was also a big-time gambler and Republican boss of the Tenderloin's many vice enterprises. Beauteous Tessie was one of San Francisco's most prominent madams. Because listing yourself as a boarding house owner or seamstress was the only way for "femmes de joie" to advertise, city directories and newspapers bulged with long lists of hookers.

Alas, the loving couple's honeymoon did not last long. Soon Frank's attentions wandered elswhere, to the point that he filed for divorce. Tessie was more single-minded. She was determined that if she could not have him, no one else would either. So she shot him dead on the corner of Anna Lane. Their Powell Street honeymoon nest is now a private club.

Union Square has always denoted the heart of downtown San Francisco. There are 40 hotels within three blocks. Flower stands, a San Francisco institution as old as the cable cars, stand colorfully on almost every corner. The square itself was dug up in 1942 for a garage to be built underneath. The park was laid back on top. It was the first under-the-park garage built like that in the country. Fortunately, this one still looks good.

## Westin St. Francis

There was an alcoholic party in John Barrymore's suite the night of April 17, 1906. When the first shock of the earthquake hit at 5:12 am, he staggered out into the Square with all the other guests of the St. Francis. The militia soon pressed him into service stacking bricks. Later, his uncle, famed thespian John Drew, remarked, "It took an act of God to get Jack out of bed and the United States government to get him to work." A decade before that, in 1897, Charles Crocker died leaving three small children and $8 million. Their guardians needed to invest the money and decided to build a hotel patterned after the best features of Claridge's in London, the Ritz in Paris and the Waldorf-Astoria in Manhattan. They bought land on Powell Street facing Union Square and opened the St. Francis in 1904. (St. Francis of Assisi is San Francisco's patron saint.) From the beginning, the hotel attracted society, famous actors, Presidents and kings. A typical dinner menu offered a choice of 14 cheeses, 20 clam or oyster dishes, 11 soups, 24 relishes, 17 kinds of fish and 58 entrées, from hamburger to Bohemian ham. These could be accompanied by any of 27 vegetables and 23 variations of potatoes. As a result of this kind of lavish expertise, the hotel's chef, Victor Hirtzler, changed the course of American history. In 1916, Democratic President Wilson was in a close election race with Charles Evans Hughes, the bearded and dignified Republican Governor of New York. Because it looked as though California would be a crucial state, William Crocker, uncle of the owners of the St. Francis and chairman of Hughes's campaign, brought him to San Francisco and ordered a special banquet with Hirtzler as chef. The guests were seated and the meal scheduled to begin in 20 minutes, when the waiters, members of the new culinary union, walked out on strike. Hughes would have left as well, but Victor insisted his meal would be served, regardless. Nonunion waiters were rushed in from nearby restaurants and the banquet went on. The next day, local union leaders printed thousands of handbills denouncing Hughes for violating a picket line to eat dinner. Wilson won the election. Hughes had lost California by the razor-thin margin of 3,673 votes, approximately the number of union waiters in San Francisco.

San Franciscans have always had affection for the St. Francis because it maintains the old traditions, fiercely valued in this city. For 90 years, a favorite phrase for couples was, "Meet me under the clock" – meaning a date in the Powell Street lobby by the large, ornate 1856 Magneta clock. Made of rosewood, it has stood in this opulent room with its elaborate carvings, coffered ceilings and black marble columns since 1907.

The St. Francis in 1910 was the first hotel in San Francisco to decree that it was "permissible" for women to smoke in the lobby and dining room. Every day from 1962 to 1993, Arnold Batliner used a machine to wash and polish every coin used by the hotel. The tradition still goes on to this day. Every cashier and taxi driver in town always assumes, when handling shiny, clean coins, that they have come from the St. Francis.

In 1921, Fatty Arbuckle was right up there with Charlie Chaplin, Mary Pickford and Tom Mix. He was the highest paid star in Hollywood. On Saturday, September 23rd, he checked into the St. Francis and was given the best suite in the hotel, 1219-20-21, overlooking Union Square. Two days later, some pals from Hollywood came up and brought with them a dour, former showgirl named Maud Delmont and a pretty, dark-haired young woman named Virginia Rappe (a wannabe film actress who was currently a "model"). They all decided to have a party. Fatty sent down to the desk for food, a gramaphone and a stack of records. The friends had brought bootleg booze. Fatty, because of a burn he had gotten on the set a few days before, was romping around in loose fitting pajamas. The party was going strong when Rappe, after drinking at least three gins with orange juice, left the parlor. After awhile, Fatty went into his bedroom, then came out a short time later to say she was sick. The other guests found her lying on the bed with her clothes on, moaning and in pain. They called the hotel doctor, who examined her and put her to bed in another room down the hall. Fatty forgot about it, checked out the next day and went back to Hollywood. Four days later he got a call at home from a *San Francisco Chronicle* reporter.

"Who else was at the orgy you threw at the St. Francis?"

"What?"

"How much did you pay the cops to hush it up?"

"Hush what up?"

Virginia Rappe had died that morning and Maude Delmont told the police that Arbuckle had raped her.

The story was front page all over the world for months and the press crucified Fatty. District Attorney Mathew Brady had ambitions for higher office and milked the trial for every drop of publicity, posing as the guardian of public morality, defending society against this "bestial, sordid, revolting crime." Maude Delmont claimed in court that a little while after Fatty went to his bedroom, she heard Virginia screaming and had to break the door down to try to rescue the girl. But everyone else who had been there disputed that and the District Attorney's own witnesses finally admitted they had been coerced by the prosecution into supporting Delmont's version of events. The coroner finally found that Virginia Rappe's death was due to peritonitis. After two hung juries, on the third trial Arbuckle was finally acquitted and declared innocent.

It was way too late, though; he'd been found guilty by the press and public opinion long before. He never appeared on the screen again. The only work he could get after that was directing a few films under the pseudonym Will B. Good. Fatty Arbuckle died 10 years later at age 46 and was buried in the Bronx, far from San Francisco and the St. Francis Hotel.

The hotel increased in size until, by 1913, it occupied the entire block on Powell facing the Square between Geary and Post. The

32-story modern gray tower behind the building was added in 1972 and linked internally with the original. The management contends that the appearance of the new tower is "in harmony" with the old building. Oh, yeah?

## Grand Hyatt on Union Square

On the northeast corner, the Square is dominated by a much taller 36-story newcomer, the Grand Hyatt, built in 1973. Its second-story Plaza Restaurant overlooks the Square with big windows (see Restaurants) and the Club 36 (guess what floor it's on) is one of the town's most popular for an after-dinner or after-theater drink. (See page 161.)

But the Hyatt's real hold on San Francisco's affections is seen in the little plaza just around the corner from the Square on Stockton Street. Sculptor Ruth Asawa created a fountain that, San Franciscans believe, "bubbles with the city's spirit." There are 41 wraparound bronze friezes. Some 250 residents aged three to 90 collaborated under Asawa's direction on these bas-reliefs – originally molded in bread dough.

## Inns

### Campton Place Hotel

If you are celebrating a wedding, anniversary or birthday, and order dinner in your room, you will find the menu is printed with your name, the occasion and the date. It is something for your scrapbook. One of the things we like about this place is that, although there are over 100 rooms, there is never the feeling that this is a large hotel. Some floors have only four rooms, and there are no VIP floors. All guests receive the same high level of service. All rooms have a TV, minibar and AM/FM clock radio. Bathrooms are fully equipped with the usual hotel amenities plus extras to make the guests feel right at home. You will find a blow dryer, plush terry cloth robes, French milled soap, a scale, a thermometer to test the bath water and more, including a complimentary overnight shoe shine. All rooms are decorated in muted tones and all halls have a thick, soft peach carpet.

The hotel was originally two buildings put together as the Drake-Wiltshire Hotel. They are on slightly different levels, so you will find yourself going up or down four or five steps in some of the hallways.

There are quite a few different kinds of rooms, with seven categories ranging from Junior King to Luxury Suite. Most rooms either have king-size beds or, when they are listed as doubles, actually have two double beds. The suites mostly have two rooms and extras like wet bars. Even in the Executive Suites, the rooms are not very large, but all are extremely comfortable.

Room service is available 24 hours a day, without the restricted menu of most hotels. It is wonderful for romantic dinners *en suite*. The public bar, in a small lounge off the lobby, has a light snack bar menu that runs from onion soup or chicken wings for $7, through quesadillas or tamales for $9.50, to smoked salmon and caviar club sandwich for $14.50. That is a light snack? Wednesday night is martini night. The bar's everyday martinis (made with Skyy vodka) were voted "best in San Francisco" by *The New York Times*, if that means anything. Every good hotel and cocktail lounge in San Francisco makes an almost indistinguishable one. But they *are* good here and go for $6.

There is live jazz by a small combo, the Martini Brothers, playing music from the 1940s.

A lot of people who work around here drop in by the late afternoon or early evening to de-stress on martinis. It has become such a fad that the lounge now has Martini Nights every Wednesday from 5:30-7:30, when martinis are only $4.

Some people get so de-stressed, they stay on for a special $29 three-course *prix-fixe* dinner menu in the dining room from 6 pm-7:30 pm. Reservations at ☎ 415-955-5555. The dining room has quite a few tables for two, a small lamp on each table, dim lighting and fabric-padded walls to insure quiet. It consistently gets high ratings as one of San Francisco's best restaurants. It is romantic and expensive.

The conclusion is that Campton Place has all the amenities and services possible in a big hotel, cut down to a human scale. It is quiet, elegant and in a wonderful location.

- *340 Stockton St., San Francisco, CA 94108; ☎ 800-235-4300 or 415-781-5555, fax 415-955-5536, e-mail reserve@campton.com.*
- *Rooms: 117, including 10 luxurious suites.*
- *Rates: $225-$980.*
- *Credit cards: AE, Diners Club, MC, V.*
- *Packages: Romance package is $265 first night, $225 additional nights, including rose, champagne, breakfast in bed first morning.*
- *Reservations: Needed, especially September-October, and weekends.*
- *Amenities: In rooms are TV, minibar, AM/FM clock radio, robes, hair dryer, scale, safe. Complimentary shoe shine. Cocktail lounge, dining room, concierge.*

- *Breakfast: No complimentary breakfast, though breakfast, lunch and dinner available in dining room. Room service 24 hours with full menu and romantic dinners served in your room.*
- *Handicapped accessible: Yes, several rooms. Special elevator to dining room and bar.*
- *Smoking: No, except at bar itself, where there are four seats.*
- *Children: Yes.*
- *Pets: Yes.*
- *Parking: Valet.*
- *Walking distance: Half a block from Union Square in the middle of San Francisco.*

## Hotel Monaco

Hotel Monaco.

Here is a hotel with the imagination to offer a package called, "An Affair to Remember." The package includes a special room, iced champagne and late checkout. Whether the occasion to celebrate is a dalliance, liaison, intimacy or simply a long, happy marriage, this is a place with the right mind-set.

With a good downtown location, the Monaco is two blocks from Union Square. It is only one block from the American Conservatory Theater (ACT) and the Curran Theater. It is two blocks from the Powell Street cable car line and one block from a slew of art galleries. As you walk in, the lobby opens up to a long, high-ceilinged room that is likely to bring out an admiring "wow!"

This part of town was destroyed by the earthquake and fire of 1906. In 1910, the Belvue Hotel rose from the ashes on this corner of Geary and Taylor. It is a landmark American Beaux Arts building. That cut glass chandelier just over your head is from the time it was built, as is the sweeping staircase and the fireplace big enough for four people to sit on the benches inside.

Those now-closed archways between the tall, fat pillars opened into the Grand Ballroom. Wait until you see the Grand Café that has been made out of that! It is easy to picture pre-World War I days and bejewelled, becoiffed women sweeping down that staircase into the ballroom for the next dance.

Over the years, the Belvue gradually went downhill. Murals were painted over. New, lower ceilings hid the originals; rich panelling disappeared under coats of whitewash. Fortunately, Bill Kempton bought it in 1993 and restored everything. Rooms were eliminated so that others could be made larger. It is decorated in a vaguely French theme. The halls, for instance, are wallpapered in a rusty-red fabric, sort of a bordello red. It sounds like something that could look garish. Actually, it is striking in a low-keyed way and fits admirably.

Standard rooms have queen-size, half-canopy beds, and often charcoal and cream wallpaper. You have to see it to realize how well it's been done. The TV and minibar are in an armoire.

Junior suites have king-size, half-canopy beds and a small sitting area at one end. Many have pistachio and yellow striped wallpaper – a great combination.

Luxury suites have a separate bedroom, a large bathroom with a whirlpool tub big enough to hold a romantic couple and a separate, glassed, oversize shower.

At the other extreme, there are a few small rooms, and we do mean small. The bed takes up most of one wall, leaving room only for a chair and an armoire, which conceals the TV set. But, they are inexpensive. If you are not going to be in your room except to sleep, you might find these to be the coziest, most romantic spaces in the hotel. Ask for a Canopy Queen.

Dinner in the Grand Café (the old ballrom) is recommended. The food is good and the room is striking. See page 153 for more details.

Lunch or a light supper after the theater is fun in Petit Café, which has its own menu, a good bar and an oyster bar. See page 154.

- ❑ *501 Geary St., San Francisco, CA 94102;*
  ☎ *800-214-4220, 415-292-0100, fax 415-292-0111.*
- ❑ *Rooms: 201, including 34 suites; 23 suites have whirlpool tubs large enough for two.*
- ❑ *Rates: $170-$210 for Canopy Queen, Double (Standard), Double Deluxe or King Deluxe; $235-$335 for suites, most with jacuzzis.*
- ❑ *Packages: "An Affair to Remember" with Deluxe King room, champagne and late checkout, $205; for Luxury Suite with jacuzzi for two, $355.*
- ❑ *Reservations: Two weeks advised, but sometimes two days will do it.*
- ❑ *Breakfast: Complimentary continental breakfast in lobby. Breakfast, lunch and dinner available. Room service, 6 am-11 pm.*
- ❑ *Wine: Wine and cheese in lobby, 5-6 pm.*
- ❑ *Amenities: Complimentary shoe shine, two robes, morning newspaper, cable TV, a small health club, steam room and sauna. Massages available in fitness center or in your room.*
- ❑ *Handicapped accessible: Seven rooms.*
- ❑ *Smoking: 50% are non-smoking rooms.*

□ *Children: Yes, in fact, 18 or younger stay free.*
□ *Pets: No.*
□ *Parking: Valet, $20 per day, 24-hour access. No self-parking.*

## Monticello Inn

*Monticello Inn.*

Here is a place with a definite interest in romance. We first noticed their "Gone With The Wind" package. It includes a deluxe guest room with sparkling wine waiting in an iced bucket. A single perfect red rose and a new copy, just for you, of that book about a confused Southern gal named Scarlet, also awaits. Perhaps you could read it to each other in bed.

The welcoming lobby, furnished in federal period colonial decor, features a grandfather clock with a brass face, and a blazing fireplace to greet you. There are reproductions of Chippendale furniture to make you comfortable and an attractive library where you can relax. Coffee and tea are available throughout the day at no charge. A complimentary breakfast is served every morning in the same library, with complimentary Napa wines every evening.

Your room has a colonial decor, too, and features early American themes. Colors are muted blues, yellows and floral patterns with an occasional splash of red for emphasis. There is a refrigerator in each room, cable TV and both smoking and non-smoking rooms.

The inn is convenient to everything. Union Square, the cable cars to Fishermen's Wharf and Ghirardelli Square, and the theater district are all within just a few minutes walking distance.

This inn seems to be well known in Europe. You will hear many languages spoken in the lobby. While having breakfast or wine in the evening, you may fall into conversation with someone from Germany or France, as we did. There is a definite cosmopolitan atmosphere that thoroughly fits San Francisco.

□ *127 Ellis St., San Francisco, CA 94102;*
  ☎ *415-392-8800, 800-669-777 in US.*
□ *Rooms: 91.*

❑ *Rates: Deluxe twins $129; queens $139, two double beds $149; suites $169-$209 (Jefferson Suite at $209 has fireplace and jacuzzi).*
❑ *Credit cards: All.*
❑ *Reservations: Three to four weeks ahead most of year; only off-season is mid-November to January.*
❑ *Breakfast: Complimentary continental.*
❑ *Wine: Complimentary in evening.*
❑ *Amenities: Refrigerator; Puccini and Pinetti Italian Grill and American Bar in building for lunch and dinner.*
❑ *Handicapped accessible: Four rooms. Entire hotel accessible.*
❑ *Smoking: Smoking and non-smoking rooms.*
❑ *Children: Up to age 12 stay free with existing beds (charge for rollaways).*
❑ *Pets: No.*
❑ *Parking: Valet, $16 per day, 24 hours in and out.*

## Warwick Regis

The Warwick Regis has some great advantages. It is a downtown hotel with a wonderful location. It is small enough for the personal touches, but large enough for the advantages that come with size (i.e., a restaurant and 24-hour room service). Most people like it because it has low rates (compared to the Campton Place and other deluxe hotels) and yet the ambiance of an upscale, expensive hotel.

It was opened as the Maryland Hotel in 1913 and became the Regis nine years ago. A 2½-year renovation included tearing down and rebuilding the hotel next door to enlarge the original. Then Warwick International bought it. They attached Warwick to the name and took on this elegant little place as its fifth in the United States. Warwick, based in Paris, has a carved gargoyle over the doorway of every room and suite, the symbol of Warwick Hotels. All rooms have antique mirrored armoirs and most have a queen bed, either four-poster or crown canopy. All rooms also have a sitting area, four have fireplaces, a few have private balconies. The honor bars are built into a piece of antique furniture so as not to be intrusive. There is 24-hour room service. The original owner of Warwick International was Chinese. That explains the Oriental touches.

David Razon, the friendly and very knowledgeable manager, showed us around his hotel; he is understandably proud of it. There are two types of suites: studio and one bedroom.

The Regis Executive is for you if you are here on a honeymoon. It is the quietest and has both a full bathroom and a vanity room with sink and closet. The cost is $200.

The Front Suite is the largest room, with a separate sitting room separated by French doors. There are two TVs, two armoires and two bathrooms. Cost is $215.

Deluxe Queen is the standard room, smaller than some but with a queen bed with crown canopy and a large sink and counter in the bathroom. The rack rate is $135, but in the off-season it goes down. Always ask.

Regis Deluxe is the favorite room for many guests who come back again and again. It is only $5 more than the standard room. Because it is on the corner, there are six windows, making it a very bright space. A four-poster canopy bed rounds out the room, which costs $140.

The smallish, good looking Scene Restaurant off the lobby is open for breakfast and dinner. On its walls are photos of actors and actresses who have played the theaters on Geary, just down the street, and stayed here. There is also a small, friendly bar, popular with local people. It is nice for a drink after you return from dinner, before you go up to your room.

- *490 Geary St., San Francisco, CA 94102;*
  **☎** *800-827-3447, fax 415-441-8788.*
- *Rooms: 70 on eight floors.*
- *Rates: $105-$200.*
- *Credit cards: All.*
- *Packages: A romance package with roses or champagne and a special room. It will not ordinarily be mentioned. You will have to ask.*
- *Reservations: Six weeks ahead for weekends, less for weekdays.*
- *Minimum stay: Weekends, June to October, two nights.*
- *Amenities: Robes, minibar, restaurant, 24-hour room service.*
- *Breakfast: Complimentary continental breakfast served in dining room; you can also order from menu or get room service (regular prices).*
- *Handicapped accessible: Four front suites, ordinarily more expensive, but the rate will be the same as for a standard room.*
- *Smoking: Yes, one floor.*
- *Children: Yes.*
- *Pets: No.*
- *Parking: $19 for 24-hour garage, in and out service.*
- *Walking distance: Hotel is in a great area for shopping, restaurants, theaters. Two blocks from Union Square.*

# Restaurants

## Cityscape Bar & Restaurant

(Sunday buffet brunch)

This is in the San Francisco Hilton & Towers. When you step off the elevator on the 46th floor, you are right up there with the angels or the high financiers. Because there are big windows all around, the view is magnificent.

Tables for four, and an occasional two, are set on two sides of this large room that takes up the entire 46th floor. No matter where you are seated, there are 18-foot-tall windows. There is more to Cityscape than the view. First, as soon as you are seated, freshly squeezed orange juice and champagne arrives, and it keeps on coming. In the case of the champagne, it is from Armstrong Ridge, Napa, and it will continue coming throughout the meal, if you wish. Whenever you go back to the buffet for the third (fourth, fifth?) time, your glass is filled up again as if by magic. One could get schnockered. For us, it is like flying first class, which is where we got the habit of starting with a mimosa. If you try it and find it an exceedingly pleasant way to get your vitamin C, here is the Cityscape bartender's recipe.

## *Mimosa Cocktail*

2/3 champagne
1/3 freshly squeezed orange juice

Pour champagne first, into a tall, fluted champagne glass. Add orange juice. Serve. Have enough champagne and orange juice to keep them coming. (Note: freshly squeezed orange juice has an intense flavor. If you are using frozen, change proportions to half and half. If you're using canned, you should be ashamed.)

The buffet is lavishly spread out on tables in a horseshoe shape in the center of the room. The number of different foods is hefty and changes weekly to take advantage of what is fresh in the Northern California fields. But, to give you an idea, many think it is best to start the meal by dipping the huge fresh strawberries in the dark chocolate fondue. Then, there are those who ladle the chocolate over the chocolate cake at the end of their meal. We see no reason not to do both. There are a dozen freshly baked breads, muffins and coffee cakes, several unusual pâtés, scores of cheeses and fresh fruit. There is a chef making omelets to order. Belgian waffles, ham, bacon and poached eggs with tomatillo salsa are all enticing choices. There are cheese blintzes, chicken curry with peanut salad and Sonoma breast of chicken. In the seafood line, we see smoked Pacific salmon with condiments (onions, capers, etc.), house-smoked tuna, peppered trout, sturgeon, chilled jumbo prawns with cocktail sauce, San Francisco shellfish cioppino or grilled salmon, and many more options. There are dozens of pastries and chocolates to finish it all off.

All the while, there is live music with a keyboard and bass playing good popular jazz. With the view, the mimosas and the incredible array of food, it is a nice way to spend a very enjoyable two or three hours.

- ❑ *333 O'Farrell St.;* ☎ *415-923-5002.*
- ❑ *Open: Sunday brunch, 10 am-2 pm, dinner 5:30 pm-10 pm, to 11 pm Friday and Saturday. Lounge open 5:30 pm-1 am, DJ and dancing 10 pm-1 am.*
- ❑ *Price: $36, includes parking. (Thanksgiving and Christmas Day buffets are incredible – $48.)*
- ❑ *Credit cards: All major.*
- ❑ *Reservations: Recommended.*
- ❑ *Parking: Self-park in hotel garage, validated. Hilton Hotel takes up the entire block. Drive in on Eddy Street and park, then take elevator to 16th floor, cross over bridge to the other building and take elevator to 46th floor.*

## ♥ *The Compass Rose in the St. Francis Hotel*

(High tea)

The two of you sit comfortably and chat for a minute, anticipating the treat to come. Then a waiter approaches, bearing a tray, the contents of which he puts on the table. Two tea cups and saucers, two halves of lemon, a small pitcher of cream, two teapots and a wonderful selection of edibles appear on your table.

The room is called The Compass Rose. Its furnishings and museum-quality sculptures are from all points of the compass. There is an antique Burmese Buddha, a Victorian English mosaic table, 18th-century English settees and a 200-year-old bronze statue of a Thai goddess inset with precious stones. Everywhere you look, there is exotic artwork.

Lunch is served here and, most famously, tea. There are wine tastings at night. It is all very sophisticated and worldly. We come here for the tea. Served from 3-5 pm every afternoon, it is heavenly. You have your choice of 13 different teas. Start with a scone, fresh creamery butter (not Devon clotted cream, darn) and preserves. Go on to an assortment of tea sandwiches like deviled egg, olive and cucumber or a turkey triangle with a mandarin orange and a tiny sprig of parsely. The latter presented its colors so delicately that we thought at first it was another pastry. A three-tiered silver server with a half-dozen kinds of petits fours arrives. Then, there are seasonal berries. The strawberries served with a Grand Marnier cream are unbeatable. Teatime is a relaxing time, especially here. After a hard day of sightseeing or shopping, you sit by large, draped windows looking out across Powell Street to Union Square or down on Geary Street. Tables for two or four are set among the high, fluted pillars, with couches and very comfortable chairs.

There are Oriental touches in the decorations, screens, ceramics and even the pillows on the couches have an eastern flair. This decor is all under a high, coffered ceiling.

In this gorgeous room there are a couple of special, more intimate places just made for proposals and, we're sure, propositions. "The Alcove," for example, is a cushioned niche behind a large folding Chinese screen and flanked by potted palms.

We can thank the British for starting this whole business of tea in the afternoon. Except for the lack of clotted cream, the British experts would thoroughly approve of The Compass Rose.

- *Union Square at Powell and Geary;* ☎ *415-774-0167.*
- *Open: Tea 3 pm-5 pm; lunch 11:30 am-2:30 pm; wine tasting 5 pm-11:30 pm.*
- *Prices: $16.95 for complete tea service. You can order à la carte: petits fours $5.50, tea sandwiches $6.50, scone $5.50, berries with Grand Marnier cream $6.75, or tea only $3.50.*
- *Credit cards: All major.*
- *Reservations: Not necessary weekdays; recommended for weekends.*
- *Parking: Valet, $2 per hour.*

## ♥ The Dining Room in the Ritz-Carlton San Francisco

(Continental)

The Ritz-Carlton lobby is what St. Peter's anteroom must look like. It has very high ceilings, lots of room overhead, marble floors that go on and on and walls with 10-foot-high paintings of deceased society dowagers. There are immense vases on long, thin tables containing enough flowers for a gangster's funeral.

After you have traversed what seems like an acre of this gorgeousness, you come to the entrance for the Dining Room. Suddenly, the ceilings are low, the walls have muted colors, rug-tones are soothing and waiters pleasant, helpful and unobtrusive. Altogether, it makes for a very charming impression.

Tables for two, against the walls and in corners, are made for couples who simply wish to dine well and talk intimately without being overheard. Just from experiencing this extremely nice room, with its atmosphere of warmth and sophistication, we know that a thousand proposals must have been made here.

As we are writing this, *Condé Nast Traveler Magazine* has come out with a list of "Best Restaurants." The Ritz-Carlton Dining Room is ranked best in San Francisco. This is a tough call. The town is full of wonderful restaurants. Still, they may be right.

You start with the duck prosciutto with hazelnut and orange vinaigrette. Actually, this is complimentary while you are perusing the menu for more serious fare. In fact, the menu was very long and the table small, so we had them take away the menus so we could deal with the duck, which is cured by the chefs here. At too many restaurants, almost everything is done elsewhere and then simply purchased and served. None of that nonsense here. The chefs do almost everything themselves, even the most basic procedures. Everything except "mixing the salt into the caviar," as one waiter confided, is done on the premises.

Meanwhile, martinis arrived. These were very, very good, both vodka and gin. These glasses, thin and classic, will never see the inside of a dishwashing machine.

A good way to start is with the lobster salad, accompanied by haricot verts, tomato, avocado, chives and a dreamy caviar cream. You could make a meal from this. Perhaps you would prefer the crayfish velouté, a fine, silky soup with an intense flavor, or a risotto with butternut squash. Baked monkfish with onion, baby capers and "crushed potatoes" is a great dish, not too heavy. Or try a scallop of peppered salmon on scented lentils.

Gary Danko, an American chef who is French-trained, is behind all this. He also created the flexible *prix-fixe* carte. You can choose as few as two courses or as many as five and the kitchen will adjust the size of the portions accordingly. Thus, you can load up on one or two dishes you particularly like, or lightly graze from five as your own personal tasting menu. Sommelier Emmanuel Kemiji, will suggest a different wine (by the glass) to go with each, if you wish.

You might want to finish with the cheese tray; 20 or so varieties of exotic and more familiar cheeses. There are cheeses you have never heard of, let alone tasted. The dense brown nut bread seems too intense, though often called for by European protocol. We asked for some French bread, which allowed us to taste every flavor.

As we surfaced between courses, we looked around the room, which is furnished in blond wood. There is an immense outburst of roses and ferns in the center, wall sconces, and candles on the tables. One perfect rose on each table is in a tall, slender vase, but has no scent. Tsk, tsk!

The waiters are extremely knowledgable. Not only do they know how the food is prepared, but where it was purchased and why. How about the origin and history of two dozen cheeses? We were impressed.

After we had finished and could not possibly eat or even look at more food, a silver tray of chocolates, made in-house of course, arrived. They were yummy.

- ❏ *600 Stockton St. (at California);*
  ☎ *415-296-7465 or 800-241-3333; fax 415-986-1268.*
- ❏ *Open: Dinner only, 6 pm-9:30 pm*
- ❏ *Prices: Three courses $35; five courses $69. There is no à la carte per se; instead, simply order from the prix-fixe menus and pay by the course.*
- ❏ *Reservations: Recommended.*
- ❏ *Parking: Valet, $9 if eating in restaurant.*

## Grand Café in Hotel Monaco

(American 1920s-30s)

This was the ballroom of the Hotel Belvue back when it was built in 1910. The arches of the side wall, to the right as you walk in where the open kitchen is now, were not blocked off then. The room flowed into what is now the lobby of the Hotel Monaco. Women in long gowns and sparkling jewels swept down the grand staircase, through the archways and into the ballroom to dance where the diners sit now. The room itself has an immensely high ceiling and large pillars. By the entryway are imaginative sculptures of elongated, super-size rabbits as acrobats, by Albert Guibara. You may have seen them pictured in magazines.

There are both booths and tables. Almost immediately, a dish of smoked salmon arrives stuffed with goat cheese and capers, drizzled with basil oil. This is just to hold you over while you study the menu. In case that is not enough, the waiter brings a long, thin loaf of homemade bread accompanied by a tapenade of sun-dried tomatoes, capers, anchovies and oil.

There was a creamy onion soup with a huge Gruyère crouton that lets the taste of the cheese come through with the onions. The meld of the two was terrific. A ravioli was stuffed to the gills with Dungeness crab and shrimp. "Day boat" scallops were pan-seared, which we had not tried before, but they turned out crusty on the outside and juicy and tender inside, served with angel hair pasta. They serve a duck confit with potato cakes and an orange sauce; the duck is perfectly preserved and flavorful, the cakes crisp and tender. Grilled prawns come with a spicy orzo. It is a delicious combination with that picante Mexican sausage, chorizo, and an oregano pesto sauce that bears repeating at home.

While the food is excellent, this is definitely not a very formal restaurant. Most men do not bother with a tie or jacket unless they are going to one of the nearby theaters after dinner. Medium casual seems to be the drill, although it is a good place for a pre-theater dinner.

We are told that the holiday season is a nice time to be here, with the room resplendent in wreaths and a decorated tree. One small caveat: The room is noisy, possibly because of the high ceiling.

❑ *501 Geary St., enter from lobby of Hotel Monaco;* ☎ *415-292-0101.*
❑ *Open: 7 am-9 pm, Monday-Friday; 8 am-9 pm Saturday and Sunday.*
❑ *Prices: Starters, soups and salads from $4.75; pastas and entrées from $9.95.*
❑ *Reservations: Dinner only; not needed for lunch.*
❑ *Parking: Valet, $7.*

## Petit Café in the Hotel Monaco

(Oyster bar, contemporary American cuisine)

This really attractive place is always jammed before and after the performances at the ACT and Curran theaters, a few hundred feet down Geary. It is also fine for a light lunch, if you are around Union Square (two blocks away), an afternoon snack or just a drink at the bar. We discovered it the first time we checked into the Monaco and had to wait while our room was being cleaned up. This is part of the hotel and a few steps took us from the lobby to the long mahogany bar, with dozens of beers on tap, where we looked out through big windows onto both Geary and Taylor.

In addition to the beers and ales, also featured are a dozen-and-a-half single malt scotches and a dozen exotic martinis. Some of the martinis sound pretty disgusting, like the Blue Skyy Martini made with "Skyy Vodka and a splash of Blue Curacao." You can ignore things like that, unless you are feeling foolishly adventurous.

There is also an oyster bar that serves fresh Pacific oysters on the shell and a charcoal grill to cook the fish, filets and hamburgers for a few booths and a dozen very small tables, better for drinks than food.

We found the starters are particularly good. Bruschetta misto is four pieces of grilled and oiled French bread with a different topping on each: egg plant, sun-dried tomatoes, anchovies, etc.

It is rare to find raclette on any menu. It is a cheese from Switzerland with a low melting point. Traditionally, it was put by a fireplace and the cheese scraped off as it melted, then smeared on small half-potatoes to eat out of the hand. The same thing is accomplished by an electric heating gadget now in some restaurants. We ordered it and shared. The rest of the menu includes several good salads, a few pizzas and things like grilled salmon. It is hard to go anywhere in San Francisco and not find seafood on the menu.

This is not the place for a big, fancy dinner. For a snack or light meal, it is just fine.

- ❑ *501 Geary St. at Taylor;* ☎ *415-292-0100.*
- ❑ *Prices: Starters $2.50-$8.95; soups, salads and pizza $4.75-$9.95; entrées $7.25-16.95.*
- ❑ *Open: Breakfast 8 am-10 am. Lunch 11:30 am-3 pm. Dinner 5 pm-10 pm. Bar closes at 11 pm, though that depends on theater crowd.*
- ❑ *Credit cards: AE, Diners, MC, V.*
- ❑ *Reservations: For dinner.*
- ❑ *Parking: Valet parking $7 for two hours, but parking is validated.*

## Plaza Restaurant & Bar

Plaza Restaurant.

(Contemporary California, with continental touches)

The Plaza Restaurant & Bar is at the Grand Hyatt on Union Square. We sat by a wall of glass, at least it seemed that way. Huge floor-to-ceiling windows overlooked Union Square with its wintertime skating rink in full swing. The skaters were doing their thing and we enjoyed it almost as much as they did. The room is large and irregularly shaped so that tables are not right next to each other. There is a fountain near the center and lots of live palm trees to soak up any noise there may be. There are no overheard conversations here. The furniture is golden rattan, very comfortable, and soft green tile trim works nicely. Dress seems to be casually chic.

Appetizers like prawns and Dungeness crab cakes with fruit chutney and a cucumber vinaigrette or crostini of smoked duck with tomatoes, mushrooms, olives and capers are typical. If you are in a mood for soup, the judicious use of herbs brings out the flavors of their vegetable soup beautifully.

Sometimes the most difficult thing for a chef is to cook a simple dish perfectly. That is what Kurt Alldredge, the chef here, is known for. Try the herb-crusted rack of lamb, served with couscous. It's a good example. Sea bass is sometimes roasted instead of grilled, which gives it a whole new flavor.

There are seasonal *prix-fixe* menus which always include appetizer, entrée and dessert. They are $28 and include validated parking that is good until 2 am. It is popular as a before-theater dinner, since it starts early and the parking is still good well after the theater is over. The theaters are across Union Square and up a block on Geary; a five-minute walk. You can come back for a drink at **Club 36** upstairs without worrying about spending a fortune on parking.

When we make reservations, we always request a table by the windows on the Post Street side. We especially like to eat here because we can look down on Union Square and all its activities.

❑ *345 Stockton St. (at Post);* ☎ *415-403-4854.*
❑ *Open: Breakfast 6:30 am-10:30 am; lunch 11:30 am-5 pm; dinner 5 pm-10 pm.*
❑ *Prices: Appetizers $6-$9, bouillabaisse $19, pastas $15-$16, fish and seafood $17-$18, chicken $16, meat $16-$22. Prix fixe menu $28 (includes parking).*
❑ *Reservations: For dinner, same day or day before.*
❑ *Parking: Valet, $11 for two hours, $16 longer.*

## *Belden Street*

We are downtown, around Union Square and it is time for lunch. Yes, there are restaurants, but they're spread out. If only there were a place where a number of restaurants were all together and you could walk along, look at menus posted outside and make up your mind. In fact, there is just such a place! It is called Belden Street, although it is more of an alley. It stretches one block between Bush and Pine, just south of Kearny, which it parallels. It is a little piece of Paris, with one restaurant after another, side-by-side, all the way down the block.

During the 1890s, Belden was the southwest end of the Barbary Coast, which extended in a long crescent from here through Chinatown and North Beach. There were heavy iron gates stretching across the street at each end of the block. Inside were 50 cribs (see page 159) and no other businesses. All the prostitutes working in Belden were French. It was relatively expensive in those days, up to a dollar a trick. In 1903, a more fervent than usual morality crusade actually expelled the women, but rents and graft were so profitable for the city fathers when the red lights were burning that the femmes de joie soon returned and it was business as usual. The fire of 1906 spelled the end of Belden Street's sinning ways, once and for all.

But now, after all these years, the one-block alley is once again as crowded with eager customers as it ever was in the 1890s. There are a few differences. Now it is women as well as men flocking here. It is food they are after, rather than sex. The big rush is at lunchtime, when starving office workers descend on the street. Some places are only open for lunch, or breakfast and lunch; some are also good for dinner.

❑ *Parking: Stockton-Sutter Public Garage is nearby; enter on Bush Street going north.*

## Boudin Café

Boudin Café is the famed originator of San Francisco's sourdough bread "since 1849." Boudin Café stretches through from its main entrance on Kearny.

- ❑ *318 Kearny, another entrance on Belden; ☎ 415-781-1849.*
- ❑ *Open: Breakfast and lunch, 7 am-5 pm.*
- ❑ *Prices: Soups, salads $3-$5; sandwiches $5.75; nothing over $6.*
- ❑ *Reservations: Not necessary.*

## Café 52

(Mediterranean food)

It looks small from the outside, but there is an upstairs and a downstairs. It has an intimate atmosphere, serving some French dishes and some Greek.

- ❑ *52 Belden St.; ☎ 415-433-5200.*
- ❑ *Open: 11 am-3 pm, lunch only.*
- ❑ *Prices: Soups, salads $4-$4.50; entrées $7.95-$12.95.*
- ❑ *Reservations: Not needed.*

## Café Bastille

This is a small place with a jazz trio that comes in to play for dinner.

- ❑ *22 Belden St.; ☎ 415-986-5673.*
- ❑ *Open: Lunch and dinner, Monday-Saturday, 11:15 am-10 pm.*
- ❑ *Prices: Lunch, entrées $8; dinner, entrées $9-$10.*
- ❑ *Reservations: Not necessary for lunch; you can call same day for dinner.*
- ❑ *Music: 7 pm.*

## Plouf

(Seafood Provençal)

Plouf has a few tables for four and a dozen just big enough for one couple. There is a full bar and the menu is primarily seafood Provençal style, with some meat dishes. Talk to Jocelyn Bulow if you have special requests.

- ❑ *40 Belden St.; ☎ 415-986-6491.*
- ❑ *Open: Lunch, Monday-Friday, 11 am-2:30 pm; dinner, Monday-Saturday, 5:30 pm-10:30 pm.*
- ❑ *Prices: Appetizers $5-$10, entrées $10-$15.*
- ❑ *Reservations: Not necessary for lunch; dinner yes.*

## *Thanks a Latte*

(Coffee shop)

If you just need a coffee fix, this is at the corner of Belden and Pine. Besides the usual fare for caffeine junkies, there is pastry, juice, soups, ice cream and frozen yogurt.

- ❑ *485 Pine St.; ☎ 415-398-6999.*
- ❑ *Open: 5:30 am-4 pm, Monday-Friday.*
- ❑ *Prices: Latte $1.25-$2.25; soups $2.25; ice cream $1.85-$2.75.*

## *Tiramisu*

(Northern Italian)

This restaurant is an exception to the typical Gallic fare here, offering strictly northern Italian food.

- ❑ *28 Belden St.; ☎ 415-421-7044.*
- ❑ *Open: Lunch, Monday-Friday, 11 am-3 pm; dinner, Monday-Thursday, 5 pm-10:30 pm, Friday and Saturday, 5 pm-11 pm*
- ❑ *Prices: Dinner, pastas $8-$12, entrées $13-$16.*
- ❑ *Reservations: Advisable for both lunch and dinner.*

## *Vic's Place*

(Saloon food)

Vic's Place is "a saloon of good food and fine spirits, est. 1978." It's a friendly bar with some Italian dishes. We recommend that you try the soups.

- ❑ *44 Belden St.; ☎ 415-981-5222.*
- ❑ *Open: 10 am-10 pm, lunch served only. Thursday-Friday, bar snacks from 4:30 pm, "until they're gone."*
- ❑ *Prices: From $4.95 for a hamburger to $10 for a New York steak.*
- ❑ *Reservations: Not necessary.*

# *Maiden Lane*

❦ *There are no people in the world who so practically ignore and hold in contempt the legal marital relations as do Californians.*

New York newspaper, 1874

There is a narrow street across from Union Square, between Geary and Post, which runs only two blocks to Montgomery. Because it is used mostly by pedestrians, it is a pleasant place to stroll. There are tables out in the street in front of the cafés, chic jewelry shops and fashionable boutiques. We sometimes come this way by choice, hand in hand, unhurried and unjostled, pausing to admire a rare and expensive oriental objet d'art in a store window. Or, we will look again at the building that Frank Lloyd Wright designed. If it is later than 5 pm, everything is locked up tight and Maiden Lane is deserted.

There was a time when, night after night, this narrow lane was jammed with crowds of jostling men. The buildings on both sides of the street were some of the busiest houses of prostitution in the city. If you had tried walking through here in the daytime back then, you would have seen the women lounging in their doorways and seated on their balconies naked from the waist up, as a way of advertising their wares. If you were the female half of a couple, they would shout, "Get smart, dearie. Stop giving it away!"

It was not uncommon for the luckiest, or prettiest, of the girls to entertain 80-100 men on a good night. That was not by choice though. The price structure was low, ranging from 25¢ to $1 per trick, depending on age, looks, race and ethnicity of the girls. Hundreds of girls were packed into these two blocks of mostly three-story buildings. So many could be accommodated because the "cribs," their rooms, were only 4½ by seven feet, like a corn crib. The furnishings were pretty simple. A single bed, a chair, a basin for water. An oil cloth was laid over the foot of the bed because these tricks, mostly miners and laborers, did not take off anything but their hats. The streets were not paved, so their boots were usually muddy.

Morton Street, as it was known then, was leveled by the earthquake in 1906. Most of the buildings you see now were built between 1906 and 1909, when the street was renamed Union Square Avenue. For awhile, it was called Manila Street in honor of Admiral Dewey. The 90-foot-tall monument in the center of Union Square was erected to commemorate his victory over the Spanish Navy in 1898. Finally, when the street had become the center of the diamond trade, it was the jewelers' idea to call it Maiden Lane. That was meant to make it sound like the jewelry center in Manhattan, which in turn took its name from the jewelry center in London.

Walking this short stretch from Montgomery toward Union Square, you will come to **Gump's**. You may reach them at ☎ 415-982-1616. The first Gump became successful in Gold Rush days by selling mirrors to saloons and casinos on the Barbary Coast. The present store, at 135 Post St., which comes through to Maiden Lane, sells fine arts from the Far East. Another establishment, **Orientations** at #134, ☎ 415-981-3972, also has several floors of fine Asian art and antiques.

In the second block is **Pierre Duex French Country Fabrics** at #120, ☎ 415-296-9940. Among several other rather pricey clothing shops is **Laura Ashley**. The address is #253 Post and this store also comes through the block, ☎ 415-788-0190.

**Circle Gallery** at #140, ☎ 415-989-2100, is notable mostly because it is in a building Frank Lloyd Wright designed for the V.C. Morris china and crystal shop. The Morris sign copied in Wright's script is still visible. In completely rebuilding a 1911 structure that had stood here, Wright introduced in 1949 the idea of a ramp that curves from the ground floor up to a skylight. The idea was to make the exhibit easily accessible and to flood it with light. This pre-dates by 10 years the building of the acclaimed Wright-designed Guggenheim Museum on Fifth Avenue in New York, with its similar circular ramp and glass dome over a central court.

# *Restaurant*

## *Mocca on Maiden Lane*

(French-American charcuterie)

It is like a little bistro in Paris. A warm, friendly place, it is narrow and very busy with the lunch crowd. Choices are soups, salads, sandwiches, wine and beer. There are a dozen and a half tables for two and more out on Maiden Lane. Posters of gallery openings in France are on the walls. By the way, Mocca is a made-up name; it means nothing.

The soups change every day and those we have tasted have always been rich and flavorful. Sandwiches are on a baguette piled high with meats, tomatoes, lettuce and the like. The place is very good for a simple lunch, not to get too complicated. There are great salads of every kind; just look in the refrigerated cabinet and choose. There is no table service. You pick it out and you pay your genial host, Khadjenouri Bahran, at the cash register, where you also pick up your wine, beer or soda. There is a tiny bar for wine and beer, but it is standing room only (no chairs). Very often, there are street musicians playing for the guests at tables outside, especially at lunchtime.

❑ *175 Maiden Lane;* ☎ *415-956-1188.*
❑ *Prices: Inexpensive.*
❑ *Open: 9:30 am-4:30 pm, lunch only, or a cup of coffee and a bite to break up the morning or afternoon.*
❑ *Reservations: No.*

# Nightlife

## Club 36 in the Hyatt on Union Square

"Of all the gin joints in all the world, she had to pick this one." No, no, that is the wrong line. It wasn't Sam at the piano. The music we heard as we came through the door was *Isn't It Romantic?*, played wonderfully by beret-wearing Larry Vuckovish. His back was to the wall of windows, with a heart-stopping view of San Francisco and the Bay behind him. We had found Club 36, surely one of the coolest, most sophisticated, romantic places to have a nighttime drink in all San Francisco.

It is way, way up on top of the Hyatt Union Square. There is wonderful piano music all week with lots of Cole Porter and Rogers and Hart. When we sat at a small table for two by a window near the piano and hesitated over what to drink, Jesus Garcia, our friendly waiter, suggested the house drink. It is called the "Naughty Irishman." Who could resist something with a name like that? It turned out to be an unlikely mixture of Bailey's Irish Cream, Frangelico, Amaretto and cream. You will not believe how good it tastes until you have had two, three or four yourselves.

If you end up around Union Square at night, do not deny yourself the opportunity to drop into this really pleasant gin joint.

- □ *345 Stockton St. (at Post, on Union Square);* ☎ *415-398-1234.*
- □ *Open: 4 pm-2 am.*
- □ *Prices: Drinks $6.50.*
- □ *Entertainment: Larry Vuckovish on piano Tuesday-Saturday.*
- □ *Parking: Valet at Hyatt.*

## The Lobby Lounge in the Ritz-Carlton

If you prefer to hear your jazz in a noisy, crowded, smokey boite, preferably a cellar, this is not the place for you. This is a big, gorgeous room with high ceilings open to the Ritz-Carlton lobby. The paneled walls have 10-foot-high paintings of 1890s women gowned all the way up to their perfect teeth. We were admiring the oils and wondering who these grande dames of San Francisco's turn-of-the-century Victorian society were. Then we learned, from a helpful waiter, that the art work had been shipped from Ritz-Carlton headquarters in Atlanta. Ah, well.

The music is provided by the John Moriarity Trio with vocalist Bonet. This is a good place to hear sophisticated jazz, a lot of not-quite standards that live on the edge of memory. If you are under 40, these will not mean as much, except that you are hearing some good music. If you have been around a bit longer, well, how long has it been since you've heard "All My Tomorrows"?

Before dinner, from 5:30 pm-8 pm, you can get fresh, fresh sushi straight from the hands of Chef Hiroshi Takama and his sushi cart. You can try any of the Chef's more than 30 variations on the two most popular types: Nigiri-sushi and Maki-sushi. Just think of this as the original fast food.

- *600 Stockton St. (at California);* ☎ *415-296-7465.*
- *Open: 7 pm to midnight.*
- *Prices: Individual sushi $4, plate $16-$18. Drinks $8.50.*
- *Parking: Valet.*

## Ritz-Carlton Bar

If you are a man who likes single malt scotch, you will love the vast array of choices here. If you are a woman who has taken up smoking cigars, you will adore this elegant, comfortable room. Gee, you two make a nice couple!

If your idea of scotch is blended and mixed with water or soda and/or ice, you have come to the wrong saloon. Oh, you can have it like that, sure, but it will not be one of the 100-odd single malts kept on hand here. Those come straight and have a dark, strong taste. The drinks start at $6, but what would you say to $36 a drink? Or $66? Bob was served a 35-year-old Strathisia, a smokey-tasting scotch in a Riedel glass made in Austria especially for single malt scotches. They even have their own glasses!

The room is also for cigar afficionados. We do not know the prices, although we were solemnly assured that they do not sell Havanas. Of course, who knows what politically incorrect stogies may lurk in the private humidors kept for regulars.

This is a nice, quiet, full bar. Remember, for those who are bothered by it, the air conditioning is good but there is still a hint of cigar smoke in the air.

- *600 Stockton St. (at California);* ☎ *415-296-7465.*
- *Open: 5 pm-10 pm.*
- *Prices: Scotch $8.50-$65. Cigars $7-$26.*
- *Parking: Valet.*

# *Things to Do*

## *International Deli*

(Middle Eastern deli)

This is a Middle Eastern deli – two blocks west of Union Square and rather nondescript from the outside. Just ask for a made-to-order sandwich and you will discover they pile it high with terrific food. There is a choice of several breads, meats, a half-dozen other ingredients and finished off with a subtle, herby "Middle Eastern sauce." A good selection of wines and expensive cigars is available.

- ❏ *587 Post St.; ☎ 415-771-1558.*
- ❏ *Open: 9 am-9 pm, seven days.*
- ❏ *Prices: Sandwiches $2.95-$3.75 (This can't be beat!)*

## *The World's Best Drink*

Was the world's best drink invented in San Francisco? Of course it was. That is, unless you are English and believe the martini was named after the Martin and Henry army rifle, famed for its kick. Maybe you are of Italian descent and believe the drink is named after Martini and Rossi, the Italian dry vermouth that was first used to make it. If you were a true San Franciscan, you would have faith and believe the story that a San Francisco bartender whomped up a drink of gin, vermouth and bitters for a customer who wanted something refreshing to send him on his way by ferry to Martinez across the Bay. It seemed to the bartender that he had concocted something special, so he kept on making them for other customers. Time passed and so did the bitters. The drink, known first as the Martinez, grew in popularity and came to be known as the martini.

To this very day, Martinez claims it is "the birthplace of the martini." There has long been a rumor around San Francisco that once a year Martinez holds a Martini Festival in honor of the great event. As soon as we heard about it, we wanted to attend, thinking it would be a strange and wonderful festival indeed. Rain was dashed on that parade when the Martinez Chamber of Commerce told us that there was no Martini Festival and there had never been a Martini Festival. Yes, they had considered the idea, but when their attorney mentioned the possibility of liability, well those plans evaporated. Alas, another bubble burst.

## *Walking Tour of Maiden Lane*

We had an enjoyable hour-and-a-half walk here with Mary Grainger as our guide. She is a mature woman whom we might expect to see at afternoon tea in the St. Francis Hotel. Instead, we spent the time being entertained and educated on the history of Maiden Lane.

This lane's history is flamboyant indeed; salacious is really a better word. We were a bit surprised, at first, to hear such words from such a proper looking lady. This is just one of the Public Library's fine and free walking tours.

- ❑ *San Francisco Public Library Walking Tour Program;* ☎ *415-567-4266.*
- ❑ *Tour listings on the Internet at http://sfpl.lib.ca.us/drafil/ctguides.txt.*
- ❑ *City Guides info: http://www.hooked.net/users/jhum.*
- ❑ *Price: Free (contributions to Libary accepted).*
- ❑ *Meets Monday at noon, off Kearny, between Post and Geary. It lasts 1½ hours. Phone first to check that the tour will be conducted. The City Guides have many other walking tours (23 in all) of San Francisco.*

# *Dashiell Hammett's San Francisco*

❦ *It's the stuff dreams are made of.*

This is perhaps the most famous final line in all American movie history. Sam Spade says it standing in his apartment in San Francisco while he holds the black bird at the end of *The Maltese Falcon*. It is the first and still considered the best of the modern mystery novels.

To afficionados of the detective novel genre, San Francisco is still the place where the lean, hawk-faced private eye walked the fog-shrouded streets with Joel Cairo sleazing along behind him.

If you've read the book or seen the movie, you might be interested to know that Dashiell Hammett, the author, lived at 891 Post St. in apartment 401 while he was writing the first draft of *The Maltese Falcon*. That's where he put Sam Spade's apartment. Spade's office was, by consensus, in the Hunter-Dulin Building at 111 Sutter Street. A lot of this was compiled by Don Herron, who used to conduct a Dashiell Hammet walking tour and wrote a book, *The Dashiell Hammett Tour* (City Lights Books, 1991).

Hammett moved around a lot, but always stayed in downtown San Francisco. Early on, he lived at the Locarno Apartments, 1309 Hyde Street. If you are on Leavenworth and pass 1155, the San Loretto Apartments is where Hammett had a studio apartment and where he finished writing *The Maltese Falcon*. At one point, he rented a room at 20 Monroe Street. You will not find Monroe anymore. In 1988, the Board of Supervisors renamed it Dashiell Hammett Street. It is only a block long, running between Bush and Pine and closer to Powell than Grant. Here is a perfect description of how to find it: The tall, black pedestal phone jangled harshly at 2 am, waking Spade. He picked it up, said, Hello... Yes, speaking... Dead?... Yes... 15 minutes. Thanks." He dressed, phoned the Yellow Cab Co. for a taxi. It dropped him "where Bush Street roofed Stockton before slipping downhill to Chinatown." Dashiell Hammett Street is just up Bush from that, near and across from what is undoubtedly the most famous Sam Spade location in San Francisco – Burritt Alley. It is a short, stubby cul-de-sac above the Stockton Tunnel. On the wall of the building there is a plaque with the words, "On approximately this spot, Miles Archer, partner of Sam Spade, was done in by Brigid O'Shaughnessy."

There is one more place everyone should visit, whether mystery fan or not, because it is a San Francisco landmark. It was already a landmark over 60 years ago when Hammett had Spade phone a cab company. "'Have him pick me up at John's, Ellis Street'.... He went to John's Grill, asked the waiter to hurry his order of chops, baked potato, and sliced tomatoes, ate hurriedly, and was smoking a cigarette with his coffee," when the driver came in.

# ℛestaurant

## John's Grill

(1920s American)

This is a chop house and bar and grill. In fact, it is one of the oldest in San Francisco. It has more than just tradition and substantial food to recommend it, though. For Dashiell Hammett fans, it is a treasure trove of Hammett and Sam Spade memorabilia.

Ask if they are serving in the second floor dining room. If they are, you'll be able to eat "Sam's Chops" – rack of lamb, baked potato and sliced tomatoes – while you look around at your leisure. If they are not serving up there, take a booth downstairs and later go up and see the fine replica of the black bird, the Maltese Falcon, along with stills from the movie and pictures of San Francisco as it was in those days.

We have been coming here for years. The walls are oak-paneled and dark, exactly the way they were in 1908, when it opened. The waiters could be from that time and the food is substantial. It's what you would expect in a chop house 90 years ago. There is a good menu of salads, pastas and meat and potatoes. One time we had

Sam's Chops out of nostalgia and they were meaty and juicy, cooked just to the pink. There was a real, unadorned baked potato, not foil-wrapped and re-wamed at the last moment. So thanks to the author and his unforgettable character for leading us to this downtown place that we have become so fond of.

In June 1997 John's Grill was declared a National Literary Landmark. A plaque over the door cites the building as the "site where Dashiel Hammett wrote *The Maltese Falcon*." That's not exactly true, but it's close enough. What's important is that San Francisco's literary landmarks are honored.

We have always loved *The Maltese Falcon* because, along with being a fine mystery story, it is an intriguing love story. "I won't play the sap for you," Sam says in that climactic scene. Is it still all an act on Brigid's part? Or does she actually love him by then? We both tend to think the latter. But then we're romantics.

- ❑ *63 Ellis St. (just off Market);* ☎ *415-986-0069.*
- ❑ *Open: 11:30 am-10 pm.*
- ❑ *Prices: T-bone steak is a good example – $12.95 to $26.95.*
- ❑ *Parking: Street.*

# The East Bay

*T*he flat land by the Bay and the rolling hills behind were carved up into vast land grants by the Spanish government, and still later by the Mexicans. The grantees, at first, were mostly retired soldiers from the Presidio at San Francisco. Then, a handful of American and British sailors, who jumped ship long before the Gold Rush, married into the Spanish families and received their own immense rancheros.

After the gold hysteria began, wheat was grown here when enterprising Americans saw there was more money to be made feeding the miners than joining them. The East Bay continued to be the granary of San Francisco throughout the 19th century.

Far more tourists visit San Francisco than the towns across the Bay. Yet they have a great deal to offer – as those who do get here discover.

## Oakland

 *There's no there there.*

Gertrude Stein

Gertrude said that about Oakland, and she was born here. But let's not forget that she had been living in Paris for many years when she wrote it. She was looking back on an earlier life from a now lofty, intellectual viewpoint.

San Franciscans have been looking down on Oakland since about 1850. Oaklanders have had a suspicion that they are second-class citizens for the same length of time. It is infuriating to know that the world-class city across the Bay cannot be bothered even to notice you most of the time, which is why Oakland is forever taking pot shots from across the water.

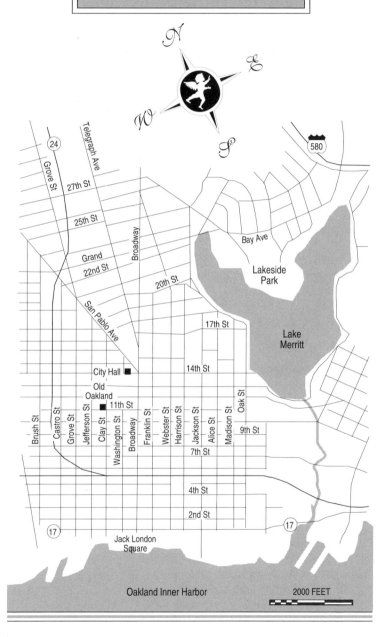

Downtown Oakland

Here is an official pronouncement from the City of Oakland about the weather. "For those die-hard fog, mist and dampness lovers, San Francisco is only a short commute away across the Bay Bridge. Experience her seven hills and all the wonders they hold, and then return to Oakland and realize why our sunny, temperate climate is the envy of the Bay Area."

A few years ago, after years of writing about San Francisco because that was the city tourists most want to know about, we decided to write an article about that place across the Bay no tourists ever asked about. We were absolutely amazed to find out how much there was to see and do in Oakland. We have a feeling you'll be amazed too.

For more information, contact the **Oakland Convention & Visitors Authority**, 550 Tenth St., Suite 214, Oakland, CA 94607; ☎ 800-262-5526 or 510-839-9000.

## Getting Here

**By Air**: Oakland International Airport is a relatively short distance from downtown. Shuttles, limos and buses connect with the BART (Bay Area Rapid Transit) system for reaching Oakland, Berkeley and San Francisco.

**By Train:** Amtrak arrivals from Southern California, north to Seattle and the east come to a new station in Jack London Square, convenient to cross-bay ferries. ☎ 800-USA-RAIL.

**By Auto:** Driving up from Southern California, take Highway 5 or 99, and get onto 880, which goes into downtown Oakland. From the north, coming down on Highway 101, take 580 (Richmond-San Rafael Bridge) to 880 and continue. If you are on Highway 5, take 80 to 580 to 880. From San Francisco, cross the Bay Bridge (20 minutes) and here you are.

**By Ferry:** Ferries run to and from San Francisco (both Ferry Building and Pier 39), Alameda and Angel Island. For schedule and fare information, ☎ 510-522-3300.

## Weather

Temperatures range in the 50s and 60s during the winter months and 70s and low 80s during the summer. The warmest months are September and October. Oakland's temperature is usually five degrees warmer year-round than San Francisco's. The highest rainfall is in January, which averages 4½ inches. February and March are usually half that, April even less and May through September has a negligible amount. The seasonal rainfall starts gently in

October with about an inch. In November, there is more and
December is climbing back toward January.

## *Inns*

### ♥ *Dockside Boat & Bed*

This is the life! Lying in a big bed, being lulled to sleep by the
movement of water under the hull. What could be better? We
strongly urge you to book this experience for two nights. You will
have a full day in between. Perhaps go for a sail on your boat in the
Bay (crew provided). Or just sit on deck and watch the dozens, and
sometimes hundreds of boats. You will see silent, beautiful sailboats or noisy, speedy powerboats skimming by. Plenty of kayaks
are to be spotted, or spy on the houseboats across the channel in
Alameda.

We did have time to sit and observe, so we saw the two shells
crewed by UC Berkeley men, the oars lifting and dipping into the
water in unison, like long, thin spiders. Then a whale boat came by
with a dozen women at the oars. We waved and the female cox-
swain cheerily waved back and we exchanged a few words until
the muscles of the crew drew them away.

We were on the *Voyager*, a 46-foot Trader ketch. She sits high off the
water and is beamy. She would roll like a half-filled tub in any kind
of sea, but the same qualities make her roomy when you are staying
aboard at the dock. We were at an outside slip. It was a great
location because it's right at the beginning of the channel off San
Francisco Bay, so all the boats down-channel go past on their way
out. For anyone who loves boats or who just likes to read Horatio
Hornblower, this is heaven. Late at night, we woke with the feeling
that something nice was happening. A boat had gone by. The waves
slapped up against the counter, right under our heads. The stern
bobbed up and down and the *Voyager* rolled a bit from side to side
gently and what do you know? We were asleep again.

From the aft deck, open the cabin door and go down four steep
stairs to the main cabin. The builder's plans probably called it the
"saloon." A big table in the center with a cushioned bench flanking
it against the bulkhead is along one side. Opposite is the galley with
a sink, refrigerator, microwave, dishes and glasses stowed neatly
beneath. A few wine and champagne glasses were hanging upside
down in a rack above.

Forward starboard is the wheel, but we would not be using that.
Next to it, a few more steps lead down to a head (bathroom to
landlubbers), and a small two-berth cabin. A larger cabin in the bow

has berths in the vee. We would not use those either. The master's cabin, the one we claimed, is down from the saloon and takes up the entire aft of the boat. It is about 15 feet long and the entire width of the *Voyager*. A queen-size bed is all the way aft under two square windows in the transom, just like in the pirate flicks. Four more square windows are in the sides and a hatch with clear plexiglass top serves as a skylight overhead. There is lots of light here, but it's dark at night. Everything in the cabin is wood, including the snug cupboards lining both sides, the paneling, overhead beams and the carved doors. There is a dressing table with a big mirror and a TV with VCR and a dozen tapes. The bathroom has a tub/shower (the hand-held European kind).

Some couples go the whole route: an afternoon cruise with a picnic basket, complete with a bottle of wine. A professional skipper takes care of the sailing. Then the boat ties up at the slip in the evening for a catered candlelight dinner. The next day, a masseuse comes to give each of you an hour of prime time massaging.

The other boats in the rental fleet are much the same. A few are larger. Several are smaller and thus less costly to rent. With a snug sailboat, what romantic couple needs more?

- ❑ *77 Jack London Square, Oakland, CA 94607;*
  ☎ *510-444-5858, fax 510-444-0420.*
- ❑ *Boats: Eight.*
- ❑ *Rates: Weekdays $95-$225; weekends $125-$275.*
- ❑ *Credit cards: All major.*
- ❑ *Reservations: Summer weekends, 3-4 weeks; winter weekends, 2-3 weeks; weekdays, much less. Try calling. Sometimes boats are available on short notice.*
- ❑ *Minimum stay: Two nights over holidays.*
- ❑ *Breakfast: Continental, delivered to boat.*
- ❑ *Handicapped accessible: No wheelchair access.*
- ❑ *Smoking: On deck only.*
- ❑ *Children: Discourage toddlers because of danger to them.*
- ❑ *Pets: No.*
- ❑ *Parking: Public lot on dock. Validates.*
- ❑ *Directions: Drive across Bay Bridge, off at first ramp to Jack London Square.*
- ❑ *Walking distance: On the watery edge of shops, boutiques, largest bookstore in Northern California (Barnes & Noble).*

## Waterfront Plaza Hotel

This is *the* hotel in Jack London Square, located right at the head of the channel and on the water. Sailboats sail by, ferries come in and dock at the next pier, tugs grunt their way past, pushing big barges, and a freighter unloads right across the channel. It is busy, colorful and interesting all at the same time.

Our room was on the top floor, the fifth, on the end of the building. This means it has a private veranda on two sides. It is large and in a great location. There is room enough for an extra table with flowers and several comfortable chairs by the fireplace (only a few rooms have them). It is a comfortable room, almost a suite. Any couple could be happy here. Standard rooms are considerably smaller and do not have fireplaces. There are some very nice rooms and some pretty ordinary ones. Even the ordinary ones are enhanced by being on the water. For your weekend to be enhanced, ask the right questions about the room you are booking.

Here is what you want when you call for a reservation: junior suite or better, Bay side ("Courtyard side" overlooks the parking lot) and preferably on the fifth floor. Why the fifth floor? That is where the hotel's owners, Joan and Buzz Gibb live. All the rooms are different on that floor, subtly better. The sauna, a really nice one, is just the right size for a couple; it's on the fifth floor.

All rooms have VCRs, minibars, voice mail, hair dryers and coffeemakers. There is twice-daily maid service and room service.

- ❏ *Jack London Square, 10 Washington St., Oakland, CA 94607;*
  ☎ *800-729-3638, 510-836-3800, fax 510-832-5695.*
- ❏ *Internet: http://www.waterfrontplaza.com.*
- ❏ *Rooms: 144, including 27 luxury suites.*
- ❏ *Rates: $150 cityside, $170 over the water. Romance package includes champagne, chocolate-dipped strawberries, continental breakfast in bed, gift, waterview room $175; with suite $225.*
- ❏ *Credit cards: All.*
- ❏ *Reservations: Recommended.*
- ❏ *Amenities: Sauna, fitness center, outdoor heated swimming pool, room service; in-room amenities are hair dryer, voice mail and coffee-maker.*
- ❏ *Restaurants: Jack's Bistro, in the hotel, serves breakfast, lunch, dinner.*
- ❏ *Handicapped accessible: Four suites, some on upper floors with sweeping views of the Square and harbor.*
- ❏ *Smoking: Yes. If a non-smoker, ask for a room in the non-smoking wing.*
- ❏ *Children: Yes.*
- ❏ *Pets: No.*
- ❏ *Parking: On premises, no charge.*
- ❏ *Directions: Cross Bay Bridge from San Francisco, off at first exit, Jack London Square to right. Ferries dock next door.*
- ❏ *Walking distance: Shops, gifts, large bookstore, nine-plex cinema, restaurants.*

# *Restaurants*

## *Il Pescatore*

(Italian)

This place is a joy and a delight. Il Pescatore is right on the water in the Marina. It's crowded but not noisy. We got a table by a window and felt apart from all the others who were tending to their own business. We had barely sat down when a half-loaf of sourdough bread arrived, complete with a bottle of good, green, extra-virgin olive oil, cold pressed and rich. "Deeelicious." Then, the antipasto misto per due arrived, and we switched loyalties. Oh, we kept up with the bread and olive oil, all right, but it took second place to the mozzarella on tomato slices, anchovies, crab and shrimp on little toasts and a host of other goodies. It kept us busy for quite awhile.

The room is warm and friendly, filled with locals who seem to know each other and enjoy the whole food experience. There are some tourists and more than a few boat owners in the crowd, with much talk about the day's sailing and fishing adventures.

When we surfaced after the antipasto, it was time for the primi piatti – a couple of dozen pastas to choose from. Phyllis had the fettucini alfredo and Bob had the linguini aglio olio.

There is a long list of secondi piatti, starting with fish like trout, sole or salmon. Also offered are shellfish and chicken baked, broiled or sautéed a half dozen different ways. Too bad we couldn't arrange to be here on the last Thursday of the month, when opera singers from all over the Bay Area congregate here to sing. It is a great night, we understand, with guests often singing along as they feel the urge. One person told us the restaurant was sold out weeks ahead and it was standing room only. Another said not to worry, we could get a reservation up until a few days before the event. We would advise that if you are going to be here on the last Thursday of a month, call well ahead, just to be sure.

- ❑ *75 Jack London Square;* ☎ *510-465-2188.*
- ❑ *Open: 11:30 am-10 pm.*
- ❑ *Prices: Antipasti: bruschetta $4.25, antipasto misto per due $13.50, most $6.25-$8.75; a simple house salad $3.75, others mostly $6.25, a few (crab Louis) $15.25; pastas $9.75-$14.25; entrées $13.50 for melanzana alla parmigiana, to $21.75 for broiled lamb chops with porcini mushrooms.*
- ❑ *Credit cards: All*
- ❑ *Reservations: Wise to call before leaving your hotel. Very busy on weekends.*
- ❑ *Opera Night: Last Thursday of month, 7:30 pm-10 pm. Call for a reservation more than a week ahead.*

- ❏ *Parking: In public lot.*
- ❏ *Directions: Drive over Bay Bridge, off at first exit, right to Jack London Square. By ferry, near the dock in Jack London Square.*

## Kinkaid's

(Seafood)

The dining room has the best location of any eatery in Jack London Square, right on the water. There are big windows along two sides, practically floor-to-ceiling, and the ceiling is high and beamed. All tables have a good view of the channel, the boats going by and the lights at night.

Pan-fried sesame bread is delivered, about the same time as the menus. It is baked daily by Maggiori Brothers Bakery and is toasted just before it gets to your table. Clam chowder is served with a meal or salad and is New England style, thick with clams and with flavor. There is a fillet of sea bass sautéed to a crisp, juicy finish and a Dungeness crab with a Louis dressing that is not at all gloppy, as so often happens. It's served as an entrée salad. The finely balanced jambalaya has tiger prawns, Alaskan sea scallops and andouille sausage that meld right in with the other flavors, especially enhanced by a spicy sauce. The dish is not extremely hot if you're sensitive to that. Even though the cajun fettuccine with chicken is billed as "very spicy," we thought the seasoning was about right, allowing the taste of the chicken to come through and not overwhelming the noodles. On the meaty side, there is a spit-roasted pork loin done over applewood coals, that is served with a creamy mushroom sauce, setting the dish off beautifully.

Our suggestion is to come here for a drink in the evening, perhaps have an appetizer from the long list of bar snacks and take a look at the dining room. If you decide to stay, you can't go wrong.

- ❏ *1 Franklin, Jack London Square;* ☎ *510-835-8600.*
- ❏ *Open: Lunch 11:15 am-2:30 pm, dinner 5 pm-10 pm.*
- ❏ *Prices: Soups and small salads $3.50-$4.95; big salads $5.95-$15.95; pastas $8.95-$13.95; entrées $8.95-$18.95.*
- ❏ *Credit cards: All.*
- ❏ *Reservations: Recommended.*
- ❏ *Parking: Street or public lot.*
- ❏ *Directions: From San Francisco, drive across Bay Bridge, take first Oakland off-ramp, right to Jack London Square. Ferry comes to next dock.*

## *Yoshi's*

(Japanese)

This is a really popular Japanese restaurant, so it is best to call and make reservations. It is a low, one-story building on Claremont Avenue, not far from The Claremont Hotel. The look is very Japanese inside and out, with oversized Japanese fans separating the tables and guests – an attractive way to provide an extra bit of privacy.

The menu is fairly extensive. Dinners and combination dinners run from $13 to $17 and there are a lot of starters and à la carte selections. Everything looked interesting on the menu. Instead of interrogating the waiter endlessly, we took the coward's way out and ordered "Yoshi's Famous Dinner for Two," priced at $35. We soon realized that we had made a good choice. It gave us a taste of many different dishes, a few we knew, most we had never tried before. All were good.

There is a full bar with some local beers and some national brands. A pretty good California wine list is available and priced fairly. Yoshi's Nightclub, in the same building, is a Bay Area institution for live contemporary music. Quite a few of the people having dinner in the restaurant went on to the club. If you are a fan, it is a good idea.

- ❑ *6030 Claremon Ave., Oakland;* ☎ *510-652-9200.*
- ❑ *Internet: http://www.yoshis.com.*
- ❑ *Open: Dinner only. Monday-Friday, 6 pm-9:30 pm; Saturday-Sunday, 6 pm-10 pm.*
- ❑ *Prices: Appetizers and salads $2.75-$6.95; sushis mostly $4.25; most dinners $12-$17.*
- ❑ *Credit cards: AE, Discover, MC, V.*
- ❑ *Reservations: Advisable.*
- ❑ *Parking: Self-parking on their lot, no charge.*
- ❑ *Directions: From San Francisco cross Bay Bridge; in Oakland stay on 24 to Claremont exit, left on Claremont.*

# *Nightlife*

## *The Fat Lady*

🐾 **kitsch** *(kich): art or literature judged to have little or no aesthetic value, esp. when produced to satisfy popular taste.*

The first time we walked into this place, we did not know what to make of it. It was appalling, the ultimate "joint." There were terrible paintings on the walls, all kinds of kitschy junk on display, and an overly ornate, old-fashioned bar. But it turned out to be filled with friendly folks – a warm place to drop in for a sip and a bar snack before going on to dinner somewhere else. We came to regard it as more than a joint, but it sure is kitschy.

The Fat Lady's back bar with massive pillars and mirrors came around The Horn at the turn of the century. For awhile the bar was part of Mike's Pool Hall in San Francisco.

There is a legend that this building, earlier in the century, had a brothel upstairs and that the madame was called The Fat Lady because she was, well, obese.

They serve lunch only. Things like French fried zucchini go for $4.75, Dungeness crab cakes are $9.25, a couple of steaks are $10.50 and $16.50, and the two pastas are $8.95 and $9.95. The menu is heavy on seafood, priced at $10.50 to $13.95. There are plenty of bar snacks in the late afternoon and early evening. Available snacks include garlic bread, little hot dogs, veggies and dips; mostly things that taste good and are terrible for you, but once in a while....

The people lined up at the bar are just about all locals. Everyone seems to know everyone else. If you are looking to get away from the other tourists, you will find sanctuary here. There is a lot of slapping coins down on the bar in match games. We never could tell who won.

❑ *201 Washington St., Oakland;* ☎ *510-465-4996.*
❑ *Open: For lunch Monday-Friday, 11:30 am-2:30 pm; brunch Saturday-Sunday, 9 am-2:30 pm. No dinner, but lots of snacks. Open to midnight.*
❑ *Prices: Pastas from $8.95, seafood and steaks from $10.50.*
❑ *Parking: Street or a public garage across the street.*
❑ *Directions: On the edge of Jack London Square, a block from the ferry dock.*

## Kinkaid's

(Bar snacks and appetizers)

This Jack London Square bar, even on a slow weeknight, is jammed. Some people are waiting for tables in the restaurant through the big archway, but most are on dates. The bar is right on the channel with boats going by and Alameda just across the narrow waterway. It is very much a place for lovers of all ages.

Couples sit at long, high tables and nibble onions and seafood cocktails while drinking. There are small tables next to the tall windows, overlooking the water, where other couples sit close together and hold hands. Plenty of white wine and beer are flowing here. On all tables is a long list of bar snacks and appetizers, starting with shrimp or crab cocktails and going on from there.

There are tall windows and high beamed ceilings. The back bar goes up 20 feet or so, at least two stories. We sit sipping and wondering how they get to those bottles way up there. One bartender says, "Nobody ever orders that stuff." He is called away before we can ask what "stuff" he is referring to.

The bar is very noisy, which can sometimes be handy on a first date when you don't know quite what to say.

- *One Franklin, Jack London Square;* ☎ *510-835-8600.*
- *Open: 11 am-11 pm.*
- *Snacks: Appetizers and bar snacks. Serves snacks after Kincaid's Restaurant closes.*
- *Parking: Street or public lot.*
- *Directions: Drive across Bay Bridge, exit at first Oakland off-ramp, right to Jack London Square. Ferry from San Francisco is one dock over.*

## Yoshi's Night Club

The nightclub is in the same building as Yoshi's popular restaurant. In fact, it is billed in their ads as Yoshi's Japanese Restaurant and World Class Jazz House. That pretty much covers the subject. It's convenient to have dinner at Yoshi's Restaurant before the show, which is why the dining room is crowded so early.

This is one of the most popular spots in the East Bay. Every jazz fan in San Francisco has been here. Even though it's near the University of California at Berkeley, you won't find many college kids here. You will find adult couples around you, because it's good for dates.

It is a deceptive room, wide and thin, with the stage in the middle of one wide wall. It looks smaller than it is, but actually holds almost 250.

Peter White and his group were here the night we went. We were happy to discover that they are masters of fusion music. The audience in the packed room loved it. Most of the time, though, they book pure jazz. If you are a fan, you will be happy you made your way here.

- *6030 Claremont Ave., Oakland;* ☎ *510-652-9200.*
- *Internet: http://www.yoshis.com.*
- *Open: Shows at 8 pm and 10 pm.*
- *Admission: $15 Wednesday and Thursday, $18 Friday, Saturday, Sunday.*
- *Parking: Self-parking in their lot, no charge.*
- *Directions: From San Francisco, cross Bay Bridge; in Oakland stay on 24 to Claremont exit, left on Claremont.*

# *Things to Do*

## *California Canoe & Kayak Rental*

This shop is in Jack London Square, just steps from the channel.

- *409 Water St., Oakland;* ☎ *510-893-7833.*
- *Open: Summer 10 am-8 pm, winter 10 am-7 pm.*
- *Prices: Open-top kayaks, 4 hours $15; canoes and double kayaks $20, including paddles and lifejackets.*

## *Jack London Square*

Almost 20 years ago, this neighborhood between Chinatown and the waterfront, was mostly warehouses, saloons and a haunt of derelects. It had been that way for over 100 years. That was when Jack London, later to be known the world over, was a teenage oyster pirate, who made a precarious living raiding other people's oyster beds. He lived and drank right about here.

Oakland realized that this depressed piece of waterfront property was potentially valuable and cleaned it up. Chic shops and restaurants moved into the old buildings. New buildings were put up, like a nine-screen cinema and a huge bookstore. Now it's one of Oakland's best places for restaurants and for dating couples. There's a hotel by the water here, and you can poke around a Farmer's Market. Stores are usually open Monday-Saturday from 9:30 am-6 pm, Sunday from 12 noon-6 pm.

Below are some events in Jack London Square you might want to drop in on.

Sundays: year-round, 1 pm-5 pm, **Music in the Courtyard**. Free concerts with top Bay Area jazz artists. 10 am-2 pm, **Farmers Market**.

Second Sunday of each month, May to December: **Chefs on the Square**. Local chefs cook up free samples with Farmers Market products.

Call hotline to confirm the events listed above, at ☎ 510-814-6000.

April: **Spring Boat Show**. ☎ 510-452-6262 for dates.

May through October: Wednesday and Saturday, 10 am. Free guided **walking tour** of Oakland waterfront and Jack London Village. Meet in front of Overland House Grill, 101 Broadway, foot of Broadway at Embarcadero.

**July 4th Celebration**: Entertainment, arts and crafts, parade, pop concert, food booths, fireworks at night.

September: **Fall Boat Show.** ☎ 510-452-6262 for dates. **Italian Festa.** Italian food booths, music, dance under the stars.

Late November: **Tree Lighting Ceremony.** Choral groups, lighting a 70-foot tree, music, arts and crafts booths, food booths.

Early December: **Lighted Yacht Parade.** 100 yachts festooned with colorful lights parade the estuary; entertainment, food booths.

## Lake Merritt & Lakeside Park

This is the only salt water lake in the center of an American city, perhaps in any city in the world. As far back as 1870, Lake Merritt was declared America's first state game refuge and today is home to leopard sharks, striped bass, different types of ducks, sea anemones, mussels, herons, egrets and a resident population of Canadian geese. The lake is flushed twice a day by the tidal action of Oakland Inner Harbor and San Francisco Bay.

At night, you will see the lake's 3½-mile perimeter is ringed by a "Necklace of Lights." This was restored in 1987 after 40 years of darkness that began during World War II's blackouts. The 120-acre Lakeside Park is surrounded on three sides by Lake Merritt. You can walk, jog, bicycle, feed the ducks, relax in fragrant gardens, enjoy bird watching or just catch some rays. Many people believe a mermaid lives in the water, so please help take care of the lake.

Boat rentals are easy and no experience is needed, except for sail boats. There is a 50% discount for seniors (60 and up) and for persons with disabilities.

- *Prices: Canoes and rowboats $6 per hour. Kayaks (one person) and pedal boats (two persons) $6 for half-hour $8 per hour. Sailboats (experienced sailors) $6-$12 per hour. Catamaran (experienced) $12 per hour.*
- *Sailing class: For information and prices,* ☎ *510-444-3807.*

### The Merrit Queen

This is a replica of an old Mississippi riverboat. It sails from the Boating Center on weekends and holidays at 1 pm for 30-minute cruises. Cost is $1.50. ☎ 510-444-3807 for reservations.

### Paramount Theater

Built in 1931, when "talkies" were all the rage, the theater is an art deco masterpiece. It was the largest and grandest cinema in the East Bay all through the 1930s and '40s, until the popularity of movies declined with the advent of TV. By 1971, the theater was shuttered, badly in need of repairs. It was saved from the wrecker's ball by the Oakland Symphony, which purchased the property as a future home for a wide variety of performing arts. By 1973, a full and authentic restoration of the theater was accomplished and a rare building had been saved to become a National Historic Landmark.

Guided tours of the 3,000-seat theater take place on the first and third Saturdays of each month, excluding holidays. Tours begin at 10 am at the Box Office entrance on 21st Street at Broadway. Admission is $1. No reservations necessary and cameras are allowed.

❑ *2025 Broadway, Oakland;* ☎ *510-465-6400.*
❑ *Parking: Street or Telegraph Plaza Garage, Telegraph Avenue between 21st and 22nd streets.*

## *Preservation Park*

Here you will find 16 restored Victorian houses, built on two richly landscaped blocks. Grouped around an 1890s fountain, these were the stately homes of prominent Oakland families. This is an easy stroll for a peek at how life was lived by the upper *clahses* in the good old days. There is a free walking tour of Preservation Park with a docent – a good way to learn much more about what you are seeing.

❑ *13th Street at Martin Luther King, Jr. Way., Oakland;* ☎ *510-874-7580.*
❑ *Walking Tour: Wednesday and Saturday, 10 am, May through October. Reservations for walking tour:* ☎ *510-238-3234.*
❑ *Parking: On street on Martin Luther King Jr. Way or City Center Garage. Enter garage from 11th or 14th streets between Broadway and Clay.*

## *Redwood Regional Park*

On Redwood Road, just a few miles over the ridge from downtown Oakland, is a hidden redwood forest – almost 2,000 acres with evergreens, chaparral and grasslands, as well as 150-foot coast redwoods (*Sequoia sempervirens*). Also to be seen is the rare golden eagle, deer, raccoons and rabbits. There was originally a huge stand of redwoods that covered this whole area and more. Between 1840 and 1860, a dozen sawmills sprang up here. The first growth trees were so large that it was necessary to build platforms all around the base to support the loggers as they cut into the virgin wood. The trees here now have grown since that time.

There is hiking, bicycling on special trails, horseback riding, archery and picnicking. Access is good for disabled persons. ☎ 510-636-1684.

## *Walking Tours*

Free guided walking tours through historic downtown streets and unique neighborhoods are led by volunteers. Choose the walk(s) that most interest you and just show up. No reservations needed. See map for locations. 24-hour hotline: ☎ 510-238-3234. Oakland Convention & Visitors Authority: ☎ 510-839-9000.

**1. Old Oakland:** This area was the 1870s business district, with many grand old brick buildings that have been restored. Meet in front of Ratto's International Grocers, 821 Washington Street. Park at Oakland Convention Center, entering garage at 11th and Clay streets.

**2. City Center:** This high-rise district dates back to the 1910s. Meet in front of Oakland's Historic City Hall, #1 City Hall Plaza. Park at City Center Garage. Enter on 11th or 14th street, between Broadway and Clay.

**3. Uptown to Lake:** Tour includes uptown Oakland, a shopping district of the 1930s and the Paramount Theater. Meet in front of the Paramount, 2025 Broadway. Park at Telegraph Plaza Garage, Telegraph Avenue between 21st and 22nd streets.

**4. Preservation Park:** See hotline above.

**5. Oakland Chinatown:** Tour the historic Chinese regional center of shops, restaurants and cultural institutions. This is the fifth largest Chinatown in the US. Meet at Pacific Renaissance Plaza Fountain, 9th and Webster streets. Park at Pacific Renaissance Garage. Enter on Webster or Franklin street, between 9th and 11th streets.

**6. Jack London Waterfront:** See hotline above.

**7. Churches and Temples:** Discover Oakland's historic places of worship, their history and architecture. Meet in front of the First Presbyterian Church, 27th and Broadway. Parking at street meters.

You can also undertake a self-guided scenic tour on foot, bicycle or by car. The tour is comprised of 52 primary destinations which are starting points for other attractions. Contact ☎ 510-238-3234 (hotline) or 510-839-9000.

# *Berkeley*

❦ *The university has become the multiversity.*

Clark Kerr, Chancellor, University of California, 1952-58

In 1896, Theresa Jacquemine marched into the office of the Alameda County Recorder, read him the 14th Amendment and demanded that she be registered to vote. Cowed by the determined lady, the Recorder allowed her to do so. The District Attorney later invalidated the deed on the grounds that the Supreme Court disagreed with her peculiar interpretation of the amendment. Nevertheless, Mrs. Jacquemine was the first woman registered to vote in California. Of course, the feisty Theresa was a resident of Berkeley.

When most people think of Berkeley, they probably remember the Free Speech Movement of the 1960s, the protests and the marches that led the way for the anti-Vietnam War uprising in universities all over the country. But that was then. How about now? Fear not, Berkeley is still a determinedly progressive town, with nearly seven registered Democrats for each registered Republican. It is home to Pulitzer Prize winners, Nobel laureates and MacArthur fellows, and hosts one of the country's great places of learning, the University of California.

As for the name, the story goes that a century ago the trustees of the College of California, a tiny Oakland-based institution, were examining a piece of property they had bought on an unnamed hill. This was where they planned to move the college. As they gazed out over the Bay, with ships coming from or going to all parts of the world, one of the trustees quoted the final stanza of what seemed to be an apt poem,

❦ *Westward the course of empire takes its way;*
*The four first acts already past,*
*A fifth shall close the drama of the day;*
*Time's noblest offspring is the last.*

"Who wrote that? Was it Berkeley?" one of the other trustees asked. The quoter said it was, and then suggested that Berkeley sounded like a good name for a college town. The name was adopted unanimously at the next trustees meeting. Or, so they say.

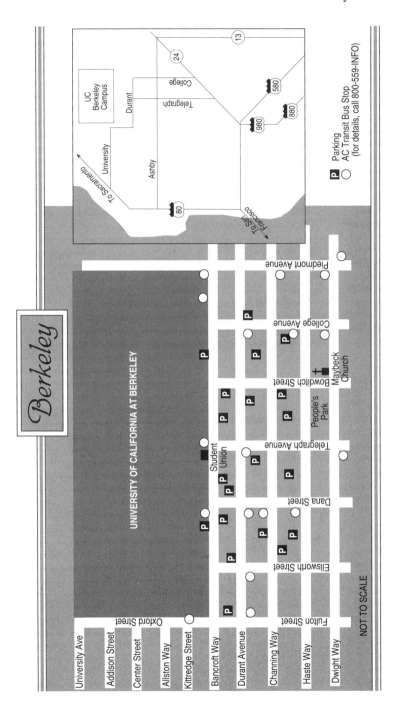

# *Inns*

## ♥ *Claremont Resort & Spa*

It is hard to believe now, but for 20 years this big, sprawling, classic white building on a hill, though a famous hotel, never served as much as a glass of wine to a guest, until a young woman took a hand. This "sprawling Mediterranean hostelry" was built in 1915 at the time of the Panama-Pacific Exposition. During those early years, Claude Gillum started as a Chief Clerk at the hotel. He worked his way up to Manager and saved enough money so that he and Mrs. Gillum could buy it in 1937 for $250,000, refurbishing it from the ground up. That is the Claremont we know today. It was named after the area, which was called Claremont long before the hotel came into being.

This hotel was one of the very few in the San Francisco area that was built without a bar because of a state law banning the sale of alcoholic beverages within a mile of the University. But one day, a female student decided to measure the distance from the University to the hotel. She found that the hotel's entrance was a few feet more than one mile away. For her trouble, the hotel awarded her free drinks for life.

*Claremont Resort & Spa.*

While the Claremont uses a Berkeley address for reservations, it attached itself to Oakland many years ago. Now both cities claim it and neither would let anything happen to it. When a fire a few years ago devastated hillside Oakland, the residents of homes around the Claremont felt perfectly safe because of all the fire trucks huddled protectively around the hotel. And there is so much wood in the building, the fear has been that if the Claremont ever burned, the fire would sweep all the way down through Oakland to the Bay.

We were in room 534. It is called a suite, although it is really one big room. But, what a room! The front wall is a large 10-foot-wide bay with a wide, thick-cushioned window seat. The rest of the wall is a huge window looking out over Oakland, the Bay and San Francisco. An added touch is the high quality telescope on a tripod standing in the window, pointing out at that fabulous view.

We left the curtains open, day and night. At night, we lay in a fully canopied, four-poster, king-size bed and looked out at the lights of Oakland and over the Bay at the lights sparkling on San Francisco's hills and towers.

Also in the large room is a tall armoire, with a TV and VCR concealed inside, space for an ice bucket and a few glasses, complimentary bottles of Calistoga water and drawers for clothes. The desk holds a big bouquet of fresh flowers. The walls are papered in a light floral pattern and the floor is thickly carpeted in a warm beige. The carpet extends through the dressing room, which has a large double closet and a long double sink with a wall-length mirror. Through a door is the toilet, bidet and tub/shower. This room has a skylight that keeps it bright. There are five rooms in the hotel like this, but this is the only one with a telescope. Every room has a phone with voice mail, TV plus pay TV movies on command, coffee-maker, hair dryer, iron, ironing board and safe. The Standard rooms are either Hill View or Bay View. There is little difference in price between them. Ask for Bayside. They are smaller than our suite was, but bright and very comfortable.

There are five true suites with a bedroom and sitting room. The Tower Suite, reached via a private staircase from the top floor hallway, is perhaps the most romantic. Most of the 360° views can be seen from the bed. But that is not all. Another stairway leads to the top of the Bell Tower. There is a sauna just for this room, with wooden benches and hot rocks on which you throw water to produce steam.

Ask for a romantic breakfast to be served in your room on lap tables, with a rose for your loved one (either loved one). Orange juice, grapefruit juice, fresh fruit and berries, assorted breakfast pastries, omelets, eggs Benedict, waffles, pancakes, smoked salmon on a toasted bagel or French toast, coffee and tea make up the delicious breakfast menu. Claremont private label California champagne tops it off.

- ❑ *41 Tunnel Road, Berkeley, CA 94705;*
  ☎ *800-551-7266, 510-843-3000, fax 510-848-6208.*
- ❑ *Rooms: 279, no two alike, even Standard rooms are all different.*
- ❑ *Rates: $199-$675.*
- ❑ *Credit cards: All major.*
- ❑ *Reservations: Recommended.*
- ❑ *Breakfast: The romantic breakfast served in the room is $34 per couple, champagne included.*
- ❑ *Amenities: Spa, massages, tennis, swimming pool, room service 6:30 am-midnight. In-room amenities include hair dryer, coffee-maker, iron, ironing board and safe.*
- ❑ *Dining: There are four restaurants. Pavilion for "casual elegance." Presto Café for creative California sandwiches, salads and soups, fresh-baked pastries. The Bayview Café is poolside, with sandwiches and salads. The Gallery Bar has appetizers, light dinners, cappuccino and espresso.*
- ❑ *Night Life: Terrace Lounge, live music, dancing., Gallery Bar.*
- ❑ *Handicapped accessible: Yes.*
- ❑ *Smoking: Two floors.*
- ❑ *Children: Yes.*
- ❑ *Pets: No.*
- ❑ *Parking: On premises.*

## *M's Bed & Breakfast*

This is a tall, narrow old house, built in 1911, on a curving residential street up in the hills. It started as a brown shingle home. After a fire in 1927, repairs turned it into an English Tudor. Although it looks rather small from the street, it cascades down the hillside in back.

The owner is Mary Leggett, who has had the house for 37 years. She is an incredibly energetic woman, forthcoming with conversation, information, directions and help of any kind. You will quickly learn to trust her about everything.

There is a hot tub out on the deck, along with a fire pit and tables and chairs where guests can sit with wine and enjoy the great view of San Francisco and the Bay. The dining room, with its shining hardwood floor, is where breakfast is served on a beautiful walnut table. The living room, where it seems natural to congregate after a day of sightseeing, draws guests with a fireplace, bar and an old-fashioned pump organ. You are free to play it, if you can. There is a small sitting room upstairs for everyone to use.

A big upstairs bedroom features a four-poster queen-size bed and a very high highboy. Three windows afford a view from the bed.

A small but nice bathroom has a shower, no tub. A second room has a low queen-size bed, a desk and lots of books. It's plain, with ordinary furniture. The third room is a half-flight of stairs farther up and is bright, with windows on three sides. It is definitely not fancy, just comfortable. These two rooms share a bathroom with a big jacuzzi and lots of plants. Staying here is like staying in a friend's home. It is a warm, nice place with portraits of Mary's daughters on the walls of the staircase. Family is what it's all about.

- 262 *Hillcrest Road, Berkeley, CA 94705;* ☎ *510-654-0648.*
- *Rooms: Three.*
- *Bathrooms: Two (two rooms share).*
- *Rates: $65-$75, $75-$95, $95-$110, depending on season and holidays.*
- *Credit cards: None.*
- *Reservations: Necessary.*
- *Minimum stay: Prefers longer than one night.*
- *Breakfast: Continental.*
- *Wine: "Please bring your own."*
- *Handicapped accessible: No, steep stairs.*
- *Smoking: No.*
- *Children: Yes.*
- *Pets: No, absolutely.*
- *Parking: Street.*
- *Directions: She will send a map when you send a deposit.*
- *Walking distance: This is the Upper Rockridge neighborhood, three long blocks to The Claremont Resort, three minutes to downtown Berkeley. Close to College Avenue for shopping.*

## *Restaurants*

Berkeley has a certain panache when it comes to food. This is a town where chains like McDonalds are not allowed. Catsup is another rarity. If you order coffee in a home-grown fast-food joint, it is sure to come in a paper cup. Styrofoam has been banned in Berkeley for almost 10 years.

### ♥ *The Pavilion in The Claremont*

(American fare)

A wonderful room to eat is the Pavilion. It runs along the side of the Claremont, with a view of the Golden Gate Bridge, San Francisco and down the South Bay.

When the hotel was built in 1915, this was a wide porch where people sat in a long row of low rocking chairs and rocked contentedly as they took in the scenery. It was enclosed and became this great room, bright and lovely. In the 1930s, Tommy Dorsey and later Lawrence Welk broadcast from here. Now the walls are pink and the tablecloths green and the view is even better at night when the lights come on all over the Bay Area. This is Oakland and Berkeley's favorite eating place, yet it is not overpriced. You can even order half-glasses of wine.

The selections for those on special diets look good, taste fine and cut the caloric percentage way down. The Claremont Hotel's spa nutritionist, Linda Prout, works with the chef on special dishes.

While all the food we have had at the Claremont over the years has been good, ranging from room service to a salad at the Presto Café or a snack at the Gallery Bar, there is an occasional slip-up. At least, some people may regard it as that. At our last lunch here, Phyllis had a Dungeness crab salad, which she raved about. Bob had a Niçoise salad and muttered something about the habit some chefs have of printing the name of a well-known dish on the menu and then putting something different onto the table. "If the chef wants to invent his own salad, that's perfectly all right. But don't call it a Niçoise salad if you are going to deliver an entire grilled filet of fish." Even though the "salad" was good, he was not happy. However, he did eat all of it. The Dungeness crab was delicious and came as ordered. Phyllis was happy.

At dinner another night, there was a marinated Portobello mushroom with sun-dried tomatoes appetizer, served with a creamy goat cheese, which brought out the earthy flavor of the mushroom. Mesclun salad, with its honey-grapefruit vinaigrette, was a refreshing change from the usual oil and vinegar concoction. Try ordering rack of lamb, medium well, and you will find it comes as ordered. It will not be blood rare as often happens, but with just a trace of pink showing. It will be juicy and taste as if it never saw the inside of a freezer. One of the several spa entrées is a seared ahi tuna that tastes fresh and not at all dietetic. That's a relief.

- ❑ *41 Tunnel Road, Berkeley; ☎ 510-843-3000, 800-551-7266.*
- ❑ *Open: Breakfast 6:30 am-10 am; lunch 11:30 am-2:30 pm; dinner 6 pm-9 pm.*
- ❑ *Prices: Appetizers mostly $8, entrées $20-$23.*
- ❑ *Credit cards: All major.*
- ❑ *Reservations: Recommended.*
- ❑ *Parking: Valet or self-parking.*

## Triple Rock Brewery

(Brew pub)

Triple Rock is a brew pub that brothers John and Reid Martin started over 10 years ago as one of the first micro-breweries in California. It still maintains its deliberately basic decor in a 1920s yellow brick building. There is a jukebox and shuffleboard table.

There are big windows looking into the adjoining room where the stainless steel brewing equipment is turning out their own fine ales and stout. Usually eight to 12 house brews are on tap.

The menu is likewise deliberately kept simple. When it comes to food, "simple" in the Berkeley sense does not translate easily. There are soups, salads, sandwiches and always two kinds of chili. You are likely to find sweet onion and garlic mayonnaise on those sandwiches, and jalapeno peppers might turn up with the lamb.

❑ *1920 Shattuck Ave., Berkeley;* ☎ *510-843-2739.*
❑ *Open: Sunday-Wednesday 11:30 am-12:30 am, Thursday-Saturday 11:30 am-1:30 am. Kitchen is open until midnight for food.*

# Nightlife

## Terrace Lounge in The Claremont

We were here recently. The band was between sets and we ordered drinks. We looked out at the fabulous view across the Bay. Then the music started and we immediately thought, this is a really great place for dancing – a special kind of dancing. As soon as the five-piece band and the singer burst into a hard-driving 1930s-40s rhythm number, half the couples got up to jitterbug! The majority of dancers were obviously born way after that era went the way of the Black Bottom. It was tremendous fun that night, whether you had jitterbugged before or not. It turns out that the entertainment varies, practically from week to week. It could be rock, swing, reggae or jazz. Phone ahead, or just go up to the Claremont and take your chances. It can't be bad.

❑ *41 Tunnel Road, Berkeley;* ☎ *510-843-3000.*
❑ *Open: Daily, 11:30 am-2 am; Sunday, piano, 6 pm-10 pm; Thursday-Saturday, piano, 6 pm-9 pm, or longer, depending on when the band starts; live band to 2 am. No entertainment Monday-Wednesday.*

# Things to Do

## Berkeley Certified Farmer's Market

Some of the chefs from the East Bay's best restaurants shop here. It is fun to wander around the stalls and see the gorgeous fruits and vegetables. They are all fresh, of course, and lots of produce is organic. You might buy one or two carrots or a tomato and find out what vegetables are supposed to taste like. Here is a suggestion.

Head first for **Uprisings Bakery**, a Berkeley collective, which sells fresh-baked cookies and muffins. Then, you can be munching something delicious while you wander. The market takes place on Saturday from 10 am-2 pm, on Center Street and Martin Luther King, Jr. Way. It is also held Tuesday from 2 pm-7 pm on Derby St. at Martin Luther King, Jr. Way.

## Good Vibrations

"1996's Sexiest Bridal Registry" is here. To quote, "Forget the toasters, blenders and china patterns. This year's sophisticated bride has erotic toys, books and videos on her mind."

If you are one of those sophisticated brides, or singles, or old-marrieds, you may be interested in Good Vibrations. This is a branch of the store in San Francisco (see page 97), and basically has the same items on display and for sale. These include massage oil, board games just for couples, videos (instructional and just fun), books to further the sexual education, audio tapes to while away the long drive home. How about a CD of *Anne Hosper's Ultimate Sex Guide*?

Rebecca Suzanne told us that the only difference between the two stores is that this one's customers tend to be slightly younger and more books are sold here. That is not surprising since this is Berkeley, the university town. The largest percentage of customers are heterosexual women under 40 (60%), but you will see lots of couples and a few single men. The atmosphere is kept at a comfort level for everyone. You can request a catalogue to see if what they have for sale is vibrating in rhythm with your vibes, by calling 800-BUY-VIBE.

❑ *2504 San Pablo Ave., Berkeley;* ☎ *510-841-8987.*
❑ *Open: 11 am - 7 pm, seven days; extended hours near Valentine's Day.*

## Telegraph Avenue

This is an area just off the University of California campus. It's constantly alive with people listening to music, reading

*Telegraph Avenue.*

books, eating food and making conversation.

Within this compact strip there are 20 bookstores holding more than 1,000,000 books. This makes it one of the best places for book browsing in the world. The largest selection of music stores in the Bay Area is right here. You'll hear the beat of jazz, pop, rap, soul, country, blue grass, even classical as you walk down the street. There are coffee houses and cafés everywhere – great places to sit on a patio and sip a cappuccino as a respite from all that walking. You will find hand-crafted goods in quaint boutiques and artists selling their wares on the street.

For more information, call the **Berkeley Convention and Visitors Bureau and Visitors Center** at ☎ 510-549-7040.

## *Transportation*

| | |
|---|---|
| BART (Bay Area Rapid Transit) | ☎ 510-465-BART. |
| AC Transit (bus lines) | ☎ 510-839-2882. |
| Ferries (Jack London Square) | ☎ 510-839-9000. |
| AMTRAK | ☎ 800-USA-RAIL. |
| Oakland International Airport | ☎ 510-577-4000. |
| San Francisco International Airport | ☎ 415-876-2421. |

# Marin County

Several hundred thousand of those who work in the City during the day retire to sleep at night just across the Golden Gate Bridge. They will tell you that they've chosen this place to live because of the climate, though much of Marin's climate is about the same as San Francisco's. Or they simply prefer to live in the country. More people are moving here all the time.

From San Francisco, those big hills that anchor the other end of the Golden Gate Bridge are Marin. Those are the Headlands. The span of the bridge that is actually over water is less than a half-mile. The freeway takes only a few minutes more to zip through the Headlands. By now you're already in Sausalito, a town oriented completely to the water. Across Richardson Bay on the right is Tiburon, wealthy and residential, on its own peninsula. Going on north, are inland towns like Mill Valley and San Rafael. You will discover that about Marin. Although its highest point is only 2,571 feet, and that's only one peak, Mt. Tamalpais, much of the rest is made up of lesser mountains. The towns are in the valleys between them and on their slopes at the water's edge. Each town, separated from the others, has its own very distinctive personality.

Across the mountains, toward the coast, everything is different. There are fewer people and much more room. A solid 40% of Marin is dedicated to parks, open space and permanently preserved agricultural land. Much of that is on the west side, with small clusters of people in places like Olema, Inverness and Point Reyes Station.

Marin is actually where California's recorded history begins. Of course, Pomo and coastal Miwok Indians have been here for perhaps 10,000 years. Then, in 1579, Sir Francis Drake landed the *Golden Hinde* at what is now Drake's Bay in Point Reyes National Seashore for repairs. He went away after a month and everyone left the Indians in peace and happiness for two more centuries. Then came the Spanish, exploring northward, and there went the neighborhood.

East Marin, starting with Sausalito, is by far the most popular destination for day-trippers and most visitors. Muir Woods is a national treasure, with ancient redwood groves. In the east are intriguing waterfront villages like Sausalito and Tiburon. But West Marin, across the mountains, has a more spectacular coastline and 65,000 acres of protected wilderness. Most people who drive over to spend a few hours, or those couples who stay a night or two, like it very much. The rest love it.

## Things to Do

**Walking and Hiking:** Call the **Visitors Bureau** for information and maps. ☎ 415-472-7470.

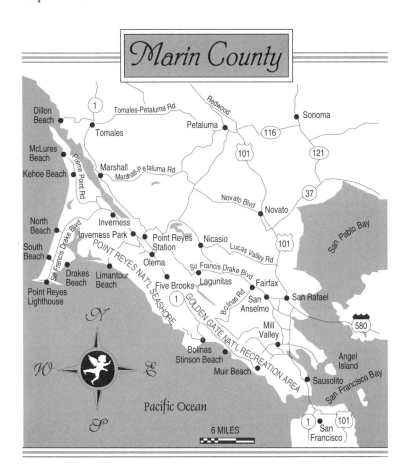

**Bike Trails:** Call the Marin County Department of Parks for a map of **Open Space trails,** ☎ 415-499-6387. Call the Marin Municipal Water District for a map of **trails in the watershed,** ☎ 415-459-0888. Call the Marin Headlands Visitors Center for a map of **unpaved trails** in Marin Headlands, ☎ 415-331-1540.

## *How to Get Here*

From wherever you are in San Francisco, go to Van Ness Avenue and turn east, toward the Bay. Go to Lombard Street, turning left onto Lombard until you see signs, "To Golden Gate Bridge." Follow the signs. No toll is charged going northbound, but $2 is charged southbound.

**The Airporter Bus** from San Francisco Airport may be reached at ☎ 415-673-2432. **Gray Line Tours** from San Francisco are at ☎ 415-558-7373. **Ferries** are available from the Ferry Building and Pier 39. Public **buses** in Marin depart from the ferry dock to most major places. Phone Golden Gate Transit at ☎ 415-455-2000. See Sausalito, Tiburon and Larkspur for ferry service to those places.

## *Weather*

As a general rule, the farther north you go from the Golden Gate, the warmer it is. Mill Valley is warmer than Sausalito and San Rafael is warmer than Mill Valley. It also gets progressively more sunny. This rule does not hold true for the coastal region, which is consistently foggier and wetter.

The coastal weather in West Marin is pretty consistent. It might be foggy along the beaches and coastal part of Point Reyes National Seashore, while the sun is shining on the valley that Olema and Pt. Reyes Station share with Tomales Bay. That is about the extent of the inconsistencies.

But East Marin is a welter of micro-climates. As a general rule, if the inn where you are staying, or the place where you are laying out a picnic has a valley to the west of it you will be in the path of any fog that comes over from the coast. If you are protected by a mountain, you will literally be in the clear. We are talking small distances here. One block can be fogged in and the next block may be sunny and warm.

# East Marin

As soon as you roll or walk off the Golden Gate Bridge, you are in a gentle land. Once it was rural and the farther parts still are. But, all the flat lands are now thoroughly suburbia. Of course, there is not much flat over here. The green mountains and blue waters of the Bay are what gives this part of Marin much of its character. We deal with the towns of East Marin in the order that you will come to them if you drive over from San Francisco. We begin with Sausalito and progress through Mill Valley, Tiburon/Belvedere, Larkspur, San Rafael and Novato.

## Sausalito

This place was first called Lewan Helowah by the Coast Miwok Indians, who lived here 3,000 years ago. Scratch almost anywhere in Sausalito and beneath the surface you are likely to turn up stone tools or arrow points. In 1769, scouts from the Portola expedition touched base briefly and called it Saucito, which means "small willow trees." Six years later, Captain Juan Manuel de Ayala showed up on the "San Carlos" and renamed it Saucelito, "place of the little willows."

The first English-speaking resident was Captain John Reed, who arrived in 1826. He ran a ferryboat from Saucelito to San Francisco – still called Yerba Buena in those days. Along came Captain William A Richardson, the one who really got things going locally. He arrived as mate of the whaler *Orion* and stayed when the ship sailed away. Eventually, he owned three schooners, was named Captain of the Port of Yerba Buena, was awarded the Saucelito Rancho and gave his name to the bay in front of the little nautical town. He is probably also the one who changed the spelling of the name. When he was using his ships to supply San Francisco with fresh water from Marin's springs, he did it through his Sausalito Water Works.

The port was bustling and an important stop during the Gold Rush. Ship Captains liked to drop anchor here, hoping their crews would be less likely to run off to the diggings than they would from San Francisco.

A few decades later, the waterfront was bustling with Italian and Portuguese fishermen who netted salmon, bass, herring and shrimp in the bay. By the 1890s, some of the wealthy from San

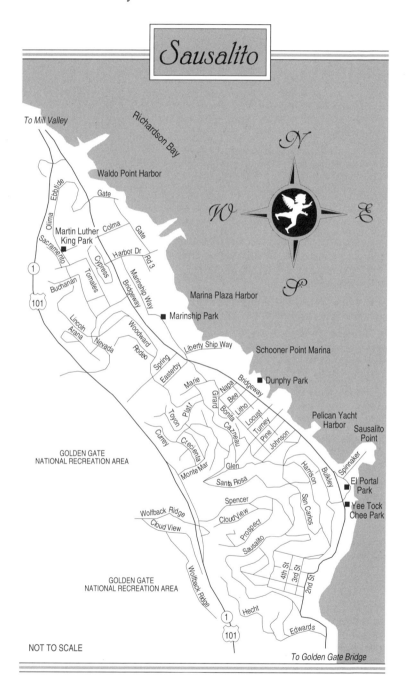

Sausalito

To Mill Valley

Richardson Bay

Waldo Point Harbor

Ebbtide

Olima

Gate

Colma

Martin Luther
King Park

Sacramento

Cypress

Gate

Harbor Dr

Rd 3

Marinship Way

1

101

Buchanan

Tomales

Bridgeway

Marina Plaza Harbor

■ Marinship Park

Lincoln

Arana

Nevada

Woodward

Rodeo

Liberty Ship Way

Schooner Point Marina

Spring

Easterby

Marie

Bridgeway

■ Dunphy Park

Napa

Bee

Litho

Locust

Pelican Yacht
Harbor

Sausalito
Point

Platt

Toyon

Girard

Bonita

Cazneau

Turney

Pine

Johnson

GOLDEN GATE
NATIONAL RECREATION AREA

Currey

Crecienta

Monte Mar

Glen

Harrison

Bulkley

Spinnaker

■ El Portal
   Park

Santa Rosa

San Carlos

■ Yee Tock
   Chee Park

Spencer

Cloud View

Prospect

Wolfback Ridge

Cloud View

Sausalito

4th St

3rd St

2nd St

GOLDEN GATE
NATIONAL RECREATION AREA

Wolfback Ridge

1

101

Hecht

Edwards

NOT TO SCALE

To Golden Gate Bridge

Francisco were building here. William Randolph Hearst, for one, moved into a grand mansion called Sea Point on the hillside. Of course, any of us who have seen *Citizen Kane* would expect nothing less than grandeur. Besides William Randolph, the house had a controversial female resident (not Marion Davies – he did not meet her until 1918). This was when Hearst was much younger and still honing his talents in the business of keeping mistresses. He met the "lovely and soft-spoken" Tessie Powers when he was a student at Harvard and she was a waitress in a Cambridge café. When he moved to Sausalito, he brought Tessie with him. There was quite a bit of controversy about it. Quiet mistress-keeping was fairly common among the wealthy of the Bay Area from the 1850s on, but William Randolph never gave a damn about public opinion. He was open and public about Tessie. Eventually his very proper mother, the stern and puritanical Phoebe Apperson Hearst, arrived on the scene with a hefty cash settlement to get Tessie out of Sea Point and out of her son's life. The remains of Sea Point are still to be seen, a bit up the hill, just south of the intersection of Bridgeway and Princess.

The town was not just about proper living. There were plenty of saloons, bordellos and gambling halls here. They made a mint whenever San Francisco gave in to a feeling of morality and cracked down on sin. That state of happy affairs went on until the good women formed the Sausalito Womens' Club in 1913 and forced the town to clean up its act.

When Prohibition arrived, Sausalito thrived once more. Baby Face Nelson had a bootlegging operation in the old Silva Mansion, smuggling Canadian whiskey to San Francisco. Some say Pretty Boy Floyd, as a cover for his real activities, tended bar at the Walhalla, then Marin's oldest continuously operated saloon. It was later owned by former San Francisco madame and Sausalito mayor, Sally Stanford.

North Sausalito became one vast shipbuilding yard during World War II. A full 93 Liberty ships and T-2s were put together there. Those big, old warehouses between Bridgeway and the bayfront are what's left from that era.

In the 1960s, writers, artists and just plain citizens attracted to casual, tolerant, waterfront-oriented living, moved into some of the warehouses. They also made their homes in a collection of abandoned tugboats, barges and whatever would float, even if only barely, and set up a unique community of houseboat dwellers. A reduced version is still to be seen in North Sausalito. This community is now augmented by some upscale residents and always threatened by city officials and real estate developers who would like to convert the waterfront into expensive real estate and private marinas. There are still plenty of artists, writers and crafts people. The annual Sausalito Art Festival attracts 50,000 over Labor Day Weekend.

## Sally Stanford

Sally was one of the town's most famous modern figures. Over the years in her pre-Sausalito days, she had many careers and a dozen names. She seems to have ended up as Sally Stanford on a whim. She first came to major notice during the 1930s and 1940s, when she was the proprietess of one of San Francisco's finest bordellos. The Pine Street address of her sporting house was well known to the carriage trade. It was frequented by Pacific Heights playboys, powerful politicians and Montgomery Street CEOs. Of course, it was a known address to every taxi driver and cop in San Francisco. A reform movement in 1949 brought enough heat to bear to make Sally close down and move to Sausalito, where she bought the Walhalla on Bridgeway Street. The respectable citizens of Sausalito were worried that Sally was merely shifting her base of operations and intended to resume her old business. She surprised everyone. Sally cleaned up the place, filled it with plush Victorian furniture, brought in the best chefs, changed the name to Valhalla and opened one of Sausalito's finest restaurants. She may have gone straight, but she remained outspoken and down-to-earth. In 1972, she was elected to the city council and when, in 1976, she was elected Mayor, newspapers all over the country broke out with stories about "Madam Mayor."

Sally died in 1982, much admired. Just to the side of the ferry dock, where every arriving visitor sees it, is a double drinking fountain erected by the people of Sausalito in memory of Sally and her beloved dog, Leland. Around the waist-high fountain is the inscription, "Have a drink on Sally." Closer to the ground on the dog-high fountain it says, "Have a drink on Leland."

The ferries from San Francisco dock in the middle of town. Sally Stanford's and Leland's drinking fountains are just to your left as you step off the ferry. The little park in front of you is Plaza de Vina Del Mar Park, named in honor of Sausalito's sister city in Chile. The vigorous fountain and two 14-foot statues of elephants are relics of San Franisco's Panama-Pacific Exposition of 1915.

Phone the **Sausalito Visitors Bureau** for more information at ☎ 415-332-0505.

# *Inns*

## *Alta Mira Hotel*

When we drove up the curving street, we saw a bride in a long, white gown and her groom. They both looked solemn, posing for pictures in front of a little, shingled church across the street from Alta Mira. We heard the pleasant sounds of a steel band and laughter as we pulled into the hotel's entrance. A wedding reception following a different ceremony was in full swing in the garden. It somehow seemed fitting that we had booked the honeymoon suite. A minutes later, we were shown to #38, a two-bedroom honeymoon suite, one of four. Wait a minute – two bedrooms? After a few lame mother-in-law jokes, we found that there is a good reason for it. Lots of people these days get married for the second or third time and bring along their kids. That's who the second bedroom is for.

This "cottage" is an 1890s Queen Anne Victorian house and our living room had the typical corner curved bay windows. A round table and comfortable chairs completed the picture. Not being very hungry, we ordered dinner in. Room service brought huge bowls of mushroom and potato leek soup. It was tasty and we spooned away, enjoying the lights of Sausalito below and the Bay beyond.

The next morning, we appreciated the sunshine and the views from Alta Mira's restaurant. Since Alta Mira is a hotel, breakfast is not included. When comparing prices of inns and B&Bs (where breakfast is included) and hotels (where it isn't), add about $15 to hotel rates for a continental breakfast for two or $20-$40 for a full breakfast. We enjoyed eggs "Alta Mira" (really Benedict) and French toast, nevertheless.

There are 14 rooms in the main building and 14 suites in four cottages spread over the grounds. The main building's rooms do not have fireplaces, but the cottages do. All of the standard rooms in the main building have private balconies and great views. The cottage rooms are all different. One room, #22, is atypical because its charming bedroom is upstairs and the sitting room downstairs. For that reason, it is in great demand.

We had lunch with Susan Satterthwaite, the manager, under the friendly eye of Joseph Antoun, the maitre d'. We asked her about rumors of ghosts here. She did not poo-poo the idea. "I have heard of something in the main building," she said. "But, since I haven't experienced anything myself...." She shrugged and looked at Joseph, who also shrugged. Who were we to argue?

- *125 Bulkley Ave., Sausalito, CA 94965;* ☎ *415-331-1350, fax 415-331-3862.*
- *Rooms: 35.*
- *Rates: $80-$209*
- *Credit cards: All.*
- *Reservations: Recommended.*
- *Minimum stay: May-October, two nights on weekends.*
- *Handicapped accessible: Very limited; some cottages are OK, but it is hilly and there are steps.*
- *Children: Yes.*
- *Pets: No.*
- *Parking: Self-park in lot or valet.*

## ♥ Casa Madrona

At first glance, the Madrona looks like a set of child's baby blue blocks piled helter-skelter on top of one another. But it all adds up, as we found out, to a charming and comfortable place to stay in what is probably the Bay Area's most delightful seaside town. Actually, we had stayed here about 10 years ago. After checking in on the ground floor, we remembered that the original 19th-century, three-story house is up the hill above it all. That old house was the inn until a few years ago. It is still much as it was. An elevator goes partway up the hillside, or you could drive up via a back street. Now, a valet will take your car and park it for you down here on Bridgeway.

*Casa Madrona, Sausalito.*

The parlor, where we had wine and cheese all those years ago, seems exactly the same. It has high ceilings (at least 14 feet), a fireplace, bookshelves, sofa and easy chairs. The front windows look out on the Bay and the yachts crowding the marina. Just outside the windows is the porch. Here, you can sip your wine and tear at your bread and cheese while you lounge in wicker furniture on a porch that sags down at an angle. There is a railing wide enough to sit on at the edge and a great view.

The rooms are all different, mostly smallish, with a few suites available. All are done up charmingly. This time, ours was the Renoir Room. It has a high brass bed, a fireplace, a really comfortable window seat and our own private deck over the bay. The eye-catching feature is the claw-footed, cast iron bathtub, perched up a few steps so a bather can look right across the room and out the windows across Richardson Bay. On the platform, along with the center-stage tub, is an equally old-fashioned pedestal sink, an armoire and a modern minibar-refrigerator with enough space to store a sandwich or two of your own. The shower and toilet are in another room.

Although the elevator has five stops, there are actually at least twice that many levels on the hillside. As a result, stairways go off at sudden angles. Rose Chalet, a suite about halfway up the hill, has a small bedroom with a high queen-size bed on a level with the full windows. Walls are rusty red and there is a fireplace, private deck, wet bar and minibar. Lots of honeymooners stay here and many request it when they return.

Lord Ashley's Lookout has its bedroom perched in an Italianate Victorian bay window nook. Double bed, fireplace, Lord and Lady Ashley in portraits over the bed, private deck, It all adds up to an intimate nest.

Le Petit Boudoir is very cozy, with a plush green carpet and delightful little sitting area. Each of the 36 rooms and suites is different, but these fairly well describe what you can expect. You can also expect from every room a splendid view of a charming seaside town that mirrors a Mediterranean fishing village more than anyplace else in the Bay Area.

- *801 Bridgeway, Sausalito, CA 94965;*
  ☎ *415-331-5888, 800-567-9524, fax 415-332-2537.*
- *Web site: www.casam.com.*
- *Rooms: 36.*
- *Rates: $138-$205, suites $225-$260. MAP: three-course dinner from Mikayla's for two, anything on menu, add $55 (does not include wine, tax, tip).*
- *Reservations: Needed for weekends all year; weekdays, June-October.*
- *Minimum stay: Two nights on summer weekends.*

- ❑ *Breakfast: Not complimentary, but available at inn's Mikayla restaurant or by room service.*
- ❑ *Wine: "Social hour," 5 pm-6 pm, serves assortment of bleu, camembert, chevre cheeses, several good wines, sourdough bread.*
- ❑ *Amenities: Outdoor jacuzzi, room service, massage.*
- ❑ *Handicapped accessible: A few rooms reached by elevator, but, alas, Mikayla's Restaurant is up two more flights of stairs.*
- ❑ *Smoking: No.*
- ❑ *Children: Yes.*
- ❑ *Pets: No.*
- ❑ *Parking: Valet, $7 in and out. This is the best parking bargain in the Bay Area. If you park it yourself in the city lot, it costs $10.50 for 24 hours, plus an extra charge every time you go out.*
- ❑ *Directions: In center of main business section of Sausalito. Park at curb in front of Bridgeway entrance.*

## ♥ *Inn Above Tide*

"Staying at the Inn Above Tide, are you?" asked an old Sausalito hand. "Well, let me warn you before you get there...." and he told us the story of a honeymoon couple who checked in at night. The next morning, the wife took a shower, then walked into the bedroom naked and threw open the drapes, just as a ferryboat packed with early morning commuters came to a halt outside the window. The passengers all cheered as they saw her in all her glory. The woman was embarrassed, to say the least. "At least," she told the old Sausalito hand, "I'll never see any of them again... I hope." Our feeling was, think how much worse she would have felt if they had all booed.

Despite the warning, we were surprised and delighted by the floor-to-ceiling window covering almost a whole wall of the Tidal Suite (the name of our huge room). The remainder of the wall was taken up by a round fireplace, ready to light. The windows look out directly to the waters of Richardson Bay, before it opens into San Francisco Bay. There was nothing between us and the water but our own private deck, as wide as the room, which is pretty wide by any standard.

Every room and suite has a view in this deluxe three-story, 30-room inn. It is right on the water, built to give guests the most dramatic Sausalito experience possible. Where it is not glass, the inn is covered with natural wood shingles. Inside, the walls are painted a pale blue and furnishings are sea-mist green or blue. In our Tidal Suite was a cabinet with a TV, next to a truly massive armoire, both with modern lines and blond wood. A model of a sailboat was in the room, to carry on the nautical theme. A really thoughtful touch is a pair of binoculars in every room so guests can use their windows and private decks to the best advantage.

King Deluxe rooms are smaller than the suites, with smaller decks. Each has a jacuzzi. Queen Deluxes are very popular, with a sitting area next to the fireplace and a bed facing the water so you see the bay when you wake up. The Grand Deluxe, on the third floor, does not have a deck or fireplace, but it is on a corner of the building with glass on two sides so you can lie in bed and see the lights of San Francisco at night. Now that is romantic!

The inn has been open only a year. Verena Zurcher-Burgoon, the manager, has designed packages to enhance the romance. The "Moonlight Serenade" includes a spacious guest room with king-size bed, sitting area, fireplace and a private deck with gorgeous views of San Francisco Bay. The Vista Suite Package includes a canopy king-size bed with a fireside sitting area in a corner suite with a panoramic view of the San Francisco skyline. In addition, there is a private deck, jacuzzi tub, original art on the walls, wet bar and fresh flowers. Both rooms include bottles of Scharfberger Champagne on arrival and fireside or deckside massage for each person.

Verena managed the Majestic Hotel in San Francisco before moving to Petaluma in Sonoma Valley with her husband Ben and two-year-old Emma. Born of Swiss parents in Mexico, she speaks five languages and is poised to handle an international clientele. If you brush up your French or Spanish, she will take a personal interest in you.

First-floor rooms are closest to the water. You can hear the waves wash against the pilings as you drift off to sleep. Some guests prefer the views from the second and third floors. Verena reminded us in parting, "There are hundreds of hotels located around San Francisco Bay. There is, however, only one on it."

❑ *30 El Portal, Sausalito, CA 94965;* ☎ *415-332-9535, 800-893-8433.*
❑ *E-mail: inntide@ix.netcom.co.*
❑ *Rooms: 30.*
❑ *Credit cards: All.*
❑ *Rates: Standard room $195, deluxe $255, suites $400.*
❑ *Packages: Moonlight Serenade $370, Vista Suite $520.*
❑ *Reservations: May-October, up to two months; November-April, four weeks for weekends, but usually not necessary for weekdays.*
❑ *Minimum stay: Two nights in summer.*
❑ *Breakfast: Continental breakfast provided.*
❑ *Wine: Yes, and cheese, 5 pm-7 pm.*
❑ *Amenities: Binoculars.*
❑ *Handicapped accessible: Two rooms.*
❑ *Smoking: Both non-smoking and smoking rooms; all rooms have decks where smoking is OK.*
❑ *Children: Yes.*
❑ *Pets: No*
❑ *Parking: Valet.*
❑ *Walking distance: Galleries, shopping, restaurants.*

## ♥ Houseboat Rentals/San Francisco As You Like It!

Don't be confused by the name. The company is definitely in Sausalito.

Here is a place that's really different – even for Sausalito. It's up along the north shore, where you will see 600 or so houseboats bobbing with the tide. A dozen are available for rental. Back in the 1850s, sailors, fishermen and shipbuilders lived on boats anchored out in Richardson Bay. That is when it was rent-free. Actually, if you look out over the upper reaches of the bay now, past the navigation channel, that is what those 20 or so boats at anchor are up to. Of course, there is no electricity or running water out there. Here, tied up to permanent piers, are a fleet of houseboats that evolved from the earlier ones and expanded as the artists and writers, who have always been attracted to Sausalito, took advantage of this wonderfully casual lifestyle.

It's a treat to watch sandpipers trotting daintily along the shoreline, picking at goodies on the bottom as the tide recedes. Snowy herons patrol for their meal. You may see a harbor seal who pokes his head out of the water beside your window to take a curious look around.

Part of the reason the houseboats are the way they are now is Sally Stanford. She is the San Francisco madam who moved to Sausalito, where she eventually became mayor. As one of her first official acts, she managed to kick all the hippies out of downtown Sausalito. They gravitated north to the edge of town where writers and artists were already living on all sorts of craft converted, more or less, into houseboats. The houseboat population expanded out into the Bay. City fathers and mothers and real estate developers, avid to get hold of all this prime bayshore, have been trying to get rid of them once and for all ever since.

Patty Cahill (San Francisco As You Like It!) has eight houseboats for rent at the moment, ranging in size from one bedroom to several. Some have nautical decorations with portholes in the doors, fishnets on the walls and hatchcover tables – we were surprised that we were not piped aboard. Others are simply "cute." All have a kitchen, a living room, a deck with a view out over the water and a fishing pole, in case all you want to do is sit and wait for a fish to come by. Some are rustic. One is very modern, with a spiral staircase to the upper deck. Several have cozy bedrooms with canopy beds.

All the floating homes are fully furnished with linens, bedding, dishes, toasters, coffee-makers, cookware, cable TV, stereo, CD and phone. All that we saw looked like an appealing way to spend a very private weekend. If you do not feel like cooking, there are menus from a dozen restaurants in Sausalito who will deliver.

There are two ways to rent. Either reserve a month or so ahead, or call at the last minute. Either way will usually work, Patty tells us.

❑ *P.O.Box 735, Sausalito, CA 94966;* ☎ *415-389-1250.*
❑ *Rates: $125-$200 per night for one bedroom.*

# ℜestaurants

## Gatsby's ℜestaurant

(American fare and pizza)

Caledonia Street is where Sausalito's residents shop and eat. Walk north on Bridgeway, a block past the Madrona Inn, to where Caledonia starts, then turn left. Gatsby's is in the second block on the left side.

We were late for lunch the first time. It was 1:30 or so when we wandered into a strangely Scandinavian looking place. There was plenty of blond wood and straight chairs. A light lunch menu offered pizza, pasta, salads and good local beer (also a full bar). Phyllis tried a young spinach salad with pickled red onions, which turned out to be a terrific combination. Bob had a big bruschetta with tomato, radicchio, eggplant, basil, garlic and very young, tender and fresh spinach.

This eclectic place also serves soups, Caesar salads, gravlax, grilled pork loin sandwiches and Chinese chicken salad at lunch time. Dinner menus are similar, but with more to offer. There is even a bar menu, with appetizers ranging from baked mussels and marinated French feta cheese and tomato to prosciutto and figs. No wonder the locals like it. The waiter knew everyone that came in except us and we made friends quickly. It's easy in Sausalito. Just start talking and you've made a new friend.

While you are on this second block of Caledonia (a gas station takes up the first shortened block), you will notice that you are on what amounts to a restaurant row. There is Café Soleil, a big, bright place; Gatsby's; the Stuffed Croissant, a bakery; Fukusuke for Japanese food; and Arawan, with Thai cuisine. On the next block, beside the cinema, is Sushi Ran, offering guess what?

❑ *39 Caledonia St., Sausalito;* ☎ *415-332-4500.*
❑ *Open: Lunch, Monday-Saturday, 11:30 am-2:30 pm. Dinner daily, 5 pm-10:30 pm.*
❑ *Prices: Pizza slice $5, small $11.50, full $14.50. Bar menu appetizers $5-$7. Soup $3.50, salads $5-$7.50. Lunch bruschetta $5.50, sandwiches $6.50, ravioli $7.50. Dinner entrées $7.50-$15.*
❑ *Credit cards: AE, Diners Club, MC, V.*

❑ *Reservations: Recommended for dinner.*
❑ *Music: Solo piano and live music played at the bar on weekends and some weekdays.*
❑ *Parking: Street (metered).*
❑ *Directions: North on Bridgeway from ferry dock to first street on left. Second block.*

## Mikayla in Casa Madrona

(American West Coast dining)

When John Patrick Gallagher ran the Casa Madrona as a "sensible residential hotel" back at the turn of the century, the restaurant was just that – sensible. When the Deschamps family took over in 1959, they renovated the hotel room by room and concentrated on the kitchen. Madame Deschamps' cooking made the restaurant famous, even outshining the hotel itself. The menu was classic French with rich sauces, lots of butter and heavy cream. When John Mays bought, renovated and added to the Casa, he did not neglect the restaurant. He glassed-in surrounding balconies and renamed the place Mikayla after his four-year-old daughter. He hired famed designer, Laurel Burch, to paint a 12-foot mural of the Goddess Mikayla gazing out to sea, her hair entwined with sea creatures. Legend has it that Mikayla gave nourishment to the villagers in time of need. The new restaurant needed a chef, so Terry Lynch, with his background of cooking at Masa's, Auberge du Soleil and Silverado, was installed as Executive Chef. The menu is now much lighter, in keeping with modern tastes.

When we had dinner here, after the latest refurbishing, we were out on the deck, but surrounded by glass, with the lights of San Francisco and Oakland across the Bay. The roof is retractable and the glass slides away on warm, summer nights for al fresco dining.

There are three menus. One is for "little plates." It is easy to make a meal by ordering a couple of these dishes. It starts with spicy gazpacho (a cold Spanish soup) with avocado. Although many people do not like cold soups, this gazpacho will convert even the most dubious. There are many variations, but it is basically made with tomatoes, onions, beef broth, lots of cucumbers and lots of garlic. The version served at Mikayla is tangy, with some great aftertastes. We can testify to the Napoleon of smoked salmon and the crab cakes. Things like ahi tuna, steamed mussels and Caesar salad "with anchovies and no eggs" are also here.

The "bigger plates" menu includes grilled mahi mahi. All the entrées come with interesting side dishes. Accompanying the mahi mahi is fried yucca and spicy Asian slaw. Also available is seared salmon with chanterelles, roasted squab with bok choy, grilled eggplant with a soy-honey glaze and several meat dishes. The centerpiece of the vegetarian offering is crispy potato galette. Galette de pommes de terre is an interesting dish, traditionally made for Twelfth Night in the provinces around Paris. It is usually prepared as a round cake and definitely a treat if you are going the non-meat route.

There is a separate dessert menu with choices like bittersweet chocolate truffle tart and charlotte of apples with brandied ice cream. The titles alone are enough to give a dieter pause.

- *801 Bridgeway, Sausalito;* ☎ *415-331-5888.*
- *Open: 6 pm-9 pm/9:30 pm, depending on guests who linger.*
- *Prices: Small plates $5.50-$7.95, bigger plates $10.95 (potato galette) to $19.75 (spice-crusted veal loin).*
- *Reservations: Recommended.*
- *Credit cards: All.*
- *Parking: Valet, $3.*
- *Directions: Sausalito exit after crossing Golden Gate Bridge. Midway along Bridgeway, the main street.*

## 737 Bridgeway Hamburgers

Shopping in Sausalito is wonderful, varied and can lead to almost anything. What may seem strange, though, the first time you see it, is a line of people outside a very little (about eight feet wide) storefront labeled, 737 Hamburgers. At one side of the door is a sign (in 10 languages) instructing you, whatever your place of origin, to "Form a line to the right." The rest of the storefront, not taken up by the door, is a window housing a big grill. On the grill are hamburgers; lots of them. Chicken also makes a grill appearance, depending on the time of day or the cooks' (there seem to be several) proclivities. Mostly, though, it's hamburgers – "the best in the world," according to those in line, waiting patiently for their orders. There is only one table inside. People take their well-wrapped burgers across the street to the park and sit, happily munching, trying to ignore the pigeons awaiting their largesse. From what we could see, there was not much largesse. People were wolfing them down. We almost wished we liked hamburgers more.

- *737 Bridgeway, Sausalito;* ☎ *415-332-9471.*
- *Open: 11 am-5 pm.*
- *Prices: $4.45-$4.93.*

## Spinnaker

(California / seafood)

Outside, it looks like a perfectly respectable restaurant; perhaps a steakhouse. But once inside, you encounter... The View! You walk into a huge room with floor-to-ceiling windows giving out over over the water. The Spinnacker is not broken up by walls or cozy booths. There are not even candles on the tables at night. The view is everything.

The restaurant is built on pilings out into Richardson Bay and the view is of Belvedere Island with Tiburon in the distance. Angel Island is to the right, beyond is Alcatraz and then San Francisco itself, the skyline and hills. In the other direction are Oakland and Berkeley. At night, it's the lights and passing boats that you watch. That's why there are no candle-lit tables. The reflections in the glass would be distracting. But a view alone does not keep a restaurant going for about 30 years. The food is what keeps locals coming back. And tourists get the word.

At lunch, we split a spring greens salad with an Italian vinaigrette dressing which did not overwhelm the taste of fresh greens. There was plenty for two. With the fish bouillabaisse, the flavors of scallops, prawns and Manila clams each had their turn in the limelight, without getting in the way of the others. There was fish and chips, lightly battered so the batter and the fish are one. Another time, we had the quesadilla for a starter with crab, shrimp and basil. The cheeses melted beautifully into the seafood. The Crab Louis had a dressing that is light both in texture and in taste; a welcome respite from the orange stuff one is usually faced with. Grilled sea bass is crisp outside and juicy inside. Lamb chops were grilled to a pink medium-rareness and came with potato-leek cakes that were light and fluffy, not like hockey pucks. All in all, it was a happy experience.

- ❑ *100 Spinnaker Drive, Sausalito;* ☎ *415-332-1500.*
- ❑ *Open: 11 am-10 pm You can order right up until 10 pm.*
- ❑ *Prices: Appetizers $5.50-$7.95, pastas $11-$13, entrées $11.95-$16, chicken $13, filets $18.95.*
- ❑ *Reservations: Recommended.*
- ❑ *Credit cards: All major.*
- ❑ *Parking: Restaurant's lot.*
- ❑ *Directions: On the Sausalito waterfront, three minutes' walk from the ferry dock.*

# Nightlife

## No Name Bar

When Sterling Hayden was a young man, he went to sea as a deckhand on sailing ships before he was snared by Hollywood to be a movie star. Years later, after he became disillusioned with Hollywood, he moved to Sausalito and lived on a boat. While here, he wrote an autobiography, *Wanderer*, which was also the name of the boat. This is from the last page of that book.

❦ *Grabbing his bag, he slips over the bulwarks and down to the heaving logs where, under the tall ship's lee, he turns right past The Tides bookstore, and steps from the storm to the warmth of the No Name Bar. He buys a drink and turns to a ship lost in the night and drinks to a life that was.*

This woody, panelled, rather beat up place is across the street and a little way north of the ferry dock. It does not have a name. Evidently, the first owner could not think of one, so it became simply the No Name Bar. There is a long oak bar against one wall serving a happy hour from 5-7 pm, with some good microbrews on tap. You can have food in the patio out back or inside if you wish. They have good sandwiches, but the food is not made here. It comes from the Venice Deli down the street. That is not why you are here anyway. If you want a light lunch right around here, try the pizza and salad place in the Hotel Sausalito, or Angelino's, a block south on Bridgeway. You are probably here because this is where everyone comes to hear live jazz. Or you may be here because there are not that many nightlife choices in Sausalito.

❑ *757 Bridgeway St., Sausalito;* ☎ *415-332-1392.*
❑ *Open: 10 am-2 pm, Happy Hour daily 5-7 pm. Live jazz Wednesday through Saturday, 9 pm on; Dixieland jazz, Sunday, 3 pm-7 pm.*
❑ *Prices: Tap beers $2.50-$4; sandwiches $5.50-$7.50.*

# Things to Do

## The Bay Model

A Congressional Act in 1954 ordered the US Army Corps of Engineers to construct this model for research to plan the future use of San Francisco Bay. It covers 1½ acres. The vast interior space was a warehouse used to build Liberty ships during World War II.

The Bay and the Delta are immensely important to California, so the model is as exact as it can be. The Bay is a third smaller now than in 1840, mainly because of soil washed down rivers, especially during the period of hydraulic mining in the 1850s-60s, and from deliberate filling in. Part of San Francisco's downtown is built on landfill in what was once the Bay.

Here is where scientists research what would happen to the Bay under different scenarios. The computerized model makes each day 14½ minutes long. You watch day turn to night and back to day again. The model is filled with water only on Friday and Saturday or when scientists are actually working on a project. Call ahead to see if water is in on the other days. Even without water, you can walk around the entire project, which is well marked and easy to understand.

- ❑ *2100 Bridgeway, Sausalito;*
  ☎ *415-332-3871, 415-332-3870 for recorded information.*
- ❑ *Open: Memorial Day to Labor Day, Tuesday-Friday, 9 am-4 pm, Saturday,Sunday and holidays, 9 am-6 pm; rest of the year, Tuesday-Saturday, 9 am-4 pm.*
- ❑ *Admission: Free. Audio tour tapes are free, available in French, Spanish, German, Japanese, Russian and English.*
- ❑ *Parking: Free, in lot at the Model.*
- ❑ *Directions: Drive north on Bridgeway one mile to sign "Marin Ship Way." Turn right and follow signs.*

## Sausalito Cyclery

All of Marin County, including Sausalito, is laced with literally hundreds of miles of bike trails. It is a great way to spend a day, perhaps taking along a picnic. Sausalito Cyclery has maps of all these trails and any directions or advice you get is based on years of personal experience. Remember, there is no law that says you have to get worn out by cycling your head and feet off. Cycle for awhile until you feel you have had it and your behind starts wondering why they make those seats so small and uncomfortable. Then stop and have your picnic, or just smell the flowers. If you're not sure at the start that you want to do this for a whole day, just rent for an hour or half a day.

Mountain bikes rent for $25 per day. Full suspension bikes, which are mountain bikes with front and rear shocks for going up Mt. Tam, rent for $40. Regular road bikes are only $25, although they do not have much call for those these days. Tandems (not just bicycles built for two, these are fully geared for rough trails) go for $70.

- ❑ *#1 Gate Six Road, Sausalito;* ☎ *415-332-3200, fax 415-332-3219.*
- ❑ *Open: Monday-Friday, 11 am-7 pm; Saturday, 10 am-6 pm; Sunday, 11 am-5 pm.*

❑ *Rates: $25 and up for full day.*
❑ *Directions: North on Bridgeway almost two miles from the ferry dock in downtown Sausalito, just before the 101 Freeway on the right.*

## Shopping

Since Sausalito has a well-earned reputation as the home of artists and writers, it only seems right that people should come here from all over to see the galleries and shop for objets d'art and lots more. Bridgeway Street is the main drag and the shops and galleries range along a very walkable curving stretch of waterfront. They are almost all on one side of the street, with a few streets branching off, but not far off. Start at the north end, next to Casa Madrona, and you will find the following.

**The Quest**, 777 Bridgeway. This is a gallery with everything on consignment from local artists. A range of oils, watercolors, dishes, sculptures, jewelry, ceramics, tapestries, hand-designed clothing and quilts are presented.

**Village Fair**, right next door, is on the site of the old, outdoor village fair. There are dozens of shops on almost as many levels. Go inside and walk up by the waterfall/pond. Candles, gifts, sports clothes and prints are all to be found. One food sign says, "We feature only 100% all-beef hot dogs (we wouldn't do that to Babe!)."

The **Sausalito Visitors Bureau and Museum** is on the top level. Interesting photos, explanations of how the town got to be the way it is and what happened along the way are just some of the topics covered here. For information, ☎ 415-332-0505.

**No Name Bar**, 777 Bridgeway (see Nightlife).

**737 Bridgeway Hamburger** (see Restaurants).

**Gene Miller**, 729 Bridgeway, sells fine clothing.

**Hanson Gallery**, 669 Bridgeway, shows contemporary oils, mostly European and American. Most buyers are not local residents, surprisingly, but are visitors off the ferry. Many are Europeans, who buy here because Sausalito's been known as an art colony since the 1930s. Word gets around, it seems.

**Scrimshaws, Nautical Paintings, Ships Models**, 30 Princess Street. Princess is a short block of shops that goes uphill on a slant from Bridgeway. The name explains the contents of this one.

**Sports and History Legends**, 34 Princess Street. There are 3,000 framed photographs here of sport figures, politicians and movie legends. It is fascinating to browse, even if you have little intention of buying. Put Albert Einstein, Clark Gable, maybe Rita Hayworth,

Marilyn Monroe or Michelle Pfeifer (pick your generation) on the wall. Prices begin at $75.

**Houlihans,** back on Bridgeway facing Princess Street, is a good spot to break your walk for a drink, for tea or whatever suits you at the time. This popular restaurant is on the second floor, with lots of tables looking out over Richardson Bay.

**Louis Aronow Gallery,** 686 Bridgeway.

**Fingerhut Gallery,** 690 Bridgeway.

As you can see, these stores are mostly for visitors. If you want groceries, a haircut or good food, go a block north on Bridgeway to the first street. It's just a few steps to the start of Caledonia.

# Mill Valley

Mill Valley is a nice little town, north of Sausalito and west of Highway 101, nestled on the lee side of Mt. Tamalpais. It was originally a logging town and takes its name from the 1836 sawmill that can still be seen among the trees in Old Mill Park. In the late 1800s, it was a vacation haven for San Francisco families. Cottages that were once summer retreats are now upgraded, year-round homes among the giant redwoods.

In 1896, a mountain railway took visitors from the town center up to the summit of Mt. Tamalpais. It was discontinued in 1931, but the old depot still functions as a bookstore and café in Lytton Square. Lytton Square is the town center where you will find a bevy of coffee houses, restaurants and boutiques.

For information about Mill Valley, contact the **Chamber of Commerce** at ☎ 415-388-9700.

## Inn

### Mountain Home Inn

Mountain Home Inn was built on the new scenic highway, now the hub of hiking and biking trails. Ed and Susan Cunningham spent four years creating the kind of place where visitors would want to drop in for a glass of wine or to stay overnight in one of the 10 guest rooms. It has been voted "one of the 10 Best New Inns in America" and counts famous musicians, actors and directors as returning guests.

This is a bed & breakfast with a restaurant that goes on through dinner. Breakfast, for those lucky enough to stay overnight, starts the day before. You are handed the next morning's menu and asked what time you'll want breakfast and what you want to eat. We tend to dislike that kind of rigid schedule, but things worked out surprisingly well. We were only five minutes late and the food appeared just a few minutes later. We sat down in a pleasant room with a fireplace and a view across the mountains and trees to San Pablo Bay.

The cheese, spinach and mushroom omelets were made with at least four eggs. Other menu items included bagels, smoked salmon and cream cheese, a freshly baked croissant filled with ham and melted cheese and French toast with bacon, sausage or ham. Very large portions were served and we found the food to be good.

Before we drove up the mountain, we were told by several enthusiastic locals that "The view up there at the inn is tremendous. San Francisco! Oakland! You can see 360°!" A few more circumspect types claimed it was only 180°. Just so you won't have unrealistic expectations, the view is of several pine-clad mountain ridges and beyond, to a bit of Richardson Bay and the extension of San Francisco Bay that eventually leads to San Pablo Bay.

The inn is built of natural wood. It looks exactly as a forest inn should. There is a small, friendly bar inside, a dining room, and a big deck for warm weather.

The Standard Fireplace Room is fairly small, with a double bed facing a wood-burning fireplace. A large oval tub in the bathroom has a window over it that opens into the bedroom. It has a view across the room and into the trees. Wide glass doors lead to a private porch, making the room bright.

The Redwood Room is larger with a bigger fireplace, jacuzzi, king bed and a sitting area with wingback chairs.

Even if you are not usually a hiker, chances are you'll want to take at least a short walk along one of the trails through the woods. Bring some comfortable shoes.

- ❏ *810 Panoramic Highway, Mill Valley, CA 94941;* ☎ *415-381-9000.*
- ❏ *Rooms: 10.*
- ❏ *Rates: $159-$215.*
- ❏ *Credit cards: AE, MC, V.*
- ❏ *Reservations: Summer weekends and holidays, several weeks ahead. Weekdays in summer easier. Off-season, phone ahead for weekends; weekdays, you can always get a room.*
- ❏ *Handicapped accessible: Yes, elevator to one equipped room.*
- ❏ *Smoking: Five rooms smoking, five non-smoking, no smoking in bar.*
- ❏ *Children: Yes, rollaway beds available, $25 charge.*
- ❏ *Pets: No.*

# *Things to Do*

## *Muir Woods National Monument*

❦ *This is the best tree-lover's monument that could possibly be found in all the forests of the world. You have done me a great honor and I am proud of it.*

John Muir

So said John Muir, the great conservationist, upon hearing of the establishment of Muir Woods. He should be proud. Some of the enormous redwood trees growing here are over 250 feet high and 14 feet across. There are dozens of species of ferns. Salmon and trout come up Redwood Creek each year to spawn. It is the most visited place in Marin.

The Park Service does a good job of handling the large numbers of people who come. The Visitors Center is a fount of information, with hundreds of books, maps and sketches of hiking trails taking off from the Center. There is a three-dimensional model of the woods and Mt. Tamalpais, and Rangers and volunteers are willing to answer questions.

There are the woods themselves, whose impact no overabundance of humanity can lessen. Thick, primeval redwoods were given to the country by the owner of this land, William Kent, who represented Marin in Congress. President Theodore Roosevelt proclaimed the redwood canyon a national monument in 1908, which has protected it from development and destruction. This is a jewel of a pocket-ecosystem.

If you have time, walk as far as possible away from the parking lot and Information Center. The number of people will lessen and a bit of quiet should descend.

Cathedral Grove and Bohemian Grove contain the largest of the majestic redwoods, some at least 1,000 years old. You probably will not spot the deer, but you will see chipmunks and Stellar's jays.

Try to avoid coming on weekends, especially in the summer when the largest number of massive, smoke-belching buses are lined up in the parking lot.

❑ ☎ *415-388-2595; Open: 8 am-sunset.*
❑ *Admission: None.*
❑ *Parking: In lot at entrance; no charge.*
❑ *Directions: Located 12 miles north of the Golden Gate Bridge via Highway 101 and California Highway One. From Sausalito, take Bridgeway to 101. Stay in the right lane; the Highway One exit comes up almost immediately.*

## *Dipsea Cross-Country Footrace*

This race was first run in 1905 by some runners who were staying in a lodge called the Dipsea Inn. Anyone seeing the terrain this race covers will suspect that those boys had hoisted quite a few by the time they dreamed this one up. The nearly seven-mile race is held annually in June. It starts in Mill Valley and ends in Stinson Beach on the southwest coast. It is strenuous and definitely for the fit. The course goes over Mt. Tamalpais and includes a long flight of redwood stairs up the mountainside en route. The Dipsea Inn, alas, is no more. ☎ 415-331-3300.

## *Hiking Mt. Tamalpais*

Just as Mt. Fuji puts its stamp on Japan, Mt. Tamalpais definitely dominates, not just Mill Valley, but all of Marin County. Even if the lower part is shrouded in fog, the upper section, covered with madrone, chaparral and oak trees, is likely to be sunny. The locals affectionately call it Mt. Tam, and everyone who lives here has walked up it at one time or another. The Old Railroad Grade and Old Stagecoach Road are heavily used by hikers. You need not spend time in the midst of crowds, though. If you are looking to be alone, there are 200 miles of trails, including those in Mount Tamalpais State Park, ☎ 415-388-2070, and the local Watershed District, ☎ 415-459-0888. Phone for information and maps.

# *Tiburon/Belvedere*

Belvedere (Italian for "beautiful view") is a small island, one mile long and a half-mile wide, just offshore. There's a causeway at each end connecting it to Tiburon on the mainland. It's quiet, residential, the most affluent area in Marin County, full of million-dollar homes and expensive yachts in the lagoon between the causeways.

The Tiburon peninsula forms the eastern border of Richardson Bay. It became a Spanish land grant and was named Punta de Tiburon, meaning "shark point."

Walk off the ferry or park on Main Street and pick up a copy of "Walking Guide to Historic Tiburon" at almost any shop or the Chamber of Commerce (96B Main Street). Many of the art galleries, shops and restaurants are housed in buildings dating from the 1880s when this was a rowdy seafaring town. **Sam's Anchor Café** is the locals' favorite. It still has a trap door to the Bay, used during Prohibition to hoist whiskey from boats below. Ark Row was once part of the lagoon. Some of the shops and businesses are actually 19th-century houseboats, now up on pilings. For information, contact the **Tiburon Peninsula Chamber of Commerce, ☎** 415-435-5633.

To get here, take Highway 101 from the Golden Gate Bridge, past Sausalito to the Tiburon exit. Or you can come direct via ferry from San Francisco's Ferry Building – a mere six-mile cruise.

## *Restaurant*

♥ *Tutto Mare*

---

(Italian, seafood)

This place is modeled after the rustic boathouses that line the Italian coast. It is two stories high and contains what amounts to two restaurants. The bottom floor is a *taverna*, casual, with a big bar and small tables. On the second floor is *il ristorante*, grander, with another bar and bigger tables in a long room out over the water. The far end is a deck looking down on the comings and goings of ferries and other boats. Across the Bay is the San Francisco skyline. On a clear day, it is great. On a clear night, it's spectacular.

Plexiglass surrounds the deck and gas heaters overhead make it comfortable on a chilly night. Inside is pretty good too. We sat outside at a table against the glass and nibbled on focaccia and tiny Niçoise olives provided to stay the pangs until martinis arrived. The martinis were a surprise, at least to us. Classic, big martini glasses arrived, but without the stems and nestled in bowls of shaved ice. The result was instant coldness, which lasted. No martinis were getting warm here. What a good idea!

Then came the antipasto misto. Be warned that the dish is fine, but it is really a meal for two. Caponata, marinated asparagus, fava beans with pecorino cheese, croutons and a seafood salad are all included.

The menu has pastas and typical dishes. Angel hair pasta is presented well with a simple sauce of tomatoes and basil. There are many seafood choices, such as fish, shrimp and lobster. Things like sea bass can be prepared either steamed or grilled. Try it steamed some time. It may not be as flaky, but when done well, as it is here, there are extra flavors that come from marinating for an hour in wine, oil and herbs. A lot of the shellfish comes from Seattle and some from as far away as the Atlantic. The fish is caught mostly by a boat that operates out of Sausalito.

- ❑ *9 Main St., Tiburon;* ☎ *415-435-4747.*
- ❑ *Open: Monday-Saturday, 11:30 am-10:30 pm, Sunday 11 am-10 pm.*
- ❑ *Prices: $7-$24.*
- ❑ *Credit cards: All major.*
- ❑ *Reservations: Recommended for lunch; usually necesssary for dinner. Without reservations, come in anyway, but you might not get a choice view table.*
- ❑ *Parking: Free, lot and street.*
- ❑ *Directions: Cross Golden Gate Bridge, 101 Freeway to Tiburon exit, follow Tiburon Boulevard to the water.*
- ❑ *Red & White Fleet Ferry Service: This is a commuter service between Tiburon and San Francisco. It runs Monday through Friday to and from the Ferry Building; noon and weekend service to Pier 43½ (Fisherman's Wharf). Wheelchair-accessible.* ☎ *415-435-2131.*

# *Angel Island*

There is a gem of an island in San Francisco Bay that makes a wonderful day excursion. No, this is not grim Alcatraz. There's nothing remotely romantic about that barren rock. Angel Island is just offshore from Tiburon, with 12 miles of easy, traffic-free hiking and biking trails. The highest point on this largest isle in the Bay is 781-foot Mount Caroline Livermore, named after the dedicated Marin conservationist who led the fight to make the island a park.

Foot trails and fire roads circle the island. There is a paved road and a dirt road, each about five miles long. All the trails are well marked, although caution should be used if you go exploring near the bluffs, which can be unstable. Keep a lookout for poison oak, native to the area and awfully itchy.

The beaches at Quarry Point and Ayala Cove are both sandy and protected from the afternoon breezes that so often blow in from the ocean through the Golden Gate. However, there are no lifeguards and swimming can be dangerous because of the strong tidal currents. The view from Perle's Beach is spectacular and, although swimming is out of the question, it is a delightful place for walking and general beachcombing.

The island has a curious background and has not always lived up to its name. The Army took it over after the war with Mexico and it was used as a quarantine station to process troops who had been exposed to contagious diseases during the Spanish-American War and the Philippine Insurrection. But the lowest point came for thousands of Chinese when an Immigration Station Detention Facility was opened in 1910. Officially, it was supposed to hold everyone who immigrated through the Port of San Francisco. In fact, more than 97% of the almost 200,000 immigrants processed on Angel Island during the next 30 years were Chinese.

Some were kept here in detention for as long as two years. Some of the detainees expressed in poetry their feelings of despair and longing for the city they could see so near across the water. These verses can still be seen carved into the wooden walls of the now-deserted barracks.

The restaurant in Ayala Cove has an outdoor patio. It is not the Ritz, but there are good soups and sandwiches. They are even trying to move away from burgers and fries and getting into more healthful food.

The **bike rental shop** has maps of trails, none of which are really strenuous and many are walkable as well as cyclable. There are short hikes to points of interest and longer ones for the more ambitious. If you do not feel like walking, there are tram tours.

Walking is a wonderful way to see the island. Most native trees and grasses have recovered from the earlier invasion of aggressive European grasses that were introduced. Firewood choppers hacked down much of the oak forest on the northeast side. Things are getting back to normal under the Park system. Bird life is greatly diverse, including everything from grebes and kingfishers to robins and hummingbirds. Salmon and striped bass migrate from the Pacific to the Sacramento River Delta through Raccoon Strait. Incidentally, this Strait is named, not for the four-legged critters on the island, but for a British warship that was repaired in Ayala Cove in 1814.

You can get to Angel Island by **ferry** from Tiburon for $6. Call ☎ 415-435-2131 for information. From San Francisco's Pier 43½ it will cost $9. Call ☎ 415-546-2896 or 800-BAY-CRUISE. The fares include the $2 state park entrance fee. Ferries run daily through the summer and weekends in the winter. It is a short trip and a nice crossing. There are picnic tables available when you get there.

**Bicycles** can be rented on the island daily through September and after that on weekends only. Costs are $10 an hour, $25 a day, tandems $40 a day. Rentals include helmets.

**Tram tours** run daily through the summer until the end of September and then on weekends only. Trams are closed December through February. Cost is $9, or $7 for seniors, including headset for narrated descriptions and history; $5 and $4 without headsets. For **Angel Island State Park** information, ☎ 415-435-1915.

# *Larkspur*

Larkspur is the little community to the west of Highway 101 and south of Sir Francis Drake Boulevard. In a way, it began as a mistake. The town was named after the blue wildflowers growing on the hillsides. Then it was found that they were not larkspur after all, but lupin. Notwithstanding that small embarrassment, Larkspur ended up with a downtown area that was listed on the National Register of Historic Places. A stroll along Magnolia Avenue's brick-lined sidewalk leads to boutiques, cafés and restaurants. For information, call the **Larkspur Chamber of Commerce**, ☎ 415-257-8338. **Golden Gate Transit Ferries** sail to and from San Francisco from the Larkspur Ferry Terminal. Fares and schedule information are available at ☎ 415-923-2000.

## Restaurant

### Lark Creek Inn

(American)

Hoo-ray! Tomatoes that taste like, well, tomatoes! Flavor that is, well, flavorful (explodes in your mouth is the cliché, but it does)!. Legend has it that all tomatoes used to taste this way.

It is the house tomato salad at Lark Creek Inn, brought to us before we had even ordered our meal, that caused that attack of ecstacy. One big plate for the two of us to share, and did we ever. Big red tomatoes, little red ones, yellow tomatoes, tiny green ones, along with a pile of watercress, were all dribbled with a balsamic vinaigrette containing lemon and herbs. The tomatoes come from Grandview Farms in Sonoma, which grows organic vegetables for a few restaurants.

Several breads also arrived; squash-buttermilk, honey wheat and plain dinner rolls (as if anything so fresh could be plain). Darcy Tizio, the baker, makes all the bread and bread puddings every day and changes them each night.

With drinks and breads in hand, we dawdled over the menu and its many choices. Bradley Ogden, co-owner and chef, is a Midwesterner and the menu reflects that culture, at least partially. It includes chicken and mashed potatoes, pork and vegetables and pan-fried fish. His relatives back in Michigan probably would not recognize what these descendents of plain American food taste like now.

Point Reyes oysters were served with a shallot-black pepper sauce, which started our serious eating. We could have made a meal out of this. There was zucchini and garden tomato soup with pesto, then a pork chop grilled to perfection. In fact, it was so juicy, we called for more bread to mop it up. The lemon tarragon roasted chicken is accompanied by mashed potatoes and garlic. The chicken is a free range bird, which gives it an almost wild game taste. This is the way chickens used to taste before they were squeezed into miniscule coops and "farmed." The garlic gives the organically grown spuds a kick that bounces the flavor right into your mouth. Fish is on the menu as well as meatloaf. It is like sitting down to Sunday dinner in a Midwestern farm kitchen, with a Cordon Bleu chef at the stove.

The room is high-ceilinged, with a 20-foot-high skylight. Part of the structure reveals the old brick walls of the original 1888 building. While impressive, it was also homey, reflecting the friendliness of the staff. Our notes say everything was "perfect," but it couldn't have been that good, could it?

- *234 Magnolia Ave., Larkspur;* ☎ *415-924-7766.*
- *Open: Monday-Thursday, 11:30 am-2 pm; casual menu, 2 pm-5:30 pm; dinner, 5:30 pm-9 pm; Friday-Saturday, casual menu to 9:30 pm, open a half-hour earlier and later. Sunday, 10 am-9 pm; casual menu to 9:30.*
- *Prices: Starters from $6.25, pasta entrées $14.50, others $17.50-$24.*
- *Credit cards: AE, MC, V, Diners.*
- *Reservations: Recommended two weeks ahead, especially on weekends. Usually no problem on weekdays.*
- *Parking: Self-park in their lot.*
- *Directions: Exit 101 at Paradise Dr./Tamalpais Dr.; turn west on Tamalpais. One mile to four-way intersection; right on Corte Madre, which changes name to Magnolia. Continue half a mile.*

# San Rafael

Downtown Fourth Street will be best remembered by many as the backdrop for the movie *American Graffiti*. It is located halfway between San Francisco and the wine country. San Rafael is the largest and oldest city in Marin. It was started when Father Junipero Serra built Mission San Rafael Archangel, the 20th mission in California's string of 21 missions. For more information about San Rafael, call the **Visitor's Bureau,** ☎ 415-472-7470. To get here, just keep going up Highway 101 past Larkspur.

## Inn

### Gerstle Park Inn

Breakfast is a full meal at the Gerstle Park Inn. Orange juice, cereal, yogurt, fruit and thick sourdough French toast are available. Co-

*Gerstle Park Inn, San Rafael.*

proprietor Jim Dowling may whip up a five-cheese scrambled egg dish for you. He and his wife Judy have spent the last year working on the property. Their project has involved knocking down walls to make rooms larger, creating suites, adding private porches that overlook the manicured gardens and finding antiques that fit the mood of each unique room.

Each room and suite has a patio or deck. All baths have hair dryers, bath robes, irons and ironing boards. The rooms have books and magazines, TVs and VCRs, with a library of moviesto choose from.

We stayed in the Oak Suite, which is on the second floor, right under the roof. The ceilings of the two comfortable rooms came in at odd angles. The bedroom is dominated by the king-size bed, covered by a black comforter embroidered with big red roses. The black wallpaper also had red roses and there was a vase of red roses on the 18th-century carved honeywood dresser. A large, gold-framed painting of an artist at his easel in a French garden enhances the mood. The Oak Suite was originally two rooms separated by a hallway. It's now one suite. The sitting room has a really comfortable sofa and a low coffee table and chairs. There is a very large closet off the bathroom, but the ceiling slopes down sharply because of the steeply pitched roof. Watch your head.

Similar units are in the carriage house. A separate cottage will be ready this year. The carriage house units are smaller than those in the big house, but cozy. The main house looks as if it must have been the mansion of the estate, but it was the servants' quarters, built around 1895. The real mansion burned down in 1953.

Gerstle and Sloff were partners in the hide trade in the 19th century, taking 100,000 seal hides a year out of Alaska. They married sisters and built adjoining homes on four acres each. Both died in 1902. Most of the acreage is now a public park, which adjoins the inn. One of the old iron rings left in the stone wall of what is now the inn's parking area was where horses used to be tied for guests at the mansion. Those were the days.

Modern guests get kitchen privileges, though. The cookie jar is always full of homemade cookies. There is an apple cobbler from trees right here on the property to take up to your room, or to have in the parlor with coffee. Other fruit from the inn's trees, juice, sodas and milk are in the big fridge. Guests can even cook their own dinner.

There is complimentary wine in the evening before guests scatter for dinner. The attractive living room has a high barrel ceiling and is a fine place to sit with wine in rainy weather. Otherwise, if it is not too cold, wine and breakfast are served on the veranda. We sat out with Jim in the afternoon, sipping Rutherford Chardonnay, talking as the sun (and the level of the bottle) went down.

We returned home late from dinner that evening and found the house locked up. No problem, we just let ourselves in with our key. Everyone was asleep, so we headed for the kitchen. There sat what was left of the apple cobbler, with a sign, "Please help yourself." All in all, it's a charming place.

- ❑ *34 Grove St., San Rafael, CA 94901;*
  ☎ *415-721-7611, 800-726-7611, fax 415-721-7600.*
- ❑ *Rooms: Eight.*
- ❑ *Prices: $129-$189.*
- ❑ *Credit cards: AE, MC, V.*
- ❑ *Reservations: Necessary; cancellation 48 hours in advance.*
- ❑ *Handicapped accessible: One room accessible, but generally a lot of stairs.*
- ❑ *Breakfast: Complimentary full breakfast.*
- ❑ *Wine: Wine and port in afternoon and evening.*
- ❑ *Amenities: Jacuzzi and steambath suites, robes.*
- ❑ *Children: Yes.*
- ❑ *Pets: Not in the house.*
- ❑ *Directions: Call.*

## *Things to Do*

**China Camp** was formerly the site of a Chinese fishing village on the shore of San Pablo Bay. It features hiking, horseback riding and biking trails. There is a preserved fisherman's cottage and a museum located in the original shrimp processing plant. ☎ 415-456-0766.

Docents lead tours of the **Civic Center**, the last building designed by Frank Lloyd Wright, during the week or by appointment.

Lovers of Shakespeare will want to go to the **Marin Shakespear Company**'s summer productions in the wooded Forest Meadows

Amphitheater, on the grounds of Dominican College. ☎ 415-499-1108 for tickets.

Chefs from the top local restaurants shop at **San Rafael Farmers' Market** behind the Civic Center. It is open every Thursday and Sunday from 8 am to 1 pm. The market is 90% fruit and vegetables – mostly organic, some exotic, all fresh. There are also live rabbits and chicks, live crayfish right out of the water, an Irish harp player (he's playing an Irish harp; he may or may not be from Eire), Bodega goat cheese and handmade ice cream. You will definitely want to take some along to have later. Coming here from the 101 Freeway, take the San Pedro East exit, go right to the Civic Center. Look for a tall gold spire and long low building designed by Frank Lloyd Wright and now used as a court building.

The **Fair Grounds** are just to the right of the Farmers' Market. These buildings were also designed by Wright. The Fair is held each year to celebrate July 4th (and the few days before and after).

# Novato

Novato is a small town whose core has been here well over 150 years. Fortunately, there is still plenty of open and wooded land, which is what attracted the Renaissance Pleasure Faire here (see below). There is also the **Marin Museum of the American Indian**, with exhibits on the Miwok Indians, at 2200 Novato Blvd., ☎ 415-897-4064. The **Novato History Museum**, built in 1850, has a collection of antique dolls, toy trains and pioneer tools. It may be found at 815 De Long Ave., ☎ 415-897-4320.

# Things to Do

## The Renaissance Pleasure Faire

"All the faire's a stage!" So says costumed Good Queen Bess. There will be jousting for her favors, jousting for a lady's hand and jousting for... well, just for the fun of jousting. "Fun" is definitely the key word here. It is a "pleasure faire" after all. There is food and drink to be had in great abundance, jugglers and strolling minstrels, plays and "jolly beggars performing bawdy songs." In addition, you will discover a very pretty tree-shaded wedding garden where people actually get married. There are crafts-makers, jewelry makers and all sorts of handicrafts for sale. You can watch metal workers metal working, potters potting and dip into the mysteries

*At the Renaissance Pleasure Faire.*

of Arcane Cove, where palmistry, card reading and all sorts of transcendental insights will enlighten you as to your future.

It is great fun to wander about, finding food stalls here and there, trying a bit of this and a bite of that. All sorts of succulent starters are available for you to carry around and taste as you go. Pick from artichokes, dolmas and pickled eggs, turkey legs, pork ribs, piroshkis, fish and chips, toad-in-the-hole, smoked venison and pasties. You can watch *A Midsummer Night's Dream* and *Twelfth Night* performed on open stages, just as in Shakespeare's time. The Newcastle Country Dancers and the Pipe and Bowl Morris Dancers perform.

All this and much, much more is packed into a few weekends from late August to early October. Last year the Faire celebrated its 30th anniversary in Marin County. Call for the dates this year.

- ❑ *Black Point;* ☎ *800-52-FAIRE.*
- ❑ *Internet: www.renfaire.com.*
- ❑ *Admission: $17.50, seniors $15.*
- ❑ *Open: Late August to early October; weekends and Labor Day, 10 am-6 pm. Call for this year's dates.*
- ❑ *Handicapped accessible: Fully wheelchair-accessible. Many stage shows have sign language interpreters for hearing impaired.*
- ❑ *Children: Yes, they will love it.*
- ❑ *Pets: No.*
- ❑ *Parking: $6.*
- ❑ *Directions: From San Francisco, cross Golden Gate Bridge, stay on 101 to Novato and take Highway 37 east to Black Point exit. Follow Renaissance Pleasure Faire signs. From Oakland and Berkeley, take Highway 580 to Richmond Bay Bridge, which puts you on 101. Turn right to #37 exit and follow Faire signs.*

# West Marin

Some call it "The land that time forgot." Some call it a paradise. Some call it the place where those damn yuppies moved in and locked the door behind them so no one else could enjoy it. West Marin is all of those things, and more.

Across the Golden Gate Bridge, Route One goes north along the coast and eventually reaches the bottom end of Olema Valley. From here on, everything to the east is the Golden Gate National Recreation Area and Samuel P. Taylor State Park. Everything to the west is Point Reyes National Seashore, Tomales Bay State Park and the Phillip Burton Wilderness Area. It is all wild and beautiful. The valley, which is where almost everyone lives because everywhere else is a park of some kind, has mountains coming down to the road for most of the way on the righthand side. Inverness Ridge is just over on the left.

This is where the San Andreas Fault plunges into the ocean. Highway One follows the fault and then, just past Point Reyes Station, the road runs along the east side of Tomales Bay – a long, narrow arm of the sea running southwest for 13 miles along the fault line. It was long a mystery why the rocks of this craggy coast matched those of the Tehachapi Mountains more than 300 miles to the south. They were nothing like the rocks on the other side of the fault. The answer was that this peninsula rides the eastern edge of the Pacific plate, which is grinding its way northwest at the rate of about two inches a year, moving over the western edge of the North American plate. From time to time, the underlying pressure becomes too great and there is a sudden violent move. That's what happened in 1906 when the peninsula jumped 20 feet north. There is an easy half-mile trail that starts at the Bear Valley Visitors Center, where you can see what happened then. Over the last few million years, everything west of this point, the entire 100-square-mile peninsula, moved here from Southern California.

Point Reyes National Seashore was created in 1962. The Golden Gate National Recreation Area was created in 1969 and covered the rest of the peninsula. The two parks occupy all the land to the west of Highway One and everything to the east of the highway south of Tomales Bay. Only a few scattered properties remain in private hands.

Not long ago, few occupied this area but fishermen and ranch families. These were mostly third and fourth generation, who ran cattle on the hills east of Tomales Bay and on land leased back from the National Seashore. Starting about 20 years ago, affluent couples from San Francisco moved here and bought up most of the old houses. They had moved into one of the most beautiful places in America. There was plenty of open space, wild animals and fish in abundance, no traffic to speak of and no crime. Understandably, the new residents wanted to keep it that way so they voted in tough zoning laws. Never will a McDonald's or a Hilton be allowed to build here. There is no sewer system – only septic tanks are used – which effectively keeps out most development.

As one frustrated visitor from Alameda told us, "I'd like to live here, too, but there's not much for sale and I couldn't afford it anyway." We asked what he thought the answer was. He hesitated, then said, "Well, I suppose I wouldn't want a place like this flooded with a mass of people and ruined, either. I guess in the end it's better kept so we can all enjoy it, even if just for a day or so." We guess so, too. For more information, contact **West Marin Chamber of Commerce**, P.O. Box 1045, Point Reyes Station, CA 94956; ☎ 415-663-9232.

To get here, drive over Golden Gate Bridge from San Francisco or, if coming from the north, down Highway 101. Highway One, which splits off at Sausalito, is scenic as you pass through forests, then along the edge of high cliffs. It's narrow, winding and steep much of the time. The other way is over Sir Francis Drake Highway, taking the exit at Greenbrae, north of Sausalito. It passes quickly through several small, pretty towns and then over the mountains on a scenic route.

Right now, **Golden Gate Transit** has very limited bus service to West Marin. For schedule information, call from San Francisco, ☎ 415-923-2000. From Marin County, ☎ 415-455-2000. Hours are 6 am-8 pm, Monday-Friday and 6:30 am-8 pm, Saturday, Sunday and holidays. The Web site address is http://www.goldengate.org.

As for the restaurants of West Marin, the quality and freshness of seafood in this area (at least at the caring places) is astounding and heartening. The argument goes on about Johnson's vs. Hog Island oysters and mussels. Johnson farms the bivalves in Drake's Estero (*estero* means estuary in Spanish). Hog Islanders come from the east shore of Tomales Bay. Ask a waiter at one of the good restaurants the difference and you are likely to get a discourse on relative salinity or the dedication (seriousness) of the particular hydro-farmer. We suggest you start with the Station House Café in Point Reyes Station and the Olema Inn in Olema.

One chef believes the water is clearer where the Hog Islanders are grown, because a spring runs into the cove there. Another chef swears the Johnsons are grown in tules and have more flavor. The best thing is to order a half-dozen of each and reach your own conclusion.

A note about the inns of West Marin. At the start of this latest visitor boom, there were not enough places to stay. The Olema Inn and a few motels in Inverness were about it. A happy result of all the couples who moved up here is that, while husbands continued to commute to the city, wives often opened bed & breakfasts. There are dozens of them now, more in one small area than we have seen anywhere else. Every one that we either stayed at ourselves or

## West Marin County

inspected was nice. Some were more romantic than others and a few were less expensive. We can attest to the ones we write about here, but others are probably equally good.

In the summer, most are full, especially on weekends because people from San Francisco and the Bay Area arrive. Weekdays are a little better, but reservations are strongly advised even then. From November through May it slows down. You can get into places without advance reservations, even on weekends, though the places with only one or two rooms may be an exception. Weekdays you might find yourselves as the only guests almost anywhere you go.

If you plan to come in the winter on a weekday, we suggest negotiating whatever price is quoted. This is a time when owners would rather get a little less for their rooms than leave them empty.

Muir Beach, the place farthest to the south in West Marin, has few accommodation choices. The other small, bucolic towns about 10 miles to the north, like Olema, Point Reyes Station, Inverness and Marshall, have a mind-boggling number of inns and bed & breakfasts. There are several cooperative groups which keep central registries and know what is available. They can make reservations for you. Try **Cottages of Point Reyes**, ☎ 415-663-9445, and **Point Reyes Lodging**, ☎ 415-663-1872 or 800-539-1872. If you have Internet access, they are at http://www.ptreyes.com.

The weather generally cooperates from May to October, and some days in January can be wonderful. When there is fog, it usually covers the coastal part of Point Reyes National Seashore, but stops at the top of Inverness Ridge – leaving Inverness, Point Reyes Station and Olema sunny and warm. Most fogs stop halfway down Tomales Bay. It sometimes gets windy in the winter, making Inverness the best location, as it's nestled in the lee of Inverness Ridge.

# Muir Beach

At the south end, way below Olema Valley, this has been a popular beach for San Franciscans for more than a century. Swimming is dangerous because of the strong undertow. You will find picnic tables, grills and restrooms. There are a couple of hiking trails that start from here, one going along the coast. A mile north is an overlook with nearby picnic grounds and whale and sea lion viewing.

To get here, take the Golden Gate Bridge on Highway 101 to Sausalito. Take Highway One. The first sign of Muir Beach is a two-story inn and restaurant, the Pelican. Just south of there, a lane goes west to the beach.

## Inn

### The Pelican Inn

It looks like a bit of Tudor England from the road – two stories with dormer windows set into the thatched roof, dark brown half-timbers on the whitewashed walls and a sprawling parking lot around it. The building looks 1700s, but it was actually built in 1979. A British ex-Royal Air Force officer fell in love with the area and wanted to build a true British inn. The rich folk of Muir Beach said in effect, "No way you're going to put a tacky pub in this neighborhood." With typical British resolve, he had a model made of what the place would look like and showed it to everyone until they came around. Now they love it. They even come for dinner.

Inside are narrow beamed halls. Olde prints are on the walls, door jams are low and there is plenty of leaded glass. The pub and restaurant are on the first floor, where a "hearty English breakfast" is served to guests.

The inn's seven rooms are on the second floor. All have fresh flowers each day, antique furnishings and "half tester" (canopy) beds. Rooms are not large, but they are cozy. Room Four, for example, is taken up mostly by the bed, although there are two corner chairs and a round table with a bowl of flowers. Room Seven is the largest and most charming; not surprising as it belonged to the owner and his wife. It has a king-size bed and a deep window nook complete with window seat. The bathroom is a few steps up, as the ceiling peaks on this side of the house.

"Is there another way back?" That was the first question we asked when we arrived. You should know that the drive over here on Highway One is narrow, twisting and mountainous.

- ❑ *10 Pacific Way, Muir Beach, CA 94965;* ☎ *415-383-6000.*
- ❑ *Rooms: Seven.*
- ❑ *Rates: $143-$165, plus 10% hotel tax.*
- ❑ *Credit cards: All.*
- ❑ *Reservations: Two to three months in advance.*
- ❑ *Amenities: Wine and beer bar, restaurant.*
- ❑ *Breakfast: "A hearty English breakfast."*
- ❑ *Handicapped accessible: No.*
- ❑ *Smoking: Yes.*
- ❑ *Children: Yes.*
- ❑ *Pets: Yes.*
- ❑ *Parking: Complimentary.*
- ❑ *Directions: Follow Highway One off 101, 16 miles from Mill Valley.*
- ❑ *Walking distance: Beach, woods.*

# ℛestaurant

## The Pelican Inn

(British country inn fare)

The pub is very English, with a low-beamed ceiling, small bar and a few tables to sit at while waiting to be seated in the dining room. There is a well-used dart board and beer and wine, with British and Irish ales on tap.

A few steps down from the pub, through a small, low door, is the Snug. Guests can also wait here, much more quietly and privately.

You will find a couch and comfortable chairs in front of a deep fireplace with logs stacked at the sides. Bellows and tongs hang from the dark, smoked mantel with a three-legged pot ready to put over the flames for cooking. We found nothing in the pot, so it seems to be merely for show. An ancient musket or two is mounted on the sides of the smokey ceiling beams. An upright piano completes the perfect picture. We can just see a couple who have the room to themselves after a late dinner singing something like, "I'll See You Again."

The dining room has a low ceiling. There are hunting prints on the walls, candles on the tables and a big walk-in fireplace with nooks on either side where a couple can sit and have a sherry before dinner, out of sight of the other diners. Over the mantel is painted in old script,

*Fear knocked at the door,*
*Faith answered,*
*No one was there.*

A reassuring sentiment!

The California salad comes in several designer greens, with good tomatoes, red peppers and goat cheese. Dressings are automatically served on the side. A nice touch is that they offer half-portions of everything in addition to the regular portions. The child-size portion of the day's pasta, for instance, is still large. Linguine with prawns and smoked trout in a cream sauce has just the right hint of smokey trout flavor. A Cornish game hen with the traditional walnuts and bread stuffing was served with an unusual gooseberry sauce that enhanced its delicate taste. There is also a whole rack of lamb with a tarragon and brandy sauce and an herb-crusted salmon fillet served over a potato pancake with crème fraiche.

Finally, choose from a dessert cart of pastries or stilton cheese and crackers.

We have one cautionary note. The place is romantic, there is no question of that. But if you are driving over from San Francisco, it is about 1¼ hours, the last half of which is narrow, mountainous and extremely tortuous. If you drive over in the daytime, you see lots of scenery and woods, but it can be unnerving at night. If you come down from Olema or Point Reyes Station, as we did, Highway One is narrow, twisting and skirts the edge of a cliff above the ocean half the way. This is even worse at night.

- ❑ *10 Pacific Way, Muir Beach;* ☎ *415-383-6000.*
- ❑ *Open: Tuesday-Sunday, 11 am-11 pm.*
- ❑ *Prices: Appetizers $2.95-$7.95; entrées $14.95-$22.95.*
- ❑ *Credit cards: MC, V.*
- ❑ *Reservations: Not necessary.*

❏ *Parking: Complimentary.*
❏ *Directions: Follow Highway One off 101 to Muir Beach.*

# Olema

This town was really jumping over 100 years ago. Before the railroad created the nearby town of Point Reyes Station, Olema was the commercial and recreational hub for the ranchers. The Olema Inn was the place to stay for folks up from San Francisco. Around the turn of the century, it was known as the town with nine saloons and one hotel, not to mention all the bordellos. Those days are long gone.

Now, it is a collection of a few buildings at the intersection of Highway One and Sir Francis Drake Boulevard, with a population that has dwindled to only 125 souls. There are two inns, a couple of small markets with deli counters and a boutique with designer clothing called the Epicenter, in honor of the 1906 earthquake. There is a bigger food selection at the Palace Market in Point Reyes Station, just a half-mile away.

# Inn

## Point Reyes Seashore Lodge

This is a rambling building on Highway One, about where Sir Francis Drake Boulevard comes in. It is across from the Olema Inn, in the middle of Olema. The Seashore Lodge, which is not near the seashore but rather next to Pt. Reyes Seashore Park, has hardwood everywhere. Wood floors, staircases and trim are all in honey-colored, vertical-grain fir. A porch in the front leads to a small lobby with a refrigerator case of wine in the wall behind the desk. You can buy a bottle at a low price to take to your room, where you will find glasses and corkscrew waiting.

Up a few steps from the lobby is a library with many books and magazines devoted to West Marin. Down a few steps is the guest lounge. Complimentary breakfast (cereal, yoghurt, fruit, juice and fresh sweet breads) is served here in front of the big stone fireplace. Down a few more steps is the game room with a pool table, cards, backgammon and so forth. A broad lawn in back slopes downhill to Olema Creek. It is not large, but it does run into Tomales Bay. From November to February, Coho salmon come up the creek past the inn to spawn. This is the real "front" of the inn as all rooms face out this way. The day we arrived, there was a wedding party rehearsing the ceremony on the lawn, drinking champagne and laughing. They were in the breakfast room the next morning. A bride and groom in their 20s were with friends, making jokes. That afternoon, after the wedding, a large group was at tables on a side lawn with food, drinks and music, provided by the inn.

We had a Terrace Room on the ground floor, opening out onto the lawn with a small patio, a white cast iron table and chairs. It was just right for when the sun goes down over the ridge across the valley, a lovely place to linger while a thousand stars come out at night.

The room was big, with a queen-size bed facing a table, chairs and an armoire by the opposite wall. At the back of the room was a wall-to-wall raised platform with a sink, a long counter and a double whirlpool bath. The toilet was in a separate room. Sliding screens could close the whole thing off if you wished.

The fireplace rooms on the second floor have queen beds. Some have jacuzzis and porches overlooking the lawn and creek. A couple of suites have beds in the lofts.

Our only quibble was the drapes covering the windows in our room. They were too thin, letting in the early morning sun. But that's a small reservation.

- ❑ *10021 Coastal Highway One, PO Box 39, Olema, CA 94950;*
  ☎ *415-663-9000, 800-404-5634.*
- ❑ *Rooms: 21, plus cottage.*
- ❑ *Rates: Holidays and weekends $115-$195; in-season weekdays $105-$185, off-season weekdays $85-$120.*
- ❑ *Credit cards: AE, MC, V.*
- ❑ *Reservations: June-September, weekends, from two weeks to two months in advance recommended; for weekdays, reservations are helpful as they are usually 90% full. October-May, two weeks ahead for Saturday nights; other days are no problem.*
- ❑ *Amenities: Game room, pool table.*
- ❑ *Breakfast: Augmented continental.*
- ❑ *Wine: No, but tea and coffee available all day.*
- ❑ *Handicapped accessible: Yes.*
- ❑ *Smoking: No.*
- ❑ *Children: Yes.*
- ❑ *Pets: No.*
- ❑ *Parking: Complimentary.*
- ❑ *Directions: At intersection of Highway One and Sir Francis Drake Blvd.*

# ℛestaurant

## ♥ Olema Inn

(American fare)

The Olema Inn looks as though it were magically transported from New England, which prompts Californians to call it European. The building is yellow with a wide, wrap-around porch and a well-kept garden where marriages are performed, followed by receptions. There is a comfortable wine and cheese bar, where guests sit while waiting for a table on weekends.

*Olema Inn.*

The inn was built in 1876, when Olema was the end of the railroad tracks. In the 1880s and 1890s, when it was primarily a vacation destination for San Franciscans, as it still is today, the town consisted almost entirely of eight saloons and this hotel.

We recently had dinner with Marianne and Roger Braun who own the inn. Thomas, their son, is the chef. He might have started in the business because of nepotism, but judging by the meals served here, he can obviously hold his own anywhere now. Marianne suggested we sample a few appetizers. "A few" turned out to be a large silver platter full. We started with oysters, clams and mussels from Hog Island in Marshall, just a few miles up the road on Tomales Bay. The Brauns prefer the seafood from Marshall. It is farm-raised there in a place where a fresh water creek comes into the Bay. The taste is very sweet and clean. There is also roasted garlic, brie and house-smoked salmon.

The house salad has a creamy vinaigrette dressing. Bouillabaisse nicely holds the individual flavors of all the seafood. Medallions of lamb are cooked to a delicate pink perfection, while roasted chicken, marinated in rosemary, lemon and garlic, melds this luscious blend of flavors. After all this we were ready to quit, but the chef insisted on serving us his special Chocolate Decadence. After the first bite, we were glad he insisted. Talk about sinful desserts – this chocolate cake with a chocolate sauce really is decadent!

The wine list is extensive, with well chosen selections from France, Italy and California at $18 and up.

- *10000 Sir Francis Drake Highway, Olema;* ☎ *415-663-9559.*
- *Open: Dinner every day, 5 pm-9 pm; lunch Saturday 11:30 am-3 pm, Sunday 11 am-3 pm.*
- *Prices: Lunch starters $3.50-$7.25; entrées $9.75-$13.50; dinner starters $6.75-$7.50; entrées $15.50-$19.*
- *Credit cards: MC, V.*
- *Reservations: Recommended.*
- *Parking: Complimentary.*
- *Directions: Located at intersection of Highway One and Sir Francis Drake Boulevard.*

# Point Reyes Station

Like many Spanish place names in California, this one is commonly mispronounced. Instead of REY-es, locals call it Point RAYS Station. That small matter is soon forgotten in such a nice little town. The old signs say "Population 350," but that is way out of date. The number of people here now is either double or four times that, depending on whom you talk to.

The town was born in 1875, when the North Pacific Coast Railroad opened a narrow-gauge line from Tomales to haul lumber, cheese and butter to the Sausalito ferry dock, with the ultimate destination San Francisco. On return trips, it brought San Franciscans to West Marin. Weekend vacations were especially popular. The town went into a slump after the railway went broke in the 1930s. As recently as the early 1970s, quite a few storefronts were boarded up and most everything badly needed paint. The two-story brick building boarded up across the street from the Station House Café is the Grande Building. At the turn of the century, in the town's early glory days, it was the leading hotel with a ballroom for all those city weekend vacationers to sashay in. Now, bringing it up to earthquake standards would be too expensive so it remains unused.

These days, you will find a nice mix of people on the streets here. There are artists and writers, ranch hands, former city dwellers happy to have made the move here, and visitors; but never so many as to overwhelm the town. There is one bank, one gas station, one rough-and-ready saloon (the Old Western), a couple of ordinary cafés and one really good one (the Station House). Up the block, on the same side as the saloon, is a book store and the Bovine Bakery, an immensely popular institution. Each morning, you will see dozens of people, who have just bought bread of some kind, sitting out front happily eating their breakfast.

The Station House Café is not actually in the old railroad depot. That is a few doors up the street and is now the Post Office. The old roundhouse was moved a few blocks to Mesa Road and is in use as the Lion's Club. It is the big wooden building painted red.

The fact that this is still a cow town is evidenced by the good business done by Toby's Feed Barn and the saddle shop. The Palace Market is West Marin's only supermarket and a good place to stock up for a picnic. On Saturday, there is a Farmers' Market in front of the hardware store on Main Street. It is small, selling mostly home-grown, organic fruits and vegetables. One of the local dairy farms sells its home-made goat cheese.

# *Inns*

## *Berry Patch Cottage*

This is more like a house than a love nest, though it could do double duty and often does. Jeri Jacobson says they often get anniversary couples. "Honeymooners like to be squished closer together. This is bigger," she said.

It is a large, quiet, private cottage with a big yard, a picnic table and barbecue. In the bedroom, a queen-size bed faces a Sears and Roebuck wood-burning stove and a couch. It is a big room with a window that looks out on the garden and yard. At least once a day you see deer there. They love to forage in the garden.

The kitchen, which opens out onto a large redwood deck, comes fully equipped and stocked for breakfast. In the living room is a queen-size sofa bed. Cable TV and a VCR with a good film library are also here. There is a reading alcove with area guides.

The cottage was built of thick redwood from an old barn in 1946, when this was all grassland and pastures. Jeri and Herb used to work in films in Hollywood, but escaped to West Marin just in time to save their sanity, according to Herb. They live surrounded by blackberries, raspberries, California laurel, four kinds of apple trees, plum, cherry, peach and black walnut trees. Sounds like a happy escape.

- ❑ *P.O. Box 712, Point Reyes Station, CA 94956; ☎ 415-663-1942.*
- ❑ *Rooms: One cottage.*
- ❑ *Rates: Weekends and holidays $120 per night; weeknights $100. $550 per week. Extra guest $15 per night. Half-payment due upon reservation.*

- Credit cards: No.
- Reservations: "We like reservations as far ahead as possible, but try spur-of-the-moment, especially mid-week after Labor Day."
- Minimum stay: Two nights on weekends.
- Cancellation policy: Full refund if cancel six days in advance.
- Breakfast: Kitchen is stocked with cereal, bread for toast, eggs, etc. You are the cook.
- Handicapped accessible: Not really.
- Smoking: Prohibited.
- Children: Yes.
- Pets: Dogs and other well-behaved pets OK.
- Directions: Call.

## Carriage House

Felicity Kirsch, the owner/manager, lives in the big old house about a third of a mile from the "downtown" part of Point Reyes Station. It is on the left side of Mesa Road and you can recognize it by the large magnolia tree in front.

The Sunrise Room, facing east of course, is in the front house, upstairs with a high ceiling and track lights. It is a long room with a double bed, sitting area and kitchen area with a coffee-maker, refrigerator, dishes, and a good-size bathroom.

In a separate house behind the main house there are two suites. Upstairs, the Sunset Suite faces west, so you see the sun going down over the Black Mountains, which turn red that time of day. There is a large bedroom with a queen bed, a living room with a fireplace, kitchenette with a microwave oven (no stove), fridge and dishes. It's a nice place to have breakfast. Just pick up a few things at Point Reyes Station the night before.

Downstairs is the Garden Suite with a queen-size bed in a large bedroom, a living room with a fireplace, full kitchen and dining room. French doors open out to a large garden that is very private. The only intruders may be some foxes who either live in the garden or visit it a lot.

Guests are free to pick the vegetables that co-exist along with the flowers. It is a beautiful place to sit, sip coffee and read a book. In the spring and summer, there are lots of lilacs, yellow and pink jasmine, lavender, honeysuckle, and passion vines that bloom all year.

- 325 Mesa Road, P.O. Box 1239, Point Reyes Station, CA 94956;
  ☎ 800-613-8351, 415-663-8627.
- Rooms: Three.
- Prices: $110-$140, mid-week and weekly rates. November-April, three nights for the price of two, Sunday-Thursday.

- Reservations: For summer weekends, as early as possible; weekdays are a bit easier to get. In winter, it is advisable to phone, but not always necessary; weekends are busier.
- Minimum stay: Two nights minimum on weekends.
- Credit cards: MC, V.
- Handicapped accessible: No facilities for wheelchairs.
- Smoking: Outside only.
- Children: Yes. Child care and cribs are available.
- Pets: No
- Breakfast: No.
- Wine: No.

## Cherry Tree Cottage

This property was a cattle ranch in the 19th century. Kristin Krugers is the innkeeper. Her place in front is 100 years old. The cottage she rents out is in the back and only five years old, but cozy. The cottage is all by itself, away from the main building. It is perfect for a couple who do not want to stay in a larger inn with other guests. This is Privacy Manor. Kristin told us she tries to make it "a home away from home." She stocks the cupboards and refrigerator with a wide variety of food. She serves what she calls, "an extended breakfast," providing muffins and breads that she bakes, plus fresh eggs. You cook the eggs and make the coffee. Everything else is provided. You can cook three meals a day if you like.

The place is very pretty. A fireplace faces the big canopy bed that has a thick mattress, making it so high you have to climb up into it. A small table with flowers is by the window and there are glass doors to the garden. A small bathroom opens to its own little garden with a big, private hot tub.

- 50 Cherry Tree Lane, P.O. Box 1082, Point Reyes Station, CA 94956; ☎ 415-663-1689.
- Rooms: One.
- Rates: $185.
- Credit cards: MC, V.
- Reservations: Necessary.
- Minimum stay: Weekends, April-November, two nights.
- Breakfast: Everything provided; you make the coffee and cook the eggs.
- Wine: No.
- Handicapped accessible: No.
- Smoking: Yes.
- Children: No.
- Pets: No.

# ♥ Ferrando's Hideaway (Garden Cottage) & Alberti Cottage

The main house is built on several levels. The unusual attraction in the all-purpose living room is a hanging fireplace made from a buoy that supported submarine nets across the Golden Gate during World War II. Guests gather here for tea and cookies before and after dinner.

Two large bedrooms share another living room with a fireplace and a private patio. A third room is upstairs, private, and with a view.

Best of all for a romantic couple there is the Garden Cottage behind the main house. It has a downstairs living room with a fireplace and a full kitchen. Upstairs in the loft is a king-size bed under the sloping ceiling and a walk-in closet larger than most. Doris' garden is just outside the door, full of tomatoes, strawberries, raspberries, squash, lettuce and peppers. Feel free to help yourself!

A short distance away, but with the same address and phone number for reservations, is the Alberti Cottage. The Ferrandos built this place in 1995. It has a big, high-ceiling living room with a fireplace and a full kitchen with a wide polished wooden counter to sit at. Out on its very private patio is a redwood table with an umbrella, where we immediately pictured ourselves eating breakfast. The fridge is stocked with breakfast food. Outside the front door in the early morning you will find a basket with fresh eggs from Doris' own chickens, muffins, croissants, coffee cakes (she bakes in the very early morning). An added treat is a roomy hot tub.

- □ *12010 Highway One, P.O. Box 688, Point Reyes Station, CA 94956;* ☎ *800-337-2636, 415-663-9372.*
- □ *Rooms: Three, plus a cottage in Ferrando's Hideaway, and one in Alberti Cottage.*
- □ *Prices: Rooms $110, weekends and holidays $130. Garden Cottage $150, weekly $800. Alberti Cottage $195. Midweek from November 1-March 31, three nights for the price of two.*
- □ *Reservations: Essential.*
- □ *Credit cards: MC, V.*
- □ *Breakfast: Yes.*
- □ *Wine: No, but tea, home-baked cookies and home-made chocolates are available.*
- □ *Handicapped accessible: Yes.*
- □ *Smoking: No.*
- □ *Children: In cottage only.*
- □ *Pets: No.*
- □ *Directions: Call.*

## *Knob Hill*

This is very private and at the end of a lane. There is a boarding school for horses in training next door. Janet Schlitt, owner of Knob Hill, works with the horses and loves them. Anyone interested in the kinds of horses that compete in Olympic trials will have a ball staying here and talking to Janet.

The cottage has a Waterford Irish wood burning stove. Its porch looks down on a creek at the bottom of a little valley and over to farmhouses on the next hill. The easy walk to Point Reyes Station is only 10 minutes, which is important because breakfast is not included. In the cottage is a coffee-maker, a toaster and a refrigerator in the kitchenette. Feel free to make your own meals from provisions picked up in Point Reyes Station.

The other rental in the main house consists basically of a double bed in a very small, very private room, cozy for a couple who do not mind really close quarters. Like the cottage, it has its own private bathroom, its own entrance and its own little garden with a picnic table. A coffee-maker is there for those who indulge. Finally, if you are on a budget, take a look at the price. Anyone who enjoys a bargain, without expecting luxury or even a lot of space, will gravitate here. This is why reservations are essential.

❑ *40 Knob Hill Road, Point Reyes Station, CA 94956;* ☎ *415-663-1784.*
❑ *Rooms: One cottage, one room in house.*
❑ *Rates: Cottage $85 weekdays, $95 weekends. Room in house $50 weekdays, $60 weekends.*
❑ *Reservations: Four weeks ahead. "Weekdays easier to get, always."*
❑ *Breakfast: Not included; $15 extra for Janet to provide it. Kitchenette in cottage to prepare your own.*
❑ *Handicapped accessible: No, bathrooms not big enough to admit wheelchair.*
❑ *Smoking: Outside only.*
❑ *Children: No.*
❑ *Pets: No.*
❑ *Directions: Just off Highway One on north side of Point Reyes Station, turn onto Viento St. Go to the end, then turn right onto Knob Hill to the end.*

## ♥ *Point Reyes Country Inn & Stables*

On this old Arabian horse ranch of four acres, the operative word is "space." The big white house off Highway One can be seen from the road. It has lots of windows and each of the rooms has a view of the surrounding rolling hills, dotted with fir trees and grazing cattle.

*Point Reyes Country Inn & Stables.*

There are six rooms for guests and Tom Evans boards horses as well as people. If you are a horse person, you will find a stableful to get acquainted with.

There is a porch – more of a deck really – covered with passion flower vines. The blossoms are colorful all year long. There are tables and chairs there for breakfast. Port and sherry are out 24 hours a day in the living room, where there is a wide fireplace. All the floors are Mexican tile. A huge, antique bookcase against one wall holds slews of books about travel and this area. On another wall hang old musical instruments. Each one has a story. Just ask innkeeper Evans, who will be happy to regale you. He is particularly proud that the deer all around here are not shy. Hardly! They come right up to the deck and munch the passion flower vines early in the morning.

After dinner, we came back to port, sherry and hot chocolate in front of the fire. Tom's collection of books about Point Reyes and West Marin kept us up late.

Our room on the ground floor had glass doors that opened into a garden with roses, purple primroses and lavender. A king-size brass bed dominated. The big tile bathroom had a marble counter.

Room Two is smaller, with a queen-size bed, carved headboard and a small deck looking off at the hills all around. There is a gorgeous bathroom with a high ceiling, a chandelier and marble-topped sink in an old side-board of carved wood with mirrors.

Room Three is also smaller, with a queen bed and a really cute sitting area and porch. It has green walls and the bathroom shower looks out on another porch with passion flower vines covering the railings.

Room Four has a big canopy bed, an armoir and a view from its own porch.

We stayed here just one night. Before reluctantly leaving the next morning, we got up to a breakfast of freshly squeezed orange juice, melon and thick-cut French toast covered with fresh blueberries and raspberries. Perfect!

- ❑ *12050 Highway One, P.O. Box 501, Point Reyes Station, CA 94956;*
  ☎ *415-663-9696.*
- ❑ *Rooms: Six.*
- ❑ *Rates: Weekdays $90-$120; weekends $125-$155.*
- ❑ *Credit cards: MC, V.*

- *Reservations: Generally for summer through October, you need to call at least three weeks ahead. Reserve ahead for February-April, if the weather's good. That's whale-watching time. The same is true in May-June for wild-flower time.*
- *Minimum stay: Two nights on weekends.*
- *Breakfast: Full ranch breakfast.*
- *Wine: Sherry and port, always available.*
- *Handicapped accessible: Try to accommodate.*
- *Smoking: Outside only.*
- *Children: No.*
- *Pets: No. Horses, yes!*
- *Directions: On Highway One, one mile north of Point Reyes Station.*

## Tree Frog Farm

There are only a few streets in Point Reyes Station so you are never more than a few minutes from the two-block business district. We drove along Cypress Avenue, a country road lined with cypress trees. Two horses trotted up to watch us as we turned into a lane on the near side of a brown wooden fence. Ferrando's Alberti Cottage is on the other side. We drove to the end of the lane, past Pat Healy's Morgan horse and a few other horses we did not know personally. At the end was Pat's new two-story house and, next to it, the older one-story place that is now her guest house. She sometimes rents it to visitors. The rent is negotiable.

The older house consists of three rooms, counting the small kitch-enette off the living room. The living room itself is comfortable, though not large. It has a couch, a marvelous chair with wooden armrests perfect for resting a glass and appetizers, plus a footstool. A bookcase and more shelves hold an eclectic collection, in case you feel like reading. The furniture is not antique or anything special. This is not a Victorian landmark. A Japanese lantern and a collection of woven baskets hang from a ceiling beam. There is an entry hall with more bookcases and a straw hat for a doze in the sun. No TV, radio or telephone are available. You are on your own. A dining table is by the kitchenette, which is fully equipped. There is a bathroom with shower, no tub. The bedroom has a double bed and bedside tables with lamps just right for reading.

We carried our bags in and did not bother to unpack. We poured two glasses of wine from a bottle we had prudently brought along, then laid out some cheese and crackers (from the Palace Market in town) and put our feet up. Next, we contemplated what we would have for dinner at Pat Healy's Station House Café.

Outside are apple, pear, plum and persimmon trees. Pat says the raccoons love the persimmons and plums and that deer often come around. We didn't see any.

Pat's new house and the guest house are on top of a hill and overlook the valley. We walked through a moon gate and past a small fountain where lots of small frogs live. On a flat place partway down the hill there are a table and chairs. Off to the right, Olema Creek makes its wandering way toward Tomales Bay. This was sacred land when the Miwok Indians lived here. The peace and stillness made us feel it hasn't changed.

Pat will bring breakfast ingredients to you or you can go to the Station House Café (a four-minute drive) with a $16 breakfast allowance for two. This will get you juice, coffee, toast (try the sourdough), a four-egg omelet with shittake mushrooms, gorgonzola, tomato and pesto, and an order of Hangtown Fries (see p. ).

□ *19 Cypress Road, Point Reyes Station, CA 94956;*
  ☎ *415-663-1617, fax 415-663-1925.*
□ *Internet: pathealy@nbro.com.*
□ *Rooms: One cottage.*
□ *Rates: $125 summer weekends, lower rest of season, negotiate weekdays.*
□ *Credit cards: Discovery, MC, V.*
□ *Reservations: "A couple of months."*
□ *Breakfast: Pat will bring a continental breakfast to you, or eat at the Station House Café with $16 credit for two.*
□ *Handicapped accessible: There are a few steps.*
□ *Smoking: No.*
□ *Children: "Probably not."*
□ *Pets: "I don't mind a well behaved pet. It's up for discussion."*
□ *Directions: Call.*

# ℛestaurants

## Station House Café

(Contemporary American)

Former jazz singer Pat Healy has owned this café for 23 years. "Point Reyes Station was very different then," she told us, "just a small, rural town. The park was much less popular. Now there are so many people, San Franciscans mainly, coming to the park and Point Reyes Station gets so many visitors." She seemed a little wistful.

The café is not the actual station house of the old railroad. That is located two doors down and is now the post office. The café consists of a large, friendly bar room and the restaurant itself. Inside, it's not particularly romantic in the traditional sense, but the food is so good, we think most people will forgive that. The outdoor garden is positively sensual. Every inch is filled with something growing;

hydrangeas, lilies, wisteria, flowering maple, lavender and roses. Arbors are scattered throughout to provide separate nooks for couples to enjoy. An experience we can highly recommend is to sit in an arbor, watching the humming birds and butterflies raiding the flowers while you have lunch. Our midday feast started with oysters, followed by an obese Reuben sandwich. There is a comprehensive menu.

Fortunately, the weather usually cooperates, allowing you to enjoy the garden from May to October. Some days in January can be wonderful.

The first time we went to the Station House was because a local friend recommended it as *the* place to eat in Marin. We met Pat, who urged us to start with the fresh mussels. We explained that we really didn't like mussels or oysters. It all started with a disastrous experience in Naples that ended with days of sickness. Dubiously, we tried a half-dozen of the little devils. After the first bite, Phyllis declared, "These are the best things I have ever tasted." Bob tried and had a similar reaction. What have we been missing all this time? Try them with lemon and butter. They were fresh from nearby Tomales Bay. "Fresh" is the operative word here. Seafood is still wet from the bay. Salad greens are grown nearby and delivered daily. There is vegetable soup every day, as well as other kinds of soups. The smokey roast tomatoes with garlic are a really good choice.

Dennis Bold, chef for 19 years, holds forth only in the evenings. Pat Healy says that you cannot get a hold on the food until you have tasted the results of Dennis' creativity and skill. You will find things like medallions of pork with grilled apples and a wide selection of fresh seafood on the menu for dinner. Dennis is "happy to prepare your meal without sauce or dressing." There are no heavy French sauces here. Instead, Dennis concentrates on such skills as making a really good meatloaf. It's not like your Aunt Emma's, but is deeper and more complex in flavor.

When you get to dessert, even if you think you are full, try the bread pudding. Both custard and caramel sauces are served alongside. It's soft and creamy inside with a crusty brown outside and here and there a raisin and an occasional bit of apple appear. To die for.

Breakfast here is a good move, too. Try the red flannel hash or their extravagant (some say excessive) omelet. It is made with crab, shrimp, mushrooms, avocado and Mornay sauce. This is your chance to try Hangtown Fries. (See page 258.)

❑ *Main St., Point Reyes Station;* ☎ *415-663-1515.*
❑ *Open: Weekdays 8 am-9 pm, Saturday and Sunday 8 am-10 pm.*

❑ *Prices: Starters from $2.95. Lunch, main courses $5.50-$9. Dinner, main courses $7.50-$18.50 for the New York steak.*
❑ *Credit cards: Discover, MC, V.*
❑ *Reservations: Seldom necessary, but not a bad idea.*
❑ *Parking: Street or lot.*

# Nightlife

## The Old Western Saloon

The Old Western Saloon looks like a yellow-painted hotel-saloon in a Western movie. Only it's better, because it was not built as part of a set. This actually is one of the oldest saloons in Northern California. The two-story building used to be a hotel, or a bordello, or both. Of course, the locals claim everything used to be a bordello.

On Saturday nights, it gets loud; which is OK. City cocktail lounges should be dim and romantic. Small town saloons should be loud, particularly on Saturday nights. People sitting on high stools at the bar that runs the length of this long, narrow, beat-up place can't hear each other, but they are shouting anyway, trying to be heard over the music. There are a couple of over-amplified musicians twanging guitars and the usual female singer on the slightly raised platform at the other end of the room. She is belting out something that sounds vaguely pop-country, trying to be heard over the shouting.

There are a couple of black metal tables with tops that slope upward from the center, forming big, shallow bowls with holes in the center. Your glass will tilt if you set it down. Don't. Maybe the holes are to let the spilled beer drain out. There is no sense in asking anybody. They can't hear you anyway. This is a place for locals. There are a lot of ranchers and ranch hands here on a Saturday night.

There is another room behind the bandstand with a few pool tables. On a quiet afternoon, you can hear the click of the balls running when you walk past on the sidewalk. You can, however, take a seat back there and watch the experts hustle each other.

Out front, it's actually a happy sort of place. If you stand at the crowded bar waiting to catch the bartender's eye, it's easy to get into a conversation with the friendly folk here. They'll talk to you about anything. Try it. Besides, there really isn't anywhere else to go on Saturday nights.

❑ *11201 Highway One, Point Reyes Station;* ☎ *415-663-1661.*
❑ *Open: 11 am-2 am.*
❑ *Prices: Tap beers $2 and $3; well drinks $2.75 (cheap enough!).*
❑ *Parking: On street.*

## Station House Café Bar

There is live music year-round on Friday, Saturday and Sunday. Friday night is jazz, Saturday has quieter guitar music and Sunday hosts jazz and contemporary, with local musicians sitting in. Some of the Sunday musicians play in the San Francisco Symphony.

If you like beer, Lagunitas Oat Ale on tap at the bar is one of the delights of the territory. Actually, it is brewed in Petaluma, about half an hour away.

❑ *Main St., Point Reyes Station;* ☎ *415-663-1515.*
❑ *Open: Weekdays 8 am-9 pm, Saturday and Sunday 8 am-10 pm.*
❑ *Credit cards: Discover, MC, V.*
❑ *Parking: Street or lot.*

## Things to Do

**Black Mountain Weavers** is across from the Post Office. ☎ 415-663-9130. Open 11 am-5 pm every day in summer and Thursday-Monday in the winter. Everything for sale here is individually handwoven: shawls and scarves, knitted sweaters, quilts, braided and rag rugs, knitted hats and handpainted silks. Even if you are not intending to buy, the textures and colors of these hand-crafted originals are a delight to see.

**Bicycle Rentals** are available in the Building Supply Center, Main St., ☎ 415-663-1737. It is open Monday-Friday 7:30 am-5 pm, Saturday 9 am-4 pm, Sunday 9 am-1 pm. You will find picnic utensils and supplies, bait for fishing, fishing and hunting licenses and bicycle rentals. Bicycle rentals range from two hours for $15 to all day for $25. They are 18-speed mountain bikes and the store will supply you with maps and directions.

# Inverness/Inverness Park

Take Sir Francis Drake Highway from just south of the bridge before entering Point Reyes Station. Or take Bear Valley Road out of Olema, which joins with Sir Francis Drake and runs up the west side of Tomales Bay. After a couple of miles, you will come to Inverness Park, which consists of a few, small, weathered buildings alongside the road facing Tomales Bay. The steep, heavily wooded sides of Inverness Ridge rise up behind them. **Inverness Park Grocery** is here (sandwiches, etc., for a picnic in Point Reyes National Seashore), and next to it is the **Knave of Hearts Bakery** and Coffee House. The latter has a reputation for good things to eat in the bread and pastry line, plus soups and spinach pies, which you can add to your picnic basket.

Inverness is two miles farther on, strung out sparsely along the two-lane road. Across the way, various docks and long, spindly piers poke out into the shallow water along the shore. Inverness has been called a "genteel town" compared to the others. You can't really see much of it. All the houses are on the mountainside or tucked away in narrow valleys between shoulders of the ridge, out of sight among the trees. It was started in 1889 as a resort and has held up pretty well.

# *Inn*

### ♥ *Blackthorne Inn*

The inn looks like a vast tree house. Head up a steep driveway off a narrow country road with trees meeting overhead and the rustic wood house is right in front of you. Tilt your head back, as you look up and up into the trees where the topmost room in the house seems to hang suspended.

Originally it was built as a residence, but when the owners, Susan and Bill Wigert, decided to move, they converted it into an inn. In any case, the place was certainly built to be enjoyed. Heavy double doors and big, solid beams come from the remodelled Ferry Building. The wavy glass windows come from the Jackson Street (San Francisco) school, designed by Julia Morgan. She was California's first woman architect, who designed, among many other notable structures, William Randolph Hearst's San Simeon castle.

The main level has a big living room with a comfortable leather couch facing a huge stone fireplace. A room just off that, surrounded by windows, is good for a drink (bring your own) or coffee. A big deck outside is for breakfast or just lounging. The deck is 20 feet off the ground and in the midst of trees. There are two rooms downstairs. One is a suite with a sitting room and the other a wicker-furnished bedroom. They share a bath. Upstairs, above the main level and reached by a spiral staircase, are two rooms with queen beds. The front room is brighter and out in the trees with a private bathroom down the hall. We stayed in the back room with its bathroom right off the bedroom. It was cozier and rustic.

The top level on the spiral staircase is the Eagle's Nest, where you are right in the tree tops, with windows surrounding you. Once you are up there, you can swing a wooden door shut over the top of the staircase for perfect privacy. A wooden bridge leads to a terraced deck on the hillside where there is a hot tub to be used by all the

*Blackthorne Inn.*

guests and a private bath and shower solely for the Eagle's Nest. Thick, warm robes are provided for nighttime jacuzzi visits. Robes in the other rooms are elegant silks. No matter which room you are in, everything is comfy and private. The quiet at night is so intense that the sound of a squirrel on the roof in the morning was startling to us.

The morning we were there, a breakfast buffet featured "Leonor's thing," which turned out to be an egg casserole with tomatoes, onions, chilis, black beans and sour cream. We also enjoyed freshly squeezed orange juice, coffee, tea and rolls from Sweet Things bakery in Tiberon. This place is incredibly romantic, especially if you stay in the Eagle's Nest. The other four rooms are not far behind.

- ❑ *266 Vallejo Ave., P.O. Box 712, Inverness Park, CA 94917;*
  ☎ *415-663-8621.*
- ❑ *Rooms: Five. Two rooms share one bathroom.*
- ❑ *Rates: $109-$195.*
- ❑ *Credit cards: MC, V, processed when making reservations.*
- ❑ *Reservations: "Can make anytime."*
- ❑ *Minimum stay: Two nights on weekend.*
- ❑ *Amenities: Robes, hot tub.*
- ❑ *Breakfast: Full breakfast, different specialities each morning.*
- ❑ *Wine: No license. They do provide glasses, ice, ice bucket and guest refrigerator to keep your bottle.*
- ❑ *Handicapped accessible: There are many stairs, no elevator.*
- ❑ *Smoking: Outside only.*
- ❑ *Children: No.*
- ❑ *Pets: No.*
- ❑ *Directions: Call.*

## Restaurant

### Manka's Inverness Lodge & Restaurant

(Regional cuisine and wild game)

Actually, we went to Manka's for dinner because everyone asked, "Have you eaten at Manka's yet?" Now we can say, "Yes! We have eaten at Manka's." But never again.

Manka's is touted by the locals for its fine food, and the food *is* good, though pricey. The service was another question. We were not in a hurry to go anyplace, but the wait was ridiculous. We were seated almost immediately, which we found to be a good sign. Then, 10-15 minutes later, a waitress stopped by just to see if we were alive. Seeing that we were breathing, rather heavily at that point, she deigned to take our order. We would like to see a menu and wine list to start with. She disappeared, to be replaced a few minutes later by a bus boy with bread. There was no sourdough bread this time, which was a surprise, but crusty French bread made at Knave of Hearts bakery in nearby Inverness Park. The bread was good, but we were getting hungry and thirsty. Finally our wine came and, well, it went on like that.

It took them two hours to serve a simple salad and entrée; no appetizer, soup or dessert. When we finished, long after we had finished, we waited vainly for someone to say, "Hello" or, "Oh, are you still here?" or something. No one did. So we went into the kitchen to interrupt a fascinating conversation and get our bill.

The food, as we said, is good. Salmon is grilled over the lobby fireplace. There is a room with comfortable couches to wait for your table if necessary; or maybe to get into the habit of waiting. The fish was served with a ragout of basil, garlic and mayonnaise, which was homemade. The fish was tender and flaky. On the wall, is a quotation from J.W. Pettee:

*Pray for peace and grace and spiritual food*
*For wisdom and guidance for all these are good*
*But don't forget the potatoes.*

They didn't. The salmon comes buried under shoestring potatoes – shades of Dennys!

A cobbler of wild mushrooms served with tomatoes, stuffed with local goat cheese and sautéed zucchini blossoms, gets high marks. It's inventive, combining contrasting foods in a medley of pleasing tastes. Locals would ask us, "Where have you eaten? How did you like it?" We would report that we had tried Manka's and found the food good, but the service was incredibly bad. They would invariably admit, "Yes, I know. I've been telling Margaret for years that she should do something about it." Go figure.

- *Argyle and Callendar, Inverness;* ☎ *415-669-1034.*
- *Open: 5 pm-10 pm.*
- *Prices: entrées $18-$25.*
- *Credit cards: All major.*
- *Reservations: Recommended.*
- *Directions: Continue on Sir Francis Drake Blvd., past Olema to Argyle. Turn left up the hill to Callendar.*

## Things to Do

**Blue Waters Kayaking** is at 12938 Sir Francis Drake Highway, at the Golden Hinde Inn Marina, two miles past "downtown" Inverness. ☎ 415-669-2600 for a recorded message, 415-669-7879 for a live person. Open seven days a week, Monday-Friday from 10 am-6 pm, Saturay-Sunday from 9 am-6 pm. Hourly and full-day rentals are available. A single kayak for two hours, $25; double kayaks $35; half-day, $35 and $45. Lessons for beginners, plus naturalist-led day, sunset and moonlight paddles on Tomales Bay are options worth exploring.

# Tomales Bay/Marshall

The smooth, protected waters of Tomales Bay are lined with remote beaches and lagoons. As the largest unspoiled estuary, or *estero*, as they call it here, on California's coast, it's a haul-out and pupping site for 400 harbor seals and home to 45 species of fish, as well as a spawning ground for Pacific herring and crab. A variety of rare ducks, 25,000 wintering loons, grebes, cormorants, geese and other open-water birds also call it home. Cod, perch and halibut are also found.

With all of this to see, you must try a kayak. If you have never been in one, try two kayaks for the two of you, or a double made for two. Head off with a picnic lunch to some secluded beach.

On the east side of Tomales Bay, taking Highway One north from Point Reyes Station, is Marshall. It was never much of a town, but it was handy for fishermen and the ranches in the hills around here. There used to be several very active boatworks, but they are pretty well defunct now. What's left are a few fishing boats, some private sailboats and, most of all, the oyster farming. Oyster farming has been going on here since the turn of the century. In addition, this is completely different country from the rest of West Marin. There are no redwoods and no forests – just the Bay and brown or green (depending on the time of year) rolling hills.

## Inn

### Inn on Tomales Bay

The road is scenic as it runs beside the long, thin length of Tomales Bay. The hills to the east, with grazing cattle, roll upward to the mountains that run the length of Marin, dividing it in half. The inn is down a slope on the other side of the road, among the trees and above the water.

On old maps, this was called Blake's Landing. The North Shore Boat Works was here back then. The area was originally home to cabins, near the water, for hunting ducks. A few of the old buildings still remain below the inn on the water's edge. The house numbers change along here and this one is easy to miss. Keep an eye out for the "Inn on Tomales Bay" sign.

Lynette and Bob Kahn live here and have four rooms to rent. Each has a fireplace, a large bathroom, small refrigerator, radio, tape deck and binoculars. The latter are handy since all rooms look out over the Bay and guests can watch the seals and pelicans diving offshore. Sometimes, you can watch Bob fish for salmon, which will be served for breakfast the next morning. There are walking and hiking trails. Lynette provides backpacks for day-long jaunts, but not everyone takes part in the strenuous all-day hikes. Some couples hardly come out of their room. It's peaceful and relaxing here. There is a big, comfortable room downstairs for breakfast and for gathering by the fireplace. Most guests have breakfast in their rooms.

Lynette and Bob started the inn about four years ago. They keep chickens for the eggs, which show up at breakfast. There is a small garden out back to provide herbs and some vegetables.

We looked in the Guest Book and saw comments like, "Thank you for a wonderful stay, so peaceful and quiet," "This is definitely a room with a view," and "This is lovely, a little bit of heaven." Indeed it is.

- ❑ *22555 Highway One, Marshall, CA 94940;* ☎ *415-663-9002.*
- ❑ *Rooms: Four.*
- ❑ *Rates: $130.*
- ❑ *Credit cards: No.*
- ❑ *Reservations: Three to four weeks for weekends, shorter time for weekdays and winter.*
- ❑ *Minimum stay: Two nights on weekends.*
- ❑ *Amenities: Binoculars, backpacks, breakfast room service.*
- ❑ *Breakfast: Full American breakfast.*
- ❑ *Wine: Yes.*
- ❑ *Handicapped accessible: No.*
- ❑ *Smoking: Outdoors only.*
- ❑ *Children: No.*
- ❑ *Pets: No.*
- ❑ *Directions: Almost three miles north of Hog Island Oyster Co. in Marshall, which is eight miles north of Point Reyes Station on Highway One.*

# Restaurants

## Hog Island Oyster Co.

(Oysters, mussels)

Look for the old general store on Highway One, just short of Marshall. This is home to the Hog Island Sweetwater Oyster. They grow oysters, clams and mussels from seedlings on racks lowered into the shallow water. You can see how it's done and then buy a dozen or so, which will cost $6 to $8, depending on the time of year and what's available. Step over to their picnic tables and grills and have yourself a mess of barbecued oysters. Remember to bring a loaf of bread, a bottle of wine, and we would add a lemon and a small bottle of Tabasco. They are open for visitors Friday, Saturday and Sunday from 9 am-5 pm. During the week, you can call ahead and they will be happy to show you around.

- ❏ *Highway One, Marshall;* ☎ *415-663-9218.*
- ❏ *Open: Daily, except Wednesday and Thursday in winter. Best to call ahead anytime.*
- ❏ *Directions: About nine miles north of Point Reyes Station on Highway One.*

## Marshall Store

(Seafood)

The young couple who run this place are proud of the fact that they sell organic milk and butter and local organic bread baked in brick ovens by the Village Bakery. The deli also has sandwiches, espresso, ice cream and wine for picnics. Fisherfolk come here for box lunches to take along on their odyssey. None of that is the big reason people drive about nine miles out of Point Reyes Station to get here. It's more because oysters, mussels and abalone are farmed just a stroll away, down the Bay. There are tanks of them on a deck beside the store, waiting for you to dip them out. Joyce or Stewart will open them for you, so you can eat them on the half shell, right then and there. They have some piquant sauces you might like to try such as soy ginger, cilantro vinaigrette or what they call their Marshall sauce, made from tomato, horseradish and a secret hot ingredient.

Abalone are sometimes on hand, but they are slow growers and there are never enough. Japanese tourists are especially fond of them and often clean out the supply. You just have to be here at the right time. Crab is also a seasonal dish, available mostly from November to May.

Two bottles of cold beer from the refrigerator inside the store, a dozen bivalves to split between the two of you, a splash of Joyce's sauce and a view of the Bay... it can't be beat.

- ❑ *19225 Highway One, across from the Post Office, Marshall;* ☎ *415-663-1339.*
- ❑ *Open: 8 am-6 pm daily.*
- ❑ *Prices: Oysters, half-dozen $5, dozen $10. Mussels $3 per pound. Clams $4 per pound. Local crab $4.99 per pound. Abalone $22 per pound.*
- ❑ *Directions: Nine miles north of Point Reyes Station on Highway One. This road is also called State Route One and Shoreline Highway.*

## *Tony's Seafood*

(Extremely fresh seafood)

Established in 1948, Tony's is now in its third generation of owners. Outside, a man shucks oysters, which are farmed practically next door. The fresh crab season runs from the second Sunday in November to mid-May.

Tony Konatich speaks of the "good old days" when clams, shrimp, oysters and mussels grew naturally in this bay. But, he sighs, now the oysters and mussels are delicious, but they are farmed. We comment, while munching away on our second order, that if you didn't know, you wouldn't know. Tony's place is north of Point Reyes Station on the edge of Tomales Bay. The café hangs out over the water and tables are lined up by the big windows so you can eat and watch the birds and an occasional fishing boat go by. Beer and wine are served, and the toilet, while clean and shiny, is in a place next door. Some people even go to look at the oyster farms, but those are usually passing tourists who see the place and stop.

Tony's is the kind of place where the smart thing to order is the clam chowder, homemade and very good. There is a bottle of Tabasco on every table, which the locals like to add to the chowder. Entrées are mostly breaded and deep-fried, like the fish and scallops. They come heaped on big plates with overflowing piles of skinny French fries. This is a place for gourmands, not gourmets. The combination club sandwich, with bits of bacon, is pretty good, too.

We may kid about it, but we love to drive out here and sit by the window. It's great to look out at the water, the fishing boats and birds while we eat. It's a treat we think you will enjoy, too.

- ❑ *Highway One, Marshall;* ☎ *415-663-1107.*
- ❑ *Open: Saturday 12 noon-8:30 pm; Sunday 12 noon-8 pm. No service on weekdays. Open only for lunch and dinner, but the doors close promptly at 8:30 pm. If you get here at 8:28 pm, you can still get an order in, but you will not make the cook too happy.*

- *Prices: Cup of clam chowder is $2.75, bowl $3.75; entrées $9.95-$12.95.*
- *Reservations: Are you kidding?*
- *Parking: Just get off the road.*
- *Directions: Drive about nine miles north of Point Reyes Station on Highway One along the west side of Tomales Bay to Marshall. Pay attention or you will pass Marshall without realizing it.*

## *Things to Do*

**Tamal Saka Tomales Bay Kayaking.** In the language of the Coast Miwok, "tamal" meant bay and "saka" were tule reed boats. One day each July, you can join in building a traditional tule reed kayak. Then tour the bay with local historians and paddle to former Miwok settlements. Rates are $35 for a single kayak (the plastic kind), half-day rental is $45; a double kayak, full day, $45 or half-day, $65.

Here are some special tours for kayakers (check with Tamal Saka for dates). South Tomales Bay Loop for beginners ($65) allows you to kayak among waterfowl, shorebirds, herons and egrets. Sunset and Full Moon Paddles ($45) are especially romantic. Culinary Kayaking Adventure ($95) starts by paddling across the Bay (waters are calm) to a beach feast of local oysters, abalone, vegetables and fruits. There is also a Yoga Kayak Adventure ($80), where you paddle to a beach with a yoga master for a session. A Massage Kayak Adventure ($95) goes to a secluded beach where a "massage therapist will greet you with open hands."

- *19180 Highway One (P.O. Box 833, Marshall, CA 94940 for brochure); ☎ 415-663-1743.*
- *Open: Only Saturday and Sunday in the winter. Call if you prefer a weekday and for package times.*
- *Directions: At Marshall Boat Works, eight miles north of Point Reyes Station.*

## *Samuel P. Taylor State Park*

This is a 2,600-acre reserve a few miles east of Olema. If you are driving to West Marin from the outside world, along Sir Francis Drake Highway, this is about where you start seeing the tall redwoods and no doubt start commenting on the beauty of the area. That's what we did the first time we drove over from Mill Valley. Then we came to the Park itself and knew what beauty really was.

There are campgrounds here, but there are also picnic tables among the trees and in a glen. Coho salmon and steelhead trout spawn in

Lagunitas Creek once it fills after the first good rain in winter. To protect their dwindling numbers, no fishing is allowed.

The entrance is on the south side, but the Park is actually on both sides of the road. There is an easy two-mile trail for a pleasant walk along a creeklet and through the woods on the other side. A three-mile section of the Cross Marin Bike Trail runs through the park.

❑ ☎ *415-488-9897, for complete information.*
❑ *Admission: $5 day-use fee.*

# *Point Reyes National Seashore*

This is the only national seashore on the West Coast. There are 100 square miles of park, 130 miles of trails and over 30 miles of protected coastline. Lush forests, rugged cliffs, open grasslands, vast wetlands and unbelievable views complete the setting.

Start at the Bear Valley Visitor Center, a quarter-mile off Highway One on Bear Valley Road at Olema. ☎ 415-663-1092. The Center is open 9 am-5 pm, seven days a week. There are maps and brochures, and you can view the well done displays and small cycloramas. There are lots of books you can buy to learn about the birds, plants, geology and seemingly every other aspect of the park. A 15-minute slide and sound show with great photos will give you an idea of what there is to see in the different areas.

There are three short, easy trails from the Visitor Center itself. **Earthquake Trail** is a half-mile paved path, wheelchair-accessible, following the San Andreas Fault zone. Signs interpret what you are seeing. Among the sights is a fence, half of which was on the Pacific Plate, that jumped 20 feet northwest. The other half of the fence, on the North American Plate, stayed put. The trail begins in the picnic area.

**Woodpecker Trail** is a loop just over a half-mile long. It explores forests and meadows, with signs identifying plants and animals that you might see if you're lucky. The trailhead is at the end of the parking lot.

**Kule Loklo Trail** is one mile long and leads to a replica of a Coast Miwok Indian village. A sweat lodge, acorn graneries, tepees, and a sacred roundhouse have been built using native tools and techniques. Culture and history are described and cultural events and demonstrations are sometimes held. Ask at the Visitor Center. This walk begins at the base of the parking lot.

There are many other walks, some of which can take up to a full day. Some are fairly flat, over easy meadows and chaparral. Others traverse steep, mountainous terrain, or have beaches, or *esteros* (marshy lagoons) as destinations. Get maps at the Visitor Center.

There are also organized group hikes to suit various interests. You may be interested in bird watching, geology, Indian lore, pinniped viewing (here's a chance to learn the difference between seals and sea lions), tidepool exploring and more. Schedules may be daily in summer, but are usually on weekends only in winter. Phone the Visitor Center for current schedule.

If you are interested in horses or ranching, visit the **Morgan Horse Ranch**, a working ranch in Bear Valley for horses used by the rangers in wilderness areas and for backcountry patrol. Self-guided exhibits, corrals and demonstrations. They are open every day from 9 am-4:30 pm. ☎ 415-663-1763.

If you prefer to ride the horses, you will find 50 miles of bridle trails from the woods to the seashore. To rent horses, contact **Five Brooks Ranch**, 3½ miles south of Olema on Highway One. ☎ 415-663-1570; on the internet, the address is http://www.coastaltraveler.com. It's open 9 am-5 pm, seven days a week, all year. You can trail-ride in a group of six or eight, or as a couple with a guide. Per-person prices are $20 and $30 for one hour; $35 and $45 for two hours; $60 and $75 for a half-day (3½ hours); $85 and $105 all day (six hours). The all-day ride goes to the beach.

If bicycling is your thing, you will discover over 35 miles of trail open to bikes. Get a trail map at the Visitor Center.

Once you're finished with the area around the Visitor Center, it's time to see the western part of the park. Drive on up Bear Valley Road. It will join Sir Francis Drake Highway, continue past Inverness where the road turns away from Tomales Bay and go over Inverness Ridge. After a few miles, there is a fork. Decisions, decisions!

The right fork is Pierce Point Road, which veers north. It's about five miles to the end of the road and the parking area. Before you get that far, you are already about a mile into **Tule Elk Reserve**. Big, hefty, beige-furred beasts with elegant antlers graze, sometimes right outside your car window. The elk were always here, a native species that once existed in large herds. Since there was no environmental movement in those days, they were hunted and killed from the 1850s on. Before long they were gone. In 1978, a small herd was found elsewhere and 10 of the elk were reintroduced here. Now, there are 240 and the Park Service is wondering how to get rid of some. They look wonderful, majestic and usually self-absorbed. The rangers advise to stay clear of them, especially when the males are rutting in the fall. But do not forget your camera.

While you are here, the Historic Pierce Point Ranch is nearby. There is a self-guided tour along a path among the white-washed buildings of this 19th-century dairy ranch.

If you are up to a long walk, or part of one, the parking area is also the beginning of the Tomales Point Trail. It's a 4½-mile one-way hike to the northernmost point of the National Seashore. That's over nine miles round-trip, but the terrain is level and the scenery unforgettable. The regular trail ends after three miles. There is a footpath from there on.

Much easier and closer at hand is a half-mile trail down to McClures Beach. You might see a few of the indigenous creatures along the way like badgers, hare, gopher snakes, gray fox and weasels.

Back in your car, return to the fork in the road and this time take the left branch. A mile or so along, you will come to a sign marking a road heading left to Drake's Estero – a reedy inlet off Drake's Bay. As you drive along Sir Francis Drake, those dark green clumps of unusual looking trees are called Bishop Pines. This is the only place in the world they grow.

Continuing along toward Drake's Bay, you may be surprised to see large dairy farms. The farms predate this park by more than a century; the park grandfathered them in by leasing the land back for the bovines to graze.

Roads branching off to the right go down to Point Reyes Beach North (about 13 miles from the Visitor Center) and Point Reyes Beach South (15½ miles). It's great scenery, but don't swim on any of these west-facing beaches. The surf can be brutal, and unseen are the rip currents and severe undertow.

You will probably be curious, as we were, about what those buildings and transmitting towers are off to the right. Turns out they were put in by Guglielmo Marconi in 1914 to make the first trans-Pacific radio transmission. MCI runs it now.

There is another fork in the road, just before the Point Reyes Beach South road. The left-hand fork leads to Drake's Beach. It's a nice, wide, sandy strand between high bluffs. This is the place where Drake, in 1579, careened his ship to make repairs.

There is no lifeguard, but it's safe to swim here. The water is "cold as hell," even in the summer. Don't even think about swimming in the winter. The Visitors Center, with information and displays, is open 10 am-5 pm daily. In the winter, they are open on weekends only. Winter officially starts in September. Guided tours are available on weekends throughout the year. Call ahead, ☎ 415-669-1250.

There is a little place to eat, **Drake's Beach Café**, next to the Visitors Center. It's most convenient to lunch or just a snack. Fish and chips are $5, clam chowder $3.09, oyster stew $6, hamburger $3.61 (odd pennies reflect tax). The food is nothing special, though we can testify that a bowl of hot clam chowder or oyster stew tastes wonderful on a cold, clammy day. They are open 10 am-6 pm and are closed on Wednesday, year-round. Eat inside or at picnic tables, where you can also bring your own lunch.

Back to the fork in the road, continue south about four miles to yet another, and final, fork. Take the right hand road to Point Reyes Lighthouse, 20½ miles from the Visitor Center. There is a parking lot and then a blacktop half-mile trail. The trail is wheelchair-accessible, but the lighthouse itself is not. The dome of cracked cement you see at the end of the trail is an old system for catching rain water, now unused. The lighthouse is open 10 am-4:30 pm. A tiny Visitor Center with old photos and a ranger to answer questions is open 10 am-5 pm, Thursday through Monday (closed Tuesday and Wednesday), weather permitting. Call to learn the local weather at ☎ 415-669-1534. There are 300 steps down to the lighthouse, which was built in 1870. There was a lighthouse keeper here until 1975, when it was automated. Bring a warm jacket – this is the windiest headland on the Pacific Coast, with 40-mile-per-hour winds common. The rocky shelves below the lighthouse are home for thousands of common murres and sea lions, who are at their peak numbers in spring and fall. The sea lions enjoy basking on the offshore rocks. This is also the best place to see gray whales on their

*Point Reyes National Seashore Lighthouse.*

migrations in late December/January and March/April. Even if you don't go down the steps to the lighthouse, you can see it all from above. Bring binoculars.

Back near the parking lot is a trail to the Sea Lion Overlook – another good place for viewing harbor seals and sea lions. When you return to that last fork, the other road goes to Chimney Rock on the opposite point of the peninsula's end. This is one of the best places for wildflowers, which bloom in early spring, and it's also good for seeing gray whales when they return from the Baja California calving and breeding season in March/April.

The weather out here on the peninsula is variable, to say the least. From April through October there is often dense fog. The light-house was located relatively low on the cliffs to keep the beam under the ceiling of typical high coastal fogs. When the fog is thick, at the top of the stairs (elevation 600 feet), the lighthouse (294 feet) is often clear.

Contrary to what you might expect, there is not as much to see here in summer as in winter. In the summer, the flowers are gone and the fog may visit daily. April is good for wild flowers and the last of the whales migrating north. Fall is best.

It was late October when we were talking to the ranger at the Lighthouse Visitor Center. The phone rang. Someone was asking how visibility was, wanting to know if it was worthwhile to come out. The ranger started to say, "It's fine and sunny," when she turned to the window. "Well, it was a minute ago, now the fog is thick!"

## *Hangtown Fries*

In the Gold Rush days, Placerville, California was called Hangtown (because they stretched more necks there than most places). Miners were striking it rich and had nothing to spend their money on. At the few, crude, greasy-spoon cafés along the muddy street, they began ordering the most expensive food they could think of – eggs and oysters. Oddly, it was not the eggs that cost so much. They were about a dollar a piece. It was the oysters that had to be rushed up the mountains from the Bay while they were still fresh. The local cooks concocted a way to put these two unlikely ingredients together – oysters cooked up with the eggs and some bacon for breakfast.

Some love the dish. Others can't stand it. You'll have to try it to see which group you are in.

# Have a Whale of a Time

Each winter, more than 18,000 gray whales migrate down the California coast, hugging the shoreline and touching base at the points and capes along the way. The bluffs of Point Reyes National Seashore are one of the best places to get a good look at these magnificent creatures. Probably the finest place is near the lighthouse at the western point.

The migration begins in the Alaskan waters at the Bering Sea feeding grounds. The giants travel south, 6,000 miles to reach the shallow lagoons of Baja California in northwest Mexico, where mature females give birth, usually to one calf each. The best time to see them is December through February when they are migrating south. Then, from March through May, the grays and their young move back northward. It's possible to sight stragglers as late as June. During the migration, the whales make 70-80 miles a day at a rate of three to five miles an hour. They travel in small groups (pods) of two to six and stay fairly close to the shoreline to avoid predators, mostly killer whales. Larger blue whales are sometimes seen with them, along with an occasional humpback and schools of porpoise.

The annual 12,000-mile round-trip trek is the longest distance any mammal migrates. Grays may reach up to 50 feet in length and weigh 45 tons. They have that name because of their gray coloring, though when swimming or hovering just below the surface they may appear white or slate blue. One of the gray's more distinctive traits is its lack of a dorsal fin. Instead, a low hump is followed by a series of bumps down the back.

Whales can be seen best from a fairly high vantage point. A time when the sea is calm with few or no whitecaps, more likely in early morning, is preferable. An overcast day, when there is no sun glare on the water, is even better. Watch the water for a "blow" – the water vapor exhaled when the creature comes to the surface, every five minutes or so, to breathe. The geyser of white vapor, which can reach 12 feet, is easy to see against the darker water.

You may see the whales perform a maneuver called "spyhopping," where the whale sticks its head above water one or more times. It's thought that the creature is getting its bearings from landmarks on the shore. Then, again, it may simply be using gravity to help swallow. Occasionally a whale will arch out of the water, lift its flukes (tail) and slap them down hard on the surface – thought to be a way of communicating with other whales. The most dramatic behavior is called "breaching," where the whale leaps entirely out of the water straight up and falls back onto its side or back, making a spectacular splash. The guess is that this is simply "back scratching" to rid itself of the parasites that cling to its hide. Obviously, we don't yet know everything there is to know about *Eschrichtius robustus*. Near the Point Reyes Lighthouse is one of the best whale-watching sights along the entire California coast because it's at this point that the whales turn into the shallower waters of Drake's Bay. The small parking area above the lighthouse is often full on busy weekends. In that case, the Park Service will usually provide a shuttle bus from one of the beach parking lots.

# Wine Country: Napa & Sonoma

❧ *A Book of Verses underneath the Bough,*
*A Jug of Wine, a Loaf of Bread – and Thou*
*Beside me singing in the Wilderness –*
*Oh, Wilderness were Paradise enow!*

Edward Fitzgerald

Spain ruled the roost here at first. It was cattle country, but the land is so fertile and the climate so good for certain crops that, by degrees, agriculture took over. There were early attempts at cultivating grapes. The missions always had a few vines growing to provide sacramental wine, but nothing more. General Marianjo Guadelupe Vallejo, who was a Governor of Alta California when the state was part of Mexico, planted the first commercial vineyards. You will see the site if you visit his home in Sonoma. There are grapevines there to this day.

Wine was flowing by the turn of the century. The valleys were doing better than ever until the 1920 Prohibition put the kibosh on it all. Most wineries closed, but a few survived by making sacramental wine.

One gimmick that was tried during the dry years was selling "wine bricks." They were made of crushed grapes, to be dissolved in water. The label warned, "This beverage should be consumed within five days. Otherwise, in summer temperatures, it might ferment and become alcoholic."

Wine's boom and bust cycle began again in 1933 with the repeal of Prohibition. But the boom was slow in coming. It takes four to five

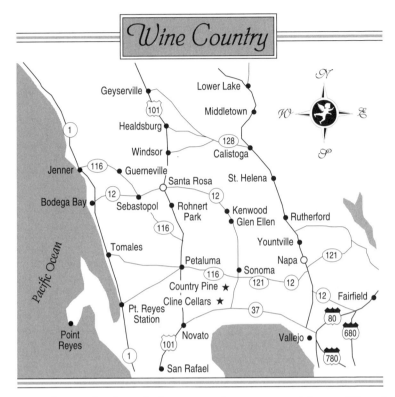

years for newly planted vines to produce commercial quantities of grapes.

After World War II, the valleys began prospering once again. It was only in the 1970s that tourists, mostly from San Francisco, began to show up for free wine tastings. When tourists appear, can hotels and restaurants be far behind? By then, Napa and Sonoma wine was selling well in California. It did not do as well in the rest of the country, which preferred European wines, particularly French. In fact, the same could probably be said for most Californians then. California's wines weren't even considered by most Europeans. Then came an event and a date that shall live in infamy (for France) and in glory (for Napa and Sonoma): May 24, 1976.

# The Paris Tasting

A British wine merchant, who had an inexplicable taste for California wines, staged a blind tasting in the patio of the Intercontinenal Hotel in Paris. Nine distinguished French oenophiles tasted from bottles covered to conceal their identities. The judges knew they were judging French and American wines, but never faltered in their patronizing attitude toward the American ones. Two and a half hours later, when the last wine had been sipped and spat, the judges sat stunned, unbelieving and mortified. The rest of wine-loving France felt the same way. Six of the eleven highest rated wines were from California, including best of the whites and best of the reds.

The fallout from that simple event was enormous and is still being felt. Napa and Sonoma wines were suddenly hot! There were huge profits to be made! Thousands of new acres have been planted and a great many of the old wineries bought by corporations – many of them French. There are now many hotel rooms for visitors in the two valleys, dozens of restaurants and way too many tourists. But, as the French say, "C'est la vie!"

## *In the Vineyards*

You are going to drive past many vineyards growing nothing but small, one- or two-year-old plants. The *phylloxera* has hit again. Some fields already had disease-resistant plants. Others have had to tear out mature vines and start over with new root stock. Most of the growers who give winery tours don't take you out into the vineyards. If it's just the two of you at a small place, you stand a better chance of seeing how things are done in the fields.

## *In The Wineries*

After showing how wine is made, from crushing to bottling, every tour ends in the tasting room. Some large wineries ask a fee (usually around $2 per person) for tasting. Few of the small places do. Some of the large wineries don't pour the "good stuff" because they get such large tour groups that they would soon be giving it all away. At Beringer, for instance, if you go into the "library" and pay a little more, they pour the better wine.

A mystique has grown up around wine. If you watch one of the experts tasting a wine, you will see there is a proper way to do it.

*1. Lift the glass by the stem so your hand is not warming the bowl.*

*2. Hold the glass in front of your eyes and look knowingly at the color of the liquid.*

3. *Swirl it in the glass and then put your nose down and sniff. You should look off into the distance at the same time and think deep thoughts.*

4. *Take a small, pensive sip. Swish it around in your mouth and let it linger on the tongue to engage lots of taste buds. If you were a real taster, you would spit it out. There is no need to do that now. It's a waste of good wine. We amateurs will never really appreciate the damn wine if we don't swallow it.*

5. *Next, and very importantly, say something like, "I detect peach" or, "A hint of apple," or even "licorish." Wine tasting, like modern art, is subjective. Who can argue with you?*

6. *At the end, especially when the wine is free, we make it a rule to say "thank you."*

## Buying Wine

Usually, there is no point in buying a lot of wine at the winery. They usually sell for the same price as stores, so as not to undercut retailers. In fact, you can sometimes buy national brands for less from a price discounter or chain drug store at home. There are circumstances where it makes sense to buy at the source. In a small winery, with limited production, you may never be able to find that brand anywhere else. Ask the winemaker if he ships to your part of the country. Sometimes, there will be a larger production of a particular vintage and variety than could be sold. In a case like that, you might spot what looks like a bargain. We have seen case prices cut almost in half. That is the time to make sure you taste the wine you are thinking of buying! Maybe there's a reason it didn't sell.

If you do buy by the case and want to ship it home, be aware that sometimes you won't be able to. It's illegal to ship to Kentucky, for example, and fines can reach $25,000. Other states simply have peculiar laws about shipping wine to individuals. Some small wineries are just not geared up to handle the paperwork. If they won't ship, ask them for the name of a professional company that will handle it for you.

If you buy any amount at the winery, don't store the bottles in the trunk of your car. The sun and heat will play havoc with the wine, and all the shaking won't do it any good either.

# Weather

Winters are moderate, with temperatures in the high 40s during January. Rains used to begin in late December and continue off and on until April. The rains were concentrated in the space between December and February, which was great for the vineyards. That dependable pattern has changed in the last decade, with years of drought followed now by uncertain rains that can come even during harvesting. In 1996, flood waters stood in the vineyards for weeks in November.

In summer, most days are comfortable, although it can get into the 90s. Nights are always pleasant. Sonoma Valley is closer to the ocean and generally cooler. Napa Valley is warmer. Fog usually rolls up the valleys from San Pablo Bay late at night, but usually burns off by mid-morning.

# When to Come

November to April is off-season for most travelers, which means no crowds and it's easy to get reservations at inns.

February and March are good for a different look at the valleys. Flowering mustard grows between the rows of dormant vines so all the vineyards are a blaze of yellow.

September and October are not only among the most crowded months. This is also the time when the wine makers are busy harvesting and crushing and may have no time for you.

# Napa Valley

❦ *Drink no longer water, but use a little wine for thy stomach's sake.*

The First Epistle of Paul the Apostle to Timothy

When Padre Jose Altimira came along in 1823, he found the Napa Indians here. The name means "plenty" in their language, which still seems apt for this fertile land. Nicholas Higuerra was awarded the original Spanish land grant and American farmers began arriving as early as the 1830s. Just a few vineyards did well making wine and selling to San Francisco during the Gold Rush. Now there are over 240 fully functioning wineries and vineyards. There are many inns and bed and breakfast places, almost all small. Of the two largest in the valley, Meadowood has only 70 rooms, and Auberge du Soleil has 50. Three or four rooms is much more common.

It's best to make reservations well ahead if you are coming in summer (April to September), or harvest season (September and October). Some resorts, like Meandowwood, suggest booking by February, if you intend to be there from April to October and want a choice of rooms. Reservations are much easier to come by over the winter, after Thanksgiving until February. Even then, if you intend to come on a weekend, you should reserve by October for the best known places.

It's common for San Franciscans to drive up for the weekend, year-round. Even people from Los Angeles and Southern California will fly up just for the weekend when there are cheap airline flights.

Napa is one of the smallest counties in the Bay Area. The valley is only 25 or 32 miles long, depending on who's doing the measuring, and from two to five miles wide (wider in the south). This makes getting around easy, as long as you have a car. Look at the map and you'll see that the road system resembles a ladder. Highway 29 runs up the west side at the foot of the Mayacama Mountains. The Silverado Trail runs up the east side, below the Vaca Mountains. The two are only a few miles apart. Running at right angles between them, from the town of Napa to past St. Helena, are a dozen roads. If you are here on a summer weekend and the traffic on 29 gets too much for you, just go over to the Silverado Trail, which is never as crowded. Many of the wineries you visit will be on the side roads.

Napa is the big city – 66,000 in population – located at the south end of the valley. The other towns cluster around Highway 29, from Oakville's 200 population to St. Helena's 6,000.

## How to Get Here

### By Car

**From Oakland:** Take 80 north to 37 west, then 29.

**From San Francisco, the scenic way** (1½ hours): Go over Golden Gate Bridge (101) to Novato, then 37 east to 121, to 29 north.

**From San Francisco, the fast way** (1 hour): Take Bay Bridge to Oakland, then Highway 80 east. Exit Highway 37, follow to 29.

**From the north, via 101:** Take 128 at Cloverdale, south to 29.

**From the north, via 5:** Take 80 west to 12 (south of Vacaville), to 29.

*Other Services*

You can use **Shelley's Airport Shuttle** from Oakland for $20. ☎ 707-259-0128. From San Francisco, **Evans, Inc.** runs 11 shuttles a day for $15. ☎ 707-255-1557.

**Bauer's Limousine Service** is another alternative. ☎ 415-522-1212.

## Getting Around

It's more difficult to see wineries by bus because stops are often in the wrong place and weekend service is limited. **Napa Valley Transit** mainly connects the towns from Vallejo up through the valley along Highway 29. ☎ 800-696-6443. **Intercity Van-Go** has service connecting the towns. ☎ 707-963-4222 and 707-252-2600.

**Yellow Cab,** ☎ 707-226-3731; **Napa Valley Cab,** ☎ 707-257-6444.

**Premier Limousine Service,** ☎ 707-226-2106.

# Wine Tasting & Wine Jargon

❧ *Let us have wine and women, mirth and laughter,*
*sermons and soda water the day after.*

Byron

The following information should help with your wine tasting. You will hear the terms below used often. Try to taste whites before reds, and dry before sweet. You will be able to appreciate a wider range of wines.

Begin with a Chardonnay. Most are dry, meaning they have little sweetness, but have enough body so they feel round and smooth in the mouth. Sniff before you taste. You want to see whether the wine is fresh and clean, without any moldy, chemical or other aromas, and how much fruit is in the wine. To experienced tasters, Chardonnays have enough aroma to suggest comparisons with green apples or ripe pineapples. They can also smell "buttery," "toasty," or like buttermilk.

A wine can be fruity and dry at the same time. Fruity refers to a high level of fresh varietal flavor in specific grapes, like "tropical fruit" in Chardonnay or "cherries" in Merlot.

Balance is the key to a wine's palatability. The body, meaning the mouth-filling quality of a wine, must be kept lively by the clear presence of acidity. A low-acid wine is flat and flabby,while high-acid wines are shrill. A well-made wine is balanced and leaves a good aftertaste, called finish.

Try a Cabernet and see how red wines differ from whites in terms of tasting etiquette and terminology. Reds extract their color from the skins of the grapes during a one- to two-week fermentation period.

Again, start with sniffing the wine. Cabernet grapes might suggest to the experienced taster aromas like black currants, chocolate, cedar, leather, roses, herbs and bell peppers. If there is a vanilla-like bouquet, it's probably from the oak barrels used to age the wine. You will expect to taste some astringency in a Cabernet due to a chemical called tannin that comes from the grapeskins. Tannin breaks down during aging. An eight- to 10-year-old cabernet should be a good deal softer than it was at age two or three. Most good reds should be dry, even astringent, with little sweetness. The flavors should linger in your mouth after you swallow.

Another aspect of maturity in red wines is a change in the "nose." Old Cabernets no longer have strong aromas. They develop a much more subtle bouquet. The chance to taste what happens to a wine over the years is one of the main reasons afficionados keep wine cellars.

Sparkling wine is especially difficult to analyze. The fragrances and flavors are subtle. Some of the best wines are often crisp with acidity. In no other type is balance so important.

---

## Ꝇapa Valley Towns

In 1831, before the town of Napa was started, George Calvert Yount, the first white settler, arrived. He wrote in a letter, "In such a place I should love to clear the land and make my home. In such a place I should love to live and die." He got his wish.

General Vallejo, over in Sonoma, arranged for Yount to receive a land grant after he became a Mexican citizen and converted to Catholicism. Two years later, he planted the first vineyard in the valley on his 11,000-plus-acre rancho in what later became known as Yountville.

Oakville and Rutherford are very small towns located mid-valley. They have their own micro-climates, suited perfectly for Cabernet grapes, which accounts for the number of wineries producing world-class Cabernet Sauvignon wines here.

St. Helena (which the locals pronouce Saint Heh-LAY-na) was a late-comer. It was not established until 1853, but now is in the center of a very important grape growing region. Main Street has some quaint shops and restaurants, many in buildings made of native stone before the turn of the century. Those street lights are antique electrolaires, installed soon after San Francisco's 1915 Panama-Pacific Exposition, where they were first seen. The big mountain towering over everything at the north end of the valley is Mount St. Helena.

## Inns

### ♥ Auberge du Soleil

(Member Relais & Chateaux)

We had the feeling here that we were in a very expensive Mexican resort. The rooms are big, with large areas functioning solely as transition spaces to other areas. A room the size of a small living room can serve mainly as a path to a big closet. But who's complaining? We love it! You will also see plenty of tile. Whoever had the tile contract for this place must be a multi-millionaire now.

Our place, Versailles One, an Auberge Suite, is typical. On entering, you are faced with a wide tile counter, a handy place to park your door key, or anything else up to the size of a Volkswagon. Big, sand-colored Mexican tiles cover all the floors. A wide living room has three sets of doors open to the private patio. Built-in couches are covered with shocking pink cushions and pillows facing each other across a large, low tile table. This is all in front of a fireplace with a tile hearth. There is a tile counter with a phone, another table and more chairs and flowers in a big vase.

A large kitchenette is off the living room, with wide tile counters and tall Mexican chairs. Sink, minibar, coffee machine, cups and glasses are all available. A closet and a half-bath are also in the suite and we are not even in the bedroom yet. A king bed, another larger TV set, a built-in desk and good-looking Mexican pigskin chairs flanking a table by another fireplace are in the bedroom. There are more tall glass and louvered wood doors leading to the patio, plus a closet with plenty of space.

The bathroom is large, with two sinks and a jacuzzi built for two. The toilet is in its own roomette and there is a roomy tiled shower. Two robes and two sets of slippers await.

This place is grand. We reveled in all that space, lit both fireplaces and watched two TV shows,

Other rooms in the cottage complex are called Auberge Kings and comprise only the bedroom part of the suite. So, you make do with only one TV and one fireplace. Auberge Standard rooms are the same, only slightly smaller, with a double tub and no jacuzzi. Two rooms in the main building above the dining room and lounge are smaller still, with no fireplace or jacuzzi.

The resort sits on a hill and all rooms overlook the valley. (The exceptions are a few ground-level units with dense foliage in front, which trade the view for privacy.) Units are built in clusters of four and six on the hillside, each level above and set back over the lower one.

There are tennis courts, swimming pool, spa and a half-mile sculpture trail through the old olive grove. The grove was here before the Auberge took form, and as many olive trees as possible were saved. The olives are still pressed and the oil can be purchased.

This all started with the Auberge du Soleil Restaurant in 1981, an acclaimed eatery from the moment it opened. (See page 275.) The resort was added four years later.

The road to the Auberge leads off the Silverado Trail. Though every inch is planted in grapes in the valley below, lots of other foliage blankets these hills. When we rose in the morning, we found big, muddy raccoon tracks tromping across the hood of our car. Nothing's perfect.

- ❏ *180 Rutherford Hill Road, Rutherford, CA 94573;*
  ☎ *800-348-5406, 707-963-1211, fax 707-963-8764.*
- ❏ *Rooms: 50.*
- ❏ *Rates: From $225 to $975 per night.*
- ❏ *Credit cards: All major.*
- ❏ *Reservations: Recommended.*
- ❏ *Minimum stay: Two nights if your stay includes Friday or Saturday.*
- ❏ *Breakfast: There is an excellent dining room, but breakfast is not complimentary.*
- ❏ *Amenities: Spa, swimming pool, tennis, dining room, cocktail lounge, robes and slippers in room.*
- ❏ *Handicapped accessible: Yes.*
- ❏ *Smoking: Yes.*
- ❏ *Children: Discouraged.*
- ❏ *Pets: No.*
- ❏ *Directions: Hill Road and Auberge du Soleil sign (big boulder) on your right.*

## *Harvest Inn*

The exterior of this building is in English Tudor style. The owner, Riehard Geier, built the first part of this inn on his vineyard in 1978 using over a million bricks (1,000,008 in fact) to construct the main building and cottages. Somebody actually counted.

Start in the main building where you walk into a large two-story lobby with a fireplace, wood floors and beams. There is a good-sized counter with two clerks working it. This is a big inn. There are 54 rooms in cottages spread out over eight acres of land and a 14-acre working vineyard to boot. The Great Room, off the lobby, is where guests gather. It has a wood floor, walk-in fireplace, deep leather couches and a beer and wine bar. An extended continental breakfast is served here, with cereals, fresh fruits, fresh pastries, coffee and juices.

Each room has a name fancifully carved in its wooden door. Gamay (some are named after grapes) is big, with a king bed, a brick fireplace (some of the 1,000,008), hardwood floor, a soft sofa beside an antique trunk used as a table, and the TV set on a butcher's block. The furniture is sort of an antique farm style. Phyllis' Midwestern ancestors would have recognized some of the pieces.

Lord of the Manor, the name of the cottage, is much more formal. A separate sitting room has a large brick fireplace and a massive brick chimney topping a wall-long hearth. There is a long cushioned window seat made for reading or fooling around, or both. The dining room has leather chairs with footstools and windows looking out on the vineyards stretching away to the mountains. A private deck is outside.

Upstairs is the bedroom, with a king bed sporting a carved wooden headboard and another big brick fireplace. The jacuzzi for two has its own private niche. There is an even larger bathroom than the one downstairs, with two sinks. The bedroom also looks out on the vineyards.

The Bluebird is not quite as grand as Lord of the Manor, but it'll do. It's another big room, with plenty of space for a table, two chairs and a brick fireplace. On the ground floor, it looks out on the vineyards from a private deck. There is also a wet bar.

These three rooms are typical of the range of accommodations. All rooms have antiques and no two are exactly alike. A very few rooms have queen beds and no fireplace, but all are a generous size.

❑ *One Main St., St. Helena, CA 94574;*
   ☎ *800-950-8466, 707-963-9463, fax 707-963-4402.*
❑ *Rooms: 54.*

❑ *Rates: Weekdays, November 10-April 10, $99-$290; rest of year $139-$329.*
*Weekends, winter to May 1, $165-$366; after May 1 $175-$366.*
❑ *Credit cards: AE, Discover, MC, V.*
❑ *Reservations: Recommended.*
❑ *Minimum stay: Two nights required with Saturday reservations.*
❑ *Breakfast: Extended continental.*
❑ *Wine: Not complimentary, but wine and beer bar off lobby.*
❑ *Handicapped accessible: Three rooms.*
❑ *Smoking: Yes, with a few non-smoking rooms.*
❑ *Children: Very welcome.*
❑ *Pets: In a few rooms only.*
❑ *Directions: South of business section on Highway 29. From San Francisco Airport, Evens Transport to Yountville, ☎ 707-255-1557; take a taxi from Yountville.*

## ♥ *Meandowood*

(Member Relais & Chateaux,
Preferred Hotels, Small Luxury Hotels.)

In the late 1800s and early 1900s, the small valley at the foot of Howell's Mountain was farmed by Chinese, who grew rice where the golf course is now. The farmers were originally brought here to build a railroad in Napa Valley and to mine silver on Mount St. Helena. Some worked in the wineries and vineyards. Most of the stone fences around Meandowwood were built by the Chinese laborers.

There is a swimming pool, spa and tennis courts, then a main lodge and dining rooms that look down on the golf course and croquet lawn. Attractive cabins are scattered around, mostly hidden on the hillside among the trees.

All rooms are painted a pleasing white, with gray trim, the same as the exteriors. There are a few large suites, some of which have beamed ceilings. Most have a fireplace, a private porch and a down comforter on the bed.

Lawn View Rooms look out at the croquet lawn. Along with the regular amenities, there is TV, hair dryer and bedroom skylight to keep things bright.

In the Hillside Terrace Rooms, the shower and tub are separate. There is a king bed and a big flagstone fireplace. Treeline Cottage has two rooms, a king bed, fireplace and a skylight in the living room.

Then there are the Studios, which are the least expensive, but still with plenty of space. They have flagstone fireplaces, large bedrooms with queen beds, a shower (no tub), a skylight and a ceiling fan. The Studios are a good buy.

They have even less expensive rooms that are not included in the brochure they will send you. These are in older buildings, have really large porches and are near the spa and pool.

If you are coming on a special occasion, like a honeymoon or anniversary, tell them when calling for reservations. There will be a bottle of wine waiting to greet you in your room. If you're coming in the winter, make sure you have a fireplace.

There are hiking trails, bike rentals, spa, massage, tennis and a pool on the resort's grounds. They have the only international croquet lawn on the West Coast. How many chances do you get to play croquet these days? Make reservations from 10 am until dusk. You must wear the traditional white or cream slacks/skirt and a collared white shirt/blouse. White tennis shoes are required.

For fine dining, there is The Restaurant (see page 277). The Grill is casual. The Pool Café is even more so. Room service is offered from 7 am-10 pm. Bon appetit!

- *900 Meandowwood Lane, St. Helena, CA 94574;*
  *☎ 800-458-8080, 707-963-3646, fax 707-963-3532.*
- *Rooms: 70, including suites.*
- *Rates: Weekdays, April 1-June 30 and November 16-March 31, $280-$395; weekends $305-$425. Weekdays, July 1-November 15, $305-$425; weekends $325-$425. Plus occupancy tax. Suite prices depend on number of bedrooms.*
- *Credit cards: All major.*
- *Reservations: For the summer (April to September) and Harvest Season (September and October), book by the previous February. Slow season is from after Thanksgiving to February. Book by October. Weekends harder to get year-round.*
- *Minimum stay: Two nights on weekends.*
- *Breakfast: Breakfast, lunch and dinner available in resort's restaurants.*
- *Wine: Cocktail lounge on premises.*
- *Amenities: Golf, tennis, croquet, swimming pool, spa. In-room amenities include robes, scale, coffee-maker, toaster. Concierge will arrange winery tours.*
- *Handicapped accessible: Yes.*
- *Smoking: No.*
- *Children: Under 12, no charge.*
- *Pets: No.*
- *Directions: From Highway 29, one mile past Rutherford, turn right on Zinfandel Lane to Silverado Trail, where you turn left and go one mile to Howell Mt. Road. Turn right and drive 500 feet to Meandowwood Lane, where you turn left and go one mile.*

## Oak Knoll Inn

The inn was originally a farm house, with locally quarried stone wings added in 1984 when it became an inn. We had one of the two end rooms of the wings and it was heaven. They call it a room, but we have been in suites that were a lot smaller than this. It has high, pitched, beamed ceilings. A king-size bed barely makes a dent in the space. Plush carpets cover the floors. A couch and overstuffed arm chairs are next to a thick black glass table, with a tall vase of fresh flowers. The fireplace is wide. There is a good radio and CD player, but no phone or TV. There is a big closet near a tall dresser. These rooms, large as they are, have no place to put open luggage (one luggage rack does not do it). A minor fault in an otherwise wonderful place.

There are two rooms in each wing and the walls between are double-thick, ensuring quiet. The end rooms (One and Six) have tall, arched windows in the end walls, with a great view of the vineyards and Stag Leap Mountains.

The Stag Leap Wine District starts north of the inn, which is on 3½ acres. Barbara Passino and John Kuhlmann, our hosts, plan to plant their land in grape vines so the inn can have its own wine label.

There are stacks of books about the valley in the "lobby" (more like a living room), with more books in each room. We found good reading – *Like Water for Chocolate* and, interestingly, *Murder in the Napa Valley*. There is a wonderful desk in the common room. If you forgot to pack something, just open a drawer and you're likely to find it. Among the accessories were a sewing kit, Bandaids and toothpaste. One time, a tiny screw came out of Bob's glasses and was lost. The magic drawer contained a glasses repair kit!

Our letter of confirmation included an invitation, "Please join us for wine and cheese from 6 to 7." We joined everyone out on the patio. In cooler weather, this get-together takes place by the fire in the dining room. We were expecting perhaps a few cubes of cheddar, but what we got was a huge bowl of different cheeses, cold cuts, crudités, and more. A selection of wines was brought by a local winemaker who conducted a tasting session. It was great fun.

The complimentary breakfasts are multi-course. Barbara has taken cooking classes in the US and in Europe and loves to cook. There is plenty of freshly squeezed juice, a fruit course that might be strawberry and rhubarb pizza, followed by big shittake mushrooms and parmesan cheese, or poached eggs and Hollandaise sauce.

One couple we know told Barbara when they reserved that they were interested in small wineries and significant local art showings. Barbara had it all arranged by the time they arrived, including winery visits, where the owner would show them around. There were also maps to the best local galleries that were having showings. This is the kind of experience you can have at small inns with caring proprietors.

❏ *2200 East Oak Knoll Ave., Napa Valley, CA 94558;*
☎ *707-255-2200 for reservations; 707-255-2296 for Barbara Passino.*
❏ *Rooms: Four.*
❏ *Rates: Rooms One and Six (end rooms) $285, Two and Five $250.*
❏ *Credit cards: MC, V.*
❏ *Reservations: "A long time ahead" or at the last minute. "By the first week in March we were almost completely booked until Thanksgiving." Much easier to book for November to April.*
❏ *Minimum stay: Guests staying Saturday night must stay one other night, Friday or Sunday. Also two-night minimum during holidays.*
❏ *Amenities: Swimming pool, two thick robes, iron, ironing board.*
❏ *Breakfast: Full gourmet breakfast.*
❏ *Wine: Complimentary wine and hors d'oeuvres.*
❏ *Handicapped accessible: No.*
❏ *Smoking: Not inside.*
❏ *Children: Infants or 14 and over OK. Not in between.*
❏ *Pets: No. "Too many guests have allergies."*
❏ *Directions: North on 29 from Napa, then right on Oak Knoll Avenue to Big Ranch Road; turn left, then right again on Oak Knoll, which zig-zags here.*

# *Restaurants*

## ♥ *Auberge du Soleil Dining Room*

(Mediterranean-California Wine Country)

The Dining Room was built in 1981, nestled in 33 forested and olive-grown acres in the hills above Napa Valley. It made a name for itself immediately. First of all, the dining room is a good looking place with a high ceiling, peeled cedar pillars and wood beams. It has lots of glass and French doors opening out on a dining terrace and a view of the valley below. Secondly, in this day of deliberately noisy restaurants, it's a relief to dine in a room where only a soft murmer is heard from the other guests. Perhaps you will hear the clink of ice as an unobtrusive waiter brings drinks or keeps a water glass full.

Starters include the Petaluma exotic mushrooms with chive waffles on polenta, and the Fig and Foie. The latter is an imperial fig stuffed with compazola, a mild, domestic blue cheese and foie gras. It has a thickened sauce with multiple overtones, oregano being the most obvious. The mushrooms actually taste like mushrooms and the chive waffles enhance the flavor. The stuffed figs are a bit rich, though mighty tasty.

For an entrée, you might try a cedar-planked golden trout, light and crusty, and a multi-grained pilaf with chanterelle vinaigrette. Or select an oven-roasted swordfish with grilled onions and merlot-lobster sauce. The horseradish whipped potatoes with snipped chives are much better than the mashed potatoes of childhood memory, thank heaven.

Good as much of the food is, we have a sneaking feeling that executive chef Andy Sutton may try too hard. Everything is very rich, with many flavors are in every bite. You can end up, at the end of the meal, with a confusion of tastes and no clear memory of what it was that you liked. The room is lovely room, and dining on the terrace above the valley on a warm evening is surely everyone's idea of a romantic occasion.

- ❏ *180 Rutherford Hill Road, Rutherford;* ☎ *707-963-1211.*
- ❏ *Open: Breakfast 7 am-11 am, lunch 11:30 am-2:30 pm, dinner 6 pm-10 pm.*
- ❏ *Prices: Breakfast $12.50-$23, lunch $23-$40, dinner $40-$95.*
- ❏ *Credit cards: All major.*
- ❏ *Reservations: Strongly recommended.*
- ❏ *Directions: From Highway 29, east on Rutherford Cross Road (121) to Silverado Trail, then left 100 yards, and right at Rutherford Hill Road.*

## *Pinot Blanc*

(California Nouvelle)

When you enter this newest Napa restaurant, you will see a tall, tall back bar full to the top with racks of wine bottles (as befits Napa Valley). Most of the beers are from local microbreweries. This is Joachim and Christine Splichal's latest in a string of Patina Pinot restaurants (all in Los Angeles, except for this newest one).

Request a table for two in one of the two end alcoves. The room is long, with both booths and tables. The booths are comfortable and have impressive dark paneling, but they face out the wide windows onto the highway, which is not too attractive. The ceiling is high and there are heavy draperies used to close off an alcove, a whole wing or simply the big-windowed bay. All this seems to cut the room up too much. There are candles on the tables at night and you can see stars and the moon through the skylight. A patio in the back is used in good weather.

Pinot Blanc chicken salad is a good example of the cooking style here. The ingredients are very fresh, local whenever possible, and are lightly dressed so as not to obscure the natural flavors. These are quite ingenious dishes put together in new ways. For example, the chicken salad starts with slices of baked potato. Perched on those is an oyster mushroom, on top of which is a thick wedge of roasted chicken. Piled on top of that is a chopped and herbed tomato. Then all of this is buried in a heap of fresh greens.

It has been said of Joachim that he practices the "crackerjack" style of cooking. There is a prize in every dish. An example is the "potato and mushroom ravioli with mini white mushrooms and a truffle *à la nage.*" The surprise here is the truffle cooked in a court-bouillon broth. "Roasted corn risotto with field mushrooms, carmelized shallots and garlic" is another wonderfully flavorful dish. The carmelized shallots add a kick. To demonstrate the common touch, the lunch menu has cheeseburgers. Of course, they're made with roquefort.

- ❑ *641 Main St., St. Helena;* ☎ *707-963-6191, fax 707-963-6192.*
- ❑ *Open: 11:30 am-9 pm.*
- ❑ *Prices: Appetizers $4.95-$7.95, sandwiches and big salads $7.95-$12.95, entrées $8.95-$13.95.*
- ❑ *Credit cards: All major, except American Express.*
- ❑ *Reservations: Recommended.*
- ❑ *Directions: On Highway 29, a bit south of St. Helena.*

## The Restaurant at Meadowood

(American)

If you are wondering if the meal will be expensive, note that this is the kind of dining room where each plate is set with three glasses – for water, red wine and white wine. There is also a plate which will be withdrawn before you start to eat. That is a sure sign. There is a small bar as you enter. No more is needed. This isn't a neighborhood hangout, since there is no neighborhood around here. It's

*Meadowood.*

furnished comfortably with a few couches and chairs before a fireplace where people wait for their tables.

The dining room is high-ceilinged and open-beamed, with fewer than 20 tables that overlook the championship croquet lawn, the last hole of the golf course and the trees around it all. Home-baked rolls and salt-free butter come first. A spray of orchids decorates every table and the watercolors on the walls are of vineyards in the area. There is one appetizer we especially like – a risotto with wild mushrooms, cepes, morels and reggiano cheese. It's buttery soft with a flavor that is delicate but strong. Next time, we'll ask for the order to be tripled and served as an entrée.

You will find a roasted and sliced Colorado lamb on the menu. What they do with lamb in Colorado should be patented. It's unbelievably tender, set off by the white truffle essence it is bathed in. The honey-glazed pork loin may tie it for satisfaction, with polenta, carmelized apple and a good grainy mustard. There are several fish dishes, prepared in various ways. The only beef is a Black Angus tenderloin served in a Cabernet reduction. They always have one soup. The pumpkin soup with roasted chestnuts and black truffles is unexpectedly good. There are a few salads and some appetizers to try as well.

The wine list is good and fairly comprehensive. It surprised us with moderately priced vintages along with the ones in the upper stratosphere. We ordered a bottle of Bayview Cellars Gewürztraminer. It was, we are happy to say, a pulled-back Gewürtz, not overly spicy, and went nicely with what we were having.

The last time we were here, a local newspaper had just published a review of the food. Management had been so pleased that they had copied it and placed it in every room. If it's still there when you arrive, don't read it. No restaurant can be five-star perfect in every category: ambiance, service, food and wine. If you read the review, you may find yourself expecting more than they can deliver, and you might be disappointed. That would be a shame, because this *is* very close to perfection.

Meadowood also has The Grill (casual), serving breakfast 7 am-11 am, lunch 11:30 am-3 pm, dinner Friday and Saturday 5:30 pm-8:30 pm.

- ❑ *900 Meadowood Lane, St. Helena;*
  ☎ *707-963-3646, 800-458-8080, fax 707-963-3532.*
- ❑ *Open: Dinner only, 5 pm-9:30 pm, and Sunday brunch, 11 am-2 pm.*
- ❑ *Prices: Appetizers $9-$12.50, soup $8.50, salads $7 and $8.75, entrées $19-$26, all desserts $7.50. Four-course tasting menu $48 or $75.*
- ❑ *Credit cards: All.*
- ❑ *Reservations: Required.*
- ❑ *Directions: Highway 29 to St. Helena, right on Pope Street to Silverado Trail. Immediately left is Howell Road on your right; 50 yards along that to Meadowood Lane on left.*

# *Wineries*

❦ *I may not here omit those two main plagues and common dotages of human kind, wine and women, which have infatuated and besotted myriads of people; they go commonly together.*

Robert Burton, 1577-1640

The small wineries don't have scheduled tours, but the owners guide you around and explain things . If possible, call ahead for an appointment. On the other hand, you can always drop in and hope for serendipity to work its wonders.

While the vast majority of vineyards and wineries are located in a number of appellation districts along Highway 29, the Silverado Trail or in between those two. Carneros is a very large appellation district in the extreme south of the Sonoma and Napa valleys. Because they are closest to San Francisco, Marin and the East Bay, and can easily be visited on day trips, we have chosen several wineries there.

## *Acacia Winery*

Little wineries are the most interesting, mainly because you can talk to the owner about the business. There is usually a tasting room, or simply a counter, and you'll be oured some of the best vintages. Some of the big wineries even charge for tasting, but that is because they have tour buses coming by every 15 minutes or so. With that kind of volume, they would soon give away too much profit.

One of the first small, good wineries you come to driving out of San Francisco is Acacia. No tour buses visit. Acacia is owned by Chalon Wine Estates, with 40 acres planted here in Chardonnay. This is not surprising, since it was their Chardonnays that put them on the map. The 1995 Carneros label Chardonnay had just been released when we tried it here. It was silky smooth and not pushing a big taste.

Now, they are bottling some Pinot Noir and getting great reviews for it. They recently bought another 50 acres to plant Pinot Noir grapes. Acacia's sparkling wine (champagne) is made up of 70% Chardonnay right now, although that varies slightly from year to year. Most (70%) of what they bottle is distributed to restaurants and only 30% goes to retail stores, where you may be able to find it when you return home.

❑ *2750 Las Amigas Road, Napa;* ☎ *707-226-9991, fax 707-226-1685.*
❑ *Open: Monday-Saturday 10 am-4:30 pm, Sunday 12 noon-4:30 pm.*

❑ *Directions: Drive about 10 minutes from Highway 39 on 121; that brings you to Las Amigas Road (just past the big Domaine Carneros chateau on your right).*

## Carneros Alambic

*Picnic in the vineyards, Napa.*

How about going to a "winery" with no wine tasting? This is one of the few. It's a brandy distillery. Sorry about that, but there is a state law.

Carneros Alambic does accept a few bus tours. Since they average about 100 people spread over five to 10 tours each day, you will probably find yourself with only a few others.

This distillery makes use of six different wines from various parts of the state to blend into brandies. This one is in the Carneros District, so the appellation is Carneros. "Alambic" is the Arab word for "still."

Here they use the original "pot still" method of double distilling, rather than the cheaper way some brandies are made. This is the first time the pot still method has been used in the US since Prohibition. The huge copper pot stills were imported from France where brandies and Cognacs are all made this way. Your tour starts at an animated miniature still which demonstrates the process.

You probably will not find this brand in your liquor store when you get home. A full 60% of the output is sold here at the distillery. It's best to pick up a bottle or two here.

When you are outside the building, look at the amazing mud nests that the swallows return to each spring, as at Capistrano. Perhaps it's the aroma that draws them.

❑ *1250 Cuttings Wharf Road, Napa Valley;* ☎ *707-253-9055.*
❑ *Open: May-November, 10 am-5 pm; December-April, 10:30 am-4:30 pm.*
❑ *Reservations: Not necessary; tour every 45 minutes, seven days.*
❑ *Directions: From San Francisco, stay on 121 to Cuttings Wharf Road. From Napa, drive south on 121 to Route 12, right two miles to Cuttings Wharf Road, left to distillery.*

## Goosecross Cellars

This is really a small winery run by partners Geoff Gorsuch and David Topper, who take great pride in their work. They even run a Wine Basics class on Saturday mornings – a crash course in the hows and whys of wine making and appreciation. One of them lives on the property in a farmhouse about 20 feet from the small building where the tanks and barrels are kept. Your tour will take about two minutes. When you step into the small winery building, you are already standing in the middle of everything. This is it!

But tasting, learning about wine making and just generally chatting with these friendly folk can take hours, if they and you have the time. This is also one of the few places where you can get away from the tasting counter and out into the vineyards among the grapes that justify the whole enterprise. During September or October, any winemaker you visit will be really busy. The off-season is a better time.

Goosecross buys half their grapes from Carneros and St. Helena appellations, growing the rest themselves on 10½ acres planted in Chardonnay here. All of this adds up to 5,500 cases bottled annually. That is small for Napa. It's distributed to restaurants throughout the country and to very few retail stores. The only chance to buy is really here at the winery.

We talked to Collenn Tatarian who is billed as the Director of Hospitality (she calls herself the "wine pourer") and Geoff. He was busy (we were here in September), but not too busy to chat a bit. He insisted we taste their latest release.

Technically, Goosecross Cellars' Chardonnay is a French-style wine and if you have good taste buds, you may detect soft peach or ripe pear flavors. If you have real tasting acuity, you may even pick up green apple undertones and, according to Geoff, "a delicate touch of oak."

They age half their product in tanks and only half in wooden barrels, to be sure the resulting wine does not have an overpowering oak flavor. Don't feel like a clod if you don't pick up on any or all of those subtle nuances. As for us, we found it to be fruity but dry, a really fine, balanced blend.

- *1119 State Line, Yountville; ☎ 707-944-1986, 800-276-9210.*
- *Open: 10 am-5 pm daily.*
- *Tours: No regular times; each tour personal.*
- *Directions: Take Highway 29 to Yountville, turn east on Madison (toward the Silverado Trail) to Yountville Crossroad. Follow to State Line, turn left, follow to winery on your left.*

## Merryvale Vineyards

The tasting room is open 10 am-5:30 pm, with a tasting fee of $3. You can see, behind an iron gate, the cask room with a massive 100 year old aging tank. Tours are by appointment only. It's in an old building and was the first winery put up around here after Prohibition. It has new technology. The tasting room sells gifts and gourmet foods. Robert Levy, the winemaker, conducts a wine appreciation class Saturdays.

- ❑ *1000 Main St., St. Helena;* ☎ *707-963-7777.*
- ❑ *Open: 10 am-5:30 pm daily.*
- ❑ *Tasting fee: $3.*
- ❑ *Directions: Highway 29 to St. Helena. It's on Main St.*

## Mont St. John

This vineyard is different. Andrea "Buck" Bartolucci has created an organic vineyard, where no pesticides or herbicides are used. Sulfur dioxide is added to the bottle to preserve the shelf life of the wine. All wineries do that. But, because of that, although the grapes are grown organically, the wine can't be called organic. This is one of a few, but growing, number of wineries, that produce all organically grown grapes.

Grandfather Andrea "Andy" Bartolucci started the vineyards in 1922. His son, Louis, came into the wine business and took over in 1932. Now, Louis' son, Buck, has planted Pinot Noir and Chardonnay grapes in the heart of the Carneros country in Napa.

This vineyard is different also because it's "dry farmed," which means that there is no spraying. They let nature take its course. Buck patiently waits for the grapes to become mature enough to make fine wine and does not hurry them at all. The Bartoluccis have been in the Napa Valley for 75 years. They have learned to be patient.

Mont St. John is the second tallest mountain in the Napa Valley. It's in Oakville, where Grandfather Andy started the winery; hence the name. Very few tour buses stop here. There is not a big staff. If you're here when there are a few others, you will get a tour. Otherwise, you'll just be able to taste some of the vintages.

Chardonnay and Pinot Noir grow well here and are the most popular of Buck's wines. He also grows some Reisling and Cabernet. Buck has been lucky. He hasn't had to tear out any diseased vines and replant because years ago he planted phlox-resistant root stock.

Buck has a pasta recipe that he swears is the best ever, especially when served with his Pinot Noir. You might want to try making it at home. When you drop into the winery, you can tell him how it turned out.

---

## Pasta Rustica

½ bunch parsley, chopped fine
3 cloves garlic peeled
¼ cup extra virgin olive oil
4 anchovy fillets mashed
1 large can chopped tomatoes
1 lb penne pasta

Sauté garlic cloves in olive oil until golden brown over medium heat. Remove garlic from pan and add chopped tomatoes. Cook for 15 minutes. Add chopped parsley, cook another 10 minutes and add mashed anchovies. Cook another 15 minutes. Add salt and pepper to taste, but be careful – the anchovy is already salty. When the pasta is cooked, immediately toss with sauce and serve with a bottle of Mont St. John 1994 Estate Bottled Pinot Noir. Serves 4.

---

- *5400 Old Sonoma Road, Napa;* ☎ *707-255-8864, fax 707-257-2778.*
- *Open: 1 pm-5 pm.*
- *Tours: No.*
- *Directions: On 121, just past Las Amigas Road.*

## Pine Ridge Winery

Tours are usually at 10:15 am, 1 pm and 3 pm. They are strictly by appointment and are restricted to eight-10 people. They take plenty of time on the tours, give lots of information and, as a highlight, go into the aging caves, where they do barrel-tasting. There is also a picnic area.

- *5901 Silverado Trail, Yountville;* ☎ *707-253-7500.*
- *Open: 11 am-5 pm.*
- *Tasting fee: $3.*
- *Tours: Phone for appointment.*
- *Directions: From Highway 29, turn right on Oak Knoll Drive to Silverado Trail, then left about four miles.*

## *Tudal Winery*

We met Arnold Tudal when he was conducting a tasting of his own wines for the guests at Oakville Inn. Tudal Winery is a very small, one-man operation. About 10 years ago, Arnold retired from business, bought a walnut grove and built a house on it near a century-old barn. All his neighbors were growing vines and after a few years he was interested enough to take out the trees and put in Cabernet vines on his seven-and-a-half acres. Now he turns out around 2,000 cases a year (he calls it "a hobby run amok"), most of it sold right here to people who drop in. You'll also find it at a few good valley restaurants like Meadowood and Auberge due Soleil. He's a great raconteur and loves to show people around his place. Visitors have been known to spend two hours, but he can cut it to 20 minutes if you're in a hurry. Be sure to phone ahead.

- ❑ *1015 Big Tree Road. St. Helena;* ☎ *707-963-3947.*
- ❑ *Open: 9 am-4 pm.*
- ❑ *Directions: Highway 29 at St. Helena; turn right on Big Tree Road; go to end. You will see winery sign.*

## *Vichon Winery*

Vichon just planted this hillside vineyard last year with their own Cabernet vines. Until now, they have been using grapes from other vineyards for their label. Their wine is priced at $10 to $45. There is a gift shop where you will find olive oil, fine mustards and wine glasses. This is a popular place; the regular tours are usually large, from 30-40 people. It's best to phone for reservations for a private, or at least smaller, tour. Also reserve a picnic spot while you are on the phone. Tours end with a wine tasting, usually four of their good wines. You will probably buy a bottle or two – so why not bring along a picnic and enjoy?

One of the big lures here is the nice picnic area, with tables, grass and trees, though it's rather heavily used. You can get picnic supplies at Pometta's Deli, two minutes east on Oakville Grade at the intersection of Route 29. Even better is to go about one mile further to the Oakville Market. (See page 286.)

- ❑ *1595 Oakville Grade, Oakville;* ☎ *707-944-2811.*
- ❑ *Open: 10 am-4 pm, seven days.*
- ❑ *Public tours: 11 am, 1 pm and 3 pm.*
- ❑ *Directions: From Highway 29, turn left a quarter-mile at Oakville Grade. Oakville is a small place between Yountville and St. Helena. From Sonoma Valley, take Oakville Grade east from Glen Ellen.*

# Things to Do

## Bothe-Napa State Park

The Wappo Indians were here first, as they were everywhere in the Napa Valley. It was their land, after all. Despite that, during the Mexican period this part of the valley was given to Dr. Edward Turner Bale, an English ship's surgeon, who left that profession when he saw the San Francisco Bay Area. Though foreigners could not own land, Bale wooed and won Salvador Vallejo's niece in 1838. Salvador was General Mariano Vallejo's brother and what is now the Swiss Hotel on Sonoma Plaza was built as his home. After Bale took Mexican citizenship, he was permitted to own the land. Bale's Grist Mill, which he built in the early 1840s, is still standing. Your entry fee into the park provides free admission here as well.

After Bale's death, the land went through many hands, ending up with Reinhold Bothe. The state acquired Bothe's estate and has preserved it as a beautiful, wild region to be used by everyone. There is picnicking and swimming (pool is open only in summer), horseback riding and hiking trails through forests of coastal redwoods, Douglas firs, oak and madrone. Wild flowers bloom extravagantly in the spring and early summer. There are birds, raccoons, grey squirrels, deer and foxes. Many vacationers camp here year-round.

With 2,000 acres, the park ranges from about 400 to 2,000 feet in elevation. Six miles of trails allow short, easy walks and more challenging hikes. For horseback riding in the park, see Napa Valley Trail Rides, and Sonoma Cattle Co. (See pages 286 and 305.)

Try the History Trail for a pleasant walk of about an hour. You go past Pioneer Cemetery, up an easy slope through woods and meadows and down again to the Mill Pond and Bale's Grist Mill. The Coyote Peak Trail is more strenuous. It takes two to three hours and climbs to almost 1,200 feet, reaching a spot where there is a tremendous view of the valley.

- ❏ *3801 Highway 29 at Larkmead Lane, St. Helena;* ☎ *707-942-4575.*
- ❏ *Open: Year-round for camping and day-use.*
- ❏ *Fee: Day use $5; camping $15.*
- ❏ *Directions: North of St. Helena on 29, between St. Helena and Calistoga. From San Francisco, take 101 to Calistoga exit, right.*

## Goosecross Cellars Wine Basics Class

This is an easy, friendly crash course in wine appreciation and the basics of wine making. Spend time with the winemaker at the barrels, in the vineyard and the tasting room of a small, rural winery.

- ❑ *1119 State Line, Yountville;* ☎ *707-944-1986, 800-276-9210.*
- ❑ *When: Saturday 11 am-12:30 pm.*
- ❑ *Cost: Free.*
- ❑ *Directions: Highway 29 to Yountville; take Madison east to Yountville Crossroad, to State Line, then left to Goosecross Cellars.*

## Napa Valley Cyclery

- ❑ *4080 Byway St. East, Napa;* ☎ *707-255-3377.*
- ❑ *Open: 9:30 am-6 pm.*
- ❑ *Rates: $7 per hour, $22 per day (until 6), $28 per 24 hours.*
- ❑ *Directions: In the town of Napa, on Highway 29 where Trower St. crosses. Look on east side for water tower and Bicycle Rentals sign.*

## Napa Valley Trail Rides

Ride through forests and meadows of a beautifully preserved area. (See Bothe-Valley State Park, above.)

- ❑ *P.O. Box 877, Glen Ellen;* ☎ *707-996-8566.*
- ❑ *Open: April 1 to November 1.*
- ❑ *Prices: One-hour ride $30 (need to call and make arrangements); two hours $40; sunset ride $45. Private ride $40 per hour. Admission to park $5 additional per vehicle.*
- ❑ *Reservations: Required.*
- ❑ *Directions: Bothe-Napa Valley State Park. On Highway 29 north of Yountville, look for sign on left.*

## Oakville Market

(Deli)

This must have been a hand-pumped gas station a few eons ago, when a Model T might have pulled in every hour or so. It still looks like that in front. When we stopped to ask directions, there was an elderly man sitting on a wooden chair tipped back against the front wall. From the looks of him, he could have been there 10-12 years. We asked directions to somewhere and he jerked his thumb to the back, indicating we should go inside and not bother him – all without a word.

Inside, another world opened up. It turned out to be a deli. What a deli! There are shelves crowded with dozens of mustards, walls of Napa and Sonoma wines and a cheese counter at least 30 feet long. Another counter of the same size had sliced meat and other goodies.

Even if you're not going to buy anything, it's worthwhile stepping inside just for that marvelous deli aroma – a mixture of salami, gorgonzola, pickles and spices.

❑ *7856 Highway 29, Oakville;* ☎ *707-944-8802.*
❑ *Open: 10 am-6 pm.*
❑ *Directions: Oakville Grade takes a jog at Highway 29; it goes off to the east about a quarter-mile north of where it goes west. Oakville Market is at the corner where it goes east.*

## Seguin Moreau

(Cooperage)

Actually, it's Seguin Moreau USA, Inc., started by two families who have been making wine barrels in the French Champagne district since 1820. They opened this branch a few years ago. It's just off Highway 39, south of Napa. After seeing hundreds, maybe thousands, of barrels containing aging wine, we wondered where all the barrels came from. We asked a few questions and found that they were made by a dozen skilled coopers close by.

It's an absolutely fascinating process to watch. The staves are shaped, then placed over a fire that chars them to a predetermined hue, depending on the type of wine they will hold. There are 300 species of oak trees in the world and only three are suitable for wine barrels.

Wine barrel makers have always used white oak from the Mediterranean. (American white oak was thought to have too strong a tang; so much so that it would overpower Pinot Noirs and similar wines.) But now, the coopers here are using American oak for Chardonnay and Sauvignon Blanc. The flavor imparted by the wood does not overshadow these wines.

A few men turn out hundreds of barrels a day. A platform runs along the length of the workroom and you watch the entire process from beginning to end.

❑ *151 Camino Dorado, Napa;* ☎ *707-252-3408.*
❑ *Open: 10 am Tours at 10 am and 2 pm.*
❑ *Directions: Off Highway 29 south of Napa. Turn onto North Kelly Road, then turn right on Carmino Dorado.*

## St. Helena Cyclery

These bikes are hybrids. They have mountain bike frames with a roadbike's bigger, skinnier wheels. Rental includes helmet, lock and pannier (to carry your lunch). The cyclery is good at providing maps and helpful directions.

- ❑ *1156 Main St., St. Helena;* ☎ *707-963-7736.*
- ❑ *Open: Monday-Saturday, 9:30 am-5:30 pm; Sunday, 10 am-5 pm.*
- ❑ *Rentals: $7 per hour or $25 per day; tandem $15 and $40.*

# Sonoma Valley

❦ *Come live with me, and be my love;*
*And we will all the pleasures prove*
*That valleys, groves, hills, and fields,*
*Woods or steepy mountain yields.*

Christopher Marlowe,
*The Passionate Shepherd to his Love,* 1589

*N*apa is the chic valley, with an international reputation and the crowds that go with it. Sonoma is the quieter, more leisurely place. It has fewer people and less traffic. You can feel there is a slower, rural pace to life here.

While there are many vineyards in the Sonoma Valley, wine is not the be-all and end-all to life here. Sonoma also produces crisp apples, peaches, berries, vegetables of all kinds and a dozen different types of greens. You will be able to identify a few of the exotic varieties in your salad at one of the restaurants. The locally produced mustard and cheese are recognized all over the country.

Sonoma Valley is seven miles wide and 17 miles long. The Mayacama Mountains to the east separate it from Napa Valley. The Sonoma Mountains on the west side keep it apart from Marin. Highway 12 runs up the center of the valley and all the other roads run off that.

In 1834, the Mexican government secularized the Missions, took over the vast church lands and sent a young lieutenant, Mariano Guadelupe Vallejo, to Sonoma to take over. We have mentioned

Vallejo before, but in Northern California you run into him wherever you turn. He was vitally important in the development of the area. He laid out the town of Sonoma, established a *presidio* and graciously accepted more than 100,000 acres of land for himself. Mexican laws would not allow foreigners to own land, so when large numbers of Americans arrived in the 1840s, there was a lot of resentment about that. It came to a peak in 1846, when 30 armed Americans took over Sonoma. They tied Vallejo to a chair, proclaimed the "California Republic," and raised a home-made flag with a drawing of a bear. The new nation lasted only 23 days before Commodore John Drake Sloat took possession of California for the United States.

The Bear Flag that flies over state buildings today is the California state flag and commemorates that Bear Flag revolt.

## *How To Get Here*

Sonoma Valley is an hour's drive north of San Francisco. Cross Golden Gate Bridge on Highway 101, then turn right onto Highway 37 at Novato. Continue east to Highway 121 and go left to Highway 12 on the left. Take 12 to Sonoma Plaza and on up the center of the valley.

If you are traveling from the San Francisco International Airport, take the shuttle. It's called the **Sonoma Airporter** van and costs $20. It makes several regular dropoffs in the valley or will take you door-to-door for $25. Reservations are essential. Call ☎ 707-938-4246.

For more information, contact the **Sonoma Valley Visitors Bureau,** 453 First St. East, Sonoma, CA 95476. ☎ 707-996-1090 or on the Web at http://www.sonomavalley.com. The Web site is 46 pages deep and offers a free 56-page visitors guide.

## *Wine Country*

🍷 *Wine that maketh glad the heart of man.*

Psalm 104:15

Sonoma is the birthplace of California wine. General Vallejo (he was promoted by this time) started the first commercial vineyard, based on the miserable mission sacramental grapes. But the real "father of California viticulture" (a plaque in downtown Sonoma says so) is a Hungarian aristocrat, Agoston Haraszthy, who arrived in 1857 and founded Buena Vista Winery.

Haraszthy, too, was at first dependent on mission grapes. His great accomplishment was to travel to Europe and return with cuttings from several hundred varieties. His experimentation with these laid the foundation of the present-day wine industry. Haraszthy lived a colorful life and came to a colorful end. After both his sons married General Vallejo's daughters, he moved to Nicaragua and became a successful sugar grower. He died while crossing a stream. The branch he was holding onto broke and he fell into the mouth of a waiting alligator. So they say.

The entire valley has been designated by the federal government as the "Sonoma Valley Appellation." This means at least 85% of the wine in any vintner's bottle with the "Sonoma Valley" name on the label must come from here. As you drive through the valley, you'll see white oval signs posted at the entrance to many of the vineyards. They give the name of the winery and the name of the grape varietal growing there. Zinfandel is making a comeback, but the valley's best known wine is still Cabernet Sauvignon.

At the south end of the valley, the first area you'll drive through on the way here from San Francisco or Oakland is the "Carneros Appellation." It's a land of gentle hills with an entirely different soil composition. Carneros is cooled by the fog drifting in from San Pablo Bay. You will see early-ripening varieties like Chardonnay and Pinot Noir, with some Johannesberg Riesling and the spicy Gewuerztraminer.

## Sonoma

Journey up Highway 12 through the southern part of the valley. When you reach the town of Sonoma, park your car somewhere around the plaza, get out and stroll. Most of the story of Sonoma County is to be seen in the plaza and on Spain Street along its north side.

The surprisingly large plaza was laid out by General Vallejo in 1835 for troop maneuvers. It was the site of an Indian uprising and several duels. The larger-than-life bronze statue of a figure unfurling the Bear Flag is on the spot where the homemade flag was raised June 4, 1846. The large stone building in the center is City Hall. On the east side facing First Street East is the Visitors Bureau, where you can get maps, brochures and information, starting February, 1998. Until then, they are at 10 East Spain St., around the corner from the plaza, ☎ 707-996-1090.

Start with the **Mission San Francisco Solano de Sonoma**, diagonally opposite the plaza's northeast corner at First Street East and

Spain Street. Founded in 1823, it was the last and most northerly of the 21 missions. This is the end of El Camino Real, "The King's Highway."

Much of what is here now is a re-creation of the original. After the missions were secularized, a great deal of neglect and decay followed. The padres' quarters, the long, low building next to the adobe church, is the oldest building in Sonoma, built in

*Adobe at 139 E. Spain St. just off Sonoma Plaza, believed to have built by General Vallejo in 1840.*

1825. The church was built by General Vallejo in 1840 for his soldiers and their families. It's open daily from 10 am-5 pm; admission $2 (also good for admission to the Sonoma Barracks and General Vallejo's home).

Across First Street East, on the opposite corner, is **Sonoma Barracks**, built by Vallejo in 1836 for his troops. It was taken over by the Bear Flag "soldiers" 10 years later, and then served as US Military Headquarters through the 1850s. The courtyard out back is where spectators gambled on the outcome of fights to the death between bulls and grizzly bears. The bears usually won. It's open daily from 10 am-5 pm; admission $2 (also good for admission to Sonoma Mission and General Vallejo's home).

Next door at 20 Spain St. is the **Toscano Hotel**, built as a general store in the 1850s. It was converted in 1886 to a hotel for Italian immigrants, hence the name Toscano. Free docent tours are held on Friday, Saturday and Sunday from 1 pm-4 pm.

Next to that is **Casa Grande**, the site of General Vallejo's first home, which he built in 1836. It was an imposing building with a three-story tower, but was destroyed in 1867 by fire. The main building was undoubtedly much grander than the unpainted adobe servants' quarters, the only structure remaining.

**Swiss Hotel** was built of adobe by General Vallejo's brother, Salvador, in the 1830s as his home, but was converted to a hotel in the 1880s. It has a bar and restaurant, popular with the locals. 18 Spain St., ☎ 707-938-2884.

Diagonally across from the northwest corner of the plaza at Spain Street and First Street West is the **Sonoma Hotel**. Built about 1872 by a wine merchant, the hotel has a restaurant and bar. The rooms are furnished with antiques. Its most recent fame is when Maya Angelou holed up here to write a novel. 110 Spain St., ☎ 707-996-2996. (See *Nightlife*, page 296.)

*Home of General Vallejo.*

**El Dorado Hotel** is across Spain Street, facing the plaza, also built by Salvador Vallejo, around 1840. Now, it's a pleasant hotel. (See *Inns*, page 293.)

Away from the plaza is the **Home of General Vallejo**. It's a 10-minute walk or a roundabout five-minute drive. The reason this home is so interesting has a lot to do with the fact that Vallejo was a fascinating person and consummate politician. Before the American victory, he was named Commandante General of all Mexican military forces in California. As soon as the Americans took over, he switched sides and served with distinction in first the local and then the state government. His new home went with his changed persona. In 1851 he moved a half-mile from the Casa Grande adobe on the plaza to the foothills, where he built an estate called Lachryma Montis. It means "tears of the mountain" in Latin, which is what the Indian name for the area had meant – so called because of the abundant hillside springs.

Vallejo put up a classic Yankee-style, two-story Gothic house with steep-pitched roof and dormer windows. It has a large Gothic window, carved, ornamental eaves, a white marble fireplace in every room and furnishings imported from Europe. It was in fact prefabricated, built of spruce in New England and shipped around the Horn. But it certainly demonstrated his new-found allegiance to America. The big building used to store the wines and olives he grew on the property was made of prefabricated timbers imported from Europe. It's a museum now.

To get here, go to the bicycle path behind the public parking lot off Spain Street. It starts by the Historical Society building and the old depot. Take the bike path to the left and go about a half-mile. The house is at the end of a long, tree-shaded country lane, nestled against the foothills, with Vallejo's vineyards spread out in front. It looks exactly as it did 150 years ago. By car, drive left on Spain Street. Look for the sign to turn right onto the lane. Open daily from 10 am-5 pm; closed Thanksgiving, Christmas and New Year's Day. Admission is $2 and good for Sonoma Mission and Barracks. For more information, ☎ 707-938-1519.

# *Inns*

## *El Dorado Hotel*

This is a two-story white frame building facing the plaza, over 100 years old and steeped in history. This was General Mariano Vallejo's house at one time. Later it was a school. It has been renovated more than once and drastically redone in 1979.

While the outside is the same as it always was, the inside is modernized. On the ground floor, the lobby, shops and restaurant flow together cleanly with a floor of big, beige Mexican tiles. There is a restaurant with a patio for dining. A gift shop has souvenirs of Sonoma and there are other shops as well.

Almost all of the rooms are identical. They are spare, modern and attractive. There are 18 rooms with king beds and nine with queens. All have balconies of varying sizes looking out on Spain Street or the swimming pool in the rear. Rooms in front have large balconies overlooking the famed plaza. Rooms in the rear have tall, sloping ceilings.

- ❑ *405 First Street West, Sonoma, CA 95476;*
  ☎ *707-996-3030; reservations 800-289-3031; fax 707-996-3148.*
- ❑ *Rooms: 27.*
- ❑ *Rates: Winter $90 weekdays, $110 weekends; summer $115-145.*
- ❑ *Reservations: Recommended, especially for summer. Call five to six months ahead.*
- ❑ *Minimum stay: Two nights for summer weekends.*
- ❑ *Credit cards: AE, MC, V.*
- ❑ *Packages: Wine country getaway – one-night stay plus $50, includes dinner at Piatti for two.*
- ❑ *Breakfast: Continental breakfast included.*
- ❑ *Wine: Split awaits in room.*
- ❑ *Amenities: Swimming pool.*
- ❑ *Handicapped accessible: Four rooms on ground floor by pool.*
- ❑ *Smoking: No.*
- ❑ *Children: Yes, if in separate room.*
- ❑ *Pets: No.*
- ❑ *Parking: Limited private parking, plus street.*
- ❑ *Walking distance: Hotel is on the plaza, with interesting shops, restaurants, sightseeing steps away.*

# Restaurants

## Bear Flag Café

(American Continental)

A small bowl of green manzanilla olives from Spain, immediately addictive, comes automatically as soon as we sit down. Then, Italian-style bread arrives, baked by Mezzaluna in nearby Santa Rosa. The meal starts well.

The Bear Flag Café is in a small white building on Highway 12, north of Sonoma. Most customers here are locals, with a few visitors from out of town who are staying at local inns.

The wine list is about 70% Sonoma wines. Peter Stewart, the tall, wise-beyond-his-years owner, told us that he has tried French wines from time to time, but the people in the valley are not that fond of them. People in the wine regions of France told us the same thing about Sonoma wines. Locals consider themselves experts, testing and comparing different wines.

Salad can be the first real test of the food to come. The spinach salad here comes with gorgonzola, walnuts and a lemon-tarragon vinaigrette. As soon as the dish was set down, we saw the tiny, tender spinach leaves (not eight-inch-long tough ones). We knew the rest would be excellent, and so it was.

Crab cakes were light and crusty. As for the lamb entrée with polenta and carrots, the lamb was full of flavor. The polenta was crusty on the outside and beautifully squishy inside. The sauce was a lovely mixture of mustard, mint and meat juices. The baby carrots really were taken from the earth at a tender age – unlike most, that are cut down from older, tougher carrots. Also recommended is the ravioli stuffed with porcinis, Swiss chard and ricotta. Its cream sauce is "herb infused," which means savory, but light, and enhances the flavor of the ravioli. There is a flatbread pizza every night, which gives you a chance to try things like gorgonzola and carmelized onion pizza. You aren't likely to run across that at Shakey's.

This is a small place. Even with two rooms, there are only about a dozen tables in all. There are lots of windows, white walls and big, bright Impressionist paintings. It may look unimpressive from the outside, but don't let that deter you.

❑ *18625 Sonoma Highway (12), Sonoma;* ☎ *707-938-1927.*
❑ *Open: Dinner only, Tuesday-Thursday, 5 pm-9 pm; Friday-Saturday, 5 pm-10 pm; closed Monday.*

- Prices: *Appetizers $6 and $7; local lettuce salads $5 for a large one, $3 for small; spinach salad $6; main courses $9-$14; flatbread pizza $8.*
- Credit cards: *MC, V.*
- Reservations: *Recommended.*
- Parking: *Complimentary lot.*
- Directions: *A mile north of town of Sonoma on Highway 12.*

## Zino's Ristorante

(Southern Italian)

This is a small, attractive place on the plaza. The real attraction is not the location, which is convenient to everything, but its food. We should point out that if you really prefer classic French fare or high-style California nouveau as a steady diet, then you won't like Zino's. If you feel like sitting at a table with a red-checked cloth and slurping up some old-fashioned southern Italian cooking, you'll love it here.

Much of its attractive look comes from the brick walls that have been left bare. There is a small dining room with only eight or 10 tables. There is a long bar in a separate room, with a few more tables for two along the opposite wall. This is a good place to wait for a table (which you will probably have to do at lunchtime), with Lagunitas beer on tap. It's made locally in Petaluma, a hoppy beer with a strong, bitter aftertaste.

When we had lunch at Zino's recently, we waited at the bar. We sampled local microbrew beers – a recommended way to kill time. Cesare, who runs the place for Zino, was distressed that we had to wait. He wondered if we would mind a table added opposite the door and next to his podium. It was fitted in somehow and we found ourselves center stage, watching everyone else who came in and had to wait.

As soon as we got settled, a basket of fresh focaccia and a small bowl of extra virgin olive oil, for dipping purposes, arrived. After that, if you are not really hungry, try a half-order of pasta Bolognese or marinara with soup (often minestrone) or salad.

Prices are reasonable. A bowl of "today's soup" is $3.50. There is a lettuce, tomato, onion and mushroom salad. Pastas include Bolognese and pasta marinara. Fresh steamed clams are succulent. The most expensive items on the menu are pepper steak or baby lamb chops at $16. There is a modest wine list. The house wine has Zino's own label, called simply "red table wine" and "white table wine."

The night before, we'd had dinner at a place where everything was very nouvelle and cost four times as much. We wished we'd come to Zino's instead. When we were last here, a big room in back was being remodeled with the expectation that it will cut down on the waiting time. Don't count on that. It's like adding lanes to a freeway that moves too slowly. As soon as the new lanes open, more people arrive in more cars and you are right back where you started.

- ❏ *420 First Street East, Sonoma; ☎ 707-996-4466.*
- ❏ *Open: Lunch 11 am, dinner 4:30 pm-10 pm.*
- ❏ *Prices: Appetizers $4.50-$9.50, entrées $9.50-$16. Zino's wine $3 a glass, $12 a bottle.*
- ❏ *Credit cards: AE, MC, V.*
- ❏ *Reservations: Recommended at lunch, but there will still probably be a wait. At dinner during the week not necessary; yes on weekends.*
- ❏ *Parking: Street.*
- ❏ *Directions: On the plaza, downtown Sonoma.*

## Nightlife

**Sonoma Hotel** has live jazz and blues on Friday nights in their attractive bar and restaurant. 110 Spain St., ☎ 707-996-2996.

**Swiss Hotel's Gray Fox Saloon** is popular with the locals. Drop in, perhaps after dinner, and try the noted Bear's Hair sherry. There's also a restaurant. 18 Spain St., ☎ 707-938-2884.

## Wineries

### Buena Vista Winery

This was the first winery to be established in the Wine Country by Agoston Haraszthy, the "father of California wine." Others had tried and made wine with the coarse grapes brought by the mission friars. Haraszthy was the first to believe that the grapes of Bordeaux and Burgundy would grow and prosper in this valley. The wines have varied over the years since 1857, but in the 1980s, Cabernet Sauvignons and Chardonnays evolved to become worthy of their history.

- ❏ *18000 Old Winery Road, Sonoma; ☎ 707-938-1266.*
- ❏ *Tours: Daily at 2 pm.*
- ❏ *Directions: From Highway 29, left on Highway 121-12, then north on 8th Street East. Dead-ends at Napa Road, turn right to Old Winery Road. Go to end.*

## Gloria Ferrer Champagne Caves

"We have a saying in my family – a wine won't please the palate unless it comes from the heart," says Jose Ferrer, who named the champagne after his wife. Gloria Ferrer is set in the Carneros District, off the high traffic areas. The tours have a great appeal for visitors, particularly the caves carved into the hill where the sparkling wines age.

❑ *23555 Arnold Drive (Highway 12), Sonoma;* ☎ *707-996-7256.*
❑ *Tours: 11 am-4 pm on the hour, daily.*
❑ *Tasting fee: Sold by the glass.*
❑ *Directions: On Highway 12 at Arnold Drive.*

# Things to Do

## The Farmers' Market

This is held in the plaza on Tuesdays from May to October, 5:30 pm to dusk.

## The Goodtime Bicycle Company

There is good bicycling in the Sonoma Valley, through parks and meadows and to the wineries. The valley is small – narrow east and west and not very long north to south. You can get almost anywhere in about an hour from the centrally located town of Sonoma.

Gourmet lunch rides with the pedaling gourmet, "The Bikeman," are Monday to Friday, 10:30 am-3:30 pm. You ride either north of Glen Ellen and Kenwood wineries or south to southern Sonoma wineries. The price includes good food (The Bikeman sees to that). No more than six riders on these lunch rides. Call about private rides for couples. Price includes a new bike, helmet, lock, cable, maps and any road service or repair during regular working hours. Free delivery and pickup in the valley, along with a minimum two-hour rental, is part of the package. Rates are $5 per hour, $25 per day; gourmet lunch rides $55. Rollerblade rentals are half-day, $10; 24-hours, $15 (includes knee pads, elbow pads, wrist guards, helmet and map).

❑ *18315 Highway 12, Sonoma;* ☎ *707-938-0453.*
❑ *Open: Monday-Friday, 9 am-5 pm, Sunday, 10 am-4 pm.*

## Plaza Books

This bookstore is located between the Swiss and Sonoma hotels. It's a good place to browse, with both used and rare books, plus lots of California books on the shelves.

❑ *40 Spain St., Sonoma;* ☎ *707-996-8474.*
❑ *Open: Every day, 11 am-6 pm.*

## Self-Guided Tour

This starts at the Vasquez House across from the plaza. It covers 59 historic buildings surrounding the plaza, sponsored by Sonoma League for Historic Preservation. You can pick up a guidebook at 414 First St. East, in the El Paseo complex. ☎ 707-938-0510. It's open Wednesday-Sunday from noon until 3 pm. When this is closed, get a guidebook at Sonoma Visitors Bureau, 10 East Spain St. (after February, 1998 their office will be on the plaza itself, facing First St. East).

## Sonoma Cheese Factory

This is a prize for deli-lovers who might have picnics in mind, or for those who just want to take some cheese home. Up front is a long glass case full of salads, another of sliced meats, a good selection of cheeses and some fresh French and Italian bread (not made here). Wines and mustards, including home-made types, are also available.

Celso Viviani came from Italy and opened the cheese factory in 1931. The famed Sonoma Jack Cheese has been made here ever since. Step to a big plate glass window at the back of the deli and you can see much of the cheese-making process going on – everything from pasteurizing the milk and aging, to forming the wheels of cheese by hand. We never knew how that was done!

❑ *2 Spain St., Sonoma;* ☎ *707-996-1931.*
❑ *Open: daily, 8:30 am-5:30 pm.*

## Sonoma Plaza Walking Tour

Marv Parker is doing a tour that fits many couples' plans. It's an easy 12-block walk and only takes an hour. You would be surprised at the amount of information he divulges in that short time. It goes well beyond the events you would expect, like the Bear Flag Revolt, General Vallejo's graceful surrender and what the locals thought of the flag. He puts it all in perspective, explaining how these events linked up to Abraham Lincoln, Paul Revere (Yes, Paul Revere!) and Kit Carson.

Sonoma has more still-standing adobe structures than any place in Northern California; you will be able to visit several built in the 1830s and 1840s that are still in use today.

*Sonoma Plaza Walking Tour.*

❑ *P.O. Box 15, Sonoma, CA 95476;* ☎ *707-996-9112.*
❑ *Price: $10, cash or check, no credit cards.*
❑ *Tour: Meets Saturdays, 10 am. Call to make special arrangements.*

## Spirits in Stone

An unusual shop, it's located on First Street facing the plaza. This is a gallery featuring nothing but sculpture from Zimbabwe. There are beautiful pieces executed in various kinds of stone. We learned that there was a traditional art, half a millenium old, that was almost destroyed during the 19th century when the country was under British rule. The art has been revived, with the encouragement of more enlightened Europeans and a few galleries like this one. It's definitely worth a look. The gallery features the work of some younger artists along with the well-known ones, which means that not all of the prices are sky-high. Still, if you are thinking of buying, bring a fat wallet.

❑ *452 First St. East, Sonoma;* ☎ *800-474-6624.*
❑ *Open: Every day, 10 am-6 pm. Closed Christmas.*
❑ *Parking: On the streets around the plaza and in a free public lot behind Spain St. Drive up First St. East past Spain; turn left behind the buildings fronting Spain.*

# Glen Ellen

The Indians called it the Valley of the Moon, and so did famed writer, Jack London, when he moved here in 1905. Now, Glen Ellen is a very small town nestled against the foot of Sonoma Mountain. Most tourists come here to visit Jack London State Historic Park.

Drive up Highway 12 about 10 miles north of Sonoma, then turn left at Arnold Drive. You will come first to the Gaige House Inn.

Continue 30 seconds past that and you will find Glen Ellen Inn, which is not an inn at all, but a small restaurant. Then the road curves to the right, crosses a little bridge over Calabasas Creek, and you're in the town. Glen Ellen was founded in the late 1860s and has always attracted a literary crowd. London lived here until he died in 1916, writing many books and hundreds of stories and articles. This is also where the wonderful food writer M.F.K. Fisher lived.

A new development, Jack London Village, is just south of the old town. There is a coffeehouse, Jack's Village Café, and the Glen Ellen Tasting Room and History Center, with winemaking equipment and turn-of-the-century photos. Olive Press, the valley's first olive oil mill, just opened and has a retail store attached.

If you are here on a Sunday in mid-October, you will be able to get in on the Glen Ellen Village Fair – certainly the smallest, but perhaps also the liveliest town fair in Northern California. All but two blocks of the downtown area is closed off. The fair begins at noon with a parade down Arnold Drive. Some 50 booths offer arts and crafts, local restaurant food and samples from nearby wineries.

## Inns

### Above the Clouds

We stumbled onto this place purely by chance. By going over the mountain from Sonoma to Napa, you save time and it's scenic, with grand vistas, but winding, twisting and steep. We had almost passed the long, narrow, private driveway leading off the road, when we saw the sign next to the Volunteer Firehouse. "Above the Clouds," it said and we agreed – way above. The top of a mountain is an odd place for a bed and breakfast, but enough people find it that it's full most of the time.

The original house was the first built on these Mayacama Mountains in the 1850s. That burned to the ground, leaving only the chimney and fireplace standing and another house was built around those. Claude and Betty Ganaye purchased it in 1985 and completely remodeled the place as a bed and breakfast. It was a very rustic bed and breakfast those first years, with no electricity until 1993.

The present house looks like a big, old farm house – comfortable, homey with soft beds, deep chairs in front of the fireplace and a well-used library. It's about 2,000 feet up. In the morning, when you wake, you're likely to be looking down on a blanket of clouds covering the entire valley while the sun is shining brightly up here.

Most guests eat breakfast on the veranda, overlooking the valley and mountains. Couples often eat in the library, where the one table has a view of everything below to the horizon. In the afternoon and evening, guests gather in the living room before the fireplace. Many of them have been here before. Most are in the 25-45 age group. There are five rooms, but just one is set up for handicapped guests. All have queen-size beds, air conditioning, robes and ceiling fans, but no TV or telephone. There is a great second floor veranda with a marvelous view, especially at sunset. Betty puts honeymoon couples in the corner room on the second floor in front.

The swimming pool is heated (solar heated from May to October). A year-round jacuzzi is just across the foot bridge, over a little creek that runs through the property. There are walks through woods of oak, Douglas fir, and madrone. This out-of-the-way place is well off the road. There is no sound except for the crickets. No cities are nearby, not even towns, and no lights. The stars are unbelievable.

There is only one possible problem and it may not be a problem for you – the meals. Betty does not serve lunch and the closest restaurants are over three miles down the mountain road to Sonoma or over seven miles down a similar mountain road on the other side to Napa. Better hold off on the booze at dinner if you go out to eat. You'll have to drive back up that mountain at night. Cheers!

- ❑ *3250 Trinity Road, Glen Ellen, CA 95442;*
  ☎ *707-996-7371 or 800-600-7371.*
- ❑ *Rooms: Five.*
- ❑ *Rates: Monday-Thursday $135; Friday, Saturday and holidays $155. Add 9% tax.*
- ❑ *Reservations: For September and October, reserve by April; November to April, reserve two weeks ahead, longer for weekends; May to August, four weeks ahead. Every once in awhile, there is a cancellation; it's worth trying.*
- ❑ *Minimum stay: Two nights minimum in regular season; two nights on holiday weekends year-round.*
- ❑ *Credit cards: All major cards or personal check received 48 hours before arrival.*
- ❑ *Breakfast: Coffee, tea ready at 8 am. Gourmet breakfast 9 am-10 am.*
- ❑ *Amenities: Swimming pool, jacuzzi, robes.*
- ❑ *Handicapped accessible: Yes, wheelchair accessible.*
- ❑ *Smoking: Outside only.*
- ❑ *Children: By special arrangement.*
- ❑ *Pets: No.*
- ❑ *Directions: On Highway 12, turn east on Trinity Road (it's a half-mile north of Arnold Drive); go three miles. The Mayacama Volunteer Firehouse sits to the left of a lane leading to Above the Clouds.*

## ♥ Gaige House Inn

*Gaige House Inn.*

The inn was originally built for Mr. Gaige, the town butcher, in 1890. The front lower floor was the butcher shop and the Gaige family lived upstairs. Several lifetimes later, it has gone through a rebuilding or two. The property goes all the way from Arnold Road, at the front, back to Calabasas Creek. The main house is big, with a front porch and a large back deck that overlooks a pool in the middle of the lawn. A wooded hill rises up behind the creek. Squirrels scurried up an old live oak tree as we stood by the pool and thought about a dip. Ken Burnet told us they often see deer on the banks of the creek and on the hill behind the house.

There is a large herb and tomato garden back here. We had a feeling the harvest was going to show up at breakfast one way or another.

The front parlor is used for wine, cheese and snacks in the late afternoon and evening. A pleasant sitting room on the other side of the central hall has books, games and TV for the seriously addicted, although Ken reports that most guests don't even turn on the TV (there are no sets in the rooms). The landscape around here is what's real.

A "hospitality room" has a cookie bowl to raid, which is easy to do. The home-made macaroons were too good to resist. There's a refrigerator with help-yourself Cokes and such, plus ice and glasses of all shapes and purposes from wine to highball to martini.

Room Four is very large, with a fireplace across from the queen-size bed. The bathroom has a sink in an oak cabinet and the toilet has an oak reservoir mounted high on the wall. Actually, these are not old, but rather replicas. There is also a ceiling fan.

Room Two is the front room upstairs with a four-poster bed and bay windows in front, bright and cheery.

The Gaige Suite, second floor rear, is the pièce de résistance – another very large room with a king-size four-poster bed and a tall armoire with full length mirrors. Because it takes up one whole corner of the house, there are windows on three sides and a private balcony with lounges that overlook the pool and the hills rising steeply behind the property.

Room Six, off the back lawn and near the pool, is the bargain room. It's smaller, but large enough for a couple and the only room with no tub, only a shower.

All rooms have gorgeous big, polished wood dressers. All have boxed sets of Jack London's books. After all, we are only two miles from where the author's house stood. The porch in front of the main house is where the smokers gather to rock and smoke and watch life go by – or as much as goes by on Arnold Road.

For early risers, coffee, tea and freshly squeezed orange juice is waiting in the front parlor from 7:30 on. We took ours back to the room. Our breakfast later was fluffy, moist scrambled eggs on smoked salmon and puff pastry.

The art work on the walls is almost all by local artists and for sale. Two oil portraits in the upstairs hall are of Mr. and Mrs. Gaige. They are not for sale.

- *13540 Arnold Drive, Glen Ellen, CA 95442;*
  ☎ *707-935-0237, fax 707-935-6411.*
- *Rooms: Nine, with plans to add two more.*
- *Rates: Sunday-Thursday and winter $125-$225. Friday, Saturday and Holidays $145-$245. Add 9% tax.*
- *Minimum stay: Two nights over Saturdays and Holidays.*
- *Deposit: One night pre-paid or 50%, whichever is larger. Balance due on arrival.*
- *Credit cards: Major cards accepted.*
- *Breakfast: Coffee and juice, 7:30 am. Full breakfast, 8:30 am-10 am. Picnic lunches are available.*
- *Wine: Afternoon and evening.*
- *Amenities: Large swimming pool, heated from May to October.*
- *Handicapped accessible: No, too many stairs.*
- *Smoking: Outside only.*
- *Children: Young children not suitable.*
- *Pets: No, "we have resident animals."*
- *Parking: Plenty of room in lot off the public road.*

## *Restaurant*

### ♥ *Glen Ellen Inn*

(American)

Glen Ellen Inn is a restaurant on the main and only street of Glen Ellen. It's small, with 16 tables inside and 10 outside in a lovely "sunken" garden with a fountain.

If the weather is nasty, you eat inside on what used to be a porch, now glassed in. You may be waited on by Karen Bertrand, co-owner with her husband, Chris. She is very friendly, open to questions about the menu and whatever else pops into your head. Candles on the tables heighten the romantic atmosphere. A tape playing Billy Holiday's "Lover Man" set a mellow mood.

What showed up first, before the menu, was a basket of scones made with sharp cheddar and dill. The salad was a mixture of arugula, frisée and several other esoteric greens that we could not identify. It was so good that we didn't bother. There is evidently a law against importing iceberg lettuce into Marin, Sonoma and Napa counties, which is OK by us. The salad was served with a little balsamic vinaigrette. The soup of the day was potato with garlic, chives and herbs, a blend of subtle flavors. There was an earthy foie gras served on a baguette with a wild berry port sauce that enlivened the pâté. California jambalaya with prawns, bay shrimp, chicken, sausage and honey-smoked ham is a regular item. This is simmered with vegetables in a light tomato sauce that brings out all the flavor of the fresh seafood and what actually tastes like home-smoked ham.

The linguine was creamy with feta cheese and artichoke hearts, tossed with capers, which makes for a spicier sauce than usual. We detected a hint of garlic in there too. Add a bit of parmesan to give it that down-home northern Italian touch. The roasted pork tenderloin was marinated in black truffle oil with garlic, thyme and cumin. It's served on smoked mozzarella polenta with a roasted pepper, sweet onion compote, which nicely balances the flavors of the polenta and pork. Christian Bertrand makes some fine desserts. One we especially like, and it's fairly easy to make at home.

## Kiwi Gratin

2 egg yolks

1 oz sugar

1 oz eau de vie framboise

3 tbsp semi-whipped cream

10 oz kiwi, diced

Place eggs and sugar in bowl with eau de framboise, and place over a pan of simmering water. Whisk until mixture has tripled in volume. Remove from heat and continue whisking until mixture is cool. Gently fold in cream. Divide the kiwi between two gratin dishes and cover with the mixture. Place under broiler until it turns a golden brown color. Enjoy immediately.

Framboise is raspberry liqueur. You will find it in your local liquor store or market.

There is a small, full bar; a very new addition. Wines run the gamut from A to about C. There are inexpensive local brands, like Glen Ellen Chardonnay, at only $14 a bottle.

Karen is upfront, while Chris is the talented chef. This place used to be a barber shop. A hint that the building has been here awhile: Jack London got his hair cut here. Then it became a restaurant. They bought it in 1992 and have not looked back. Good for them.

❑ *13670 Arnold Drive, Glen Ellen;* ☎ *707-996-6409.*
❑ *Open: Dinner only, 5:30 pm-closing. May 1-November 1, open seven nights a week; November-April, Tuesday through Sunday.*
❑ *Prices: Soup and salads $4.50-$6.95; entrées $10.95-$23.*
❑ *Credit cards: AE, MC, V.*
❑ *Reservations: A good idea, but they will always try to squeeze you in.*
❑ *Wine: Full bar. Limited but generally reasonable wine list.*
❑ *Handicapped accessible: Yes.*
❑ *Parking: Lot.*
❑ *Directions: Turn west off Highway 12 at Arnold Drive. Glen Ellen Inn is on the near edge of the town, a block past Gaige Inn.*

# Things to Do

## Jack London Book Store

This store probably stocks everything ever written by and about the author. London's youngest daughter, Becky, lived in an apartment attached to the store until her death in 1992 at the age of 89. Now, the place where she lived is home for the Jack London Foundation, a resource center for researchers into London's life and writings. The book store is in the village at 14300 Arnold Drive, ☎ 707-996-2888.

## Sonoma Cattle Company (horseback rides)

Ride through forests and across meadows, with panoramic views of the Sonoma Valley. You will be in the Jack London State Historic Park (see listing below). Write Sonoma Cattle Co. at P.O. Box 877, Glen Ellen, CA 95442 or ☎ 707-996-8566. Prices: for a one-hour ride, $30 (special arrangements only); two hours $40, sunset ride $45; private ride for just the two of you $40 per hour. Admission to park is additional $5 per vehicle. Jack London State Historic Park is open April 1 to November 1. Reservations for rides required.

## Village Mercantile

This is an arts and crafts store that also sells antiques and books about the valley by local authors. If you happen to be fans of Lucy Maud Montgomery's early 20th-century novels ("Anne of Green Gables," etc.), you will be delighted by the collection of books, dolls, clothing, tea sets and other items. 13647 Arnold Drive, ☎ 707-938-1330.

## Jack London Historic Park

❦ *When I first came here, tired of cities and people, I settled down... on some of the most beautiful, primitive land to be found in California.*

Jack London

Few other American writers ever achieved the world-wide popularity of Jack London. After he was already internationally famous for *Call of the Wild* and *The Sea Wolf*, London built a ranch in the Sonoma Valley, above the little town of Glen Ellen. He planned his dream house and had his most productive writing years here.

Jack London called it "The Valley of the Moon." The 800-acre park on the land that was deeded to the state has meadows and mountainsides where you can hike, picnic, take horseback rides or just stroll among the oaks, madrone, California buckeye, Douglas fir and redwoods.

The House of Happy Walls was built by Charmain London after her husband's death and is now a museum. Two stories, built of big local stones, it contains London's books, photos of the author, his personal collection of South Pacific art objects and the original furnishings.

A half-mile down an easy walking trail lie the remains of The Wolf House. The author built this and expected to spend his life here, but it burned down just days before he could move in.

There are nine miles of trails for walking, hiking and horseback riding (guided, no going off on your own if you're on horseback). Picnic tables are in the lower parking lot, but better ones can be found on the trail above. Dogs on a leash are OK, but not inside the buildings and not on back-country trails.

A great time to come is between Thanksgiving and Christmas. The park is not crowded then and the weather is (or should be) clear and warm. April to October is the most crowded and weekends are crowded year-round.

The park is very popular with Europeans because Jack London's books have been translated and read extensively in Europe for a century. You will probably run into Russian visitors – London has always been one of their favorite authors and his books are reprinted there by the millions. Everyone reads him in school.

❑ *The park is open 9:30 am-5 pm, seven days a week. Museum opens 10 am-5 pm, but is closed Thanksgiving, Christmas Day and New Years Day. The park, however, is open on those days. Fee per vehicle $5, seniors $4; includes admission to museum. Horseback riding on park trails with guide. Phone Sonoma Cattle Co.,* ☎ *707-996-8566. (See listing above.)*

❑ *Directions: From Highway 12 turn west on Arnold Drive to Glen Ellen, turn off Arnold and go uphill at north end of bridge over Calistoga Creek. There is a sign for the park.*

# Wineries

## Arrowood Vineyard & Winery

Richard Arrowood had made his name at Chateau St. Jean, which floundered somewhat in his wake. But the new winery he and his wife opened in 1986 was a success from the start. What looks like a small farmhouse is built onto a knoll; but looks can be deceiving. If you take a tour, which is given by appointment only, you will see everything and end with a tasting on the porch. Chardonnay is the big attraction here, though there is some Cabernet Sauvignon and Merlot on the menu too.

❑ *14347 Sonoma Highway (Hwy. 12), Glen Ellen;* ☎ *707-938-5170.*
❑ *Tours: By appointment.*

## B.R. Cohn Winery

Can a rock 'n' roll band manager be the working owner of a good winery at the same time? Apparently he can, because B.R. Cohn is doing it every day. A few years ago, *Bon Appetit* magazine rated B.R. Cohn Cabernet Sauvignon number two in the world. Yet Cohn still manages the Doobie Brothers rock band, Little Feat and others.

Bruce Cohn bought this vineyard in 1974. It was originally part of a Spanish land grant. Cohn became the third owner in 100 years. There are no tours at the winery, only tastings. We have tasted and agree that the 1995 Chardonnay was fruity with a nice, light French oak char. This wine is available in big city restaurants and a few retail wine stores. The winery is also known for estate Cabernets, touted as being "big and bold." You will have to taste one to see if you agree.

- ❑ *15140 Sonoma Highway, Glen Ellen;* ☎ *707-938-4064.*
- ❑ *Tasting: Daily 10 am-4:30 pm, no tours.*
- ❑ *Directions: On Highway 12 just south of Arnold Drive.*

## Valley of the Moon Winery

This is the second oldest winery in Northern California. Buena Vista was the first, started in 1856. Valley of the Moon was planted just a year later. There is not much chance of running into crowds here. It's a small operation, too small for tours of its own. There is just a wine tasting room under some big trees by the side of a country road with vineyards stretching out in every direction. Nonetheless, this small winery on Madrone Road beside Sonoma Creek has a long history.

It was originally part of the Agua Caliente Rancho, purchased by General Vallejo. The 640 acres were given to the music teacher of the General's children in payment for piano lessons. General Joe Hooker, later of Civil War fame, planted a vineyard here with Chinese labor. He sold it at the start of the Civil War when Lincoln called him back east, where he established a reputation as "Fightin' Joe Hooker." He later gave his name to history again because of the number of camp followers who trailed along behind his troops. Why do you suppose prostitutes are called "hookers" in this country? Anyway, the acreage was named Madrone Winery by Senator George Hearst (William Randolph's father) when he bought it in 1883. It passed through other hands, until Kenwood Winery bought it last year.

Small as it is, the winery has always been known for its Chardonnay. It still makes red Zinfandel from vines that are 120 years old. Grape vines are known to last an extraordinary length of time, but they don't necessarily produce good wine all those years.

There is talk of installing a big picture window to let visitors see into the barrel room. Perhaps they will even start tours. There is a little picnic area – convenient if you've brought a few sandwiches along.

- ❑ *777 Madrone Road, Glen Ellen;* ☎ *707-996-6941.*
- ❑ *Open: 10 am-5 pm (closed Thursday). No tours, wine tasting only.*
- ❑ *Picnics: Yes, small area by creek.*
- ❑ *Directions: Seven miles north of Sonoma, turn left on Madrone Road. It's the first place on the right.*

*Sonoma Valley Vineyard.*

# Kenwood

If you happen to be in town on a weekend, look over at the railroad depot. It was built of locally quarried stone in 1887. The striking old building is much in demand these days as a site for weddings.

The valley is narrow here, yet there are endless acres of grapevines, filling it from the steep wooded hillsides on the west and rolling over the gentle hills on the eastern side. Behind that are the mountains. No highrise buildings, no shopping malls, just a modest village and an abundance of beauty.

The little town of Kenwood and most of this area was once part of the 18,000-acre Rancho Los Guilicos. That's pronounced Wee-lee-cos in Spanish. It got that name because a Wappo Indian village called Wilikos was here before the Spanish came.

When the railroad line was built in the 1880s, one of the small towns along the line was named Kenwood, after a city in Illinois.

# Inn

## Kenwood Inn & Spa

*Kenwood Inn.*

A vase of red roses, a bottle of red wine with two glasses, and a CD player with a disk titled "Amore, the great Italian love arias" were in our room upon arrival. It seemed an appropriate way to start.

The very old building here was an antique store for awhile, then the Italian woman who sold antiques died, and the building was suddenly for sale. Terry and Roseann Grimm bought it and rebuilt. What was a store became the lobby, spa and library. The other buildings at Kenwood Inn are all new, but made to look aged and lovely, like an estate in Tuscany.

All rooms have queen-size beds, fireplaces, two robes and CD players. There is a big supply of CDs and VCR tapes, but no TV in the room (they will move one in if you request it). Both inn and spa packages offer in-room massages in front of your fireplace.

The honeymoon suite is like the others, but with a few differences of size and details. It's in a building that looks like a two-story farmhouse in Northern Italy. The outer walls are stained ocher. There are arches and a central courtyard, balconies outside the second-story rooms and lots of chimneys.

There are two rooms on the first floor flanking a fountain. Up the semi-open stairs are two more rooms, one on each side of the stairway. The bed has a quilted feather comforter and faces the fireplace. There are intricate triple sconces above the mantelpiece and French doors that open onto a private balcony with plenty of space for a table and chairs. It's good for sitting and sipping wine as you look at the grapevines over to the right or the ancient California live oaks on the hillside to the left. Deer can sometimes be seen. A big persimmon tree, weighed down with bright orange fruit, grows by the large swimming pool.

There is a huge complimentary breakfast at 9:30 every morning. If you want to get an earlier start, just tell them and they will fix a continental breakfast for you. It would be a shame to miss the great spread they serve. We put off leaving, so we could partake.

A few guests gathered early for coffee by the fireplace in the flagstone-paved breakfast room next to the big open kitchen. Then came pitchers of freshly squeezed orange juice, scones right out of the oven and cranberry bread from another oven. Our main fare that day, though it varies from day to day, was a winter hash of vegetables served under a poached egg with a light tomato sauce. We were ready to get up and leave when the apple baked with figs and honey-cinnamon sauce arrived. We stayed and ate every last bite.

There is hiking and walking here and bicycling and horseback riding about a five-minute drive away. It's a few minutes from the small town of Kenwood and 15 minutes from Sonoma, where there are restaurants, shopping and galleries, plus historic landmarks.

But don't forget the spa. Every kind of massage from classic full body to the togetherness massage (that's the one in your room) is available.

- *10400 Sonoma Highway, Kenwood, CA 95452;*
  ☎ *707-833-1293, same number for spa.*
- *Rooms: 12 (one suite).*
- *Rates: November 1 to March 30, Monday-Thursday, Tuscany Suite, $265, others $225; Friday-Sunday, Tuscany Suite, $315, others $265. April 1-October 31, Monday-Thursday, Tuscany Suite, $295, others $255; Friday-Sunday, Tuscany Suite, $365, others $295.*
- *Credit cards: AE, MC, V.*
- *Reservations: Weekends, four to six weeks.*
- *Minimum stay: Two days on weekends.*
- *Breakfast: Gourmet breakfast complimentary. Romantic dinner in room upon request (fee).*
- *Wine: Wine, sodas, cookies available in library all the time.*
- *Amenities: Heated swimming pool, robes, spa and massages available (charge).*
- *Handicapped accessible: One room.*
- *Smoking: No.*
- *Children: No.*
- *Pets: Not usually, but have made exceptions.*
- *Directions: Highway 12, just south of Kenwood.*

# Things to Do

## Farmers' Market

It's small but potent and held at the Village Center, April to November, Saturdays 9 am-12 noon.

## July 4th World Pillow Fighting Championships

Actually, there is a lot more to this than the name suggests. It's an all-day affair, starting with the traditional small town 4th of July Parade in the morning and going on through to the afternoon Chili Cookoff. The main event takes place when contestants, armed only with feather pillows, whale away at each other while balanced on a greased pole suspended above a muddy bog. Throughout, there is music, entertainment and lots of fun. If you need to know more, ☎ 707-571-8071.

## Sugarloaf Ridge State Park

This park has almost 3,000 acres of wilderness, meadows, fantastic views of the mountains and valley and picnic areas. There are 21 miles available for hiking or simple walking. Try the Hillside Trail. Get a map from the rangers. The park is a few miles north of Kenwood and in the foothills of the Mayacama Mountains. It was named by someone who thought the mountains resembled sugar loafs, the kind sold by grocery stores in the old days.

There are picnic tables near the parking area, and others scattered around in less public meadows and near trails where great views can be enjoyed. Squirrels, raccoons and deer are common and best seen if you are out here in the early morning hours.

Get here by driving north of Kenwood on Highway 12 a few miles. Turn right at Adobe Canyon Road, and go a few more miles to the park entrance. 2605 Adobe Canyon Road, Kenwood, ☎ 707-833-5712. Admission is $5 per car.

## Wine Country Wagons

Here you will find farm wagons pulled by Belgian horses to tour the vineyards. Pat Alexander and Heidi Dexter conduct the tour. They are both fourth-generation Kenwoodians and are great sources of information about this area. At present, they are doing weekend rides from April to October, which increase to six days a week in August and September. They will take you out into the vineyards of Landmark Winery. The ride only lasts 20 minutes, costs $5 and is part of a winery tour.

If you want a private ride on a smaller wagon with just the two of you and the driver, you can make arrangements to have a wagon ride anywhere you want to go in the valley. A possible drawback is the rate. It costs $500 for a minimum of three hours. That does not include lunch, so pick up two sandwiches and a bottle of wine to take along.

Their address is P.O. Box 1069, Kenwood, CA 95452; ☎ 707-833-2724. For the vineyard ride at Landmark Winery, ☎ 707-833-0053.

# Half Moon Bay

> 🐚 *I would win my way to the coast, apple-bearing Hesperian coast*
> *of which the minstrels sing, where the Lord of the Ocean denies*
> *the voyager further sailing, and fixes the solemn limit of Heaven*
> *which giant Atlas upholds. There the streams flow with ambrosia*
> *by Zeus's bed of love, and holy Earth, the giver of life, yields to the*
> *Gods rich blessedness.*

Euripides, 485-406 B.C.

When you drive down from San Francisco on the freeway in about half an hour you get to the coast and Devil's Slide. It's where Highway One goes through a sudden twisting, rocky patch high above the water. When you take the last curve, there it is, all at once in front of you. Green, gently rolling hills, wide beaches, wind-twisted trees clinging to rocky bluffs above the crashing waves all combine for sheer beauty from this point south all the way to Santa Cruz. "This point" is Half Moon Bay. It's the closest tranquil stretch of coastal land to San Francisco, 25 miles to the north. Much of the land down here is still available to private development, and most of the locals are worried about what could happen to their paradise.

With mountains to the north and east, this strip of coast has been isolated and little-populated from the beginning. The Spanish pushed out the Indians. The Portuguese came, followed by Italians. Their descendents are still here. Something decisive happened around the turn of the century. The Ocean Shore Railroad laid tracks from San Francisco to Half Moon Bay, building depots at Montara, Moss Beach, El Granada, Princeton-by-the-Sea, Miramar and the town of Half Moon Bay – the same hamlets you will find today.

The railroad was gone by the 1920s, although you will see some of the stations, disguised as private homes or businesses, still standing. At the time of Prohibition, these isolated beaches close to the city were perfect for landing illegal booze. Many of the roadhouses and bordellos built then are still thriving. Now, it's assumed that they are used for more respectable purposes.

## Montara

Founded as an artists' colony at the beginning of this century, Montara State Beach, just below Devil's Slide, is a pristine stretch between two high bluffs, good for walking and surfing. There is a lighthouse on one bluff with plenty of parking. The wild land that slopes up the mountains at the north end is a reserve. It can't be developed, to the great appreciation of all Montarans.

## Moss Beach

A romantically inclined fellow named J.F. Wienke and his bride apparently had an idyllic honeymoon here in 1881. In any case, he fell in love with the place and stayed. Look around and you will find Wienke Street. He is also the one who named the subsequent town for the moss he saw clinging to the rocks near the white beaches and tall cliffs.

For awhile, it was a vacation place, with hotels and resorts. Then, during Prohibition, silent film stars and politicians cavorted at the roadhouse, now known as Moss Beach Distillery, built on a bluff in 1917. Booze was landed in a cove just below, and sent on to San Francisco or guzzled on the premises.

Moss Beach's main attraction now is the James Fitzgerald Marine Reserve. There are tide pools full of live marine plants and animals.

## Princeton-by-the-Sea

Called Corral de Tierra by the Spanish, Princeton's half-dozen or so streets are named after famous universities. Some people hint that may have been a later coverup when they point out that developer Frank Brophy's dog was named Prince. At any rate, the town was laid out in 1908, another hoped-for resort town. The location was based on Pillar Point, a prominent bluff which juts into the ocean and forms a semi-protected harbor. Now the harbor, still a very active commercial fishing port, is fully protected with breakwaters and a marina. The huge satellite dish on the bluff is Pillar Point Tracking Station, which keeps tabs on NASA space shuttles and satellites. The James Fitzgerald Marine Reserve stretches all the way down the coast to this point from Moss Beach, and there is a protected shorebird habitat here.

## El Granada

Formerly plain Granada, this is another early resort town that has re-risen as a popular bedroom community for the City and Silicon Valley. Most of El Granada is on the inland side of Highway One, though El Granada Beach is the stretch just south of Pillar Point Harbor.

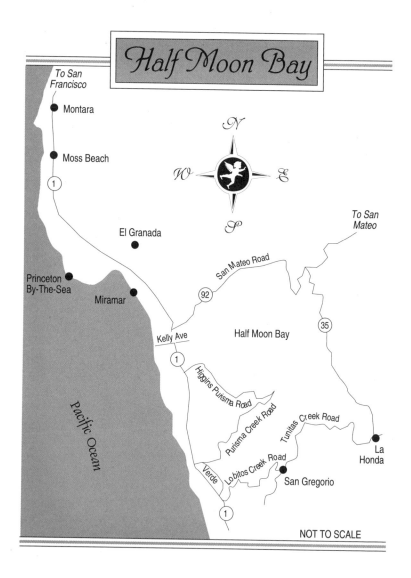

# Miramar

At one time, this town was called Amesport. Ocean Shore Railroad, eager to sell lots, gave it a more romantic and more saleable name. There was another Prohibition-era roadhouse here, now Miramar Beach Restaurant. This coast was obviously rife with them! This is a small place, an appendage of Half Moon Bay, with a dozen short streets and Miramar Beach.

# Half Moon Bay

This is the big city, with all of 8,800 people. Tiburcio Vasquez got here first, after the Indians, who soon were no more. Seeking refuge during the Mexican War, he settled on his land grant, safe behind the mountains on this isolated stretch of coast. He was followed by others like him. The town was first named San Benito, but later called Spanish Town for all the Spanish who lived here.

Later in the 19th century, there was a stagecoach that rattled along the rough narrow trail over the mountains to the east. It's still there; not the stagecoach but the two-lane, winding Road 92, still the only way to reach Half Moon Bay, except for Highway One along the coast.

It's the kind of town politicians have in mind when they spout off about "family values." Streets are named after early settlers and there is a palpable feeling of community. Most of the one- and two-story buildings date from the turn of the century or before. The oldest building on Main Street was built in 1859. Cunho's Country Store was built in 1900. Even though it was a speakeasy for awhile, it's back to being a country store now. There is a parade on the 4th of July and a Pumpkin Festival in October.

# Weather

As a general rule, expect fog in summer, crisp clear days in spring and fall, and wet windy winters. It doesn't take a meteorologist to figure out that spring and fall are the best times to come. Summer fog is most common in mornings and evenings, and summer temperatures are moderate with highs in the mid 60s. Winter lows are in the mid 40s.

# How to Get Here

From San Francisco, get on the Freeway going south: there is an on-ramp at Fourth Street, Seventh Street and South Van Ness (south of Market). Follow signs to San Jose. You'll end up on 101 if you aren't already on it. Get off at the Highway One/Pacifica exit. Follow Highway One. It's 10 miles from there to Montara, and 18 miles to the town of Half Moon Bay.

# *Inns*

## *Cypress Inn on Miramar Beach*

(Miramar)

The place was built in 1988 as an inn and it's right on the beach. The small Common Room has a fireplace, comfortable chairs for reading or just sitting and sipping in the late afternoon. You can have breakfast here if you prefer, although the honeymooners usually have breakfast in their rooms. Champagne and flowers are available for an extra fee.

Suzie Lankes and Dan Floyd bought the inn three years ago and want it to be homey. For example, all rooms have feather beds. If you are allergic to feathers, just tell Leigh Herley, the manager, and the mattress will be replaced without a problem.

The big front house is called Cypress House and has eight rooms, all with views of the water. All the rooms have southwestern decor and small, private verandas from which you can watch the waves roll in. All have phones, Mexican tiled floors and good bathrooms with a tub/shower.

The Standard Rooms have a gas fireplace, queen-size bed and bright lemon walls. El Sol, a corner room, is larger and quieter, with a fireplace, TV and stereo.

There are four rooms in back in the Garden House – three with partial views of the ocean. These rooms are larger but the view is inferior and are they are hideously decorated. As soon as you step inside the front door and see the mural on the wall, you'll see what we mean. Opt for a room in the front house, by all means.

- ❑ *407 Mirada Road, Half Moon Bay, CA 94019;*
  ☎ *800-83-BEACH or 650-726-6002.*
- ❑ *Rooms: 12 – eight in a newer beach house, four in garden house.*
- ❑ *Rates: $150-$275.*
- ❑ *Credit cards: AE, MC, V.*
- ❑ *Reservations: Three to four months for weekends; weekdays much easier. Lots of guests from San Francisco and San Jose come down for the weekends.*
- ❑ *Breakfast: Buffet or a tray in the room, with eggs, peaches and cream, always French toast.*
- ❑ *Wine: Wine and hors d'oeuvres 5 pm-7 pm; dessert and coffee after you've had dinner elsewhere.*

❑ *Handicapped accessible: One room.*
❑ *Smoking: No.*
❑ *Children: Must be well behaved. If another guest complains, parents and child will have to leave. No exceptions.*
❑ *Pets: No.*
❑ *Parking: In lot.*
❑ *Directions: Highway One to Mirada Road (2½ miles north of Half Moon Bay or a half-mile south of Pillar Point Harbor breakwater), and drive to end.*

## ♥ Mill Rose Inn

Never have we seen so many beautiful roses in a private garden. The house itself is an attractive white English country house with blue trim. Owners Eve and Terry Baldwin are responsible for the extravagant garden and for the window boxes lush with flowers outside each guest suite. Out back is a patio with a hot tub in a gazebo, surrounded by flowers and set beside a fountain. Guests reserve it if they want the hot tub to themselves.

*Mill Rose Inn.*

The Renaissance Rose Suite is the largest, but typical of them all. Many brides use this one when they are married here. The inn hosts over 50 weddings each year. The living room is large with a red carpet, a luxurious window seat, sofas and a big spray of fresh flowers on the center table. The bedroom has a queen-size bed, another window seat, fireplace and an old-fashioned chandelier.

The decor in each suite is keyed to match its name: Botticelli Rose, Burgundy Rose, etc. All have moiré curtains, 1860s needlework on antimacassars, silver dressing table sets and a view of the garden. They also have coffee, tea, bottled water, hair dryer, an iron and a bright yellow rubber ducky in each tub. All rooms have a big table by the window. Most guests have their breakfast here, brought to the room with champagne. In the evening, before going out to dinner, it's also a nice place to have some wine and cheese – delivered to the room on request.

A huge old maple tree shades the flagstones in the garden – a nice place to sit and read. No wonder couples return here to celebrate their anniversaries. This is a beautiful retreat if you're seeking quiet and privacy.

Lodie Baird, the manager, is a third generation Half Moon Bayite and is very friendly, willing to answer questions and talk about the coast. She gives full credit to the owners for the profusion of flowers and the rose garden. Half Moon Bay is an important commercial flower growing center and the inn reflects that with its poppies, delphiniums, lilies, sweet peas and... roses.

- ❑ *615 Mill St., Half Moon Bay, CA 94109;*
  ☎ *800-900-ROSE (7673), 650-726-9794.*
- ❑ *Rooms: Six luxury suites.*
- ❑ *Rates: $215-$255.*
- ❑ *Credit cards: All.*
- ❑ *Reservations: Weekends, four-six weeks ahead (all year-round), weekdays, four weeks.*
- ❑ *Minimum stay: Two nights weekends.*
- ❑ *Breakfast: Full breakfast with champagne, served in dining room or en suite. Cake, cookies and coffee are available 24 hours.*
- ❑ *Wine: Wine and cheese plate will be brought to your room.*
- ❑ *Amenities: Hot tub, robes, hair dryer, iron, rubber ducky.*
- ❑ *Handicapped accessible: Two suites, but not completely set up. Call for more information.*
- ❑ *Smoking: No.*
- ❑ *Children: Only if parents take a second room.*
- ❑ *Pets: No.*
- ❑ *Parking: On the street, but that's no problem. This is a small, quiet town, remember?*
- ❑ *Directions: Highway One to Half Moon Bay, left on Main Street (at the first signal), left on Mill Street, two blocks ahead on right.*

## Pillar Point Inn

(Princeton-by-the-Sea)

This inn is on a street that fronts the marina. Though there is a parking lot in between, all rooms have a good view of the water and the boats coming and going. The view is better from the upstairs rooms, which also have higher, peaked ceilings and larger windows.

All rooms have attractive brass beds – two are king-size, the rest queens with feather mattresses. All have blue coverlets which go well with the light blue carpets, window seats, wicker chairs with blue cushions and blue-tiled gas fireplaces. They also have VCRs, radios and refrigerators.

Downstairs, there is a comfortable room with deep sofas for reading and socializing, especially in the afternoons and evenings when all the guests are back from sightseeing. Breakfast is served in another cheery room.

The marina with its commercial fishing boats, sail boats and power boats is right in front of you here. It's a short walk to the beaches or to Pillar Point. Sometimes commercial groups use this inn for meetings. You might want to phone ahead to avoid them.

- *380 Capistrano Road, Princeton-by-the-Sea, CA 94018;*
  ☎ *800-400-8281, fax 650-728-8345.*
- *Rooms: 11.*
- *Rates: Sunday-Thursday, from $140 plus tax; Friday, Saturday and Sunday, from $160 plus tax.*
- *Credit cards: AE, MC, V.*
- *Reservations: Weekdays usually OK, weekends 1½ to two weeks in advance.*
- *Breakfast: Full breakfast with baked entrées, fruits, bread.*
- *Wine: Cookies and fruit in the afternoon.*
- *Handicapped accessible: One room.*
- *Smoking: No.*
- *Children: Yes.*
- *Pets: No.*
- *Parking: Complimentary off-street lot.*
- *Directions: From Highway One turn onto Capistrano Road (south of the airport at the marina).*

## Seal Cove Inn

(Moss Beach)

Turn off Highway One in Moss Beach on Cypress Avenue and drive toward the ocean to the end of the road, where it runs into the Marine Reserve. This imposing two-story English manor is flanked on one side by a forest, part of the Reserve, and on the other by a commercial flower grower.

The local tide times marked on a slate are prominently displayed near the door. The inn is very near Seal Cove, where the seals loll on rocks and throw themselves up out of the water, especially at low tide.

Downstairs is a large common room, complete with fireplace and comfortable chairs. Guests gather and chat about the day's happenings, trying to top each other with the number of seals seen. Next door is an equally large conference room. We are sure conferences are good business, but they certainly tend to distract from the country inn feeling. You might want to call and ask whether a conference is scheduled for the same time you would like to be there.

All rooms have wood burning fireplaces, refrigerators with complimentary wine and soda, TVs, VCRs (with complimentary videos), armoires, grandfather clocks and fresh flowers. Upstairs rooms have private balconies and all rooms also have some view of Fitzgerald Marine Reserve as well as a small view of the ocean. Bathrooms have towel warmers and tub/showers. Two of the larger suites have jacuzzis and king-size beds.

In one room we saw "Happy Birthday" spelled out in big children's blocks on the mantel; another had "Happy Anniversary." These guests will find wine or champagne in their rooms at night when they return from dinner.

Karen and Rick Herbert Brown are the owners. Karen definitely knows what guests like in an inn. She is the author of several books on the subject of inns.

- 221 Cypress Ave., Moss Beach, CA 94038; ☎ 650-728-7325.
- Rooms: 10.
- Rates: $165-$250.
- Credit cards: All.
- Reservations: Weekends year-round, four-six weeks; weekdays, April-October, one week; November-March, open.
- Breakfast: Full American breakfast in dining room. If you prefer to have it in your room, a continental breakfast will be delivered.
- Wine: Sherry and brandy is always out for you, plus wine in the evenings, and complimentary wine in the room.
- Amenities: Morning coffee and newspaper outside the door.
- Handicapped accessible: One room.
- Smoking: No.
- Children: Downstairs rooms only.
- Pets: No.
- Parking: Complimentary, on premises.
- Directions: Turn right off Highway One in Moss Beach. The inn is on your right.
- Sightseeing: Through woods, along bluff, tidal pools, walking distance to Moss Beach Distillery Restaurant.

# Restaurants

In the past, this area has had few really good places to eat. But the situation has improved. The first three below are the best.

## Mezza Luna

(Italian)

This place is very Italian. It's run by an Italian family and the waiters are usually young guys just off the boat. One of them is a dead-ringer for Antonio Banderas. That may be why you'll see so many single women customers.

Although a few years ago the cooking was uneven, it has vastly improved in the last year and now it's like eating in an Italian kitchen – very authentic and good. The wine list has both Italian and California wines. Generally the Italian wines are better choices.

- ❑ *3048 Cabrillo Highway, Half Moon Bay;* ☎ *650-712-9223.*
- ❑ *Open: Monday-Friday, lunch, 11:30 am-2:30 pm; dinner, 5 pm-10 pm. Saturday, 11:30 am-10 pm. Sunday, dinner only, 5 pm-10 pm.*
- ❑ *Prices: Pasta $8.50-$9.50, veal $11.50, chicken $11.50-$15.50.*
- ❑ *Credit cards: Discovery, MC, V.*
- ❑ *Reservations: Yes.*
- ❑ *Parking: Free lot.*
- ❑ *Directions: Highway One, 2½ miles north of town center.*

## *Pasta Moon*

(Nuevo-Italian)

This is a small, neat place in a storefront on Main Street. It has no view and is not on the highway. Most visitors never stumble on it. There are no pretensions here, but it has a good atmosphere – clean lines, art on the white walls, and a friendly ambiance. Lots of couples come here to enjoy the good food. It's pleasant, though it can be noisy.

Sit down to a bare table (no tablecloth), with a holder full of very skinny breadsticks. Soon, a delicious pepper or olive spread will arrive. The food is nuevo-Italian with California touches. The wine list contains almost all Italian wines, with hardly any California wines. This is a little unusual for a place in Northern California.

Note: Mezza Luna and Pasta Moon are about even when it comes to the quality of the food. Pasta Moon definitely has the edge for romantic atmosphere. Mezza Luna has no decor at all, but the better wine list, and it is less expensive. It will be about $60 for two, including a bottle of good Italian wine at around $25. Figure on about $80 at Pasta Moon, including wine.

- ❑ *315 Main St., Half Moon Bay (in Tin Palace Building);* ☎ *650-726-5125.*
- ❑ *Open: Monday-Friday, 11:30 am-2:30 pm, 5 pm-9 pm; Saturday, 12 noon-3 pm, 5:30 pm-9:30 pm; Sunday, 9 am-3 pm, 5:30 pm-9:30 pm.*
- ❑ *Prices: Antipasti and salads $4.25-$9.95; pastas and entrées, $10.95-$16.95.*
- ❑ *Credit cards: AE, Discovery, V.*
- ❑ *Reservations: Recommended.*
- ❑ *Parking: Two-hour parking anywhere on Main St.*
- ❑ *Directions: Turn off Highway One at first Half Moon Bay signal, then right on Main Street one block across bridge. First building on left hand side of the bridge.*

## Sushi on Main

(Japanese)

This is the hip place, very trendy and the hottest restaurant in Half Moon Bay right now. There is the usual sushi bar plus tables. The decor is terrific, all woody and art-filled, with a "new age" feeling. The food is what you might call new wave sushi. In addition to what we are all used to in the way of traditional sushi, there are some very different blends and spicy items. Some call them weird, but we think they are quite good.

If there's a wait for a table (there usually is), you can go across the street to San Benito House bar. The waitress will come and fetch you when your table is ready. How's that for service?

- ❑ *696 Mill St., Half Moon Bay;* ☎ *650-726-6336.*
- ❑ *Open: 11:30 am-2:30 pm, 5 pm-9 pm.*
- ❑ *Prices: $7-$11.*
- ❑ *Credit cards: MC, V.*
- ❑ *Reservations: Weekends and evenings.*
- ❑ *Parking: Street.*
- ❑ *Directions: Coming from the north (San Francisco), turn left to Main St. at first stoplight for Half Moon Bay, then right on Mill St. past bridge. Restaurant is on the corner.*

## San Benito House

(Mediterranean cuisine)

This is at 356 Main Street in Half Moon Bay, ☎ 650-726-3425, on the ground floor of the old Mosconi Hotel. "Imaginative Mediterranean Cuisine" is how they describe it and you'll find it very quaint. The building is turn-of-the-century and the bar came around the Horn. There is no view. The food is OK, but expensive.

## Miramar Beach Restaurant & Bar

(American – mostly seafood)

This is fairly typical of the restaurants along the coast that feature sea views. The best thing about Miramar is its history. It used to be known as the Ocean Beach Hotel and rumor has it that it also used to be a bordello. Rumors like that abound in these parts, especially if the place existed during the Prohibition years, 1919 to 1931. This was where the rum runners roved. It was a notorious drop-off point for illegal liquors brought down from Canada and then off-loaded into small, high-speed motorboats along this bayshore. The hotel was raided several times by G-men looking for the illegal moonshine. They seldom found it though. There were revolving kitchen cabinets and other tricky gadgets that hid the liquor and made this a Prohibition Roadhouse.

Now it's much calmer. The club sandwich they serve at lunchtime is ridiculously huge, the equivalent of two full sandwiches, between three slices of bread. It's hard to get it in your mouth and, unfortunately, with today's modern, improved pressed meats, it's hard to tell the turkey from the ham. But we recognized the bacon. It was brown.

We've eaten here several times, but we still haven't tasted everything on the menu. Perhaps there are some great culinary items we missed. When you are sitting at a table with a small lamp casting soft light, the ocean outside, and your significant other with you, this place can definitely be romantic. You don't even have to wait for a full moon. A spotlight on the roof shines on the waves so you won't miss a thing. It's even more romantic when there are orchids on the table and it's understood that you aren't here entirely for the food.

❑ *131 Mirada Road, Miramar;* ☎ *650-726-9053, fax 650-726-5063.*
❑ *Open: 11:30 am-close. Weekends, it's open to 10 pm or later. But, if there is a storm and no one shows up, they close early.*
❑ *Prices: Appetizers $5.95-$12.95, soups and salads $3.25-$6.95, pastas $15.95-$18.95, entrées $17.95-$21.95.*
❑ *Credit cards: Diners Club, MC, V.*
❑ *Reservations: Not necessary.*
❑ *Parking: Complimentary.*
❑ *Directions: From Highway One, turn on Mirada Road (between Half Moon Bay and Pillar Point Harbor, closer to Harbor).*

## Moss Beach Distillery

(Mostly seafood)

This was another roadhouse, with an upstairs bordello, built during Prohibition. It also lays claim to a ghost, a spectral Blue Lady who met her end mysteriously during a murder that took place on the bluff. Several claim to have seen her wafting along in the mist.

The food is only so-so, but this place is very popular with couples who drive down from San Francisco for dinner. It's usually crowded and you have to wait for a table, so sit outside and watch the seals on the rocks. (There can be as many as 50 at low tide.) In the meantime, have a bucket of clams, or oyster shooters. If it's cold, a blanket is provided. It's romantic to sit there with a glass of wine in one hand and an oyster in the other, watching the sun go down over the ocean.

❑ *Beach Street at Ocean, Moss Beach;* ☎ *650-728-5595.*
❑ *Prices: Dinner entrées $15.95-$21.95.*
❑ *Directions: Watch for sign on Highway One.*

# Nightlife

## Bach Dancing & Dynamite Society

(Douglas Beach House, Miramar Beach)

Definitely tops around these parts are the jazz or classical concerts. They are usually on Sundays, starting at 4:30 pm, or sometimes on Saturdays, starting at 8:30 pm. Call to find out what's happening. Prices vary from $16 to $20 per person, depending on the event. Usually doors open at 3 pm, music starts at 4:30 and goes to 8. There is a buffet with a wine and juice bar. This is first-class stuff, with well known jazz and classical performers. These events used to happen every week, but have been irregular lately. When concerts are scheduled, there will be flyers around town and the *Half Moon Bay Review* always publishes the details. Definitely call first. ☎ 650-726-4895.

Other places with live music (always call ahead):

❐ **Bad Offer Sports Pub and Steakhouse**, 108 N. Cabrillo Highway, Half Moon Bay, ☎ 650-726-7160, with blues or rock, dancing on weekends.

❐ **Cameron's Inn**, 1410 Cabrillo Highway, Half Moon Bay, ☎ 650-726-5705, with karaoke, bluegrass, folk music.

❐ **Café Classique**, 107 Sevilla, El Granada, ☎ 650-726-9775, with jazz, folk.

❐ **El Perico**, 211 San Mateo Road, Half Moon Bay, ☎ 650-726-3737, with occasional Mexican or country music on weekends.

# Things to Do

## Gray Whale Cove Trail

This trail is in McNee Ranch State Park at the north end of the bay. It's a mile long, one-way, over moderate terrain – flat once you climb the gentle slope from the parking lot. Park at Gray Whale Cove State Beach on the inland side of Highway One, 1½ miles north of the Chart House Restaurant in Montara.

Coastal scrub lines the trail. Look for gray-green, thread-like leaves of coast safebrush and bright green, toothed leaves of coyote bush. Watch out for poison oak – three shiny reddish-green leaves. That gray-green mountain to the north is San Pedro Mountain. Montara Mountain looms inland. For information, ☎ 650-726-8819.

## Montara State Beach

This beach is at the north end of the bay, about 12 miles from the town of Half Moon Bay. Big bluffs, crashing waves, lighthouse and foghorn all make for great beachwalking. Usually there is plenty of privacy, especially on weekdays.

## Fitzgerald Marine Reserve, Moss Beach

Explore tidepools, especially at low tide, for hermit crabs, purple shore crabs and starfish. It's a beautiful place. There is a half-mile loop trail with moderate terrain. Take California Avenue off Highway One in Moss Beach and follow signs. For Interpretive Center, docent tours and time of low tide, phone Fitzgerald Marine reserve, ☎ 650-728-3584.

## Pillar Point Harbor

It's come a long way since sailors with bags of grain on their shoulders waded out to their anchored ships in the 1850s. Now the harbor is home to hundreds of fishing boats and yachts. If you are a fisherman, try your luck for rockfish or halibut off the pier on the west inner breakwater, or go deep sea fishing. **Huck Finn Sportsfishing,** ☎ 650-726-7133 or 800-572-2934, supplies bait and tackle and has several boats that go out rock fishing year-round, salmon fishing in March and whenever other fish are running.

If you are here between October and March, when the gray whales migrate south along the coast, you can see them from the bluffs. Bring binoculars or, for a closer look, the non-profit Oceanic Society and a few local commercial firms offer whale watching trips. (See pages 259 and 329.)

Pillar Point Marsh is small, but a paradise for bird watchers. You'll spot great blue herons, snowy egrets and red-winged blackbirds. Nearly 20% of all North American bird species have been sighted here. While you're here, follow the trail around the point to the breakwater and tide pools. California sea lions bask on the offshore rocks.

The marsh is reached by continuing past the harbor entrance to Prospect Way. Turn left, then right on Broadway, left on Harvard, right on West Point Ave. and go a half-mile to Pillar Point Marsh parking lot. Up-to-date information available from the Fitzgerald Marine Reserve, ☎ 650-728-3584.

The Coastside Trail runs three miles along the bluffs between Mirada Road in Miramar and Kelly Ave. in Half Moon Bay. In addition to an unparalleled ocean view, you will enjoy bright yellow beach primroses and pale yellow bush lupines, along with small brush rabbits and long-legged, long-eared jack rabbits. There is one problem with this trail. It's heavily used by dog owners walking their pets. You will find that instead of enjoying the view, you will tend to keep your eyes down on the path to avoid stepping in what the dogs leave behind.

Paralleling the trail between Pillar Point Harbor and Half Moon Bay are public parks on Mirada Road off Highway One in Miramar, at Roosevelt Beach, Dunes Beach, Venice Beach or Francis Beach. Francis Beach, at the end of Kelly Avenue in Half Moon Bay, has picnic tables and barbecues. Parking fees are charged. Also park at these beaches to access the Coastal Trail. For more information, call Half Moon Bay Parks and Recreation, ☎ 650-726-8297.

Surfing is popular, though not very good (we've noticed that never seems to discourage surfers) at the first beach south of Pillar Harbor. This is called Surfers Beach and it's really just for kids. Waves tend to range from a few inches to a few feet. Much better surfing is at Montara Beach, where experienced surfers go. Just west of Pillar Point, beyond the Tracking Station, is where you can catch the famous Mavericks Waves. This location is for experienced surfers only. Waves here, like The Pipeline on Oahu, can be very dangerous. This spot is used for competitive events by the best surfers in the world.

**A Bicyclery**, 432 Main St., Half Moon Bay, ☎ 650-726-6000, rents bikes. Most people ride the Coastal Trail to get clear away from traffic. All mountain bikes, they rent for $6 per hour, minimum two hours, maximum four hours ($24), which actually gives you up to eight hours. You need a credit card for a deposit and must rent a helmet ($5) if you don't bring your own. Open 9:30 am-6:30 pm, Monday-Friday; 10 am-5 pm, Saturday; 11 am-5 pm, Sunday.

**California Canoe & Kayak**, Princeton, ☎ 650-728-1803, rents open-top kayaks. Four-hour rentals $15; double kayaks and canoes $20; wetsuits and paddlejackets, additional charge. Summer, 10 am-8 pm, seven days; winters on Saturday and Sunday only, 10 am-7 pm.

**Friendly Acres Ranch** or **Sea Horse Ranch** (same owners), Highway One, one mile north of Half Moon Bay, ☎ 650-721-9916, rents riding horses. A one-hour trail ride is $25, two-hour beach ride is $40. Early morning rides, 8 am and 9:45 am, are $20 for one hour, $25 for two hours. It's definitely better to ride in early morning than late afternoon, when the animals are reluctant to go anywhere. All they want in the late hours is go home to the stables and eat.

**Whale watching cruises** are offered by the non-profit Oceanic Society on Friday, Saturday and Sunday from late December through April, on a 56-foot boat. They leave from Pillar Point Yacht Harbor at 9 am and 1 pm. Duration of the cruise is one hour. Bring snack and beverage, binoculars and warm clothes. Fridays $29 (youths 5-15 and seniors 60+ $27); Saturdays and Sundays $32 (youths and seniors $29). ☎ 650-474-3385. Trips also made by Captain John's, ☎ 650-728-3377.

## Events & Attractions

### Spring

On the seventh Sunday after Easter is **Chamarita**, a holiday dating back to Queen Isabel of Portugal that has been celebrated for over 100 years in Half Moon Bay. Festivities include a Catholic mass, parade with annual Queen, carnival, barbecue, auction and dance.

### Summer

**4th of July Parade** down Main Street with antique autos, carriages.

### Fall

**Half Moon Bay Art & Pumpkin Festival.** The Pumpkin Capital of the West hosts the pumpkin weigh-off on Columbus day, always the Monday before the Festival begins. The Festival itself is open from 10 am-5 pm the following Saturday and Sunday. The Great Pumpkin Parade is Saturday at noon. There are pumpkin carving and pie-eating contests, wine tasting and good food to eat.

### All Year

**The Flower Market** is held on the third Saturday of each month, 9 am-3 pm. A wide variety of flowers and flowering plants are on display. In summer, you will find it at Kelly and Main. A block of Kelly is closed off. In the winter, it's held inside La Piazza, corner of Main Street and Miramontes Avenue.

## Transportation

**Taxis:** Coast Cab Co., ☎ 650-738-8000, based in Half Moon Bay, covers the coast and will take you to San Francisco International Airport.

**Limousines:** Gateway Limousine, ☎ 650-726-1504; Coastside Limousine, 650-728-0260.

**Buses:** SamTrans, ☎ 800-660-4BUS; hearing impaired (IDD) only, 650-508-6448. Covers coast from Montara south; has route to San Mateo, Alameda and Colma and Daly City BART stations. Buses only run every few hours along the coast. Call for schedule.

For more information about any aspect of Half Moon Bay, phone **Chamber of Commerce/Visitors information,** ☎ 650-726-8380.

# Quick Index of Accommodations, Restaurants, Nightlife & Wineries

## Accommodations

### San Francisco

### Oakland/Berkeley

### East Marin

### West Marin

## Napa Valley

## Sonoma Valley

## Half Moon Bay

# Restaurants

## San Francisco

# Nightlife

# Wineries